Performance Cycling

Performance Cycling

The Scientific Way to Improve Your Cycling Performance

Stuart Baird

Cycling Resources
books are published by
Van der Plas Publications, San Francisco

Printed in USA
First printing, 2000

Publisher Information:
Van der Plas Publications
1282 7th Avenue
San Francisco, CA 94122, USA
http://www.vanderplas.net

Distributed or represented to the book trade by:

USA:	Seven Hills Book Distributing, Cincinnati, OH
UK:	Chris Lloyd Sales and Marketing Services, Poole, Dorset
Canada:	Hushion House Publishing, Toronto, ON
Australia:	Tower Books, Frenchs Forest, NSW

796.6/0143 7306

Cover design:
Kent Lytle, Lytle Design, Alameda, CA

Frontispiece photo:
Enclosed human-powered vehicle versus road racing bike — both answer to the same laws of physics.
(H. A. Roth photograph)

Publisher's Cataloging in Publication Data
Baird, Stuart T, 1946–
Performance Cycling: The scientific way to get the most out of your bike.
224 p.   28 cm
Includes bibliographical references and index.
ISBN 1-892495-28-7
I. Bicycles and Bicycling
I. Authorship
II Title
Library of Congress Control No. 00-131377

Acknowledgments

The author wishes to thank Mark Hanback for his help with the diagrams in this book. He would also like to thank the members of the Brandywine Bicycle Club in Chester County, Pennsylvania, who over the years have helped expose him to many of the facets and follies of bicycling, and patiently put up with his steady stream of newsletter articles.

About the Author

Stuart Baird took up cycling in the early 80s and soon "went off the deep end," acquiring a couple of custom bikes, becoming active in a bicycle club, editing its newsletter (a role he still fills), and writing and publishing a well-received book of cycling routes, *Bicycling in Brandywine Territory*.

In addition to logging a few thousand miles of recreational riding each year, Mr. Baird is relatively unusual among cyclists in that he does long-distance self-contained touring and (at the opposite end of the cycling spectrum) competes in time trials. That may be the result of the liberal arts philosophy instilled in him at Lawrence University in Appleton, Wisconsin, where he earned a degree in mathematics and was elected to Phi Beta Kappa.

Computer simulations were often his focus at the University of Illinois, the U.S. Air Force, and in industry, but he is also a music lover who has performed in dozens of Gilbert and Sullivan productions. A former aerospace engineer, he is currently employed in the avionics industry. In this book he has combined his engineering and software simulation background, a healthy skepticism, perhaps a trace of Gilbertian wit, and a long-term perspective — plus of course his love of cycling.

Table of Contents

Introduction: Physical and Mental Aspects of Cycling

Sport is almost by definition a physical activity. The very word "sport" implies an enjoyable, playful diversion. A great deal of that pleasure derives from the sheer physical exertion, from the skills employed, and from their results: speed, strength, reflexes, agility, balance, control, and endurance. In a competitive sport, the physical aspects play a vital role in the outcome.

Cycling is no exception. Even the least competitive recreational cyclists delight in the physical sensations of movement, exult in the conquest of a hill, and thrill to close brushes with danger; when they return home exhausted, they collapse in satisfaction. Increased fitness and skill only intensify these physical pleasures. Cycling competitions among near-equals increase both the physical stakes and the rewards.

Yet unquestionably, part of the fascination of cycling is its mental side. It takes more than muscle to ride a bike. Even to venture on one's first bike ride, it takes a certain amount of curiosity, courage to face a sometimes hostile environment, willingness to learn new skills, stoicism to endure minor discomforts, determination to persevere, and faith that in time the rewards will overwhelm the inconveniences. Though almost all adults have enough muscle to be cyclists of some sort, the majority fail the mental test: how else can one explain the fact that relatively few adults in North America are cyclists?

The role of the mind in cycling is greater than most people (especially non-cyclists) suppose. Just to overcome laziness — to get off the couch, turn off the TV, change into cycling wear, and roll out the bike — takes a considerable mental effort. Laziness, in fact, may be the greatest intellectual obstacle to bicycling performance. Because even small children ride bicycles, adults are conditioned to believe that bicycling requires little thought. Yet adults newly rediscovering cycling quickly find themselves immersed in a sport that has developed significantly since they last rode, a sport full of unfamiliar brand names, French terminology, confusing control mechanisms, rival technologies, and uncertain legal issues. They may be unaccustomed to the determination and intellectual curiosity necessary to deal with cycling's intimidating complexities. It is difficult to admit ignorance and approach knowledgeable cyclists to learn how to ride safely, enjoyably, and well.

Even before the potential cyclist first climbs onto a bike, the mind must go to work in selecting the bicycle and adjusting it to fit, because in cycling the body and machine must be more closely matched than in any other sport. During the ride, the cyclist's mind must constantly monitor the body's feedback and each element in the eyes' kaleidoscopic view, evaluating their current states and anticipating how each may change within the next few seconds; then it must control steering, gear selection, braking points, and effort accordingly. As rides start to become more challenging, the mind must also learn to think beyond immediate sensations and plan for the longer term. And perhaps even before all these become second nature, the mind often starts to think about improving performance.

Performance

To a bicycle racer, performance means speed, more speed, maximum speed. "Maximum" may not be the right word, however, because in most racing events the objective is not to maintain the highest possible speed at all times, but merely to exceed the average speeds of one's competitors by a small margin. Besides, it is often an effective race strategy to hold back now in order to achieve greater speed later. Hazardous conditions and warning signals from an overtaxed body often also demand a prudently lowered speed for a pe-

riod of time. Yet speed is still the racer's focus — whether just a bit more, or enough for a stunning new course record.

Other cyclists may view performance very differently. A tourist with heavily loaded panniers is not interested in getting from point A to point B as quickly as possible; at least, he shouldn't be. His proper performance goal is to spend his energy wisely. Not only should he have enough energy to get to point B, but have enough all along the way for an enjoyable ride. If he passes up an interesting side trip because he feels he may lack the stamina for it, or if he becomes too fatigued to continue his tour, then his performance has fallen short of his needs. In addition, even though speed should not be his overriding concern, the tourist does have speed requirements: he must reach his day's destination by nightfall, and he may need to average a certain number of miles per day or miss his flight home.

A recreational rider has intermediate performance goals, whether attempting to do a century (a 100-mile ride) or just a weekend club ride. Yes, he needs to finish the ride, not to mention have enough energy to return to work on Monday; and yes, if the ride is a painful, exhausting ordeal rather than an agreeable, rejuvenating outing, he will soon find another way to spend his weekends. But speed also figures in the recreational equation. Most riders feel a need to keep up with other cyclists. Even when riding alone, many riders have a personal notion of what their average speed ought to be; anything less and the ride is not as satisfying as it could have been.

These differing performance goals are not as incompatible as they appear. Each is concerned with budgeting energy — a quantity of energy that may be modest or large, but is never unlimited — and parceling that energy out over a given distance or span of time. The racer has a great deal of energy at his disposal, and wants to use as much as possible to go faster, because all his competitors have similar amounts of energy and are intent on using theirs to go faster than he does. The recreational rider has less energy available for his planned ride, but also has a more moderate speed requirement. The tourist likewise has less energy, and a heavier load to boot, but perhaps also a less stringent need for speed. The key to all their performance problems is efficiency: to spend no more energy than necessary to achieve the required speed for the given length of time, or equivalently, to constrain the speed to keep energy expenditure within available limits for the duration of the ride. The fact that the speed required, the energy available, and the allotted time may not be known precisely makes the problem more difficult (and more interesting), but it doesn't change the goal of maximizing efficiency.

If the rider overachieves, finds himself nearing the finish earlier than expected or with energy to burn — why, that's seldom a problem. No cyclist needs to be told how to go slower or waste effort. Determining how to go faster or become more efficient is more elusive.

Conflicting Sources of Advice

Not that there is any shortage of advice on the topic. Cyclists in fact find themselves barraged with conflicting advice from all directions.

First comes advice from the traditional school, information distilled through the decades by championship cyclists and their coaches, almost exclusively European. A modern English or North American cyclist may legitimately wonder how much traditional advice is scientifically sound, and how much is merely meaningless custom or Continental mystique. The passage of information from generation to generation is analogous to heredity and evolution. We know from the theory of natural selection that "bad" mutations — that is, ones that reduce an organism's ability to compete in its environment — die out, while "good" ones increase the organism's "fitness" or chance of survival. Shouldn't advice that hinders performance also die out, leaving behind only advice that enhances performance? Unfortunately, it is not necessarily true that something that survives is or was more fit. In nature, the fact that one person has blue eyes and another brown does not imply that blueness was somehow a competitive advantage for one while brownness was an advantage

for the other. It may mean only that eye color had no significant effect on survival fitness and was only the result of chance. Likewise, some tidbit of traditional bicycling advice may be largely irrelevant. Poor advice could also be masked by another characteristic: for example, a rider's success may be due to brawn rather than brains. All we could hope for is that the worst advice will have been weeded out. In addition, selection takes time to operate. New pieces of equipment and innovative techniques may not have had sufficient time to be either embraced and passed down to succeeding generations, or rejected and forgotten. Traditional advice is neither infallible nor all-inclusive.

Another suspect source of advice is the bicycling industry, including its advertising agencies. If one were to believe the ads of manufacturers, increased performance is merely a matter of purchasing their latest products — but not those of their competitors, who make similar claims. Most advertising conveniently omits enough performance data to allow an informed decision. Supporting data may not exist, and often what claims the ad copy does include are inaccurate. Dealers are naturally most interested in selling something currently in their own stock. Having to special order an item is like admitting failure, and sending a customer elsewhere out of the question. In addition, dealers can understandably confuse what item is best for the individual rider with what items are merely selling well at the moment.

Journalists in the popular cycling press are yet another source. Their enthusiasm for cycling and their desire to communicate are seldom in question, and they have access to a variety of equipment and cycling personalities beyond the reach of most of us. Despite these advantages, their qualifications as reviewers are not always immaculate, and their objectivity may be undermined by the constant editorial demand to publish what is fresh, new, and exciting. A built-in bias against what is tried, tested, and commonplace can prevent a journalist from being a reliable source of advice. Unlike, say, the 0-to-60 times in automotive magazines or the total harmonic distortion figures in high fidelity magazines, there are seldom any measured, repeatable performance evaluations in bicycle magazines. Blindfolded testing being out of the question, the opinions of reviewers are also inevitably colored by slight differences in fit and feel.

Finally, individual cyclists are bound to have a variety of experiences — some relevant, some not — that influence the advice they offer. Much of even the most earnest opinion is based on subjective impression rather than objective evaluation. It is a rare rider who can keep the amount of money he has spent, pressures from friends and sponsors, ego, and other superfluous considerations from biasing his opinion. Most of us know cyclists who are repelled by the "fat" appearance of certain aluminum tubing or who equate even the highest-tech steels with pig iron, and just the idea that a frame is Italian or Taiwanese often provokes a passionate reaction. The famous cyclists in magazine interviews, almost always accomplished racers, can be just as confusing and self-contradictory as one's own cycling acquaintances, not to mention well off target for cyclists whose physiology and goals may be completely different. Performance is such a subjective topic that the most experienced, helpful, and sincere cyclist can still give bad advice, believing it to be good advice. Cycling is also a competitive activity. No competitor willingly hands his rivals the means to defeat him; some fraction of what he says may be intended to lead challengers astray. The advice of fellow cyclists is still more advice to take with a grain of salt.

The Intent of This Book

A cyclist who is seriously intent on improving his performance needs tools to cut through layers of traditionalism, hype, naivete, and guile. It is the intent of this book to provide some of those tools. Using straightforward physics and mathematics, it will examine the activity and the components of cycling, their effect on performance, and their implications upon cycling strategy. If the book is successful, the reader will acquire tools not only to evaluate prevalent advice and improve his present performance, but to evaluate future equipment and techniques in the same way.

Unlike many bicycling books, however, this one is not a training manual. The reader will find no day-by-day riding schedule, no conditioning regimen, no cross-training recommendations, no dietetic advice. It may be useful to think of it instead as training for the mind. Although much of its contents will confirm what many experienced cyclists already know and what is preached by other sources of cycling wisdom, some of it will undoubtedly contradict traditional gospel. The author suggests that neither this book nor any other source be accepted at face value. Instead he recommends examining the underlying technical data and principles to draw one's own conclusions. If this book fails to make the bicyclist-reader think, then it has failed, period.

Technical Discussions and Conclusions

Some of the discussion in this book will necessarily be technical. The reader, however, is not obligated to delve deeply into the physics and mathematics. He can, if he likes, skim through the technical discussions to arrive at the conclusions, though he should be warned that few people genuinely learn by skimming. Or he can dust off his pocket calculator and follow in detail, because the subject is not terribly difficult, and plenty of background material and examples have been included for the reader whose high school or college math and science courses are a distant memory.

Some people (men especially, it seems) enjoy technical material in and of itself. They take pride in knowing how things work, relish tinkering with machines, and like to explore cause-and-effect relationships. These tech types may appreciate this book even if (gasp!) they do not ride a bike. A larger number of readers will undoubtedly view the technical discussions in this book as a means to improving their personal bicycling performance. Still more will find the book useful in dealing with the misinformation that is unfortunately rampant in product advertising, magazine articles, and dealer sales pitches. Contrary to what many people believe, most of the technical innovations in the bicycling industry during the last several years have had zero effect on performance per se. Some, yes, have made it easier for riders with less skill or less tolerance for discomfort to perform feats formerly reserved for more experienced riders. Some have lured people into serious bicycling who were formerly unable or unwilling to ride; some have made bicycles common in places where they were formerly rare. Perhaps to certain ways of thinking, these innovations count as performance improvements. A few popular products have indeed led to gains, if small ones, while a few others have actually caused moderate losses. An informed reader is better able to assess what, if anything, the next hot product can do for him.

The conclusions ought to be straightforward enough for any rider to apply whenever performance on the bicycle is important. Most of the text will deal with fast solo riding, including time trial competition, track pursuit, the bike leg of a triathlon, "flyers" (escapes from a pack), bridging the gap to the race leaders, or trying to outrun an approaching rainstorm. Portions of the text will also cover drafting, or pacing as it is called in Britain. Even tourists pledged to abstain from speed should find much of the book useful.

A discussion in this book may lead to a conclusion — a recommendation to adopt for increased performance. It is important, however, not to interpret the conclusion too narrowly, for instance as only a way for a competitor to boost his speed in an event. Though it may be phrased in terms of speed, the conclusion almost always implies a way for any rider, competitor and non-competitor alike, to ride more efficiently, to spend less energy to achieve a certain result. After all, to use an automotive analogy, most of the car preparations and driving techniques a weekend autocrosser uses to be competitive are also useful to a driver trying to squeeze the most miles out of a gallon of gas: he tunes the engine, aligns and lubricates the chassis, jettisons unnecessary weight, pumps up the tires, and adopts a smooth driving style that maintains as much momentum as

possible. The speeds, the maximum available power, and the amount of fuel may be very different, but the principle of attaining one's goal with the help of increased efficiency remains. For bicyclists, whose engines are puny and whose fuel tanks can only be refilled slowly during overnight sleep, the principle is even more applicable.

Determining how best to apply the conclusions approaches the fuzzy realm of strategy. Competition, informal or sanctioned, heightens the need for an effective strategy, because competitors often have similar physical ability, and (besides) even superior strength is no guarantee of victory. The subject of strategy is worthy of an entire book by itself, perhaps an entire library of books. It is far too complex and intangible to be discussed as an isolated topic in a book about the technical aspects of cycling performance. Instead, the discussion of strategy must be limited to the most basic implications stemming from the technical conclusions. Yet anticipation forms the basis for strategy, and awareness of the ever-changing conditions during a ride is essential for the successful application of a strategy. Technical insight is bound to help both the formulation and execution of a successful plan. The author has tried to point out some of the implications pertaining to each of the topics, but cannot pretend to more than a smattering of strategic insight.

The calculations in this book depend on data that vary from cyclist to cyclist. Some of the physical quantities, such as rolling resistance for particular tires and road surfaces, are known only roughly. Even if the physics were perfect, these limitations would make the numbers in this book approximate. Even less is known about rider physiology. The author has made certain assumptions that may not apply well to a particular rider, or even to riders in general. Whenever possible, any such assumptions have been explicitly called out so that the reader may assess the validity of the conclusions.

Gender Terminology

Many adult bicyclists in the United States are female; by some accounts, female riders outnumber the males. The author is personally grateful that the era in which athletic females were viewed as oddities is decidedly over. Everything in this book is equally applicable to male and female riders, with the understanding that some of the results obviously vary depending on rider size and power, the two most important distinctions between the sexes as far as bicycling is concerned. Though the reader will notice that the text exclusively uses such words as "he," "him," and "his" to refer to a rider, the choice of masculine words is only an expedient. Such usage is not intended to imply that the rider in question is actually male, nor to refer nostalgically to former times. The author felt that masculine words were preferable to such awkward phrases as "he or she," which tend to distract attention from a subject independent of gender, and trusts that readers will not attempt to read any sexual bias into the text.

Trigonometry Review

Distances and angles are fundamental to most technical discussions. Geometry, specifically trigonometry, is the branch of mathematics that deals with these concepts. Because we will need to call on trigonometry often, it is time to review what we learned in high school. Figure 0101 shows a right triangle with each of its sides and angles labeled. The angle opposite side a is labeled with the lower-case Greek letter α (alpha). (Mathematicians continue to use Greek letters even though it has been two millennia since Greece was the center of mathematical enterprise. And you thought European bicyclists were traditionalists.) The angle opposite side b is labeled β (beta). The angle opposite side c, labeled γ (gamma), is a right angle, that is, one of 90 degrees. (The little square in its corner is a reminder that the angle is a genuine right angle, not merely some angle that happens to look like one as drawn.) Between the figure and the equations below, the reader has practically everything he needs to know about trigonometry.

$$c^2 = a^2 + b^2$$

$$\sin \alpha = a \, / \, c$$

$$\cos \alpha = b \, / \, c$$

$$\tan \alpha = a \, / \, b$$

$$\sin \beta = b \, / \, c$$

$$\cos \beta = a \, / \, c$$

$$\tan \beta = b \, / \, a$$

$$\alpha + \beta = 90 \text{ degrees}$$

$$\tan \alpha = \sin \alpha \, / \, \cos \alpha$$

$$\sin^2 \alpha + \cos^2 \alpha = 1$$

$$\sin (\alpha + \beta) = \sin \alpha \cos \beta + \cos \alpha \sin \beta$$

$$\sin (\alpha - \beta) = \sin \alpha \cos \beta - \cos \alpha \sin \beta$$

$$\cos (\alpha + \beta) = \cos \alpha \cos \beta - \sin \alpha \sin \beta$$

$$\cos (\alpha - \beta) = \cos \alpha \cos \beta + \sin \alpha \sin \beta$$

If α is small, then:
$\sin \alpha$ is approximately equal to $\tan \alpha$

If α is small and expressed in radians, then:
α, $\sin \alpha$, and $\tan \alpha$ are all approximately equal

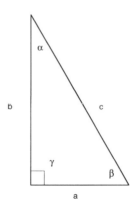

Fig. 0101. Right triangle with sides and angles labeled in the conventional way.

The 2 superscript means "square" or "squared," that is, raised to the second power or multiplied by itself: 6^2 ("six squared") is 6 x 6 or 36. The terms "sin," "cos," and "tan" are abbreviations for the trigonometric functions sine, cosine, and tangent, respectively. The phrase "sin α" (read as "sine of alpha") is a direction to apply the sine function to the angle α. The phrase "$\sin^2 α$" (read as "sine square alpha" or "sine squared of alpha") is a direction to apply the sine function to the angle α and then square the result.

In a mathematical expression, multiplication signs are normally omitted. The expression "a b" means a x b or the product of a and b. Hence the phrase "sin α cos β" is a direction to apply the sine function to the angle α and the cosine function to the angle β and then multiply the two function values together. If the order of calculation matters and may be unclear, parentheses are used to force the expressions inside them to be evaluated before subsequent calculation. Hence sin (α + β) assures that α and β are summed before the sine function is applied, because the answer is much different from taking the sine of α and then adding β. Each of the trigonometric functions has a specific value for any specified angle. See below for how to find the values of trigonometric and other functions.

These equations can also be manipulated with a little simple algebra. For example, if we know one of the sides and one of the angles (besides the right angle), it is easy to calculate the rest. The following example will give the idea.

Suppose we know c = 12 and α = 30 degrees. Then:
a = c sin α = 12 x 0.5 = 6.0 and
b = c cos α = 12 x 0.866 = 10.4.
The other angle β = 90 − α = 60 degrees.

If we know b = 26.4 and β = 40.5 degrees, then:
a = b / tan β = 26.4/.854 = 30.9,
c = b / sin β = 26.4/.649 = 40.7, and
α = 90 − β = 49.5 degrees.

Or if we know c = 13 and a = 5, then b equals the number which when squared equals the difference between c^2 and a^2; that is, b = the square root of (169−25) = 12. The angles α and β are the angles whose tangents are a/b and b/a respectively. The function for "angle whose tangent is" is called the "arctangent" (or "inverse tangent"), written arctan, atan, or $\tan^{-1}$. In this case, α = arctan 5/12 = 22.6 degrees, β = arctan 12/5 = 67.4 degrees. A piece of cake, as the saying goes.

How to Find Values of Functions

Even a couple of decades ago most math was done with pencil and paper. To find the value of a sine or square root, one looked it up in a book of mathematical tables — not very convenient, perhaps, but inexpensive and more than accurate enough for most purposes. It is, believe it or not, still possible to work this way.

Slightly more convenient was the slide rule, once the ubiquitous tool of math, science, and engineering students, but nowadays confined to attics and museums. The three-digit accuracy of a slide rule, if you can lay your hands on one, is also more than enough for the calculations in this book, considering that some of the quantities involved are not known to better than one or two digits of accuracy.

Nowadays electronic pocket calculators are fast, widely available, and inexpensive. But not just any of them will do for the sort of math in this book; for that, one needs a scientific calculator. The word "scientific" in this case means that the machine must include trigonometric functions, powers or exponents, and logarithms, in addition to the standard addition, subtraction, multiplication, and division operations. To find the cosine of 23.8 degrees, for instance, all you have to do is key in 23.8 and press the "cos" key — or something like that. Consult the manual to find out how the function keys work. Be sure the calculator is in the right mode when dealing with angles, because some calculators work with angles in radians in addition to angles in degrees. Finally, if you need to compute the nth root of something, remember that it is the same thing as the (1/n)th power. For example, the 13th root of 2 = 2 to the 1/13th power = 1.0548. The more expensive scientific calculators, with built-in engineering functions and programmability, are ideal for the math in this book once you have mastered their sometimes daunting operation.

Though they still have a long way to go before they are as inexpensive or convenient as pocket calculators, personal computers are becoming as common as televisions. People who do not own one themselves usually have access to one at their office or local library. Computers do not automatically know how to compute cosines or thirteenth roots, however. They must run appropriate software to be able to do scientific math. Back in the days when computers were more than just Internet appliances, most of them came packaged with some version of the computer language BASIC. If you have one of these, you're in luck, because BASIC includes all the trigonometric functions and has a convenient operator for raising a number to a power. Your computer manual may tell you how to use BASIC; your library and bookstore have additional material. Remember that BASIC expects angles in radians, not degrees. To convert degrees to radians, multiply by π (pi, i.e. 3.14159…) and divide by 180; for example, 20 degrees is 0.349... radians. To convert radians to degrees, multiply by 180 and divide by π.

No BASIC? Perhaps you have one of the popular spreadsheet packages. These often include scientific functions. Some computers may also have the equivalent of a pocket calculator implemented as a software program. If you come up empty-handed after consulting your computer documentation but are determined to make your computer do what its name suggests it ought to be able to, then no doubt your local computer dealer can supply software to do the trick. Most other computer languages are fully up to number-crunching tasks, too. Experienced computer programmers familiar with, say, C or Pascal should not require any advice, except a reminder that most of these languages also deal with angles in radians, and may need a function call to perform the exponentiation that BASIC easily takes in stride.

Units

Everyone knows you can't compare apples with oranges. A similar principle applies when one is mathematically manipulating quantities that have units such as miles, pounds, or meters per second. When adding or subtracting, one must make sure the quantities have identical units. For example, 12 inches minus 3 inches is certainly 9 inches. What is 12 inches minus 5.1 centimeters? In this case, one must either convert the inches to centimeters (12 inches is 30.5 centimeters; 30.5 — 5.1 = 25.4 centimeters), or the centimeters to inches (5.1 centimeters is 2 inches; 12 — 2 = 10 inches). Sometimes we convert both units to a common unit, such as meters.

When multiplying or dividing two quantities, units need not be identical; instead, the units are also multiplied or divided algebraically. Take the following examples. Ten 100-watt light bulbs use 10 x 100 watts of power. The 10 has no unit itself, so the product is 1000 watts, neither merely 1,000 nor 1,000 of anything else. Ten 100-watt light bulbs burning for 8 hours consume 10 x 100 watts x 8 hours of energy. That's (10 x 100 x 8) (watts x hours), or 8000 watt-hours, commonly expressed as 8 kilowatt-hours. A distance of 60 miles divided by 20 miles per hour is (60 / 20) [miles / (miles/hours)], or 3 [miles x (hours/miles)], or 3 hours. A mass of 4 kilograms times an acceleration of 0.5 meters per second squared is (4 x 0.5) [(kilograms x meters) / (seconds x seconds)], or 2 kg-m/s². The unit kg-m/s² is called a newton, so the result could also be called 2 newtons.

Multiplication and division of units is particularly useful whenever we need to convert one unit to another, for example before adding or subtracting. To go back to the first example, we can convert inches to centimeters using a conversion factor. (Examples of such factors are given in the Glossary.) So 12 inches times (2.54 centimeters / inch) = (12 x 2.54) (inches x centimeters / inches) = 30.5 centimeters. Or 12 inches divided by (0.3937 inches / centimeter) = (12 / 0.3937) [inches / (inches / centimeter)] = 30.5 [inches x (centimeters / inches)] = 30.5 centimeters. Notice that if we do the conversion correctly the unwanted units cancel out algebraically, leaving only the desired units. If we multiply instead of dividing, or vice versa, we will get incorrect units, something like inches squared per centimeter — an immediate tip-off to our mistake. Because this book will often perform calculations upon quantities with units, the reader should make sure he understands these examples.

Scalars and Vectors

A scalar is a quantity that has only magnitude (and perhaps a unit): 3.1416, 10 seconds, and 243 kilowatt-hours are all scalars. A quantity that has both magnitude and direction is called a vector. A bicycle may move northeast at a velocity of 18 miles per hour; in one second its position has changed 0.005 miles, also northeast; the force pressing its rear wheel onto the surface may be 130 pounds vertically downward. In all these examples of vectors, the direction is an essential part of the information. If the force holding the wheels onto the surface were to assume some other direction, the bicycle may fly off the road; if the bicycle's velocity is not toward the finish line but instead in some other direction, the outcome of the race may be very different. The direction of vector quantities must not be overlooked.

We usually represent vectors graphically by means of an arrow. Figure 0102 shows an example. The length of the arrow represents its magnitude; the arrowhead indicates its direction. Sometimes we need to add vectors together. Like

scalars, they must first be converted to identical units if necessary. Then they are added geometrically, taking both magnitude and direction into account. Figure 0103 shows vector A being added to vector B. The two vectors are first placed head to tail, being careful not to change the length or direction of either; then the sum, called the resultant (vector C in the illustration), is the vector that extends from the tail of one to the head of the other.

Suppose for example that vector A represents what the velocity of the air relative to a moving cyclist would be under windless conditions, and that vector B represents the actual velocity of the wind. The resultant vector C represents the apparent wind velocity perceived by the cyclist. In this simple case, A and B are perpendicular to each other, making the figure A–B–C a right triangle. Using the equations above, we can then calculate the magnitude (speed) and direction of that resultant velocity. If A is 15 mph east and B is 5 mph north, the magnitude of C is the square root of 15 squared plus 5 squared or about 15.8 mph. Its direction (the perceived wind direction) is the arctangent of 5/15 or about 18.4 degrees north of east; expressed as an azimuth, it's 90 − 18.4, or 71.6 degrees clockwise from north. (If triangle A–B–C were not a right triangle, it could be subdivided into two right triangles to allow the magnitudes to be calculated.)

Subtraction of vectors is almost as easy as addition. To subtract a vector from another, first reverse its direction (that is, change it by 180 degrees) without altering its magnitude. Then proceed to add. Figure 0104 illustrates this.

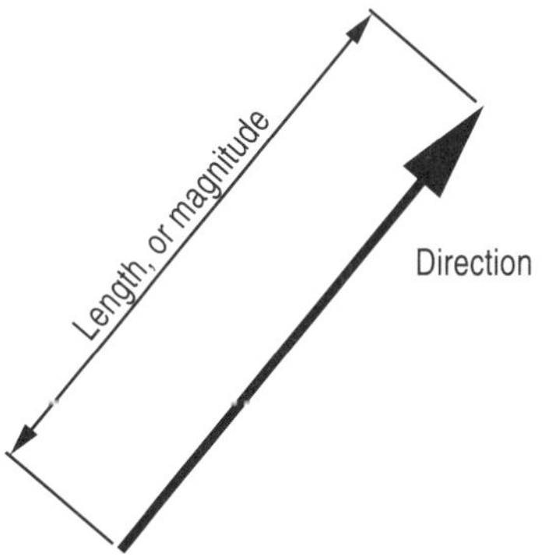

Fig. 0102. Vector representation. The elements of a vector are its length and direction.

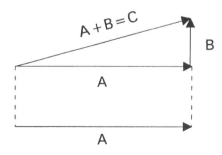

Fig. 0103. Addition of vectors. Place A and B head to tail without changing length or direction to form sum, vector C.

Multiplication of a vector by a scalar is even easier: double a downward force of 130 pounds is a force of 2 x 130 or 260 pounds in the same direction, downward.

The other operation we often need to do with a vector is to break it into its components. The components of a vector V are two other vectors whose directions are already specified and which add up to V. In practice, the components of a vector are always perpendicular to each other, for example north-south and east-west, or horizontal and vertical, or parallel to the direction of the bicycle's motion and perpendicular to the road surface. Looking back at Figure 0103, vector C might represent the bicycle's forward velocity up a steep grade. The horizontal component of C would then be A, the velocity to the right; the vertical component would be B, the velocity upward.

Accuracy and Precision

The terms accuracy and precision are often used interchangeably, but they have distinct meanings to the scientist.

Accuracy refers to closeness to the truth. A bullet near the center of a target indicates an accurate shot. A stopwatch that records a rider's time in a time trial correctly to the nearest second is usually accurate enough. A calculation of the power required for a cyclist to maintain 25 miles per hour on a level road is quite accurate if it manages to get the first three digits correct.

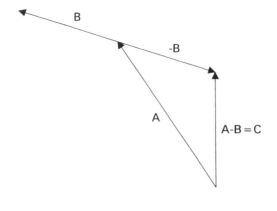

Fig. 0104. Subtraction of vectors. Reverse B to form –B, then add: A + (–B) = A–B = C.

Precision refers to closeness of tolerances, or the degree to which successive trials agree. Three bullet holes clustered together on a target indicate precision shooting, regardless of how close they are to the bull's-eye. A stopwatch may record times to a precision of one hundredth of a second, but that is no guarantee that the person operating it pushed the start and stop buttons at exactly correct times, or that the watch runs on time. An electronic calculator retains 8 or 10 digits of precision, but if the numbers it multiplies and divides are only accurate to the first 2 or 3 digits, it is unlikely that more than the first 2 or 3 digits of the result will be accurate, regardless of how many digits are displayed.

Mathematicians use the term significant digits to indicate the number of digits, starting with the leftmost non-zero digit, warranted by the accuracy of the numbers. For example, suppose you will be driving from New York to Chicago. You expect to average 50 miles per hour and know the cities are about 800 miles apart, so the trip should take 16 hours. Now suppose someone tells you that the actual distance from Times Square to Buckingham Fountain is 809.27 miles. Do you now plan on arriving exactly 16 hours, 11 minutes, and 7.44 seconds after you start? Of course not. Your expected average speed is not exactly 50.00000...; 50 is only a "ballpark" figure. The real average may turn out to be, for example, 49.60123 or 50.265. In fact, it may not even be between 49 and 51. It therefore has at most 2 significant digits. The 5 for sure, in that the number is much more likely to be closer to 50 than to either 40 or 60; but the 0 is rather less certain. Any calculations you make with it cannot be expected to have more than 2 significant digits, either.

In this book most of the calculations will be done to 3 significant digits. Many measurements cannot be made to an accuracy greater than 3 digits. For example, bicycle computers rely on the circumference of the wheel to calculate mileage: 209, 210, 211, and 212 may all be possible inputs for circumference in centimeters, but 210.3 is usually not. Therefore, only the first three digits of the computer's mileage display should be considered significant. Some numbers, such as the coefficient of rolling resistance, are not known even to 2 digits, either because they are difficult to measure, or because they vary with different brands, inflation pressures, or road conditions during a ride. And the chances are that the numbers in the examples will not exactly apply to the reader's own body and bicycle anyway. Given the limitations in accuracy, there is usually no point in carrying out calculations to greater than 3 significant digits. The reader following them with a calculator may therefore find his results differ slightly from the ones printed. It is no cause for concern.

Occasionally, however, in order to make a particular point, a calculation in the book may carry many more digits than usual. The excess precision is not to suggest that suddenly the numbers are known more accurately; it merely means that *if* a particular variable has exactly such-and-such a value (and it has to have *some* exact value, even if we don't know very well what it is), by carrying more digits we can see the effect of small changes that would otherwise be buried in the noise beyond the least significant digit.

Scientific Notation

How far is the earth from the sun? Astronomers tell us that on average the distance is about 93,000,000 miles. No wonder values such as this are called "astronomical" numbers. The many zeros readily identify the number as a sort we do not encounter every day, unless we happen to be astronomers. All scientists and engineers must, however, deal with very large or small numbers at least occasionally. When they do, they often express them in a form known as "scientific notation." Not counting a possible leading minus sign, a number expressed in scientific notation is the product of two numbers, the first in the range from 1 up to but not including 10, and the second a power of 10. See Table 0101 for a list giving examples of powers of 10. The superscript following the 10 is called the "power" or "exponent" of 10.

It shouldn't be difficult to discern the underlying principle and extend the table indefinitely far in either direction.

Table 0101. Some powers of 10

10 and exponent	value
10^{-5}	.00001
10^{-4}	.0001
10^{-3}	.001
10^{-2}	.01
10^{-1}	.1
10^{0}	1
10^{1}	10
10^{2}	100
10^{3}	1,000
10^{4}	10,000
10^{5}	100,000

What then is our original number, 93,000,000, expressed in scientific notation? Take it in two parts: the number between 1 and 10 must be 9.3 (followed by zeros if you like); the power of 10 must have the same number of digits as the original number: 10,000,000, which is 10^7. Therefore the number that represents the average distance to the sun in scientific notation is 9.3×10^7 miles. Try another example: there are 0.44704 meters per second in 1 mile per hour. That's 4.4704×10^{-1} m/s. Now try the reverse direction: the universal gravitational constant is 6.670×10^{-11} N-m^2/kg^2; when you write it all out, you should get 10 zeros between the decimal point and the first 6.

Besides preventing writer's cramp and helping guard against miscounting the zeros, scientific notation has another advantage. It helps show the precision of the number. Is 93,000,000 precise to the nearest mile, the nearest thousand miles, or what? Expressing it instead as 9.3×10^7 conveys the idea that there are two significant digits (the 9 and the 3), and that the number is therefore precise to the nearest 0.1×10^7 miles, that is 1×10^6 or one million miles. When we expressed the gravitational constant as 6.670×10^{-11}, we were deliberately implying that the zero following the seven is a significant digit.

Most scientific calculators can accept and display numbers in scientific notation, but numbers in scientific notation are also easy to multiply and divide by hand. Remember that 10^a times 10^b equals $10^{(a+b)}$, and 10^a divided by 10^b equals $10^{(a-b)}$. As an example, suppose you wanted to know how fast light from the sun reaches us. The speed of light is 3.00×10^8 meters per second. We saw the conversion factor for m/s to mph above. 3.00×10^8 m/s divided by 4.47×10^{-1} m/s per mph is $(3.00 / 4.47) \times (10^8 / 10^{-1})$ (m/s)/(m/s / mi/hr) or 0.671×10^9 or 6.71×10^8 mi/hr. Similarly, 9.3×10^7 mi divided by 6.7×10^8 mi/hr gives 1.4×10^{-1} hours. We may as well continue on in the same vein: 1.4×10^{-1} hours times 3.6×10^3 seconds per hour is 5.0×10^2 seconds, in other words 500 seconds. To add or subtract numbers in scientific notation, however, one must first align the decimal points by making the powers of ten the same. For example, $3.4 \times 10^{-3} + 1.2765 \times 10^{-1} = 0.0034 \times 10^{-1} + 1.2765 \times 10^{-1} = 1.3105 \times 10^{-1}$.

Physics Terms

A rider causes the bicycle to move by applying force to the pedals. If the pedals move, this force causes "work" to be done. "Work" here is used in the physicist's sense, force acting over a distance, and we see the result as the bicycle moves. Merely applying force to pedals that do not move — if the chain is jammed, for instance — is not work in that sense; the bicycle does not move. Work being done is the same as energy being expended. We also talk about power, which is the rate of energy expenditure, that is, energy spent or work done per unit of time. All of these concepts involve the notion of mass, a basic physical property that is closely related to but not quite the same thing as weight.

There are units for all these physical concepts. We will be dealing with a number of them, sometimes in the English (or U.S.) system, but more often in the metric system, particularly the "mks" (meter-kilogram-second) system, more formally known as the SI or International System.

All of us are already familiar with the units of time: seconds, minutes, and hours. We are also familiar with distance: in the English system, feet and miles; in the metric system, meters and the multiples of ten: millimeters (1/1,000 meter), centimeters (1/100 meter) and kilometers (1,000 meters). Force is measured in pounds, or (metric) newtons. Power is measured in horsepower, or (metric) watts. Work or energy has no simple unit in the English system; instead we see the compound units foot-pounds or (borrowing from metric) kilowatt-hours. The metric system employed by physicists simply measures work or energy in joules.

The mks unit of mass, the kilogram, should be familiar: it's 1,000 grams, another mass unit we use. Outside of physics texts, one seldom encounters the torpid English unit of mass, the slug, but some references distinguish between "lbm," pounds of mass, and "lbf," pounds of force. This book will ignore all three of those terms and use pounds only as a unit of force. Weight is an example of a force; its units are therefore pounds or newtons, not grams or kilograms. Definitions for all the units are to be found in the Glossary. There are many other units for most of these concepts, units such as years, furlongs, dynes, and calories, that we will not be using here.

The units of the mks metric system simplify our calculations. The system needs no conversion factors such as 12, 16, 5,280, or 33,000; most of the time we don't even need to multiply or divide by 10. Its units work together as neatly as a chain fits the teeth on a gear.

2
Force and Power

The bicyclist applies force to the pedals, force that is transmitted through the drivetrain to the wheels, causing the bicycle to move forward; but other forces also act on the bicycle and affect its motion. One such force is the friction between the parts of the bicycle with each other and with the road.

Rolling Resistance as a Force on the Bicycle

This friction has many sources. The chain rubs against the gear teeth, and its individual links and bushings rub against each other and against the chain lubricant — if any. In the pedals, bottom bracket, hubs, headset, and freewheel, bearings rub against each other, their lubricant, and the cups and cones that confine them. The tires and tubes deform as they compress under the rider's weight, causing the rubber and air molecules within them to collide with each other. Even the wheels, frame, axles, crankarms, and road surface deform. All these molecular collisions create heat, just as rubbing two sticks together does. While the heat produced is not enough to start a fire (unless perhaps the lubricant has dried up), it is nonethe-

less energy that is unable to be used for moving the bicycle. In this book, we label the friction from all these sources as "rolling resistance," even if strictly speaking some of the friction — such as that within the chain — has little to do with rolling. Rolling resistance is a force that acts in the direction opposite to the direction of motion.

Gravity as a Force on the Bicycle

Then there is gravity. Gravity is a factor in the above frictional forces, because almost all of them are proportional to weight, the combined weight of the rider and bicycle. Weight is itself the product of two factors. One is a local constant known as the acceleration due to gravity, the acceleration of gravity, or simply g. At any given spot on the earth, the acceleration due to gravity is constant, but its precise value varies slightly from place to place depending on latitude and altitude. The variation is a consequence of the universal law of gravitation between any two objects (see Appendix B). The most massive object in our vicinity is the earth. As we climb higher or move toward its bulging equator, we move farther from its center, weakening the gravitational attraction. The International Committee on Weights and Measures has adopted 9.80665 meters per second per second (m/s^2), or 32.174 ft/s^2, as the standard value of g, used for defining weights in terms of mass. That standard value is what the actual value would be at sea level at 45 degrees, 32 minutes, and 33 seconds of latitude. Places close to that latitude include the French coast about halfway between Bordeaux and La Rochelle, Fundy National Park in New Brunswick, the northernmost tip of Japan, the coast of Crimea, and (in the Southern Hemisphere) Dunedin, New Zealand. Almost everywhere in the United States except Alaska, the actual value of g is less than the standard value: at Atlanta, for example, it is 9.79524 m/s^2; at Austin, 9.79283; at Colorado Springs, 9.79490; at Honolulu, 9.78946; at Indianapolis, 9.80090; at Philadelphia, 9.80196; at San Francisco, 9.79965; and (one of the few exceptions) at Seattle, 9.80733.

The other factor in weight is mass, a property of an object that depends on its size and composition. The mass of an object is the same no matter whether the object is on the surface of the earth, on the moon, or out in space. While mass affects weight, which affects rolling resistance, more important to the cyclist is the direct effect of gravity on the rider and bicycle when the terrain is not flat. Gravity opposes the cyclist's efforts on uphills and assists on downhills, again in proportion to weight. Unlike, say, a tennis ball tossed before a serve, the bicycle never moves absolutely vertically. The portion of gravity that most interests us is just the vector component in line with the motion of the bicycle. Only a fraction of the full acceleration due to gravity affects that motion, and that fraction is proportional to the steepness of the grade the bicycle is climbing or descending. Sometimes gravity is lumped together with internal frictional forces and included in the term rolling resistance, but it seems perverse to call a force that accelerates the bicycle down a hill "resistance." We will keep it separate.

Aerodynamic Drag as a Force on the Bicycle

Finally, there is the force resulting from interaction with the molecules of the air. Aerodynamic drag (or aerodynamic resistance) is the component of aerodynamic force opposite to the direction of motion. (The other component is lift, aerodynamic force in the vertical direction. While lift is important for airplanes and even racing cars, we will consider it to be negligible for bicycles. Too bad — most of us could use a little lift up hills.)

There are two aspects of aerodynamic drag. One is form drag, resulting from the shape of the object and the turbulence it produces. The reduced air pressure in the turbulence behind a moving object actually creates a suction that tugs backward on the object. Some shapes are obviously more "aerodynamic" (streamlined) than others and reduce this turbulence. An aircraft fuselage and the profile of a sports-racing car approach the ideally streamlined shape that minimizes form drag. A racing bicyclist on a standard bicycle falls considerably short of that ideal, however, and an upright recreational rider or mountain biker is worse yet. The other aspect of aerodynamic drag is skin friction, resulting from the friction of the air against the surface of the moving object. For simplicity, however, we characterize both aspects with one number, the coefficient of aerodynamic drag or C_D, a quantification of how slippery the moving object is. This number is considered constant, even though in reality it varies slightly with wind speed and direction. Aerodynamic drag is proportional to C_D.

Yes, this is the same C_D that automobile commercials love to brag about, but they conveniently ignore frontal area. Aerodynamic drag is also proportional to frontal area, which obviously enough is the area of the largest cross section of the moving object as seen from the front, that is, perpendicular to the direction of motion. (Picture, for example, the vehicle coming toward you silhouetted against a background of sky.) It does little good to have a low C_D if the frontal area is large — as it is for most autos. For bicycling, both the C_D and the frontal area must include the rider in addition to the bicycle itself.

Aerodynamic drag is also proportional to the density of the air. (The density of any material is the ratio of its mass to its volume.) Although the density of air seldom changes significantly during the course of an event, for completeness we can look at the factors that influence air density. One such factor is temperature. Air is less dense at higher temperatures. Density (and therefore aerodynamic drag) drops about 3.5% for every gain of 10 degrees Celsius (18 degrees Fahrenheit). Air density is also proportional to barometric pressure. For example, density at a pressure of 29 inches of mercury (737 mm Hg) is 3% less than at a pressure of 30 inches (762 mm). The barometric pressure value one hears quoted in a weather forecast is not necessarily the actual pressure, however; it may be what a barometer would read if it were at sea level, because altitude (elevation or height above sea level) has a significant effect. Barometric pressure drops about 1% for every 80 meters (262 feet) gain in altitude. In Colorado Springs, with an altitude of 5900 feet, aerodynamic drag is typically only 80% of what it is in Wilmington, Delaware, at about 80 feet above sea level. In Mexico City (altitude 7,800 feet), drag is even less, only 93% of what it typically is in Colorado Springs. Humidity also affects air density, but only slightly. Perhaps surprisingly, at 20° C (68° F), air is 1% less dense when the relative humidity is 100% than when it is perfectly dry.

Putting these all together, for a record attempt the cyclist ideally wants a hot, humid day, possibly with rain threatening (for low barometric pressure), in a place such as Bogota, Colombia (altitude 8660 feet) or La Paz, Bolivia (altitude 11,909 feet). Most of cycling's world records were indeed set at high altitude velodromes. Lest this information cause even more cyclists to stampede to their travel agents, it is only fair to mention that not only are some of these low-density-producing conditions unlikely to occur simultaneously, but

some may reduce the amount of power a cyclist is able to develop. Temperature, for instance, drops with increasing altitude, which may be just as well, for most cyclists are either less able or less inclined to exert themselves in hot, humid air, let alone thin air. Perhaps for such reasons, the increases in speed at high altitude are not as great as one might expect. For example, both Francesco Moser and Jeanne Longo set 1-hour records in both Milan and Mexico City. Moser rode 49.80 and 51.15 km respectively, Longo 43.59 and 46.35 km respectively. By the author's calculations, had Moser managed to generate the same power in Mexico City as he did in Milan, he might have gone over 3.5 km farther. Likewise, Longo might have gone over 1.5 km farther in her hour in Mexico. These estimates do not imply that the Milan records are the greater achievements (though in some sense that may be true), but only that these outstanding athletes developed significantly less power setting their high altitude records.

Even more important to aerodynamic drag is speed, because drag is proportional to the square of the airspeed. The airspeed in turn depends on the bicycle's (ground) speed, the wind speed, and the relative direction the wind is blowing. In some cases, the wind may be blowing in the same direction as the bicycle is moving — a tailwind — and be strong enough to move the bicycle sufficiently fast all by itself. A large pack of riders may also move the air along fast enough that riders within the pack can coast. Aerodynamic drag then proves to be an asset. Far more often, however, drag acts against the cyclist, because the bicycle's own speed makes almost any wind conditions seem like a headwind. As with rolling resistance, aerodynamic drag is always viewed as a force opposite to the direction of motion, even if it occasionally has a negative value that makes the term "drag" seem a misnomer. See Appendix C for a program that makes airspeed computation easy.

Force Equations

Transforming the above verbiage into mathematics, the following are the equations for the forces acting on the bicycle, other than the rider's pedaling. For rolling resistance and gravity,

$$F_R = g\, m\, C_R$$

$$F_G = g\, m\, \%G/100$$

Here F_R is (the force of) rolling resistance and F_G is the force of gravity: the force in line with the bicycle's motion, that is, not the force pressing it onto the ground. The two equations are similar: g is the acceleration due to gravity, m is the mass of the rider and bicycle, C_R is a constant known as the coefficient of rolling resistance, a quantification of how reluctant the bicycle is to roll, and $\%G$ is the grade (or gradient) of the slope, expressed in percent, which is why it must be divided by 100. For aerodynamic drag,

$$F_D = 0.5\, C_D\, \rho\, v_a^2\, A$$

Here F_D is the drag (force), C_D is the coefficient of aerodynamic drag, ρ (the Greek letter rho) is the air density, v_a is the airspeed, and A is the frontal area. When the terms in these equations are expressed in mks units, the forces all come out in newtons. Otherwise, the equations also need some conversion factors.

Let's take some examples. For a recreational rider on a paved surface, the coefficient of rolling resistance may be about 0.0045. Suppose the rider weighs 175 pounds and his bike weighs 25 pounds. First, express the quantities in mks: total mass, (175 + 25) times 0.454 kilograms per pound = 90.8 kg. (See the Glossary for this and other unit conversion factors.) Rolling resistance is therefore 9.8 m/s² times 90.8 kg times 0.0045 = 4.0 kg-m/s² or newtons. At one newton per 0.2249 pounds, that's about 0.90 pounds of force pushing backward on the bicycle.

On level ground, computing the force due to gravity is trivial: it's zero, because the grade is zero. Up (or down) a 2% grade, one that rises (or

drops) 2 feet vertically for every 100 horizontally, the force of gravity is 9.8 times 90.8 times 2/100 or 17.8 newtons, about 4 pounds pushing backward (or forward). It is no surprise that even on a fairly easy grade, this force is a lot greater than rolling resistance. Suppose this recreational rider has his hands atop the bars and his arms are straight, not bent at the elbows. His frontal area is then about 4.3 square feet (0.40 square meters); his drag coefficient about 1.0. Typical air density is 1.2 kg/m³. Suppose the bicycle is moving at 15 miles per hour into still air; that is, 6.71 meters per second. Aerodynamic drag is therefore 0.5 times 1.0 times 1.2 times 6.71 times 6.71 times 0.40 = 10.8 newtons, about 2.4 pounds.

The total forces acting on the bicycle, forces that the rider's pedaling has to counter, are therefore 4.0 + 0 + 10.8 = 14.8 newtons on level ground, 4.0 + 17.8 + 10.8 = 32.6 newtons up the 2% grade, and 4.0 − 17.8 + 10.8 = −3.0 newtons down the 2% grade. The last one has a negative sign: gravity offsets the drag forces and would move the bike forward even if the rider doesn't pedal.

Power

Although the forces on the bicycle and rider are important, more often we will be talking about power, because the rider can change the amount of force he applies to the pedals whenever he likes, just by changing gears. At any speed, he can tailor the force to suit his preferences and riding style. He has much less freedom regarding the amount of power he must supply. As long as conditions stay the same — the same total force from rolling resistance, gravity, and aerodynamic drag — he must maintain the same power output in order to maintain the same speed.

We already mentioned that power is the rate of doing work. An equivalent definition is that power is the product of force applied to a body and the velocity of that body:

power = force **x** velocity

If the force is expressed in newtons and the velocity in meters per second, the power will be expressed in watts.

Both force and velocity imply a direction: they are vector quantities. If we are talking about the power needed to keep a bicycle moving, the direction is of course the direction along the bicycle's path of motion, which is also the way we have already defined the forces on the bicycle. A certain fraction of the power the rider applies to the bicycle at a particular speed goes toward offsetting each of the various forces we have already discussed. To counter rolling resistance, for example, the power needed is the force of rolling resistance times the speed of the bicycle. (That was easy, wasn't it?) To counter an uphill slope, if any, the power needed is the force of gravity in line with the bicycle's motion times the speed of the bicycle. (Again, easy.) A downhill slope is almost as easy to understand. Power is again involved, and it is still force times velocity, but this time the amount is negative, because according to the way we defined it, the force of gravity on a downhill is also negative. So on a downhill the rider in effect gets a credit, an amount he can subtract from the total power he owes the bike. Finally, aerodynamic drag can also be positive or negative, but here the velocity that matters is not the speed of the bicycle relative to the ground but the speed relative to the air. The power needed to offset motion through the air is the force of aerodynamic drag times the airspeed.

Add those three quantities — the power needed to offset rolling resistance, the power needed to offset gravity, and the power needed to offset aerodynamic drag — and you have the total power the rider needs to apply in order to maintain his speed under constant conditions. If conditions change — he gets a flat, or the slope gets steeper, or he goes into a tucked position, or the headwind picks up, or he decides to go faster — then no doubt his power output will change. But when conditions are stable, speed and power are locked together with an equation:

$$P = (F_R + F_G) \, v_g + F_D \, v_a$$

In this equation, P is power; the forces F_R, F_G, and F_D are rolling resistance, the force of gravity, and aerodynamic drag, respectively, just as we defined them earlier; and v_g and v_a are ground speed and airspeed, respectively.

Let's use the same examples we did above. There the rolling resistance was 4.0 N. On level ground, the force of gravity was 0; on the 2% slope it was 17.8 N or –17.8 N depending on whether the bike was going up or down the slope. Aerodynamic drag was 10.8 N. The bike was moving 15 mph into still air, so both ground speed and airspeed were 6.71 m/s. Total power needed to maintain that speed on level ground is (4.0 + 0) x 6.71 + 10.8 x 6.71 or 99 watts. Up and down the slope the corresponding power levels needed are 219 W and –20 W. Except perhaps with a track bike, it is difficult to apply a negative 20 watts pedaling; it looks like either speed will be increasing, or an additional force — braking — will have to be applied to maintain a constant speed.

It is important for the cyclist to remember that it is *power* that is locked together with speed, not merely *force*. Many cyclists seem to think that to achieve a higher speed, they must push harder on the pedals. Increased force certainly does increase power, as long as the cadence doesn't drop; but it is equally effective, and easier on the knees, to increase power by adopting a faster cadence with no increase in force. Most effective of all is to be able to apply a high force at a high cadence: that is how high power is developed.

Calculating Power

We will need to use the power-speed equation often. So often, in fact, that it can easily become cumbersome, especially because we need to substitute into it the full expressions that make up the individual forces on its right-hand side. In consequence, we won't explicitly bring this equation up again. It will still be necessary to use it, understand, but we won't drag the messy calculations out onto the printed page. We'll pretend we have a gnome down in the basement who will perform the power calculations whenever we need them. If you wish to do the calculations yourself, you will soon find that *you* have become that gnome. But cheer up — Appendix C in this book has a computer program to help make the gnome's task easier.

Now if you think the power equation is messy, try solving it for speed; that is, try to express ground speed in terms of power. A nasty task, but fortunately our gnome can be just as adept at this power-to-speed calculation if he uses another program in the appendix. If your gnome lacks a computer or programmable calculator, be prepared for a long wait as the poor fellow goes about the problem by trial and error.

Calculating Acceleration

This is as good a place as any to introduce another program in Appendix C, one that calculates acceleration. The elapsed time, distance covered, and speed attained by an accelerating bike involve more complicated calculations than merely applying "F = m a"; the reason is a physical property known as moment of inertia, a subject that will be covered in Chapter 12. In addition, air resistance is always a major factor for a bicycle, and it varies a great deal as speed changes. Our gnome will find the calculations a bit overwhelming without a computer, but the program in Appendix C makes the task easy. The program accounts for moment of inertia as well as the forces on the bike, and handles the changing air resistance by dividing the time into brief slices and treating the resistance as constant during each slice.

Calculating Deceleration

Car magazines often publish braking performance data in terms of g's: some number (such as 0.8) times the acceleration due to gravity. This assumes that deceleration under braking is nearly linear (a good approximation), and implies that other drivers ought to be able to expect similar results. Comparable performance figures for bikes are not to be found. Although bike braking is much the same,

four factors make it inadvisable to list a typical braking deceleration number. Automobile drivers do most of their braking on level ground, but most bicycle braking is done on downhills, where the grade must be taken into account because gravity reduces the effective deceleration. On steep grades, bicycle braking is further limited by the danger that the rear wheel may lift, vaulting the rider over the handlebars — a concern automobile drivers do not have. Although the weight of the driver of a car is only a small fraction of the car's weight, bicycle rider weight is very significant; it greatly affects the rate of deceleration. Finally, airspeed is almost always high on a downhill, and the coefficient of aerodynamic drag is higher for a bicyclist than a car, so air resistance is a significant decelerating force; it also varies with speed.

It helps to deal with force instead of some number of g's. Typical forces from braking, considered in the direction of motion rather than (for example) from the brake onto the rim, range up to 450 newtons on a level paved surface, somewhat less on a steep downhill, much less off-road or under wet conditions. (The author obtained this figure from a few trial runs. No doubt higher figures are possible.) Summing this force with those from rolling and aerodynamic resistance and dividing by mass gives acceleration — in this case, deceleration. A programmable calculator or computer can iterate this calculation over many fractions of a second, accounting for the changing airspeed. Sorry it isn't as simple as 0.8 g, but a program in Appendix C (the same one used for acceleration) helps make these calculations easy for our gnome. It is for this same reason that this book does not include a simple formula for minimum stopping distance.

Energy

Once we know how much power is being applied, it is easy to calculate energy expended (or work done):

$$E = P\,t$$

Here E is energy (or work), P power, and t elapsed time. This is another equation we will use often, but one so easy that we don't need to hide it in the basement. In the way we use the equation, P will be constant throughout the time interval, but the equation is equally valid if power varies and P is the average value of power during the interval t. If P is in watts and t in seconds, E will be in joules. Like power, energy is a scalar, not a vector.

A Standard Rider and Bicycle

People of course vary in size and riding styles, and bikes vary somewhat, too. Because we will need to do some performance calculations from time to time, it makes sense to pick one standard that we can use in these examples. Somewhat arbitrarily, our standard rider will be a male of average size, dressed in usual racing style clothing, in a full racing crouch upon a more-or-less standard road bike. For the record, we'll say that these conditions mean that the coefficients of rolling resistance and aerodynamic drag are 0.003 and 0.88, respectively, that the frontal area is 0.36 square meters, and that he and the bike together have a mass of 90 kilograms (that is, they weigh about 198 pounds). This may be a little higher than the mass of a world-class athlete on a state-of-the-art bike, but probably more representative of typical American male performance-oriented cyclists. Of course the data will differ for a different sort of rider, but adopting this standard rider will usually not alter the general conclusions. The author will try to point out the exceptions when it does, and the reader may of course redo the calculations with data more closely representing himself. The air our rider passes through is also reasonably standard: dry, 20° C (68° F), at sea level: density 1.205 kg/m^3, and we assume the local acceleration due to gravity is more typical of the United States, 9.8017 m/s^2.

Gearing

Why do bicycles have so many gears? Ask a few cyclists that question, and their answers will most often be "to climb hills better" and "for more performance." Neither of these answers is necessarily accurate.

For hill climbing, what the cyclist needs is a low gear, at least one gear that is low enough; beyond that, the number of gears is irrelevant. (Why a low gear? In a low gear, the bike moves only a short distance forward for each full circle the pedals make. During a climb, that means the bike and rider are lifted only a little way further up at a time. The low gear makes climbing relatively easy, for the same reason that going up a flight of stairs one step at a time is easier than making one giant step up. Of course it's also relatively slow, which is probably why the gear is called "low.")

Mountain bikes and touring bikes usually have triple cranksets (or chainsets, for our British readers), giving half again as many "gears" or "speeds" (i.e. gear ratios) as a double crankset provides, and it is true that the additional gears from this arrangement are low ones. However, it is also true that six-speed freewheels on recreational, sport, and racing bikes have been superseded by seven-, eight-, nine, and even ten-speed models, which paradoxically often provide no low gears whatsoever. The lowest gears ever commercially available were found on a five-speed freewheel. Not only is that freewheel no longer available, but five-speed freewheels as a group are obsolete.

"More performance" is closer to the mark, but again additional gears are no guarantee of better performance. To see why, we need to understand why most bicycles have multiple gears. After all, early bicycles did not. On a "penny farthing" or "ordinary" high-wheeler, for example, the pedals and cranks were solidly attached to the hub of the large front wheel; when the pedals made one complete revolution, so did the wheel. (We will see later why the wheel was so large. Please be patient for now.)

Engines and Rotation

Vehicles of all sorts obtain the power they need from an engine. The engine rotates something, such as a drive shaft or drive wheel, which may in turn rotate other parts until finally the rotation is transmitted to the vehicle's wheel(s) or some other motion-producing device such as a propeller. For bicycles the engine is of course the human rider. On a typical bicycle, the human engine's legs rotate a crankset, which drives a chain, which rotates another gear, which rotates the rear wheel.

All engines have a characteristic power curve. See Figure 0301 for a graph of three examples — pick any one for the discussion that follows. The vertical direction represents engine power, with zero power at the bottom of the graph, and more power the higher up we move on the graph. The horizontal direction represents engine rotational speed (rpm, or revolutions per minute), with zero rotation at the extreme left, and faster rotations to the right. The curved line represents the relationship of power to rpm. At the lower left corner, we see that at zero rpm, when the engine is not rotating at all, it produces zero power. Once the engine begins rotating, it starts producing power. Generally, the faster it rotates, the more power it

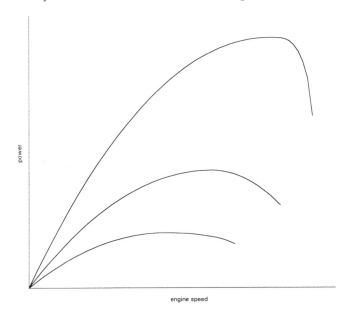

Fig. 0301. Characteristic engine power curves. Bottom: low performance, output not critical; top: high performance, peak power within relatively narrow engine speed range.

produces. As rpm goes up, however, the power produced is not quite proportional to speed: the line is not straight, but begins to curve. Eventually power reaches a plateau, in which additional engine speed increases power very little or not at all. Finally power drops off with additional rpm.

Consider what happens with two familiar engines: the internal combustion engine in a car, and a cyclist on a bike. The car's engine speed is indicated on the car's tachometer (if it has one) and by the audible pitch its exhaust makes. The cyclist's engine speed is the cadence, the number of pedal revolutions per minute, which may be indicated on a cycle computer or merely counted while a watch measures the elapsed time. At zero rpm, the engine is not yet started; the vehicle stays put. Once started, the car engine does not run at zero rpm, but instead idles at a speed well above that. Likewise no cyclist inches the pedals around over a period of several seconds — it just is not a natural motion. At very low rpm, the engine "lugs:" it does not run smoothly, and is in danger of stalling, so the driver tries to get through the low rpm band quickly. With a manual transmission, the driver may slip the clutch so that the engine can run at a higher speed, providing intermittent power until the vehicle reaches an adequate speed. (In an automatic transmission, some slip is built in.) The cyclist may do something similar, such as stand on the pedals but not attempt to pedal through the entire circle, until the bike is up to speed. If an engine is forced to run for extended periods of time at very low speeds, damage to its bearings may result. In humans, the bearings are in the joints: the hips, the ankles, and especially the knees. In any case, output power is low at low engine speeds.

At medium rpm, the vehicle responds well to power. As the driver applies more throttle via the accelerator pedal, or the cyclist increases pedaling effort, engine rpm goes up; the engine provides more power, and the vehicle increases speed. At high rpm, however, as the needle on the tachometer approaches the redline, the car engine begins to sound noisy and strained; likewise the cyclist approaching his maximum cadence becomes uncomfortable and runs out of breath. It becomes evident that a further increase in engine speed is not going to increase power. If forced to run beyond its limit, the engine "over-revs:" internally its parts cannot keep up with the speed demanded, it loses smoothness, and power drops off. In a car engine, something may even break. The freewheel mechanism on most bicycles helps prevent such damage to the cyclist, but on a fixed-gear track bike, injury would be a real possibility during a fast downhill.

Gears are used to keep engine rpm within a desirable range. What range is desirable? The range must of course exclude the very low and very high engine speeds that may provoke injury or discomfort. Beyond observing that simple criterion, the range depends on the level of performance needed. In leisurely driving or riding (like the bottom curve of Figure 0301), power output is not critical. Therefore, a wide range of engine speeds may be acceptable. Perhaps high engine speeds, which are noisy in a car and require some concentration on a bike, are less acceptable, but in that case, the driver or cyclist can always slow down. Any gear that permits operating the engine within that wide acceptable range is also acceptable. Under these conditions, a few gears with widely spaced ratios are sufficient to accommodate different vehicle speeds.

However, in a high-performance application, such as racing, power output is more critical (see the top curve of Figure 0301, for example). Through performance tuning of a car engine, or training and conditioning of a cyclist, the power curve of a racing engine has more of a pronounced peak. Not only does it produce more power than its lower-performance counterparts, but maximum power occurs only within a relatively narrow band of rpm. If the racing driver or cyclist fails to keep power output close to the available peak, he will be uncompetitive. Because the desirable range under these conditions is very narrow, racing vehicles usually have several, closely spaced gear ratios.

If many gears can help keep engine speed in the desired range, why shouldn't all vehicles have 10, 20, or 100 gears? What would it hurt to have more than enough? You know the answer already:

Extra gears add cost and complexity, not to mention weight. Table 0301 summarizes what sorts of vehicles and applications should (and do) use different numbers of gears.

Table 0301. How Many Gears?

One Gear

❏ near constant conditions and speeds: compressor, airplane, bike for a flat time trial, at the shore, around the local neighborhood, etc.

❏ minimum weight and complexity: go-kart, track bike

❏ maximum reliability, low cost, simple operation: kiddie bike, leisure bike

❏ ultra-flexible engine: electric drill, electric car, track sprint cyclist

Few Gears

❏ variable operating conditions and speeds: car for both parking lots and freeways, bike for rolling or windy country

❏ low cost and complexity, simple operation: passenger automobile, leisure bike

❏ flexible engine: big automobile V-8, untrained cyclist or one unconcerned about performance

Many Gears

❏ extremely variable conditions and speeds: heavily loaded truck, loaded touring bike, mountain bike

❏ power output critical: racing car, racing bike

- fuel economy critical: long-distance truck, long-distance cyclist

- inflexible engine: small or highly tuned car or truck engine, highly trained cyclist

Relationship between Engine Speed and Vehicle Speed

So far we have assumed that the greater the engine speed, the faster the vehicle goes. That is true as long as the selected gear ratio stays the same. In fact, there is a much more precise relationship between engine speed and vehicle speed.

Consider an ungeared bike such as a high-wheeler. The cyclist's cadence is the engine rpm, and that is the same as the wheel's rpm. (The driven wheel's rpm, that is. The other wheel, in this case the high-wheeler's small rear wheel, is not driven by pedaling and need not concern us.) Each time the driven wheel revolves one full turn, the bicycle moves the same distance as the wheel's circumference. Therefore the speed is the product of the cadence and the circumference. Suppose the wheel has a diameter of 72 inches and the cyclist is pedaling so that the cranks, and the whole wheel, turn one complete revolution every second. Every second the bike advances $\pi \times 72$ inches, because the circumference of a circle is π (about 3.1416) times the diameter, so the speed is $\pi \times 72$ inches per second. To convert to feet per second, multiply by 1 foot per 12 inches (1/12), or if you prefer, divide by 12 inches per foot: 18.8 feet/second. With further multiplications or divisions, you'll see the speed is 5.7 m/s or 12.8 mph.

Here is a clue as to why the driven wheel on a penny-farthing was so big: The bigger the wheel, the greater the speed. Yet the bike in this example, with a wheel almost three times the size of a modern bike's, goes only 12.8 mph, maybe double that if the cyclist pedals furiously. Because cyclists were as obsessed with speed back in the penny-farthing's era as they are now, even larger wheels were common, despite the fact that they made mounting and dismounting awkward or dangerous, and increased the distance of a fall induced by the abysmal unpaved or cobblestone road surfaces.

A bike with gears is only slightly more complicated. First we must understand how gears work. If two identical gears are meshed or chained together, it is clear that both must turn at the same speed. Figure 0302, like most of the figures in this book, reduces the form of the physical objects into simple geometric figures so that we focus on the geometry rather than become distracted by irrelevant details. In this case, the figure depicts a chain connecting two equal-size gears as a straight line connecting two circles (of which only the tops are shown). Inside each circle is shown an equal angle (30 degrees) through which one can imagine the gears turning and advancing the chain and the circumferences of both circles a certain amount. Figure 0303 depicts one gear twice as big as the other in the same simplified way. Here the angle shown inside the small one is 30 degrees and the angle inside the big one is 15 degrees, yet the chain motion or circumferential motion of each gear is the same distance. Then for every turn of the big gear, the small one must make two turns. Or for every turn of the small gear, the big one must make one half turn. The actual sizes of the gears do not

Fig. 0302. Two identical (and idealized) gears chained together. When one advances a certain angle, the other does the same.

Fig. 0303. One (idealized) gear twice as big as the other. When the smaller one advances a certain angle, the bigger one advances half that angle.

matter; what does matter is the ratio of those sizes, (2/1 = 2 in Figure 0303). We could determine gear sizes and therefore the ratio by measuring their diameters or circumferences, but there is an easier way. Modern multi-speed bicycles have standardized half-inch spacing between chain links or gear teeth. So all we need to do is count the number of teeth on the two gears and we have a measure of their sizes; divide the number of teeth on one by the number of teeth on the other to determine the ratio. (There is an even easier way: often the number of teeth is stamped on the gear.)

Suppose the gear to which the cranks are attached (called a chainwheel or chainring) is the same size as the gear to which the rear wheel is attached (called a cog or sprocket), and the two are connected by the chain. Then the rear wheel is being driven at the same rpm as the crank, and the situation is essentially the same as our earlier high-wheeler example: the bicycle's speed is the cadence times the circumference of the driven wheel. If however the chainwheel is twice the size of the cog, you will see that the cog, and the rear wheel, must revolve at twice the rpm of the crank, so the distance the bicycle moves per crank revolution is twice the circumference of its rear (driven) wheel. Therefore the bicycle's speed is the cadence times the circumference of the driven wheel times the gear ratio, 2. This is exactly like having a driven wheel with twice the circumference, and this is a clue to why high-wheelers became obsolete with the advent of chains and gears. With suitable gearing, the relatively small wheels of "safety" bicycles can behave like much larger wheels. With a safety, the cyclist no longer needed to climb dangerously high off the ground to obtain adequate speed.

Because wheels come in a few different sizes, and gears come in all sorts of different sizes, for comparison purposes it helps to boil these all down into one unit. That unit is called "gear-inches" — in the non-metric world, at least. For a vehicle with a directly driven wheel, such as a high-wheeler or a child's tricycle, the number of gear-inches is the same as the diameter of the driven wheel in inches. Our 72-inch-diameter high-wheeler is a good example: 72 gear-inches. For a geared bicycle, gear-inches must factor in the gear ratio, that is,

$$\text{gear-inches} = f\,w/r$$

where f is the number of teeth on the (front) chainwheel, w is the diameter of the driven wheel in inches, r is the number of teeth on the (rear) cog, and the space between the f and the w implies multiplication. For example, on a bike with 27-in. wheels, if the chain runs from a 52-tooth chainwheel to a 14-tooth cog, the number of gear-inches is 27 x 52/14, a little over 100.

While we are on the subject of equations, it is as good as time as any to relate gear-inches and cadence to speed. If g.i. is the gear-inches of the selected gear combination and rpm is the cadence in revolutions per minute, then the speed v in ft/s is g.i. x π x rpm x 1/12 ft/in x 1/60 min/s, that is

$$v = 0.004363 \text{ g.i. rpm feet per second}$$

Similar conversions for other units give

$$v = 0.001330 \text{ g.i. rpm meters per second (m/s)}$$

$$v = 0.002975 \text{ g.i. rpm miles per hour (mph).}$$

Range of Gearing

Gear ratio range is the most important consideration when choosing gears for the bicycle. The basic principle is to be able to maintain one's optimum cadence come hill or high water. Well, perhaps not high water, but certainly the steepest downhills on which pedaling is still desirable (i.e. safe), the steepest uphills encountered when the rider is already dead tired, and everything in between. With a cycle computer that registers cadence, or with an ordinary speedometer and a little math, it is easy to determine whether one's bike's gearing meets that criterion.

Competitive riders are normally in excellent physical condition. Even so, through tradition or rider vanity, most racing bikes lack sufficiently low gears for hilly country when judged by the above criterion. Because racers have been riding and winning on such supposedly over-geared bicycles for decades, skepticism is a perfectly reasonable reaction to this assertion.

Let us work some examples to illustrate. In a hilly area, such as that near the author's southeast Pennsylvania home, roads with grades of 6% and under are common, it is easy to find 10% grades with a little effort, and even a 15% grade may be lurking, though mercifully such grades are rare. (Mountain bikers will regularly encounter grades this steep and even steeper on hilly trails, and anything is possible off the trail. Fortunately, mountain bikes without a triple crankset and low gears are practically unknown.) While many recreational bicyclists try to avoid steep hills, road racing courses often deliberately include especially steep grades to test the abilities of the competitors.

Let us arbitrarily adopt 80 rpm as a good cadence for plenty of power output without endangering the knees. If we ignore criterium gearing that is clearly not intended for hilly courses, often the lowest gear on a racing bike is 42/24; with many component groups, the lowest possible gear that could be fitted is 39/26. With 700C wheels (about 26.3 inches in diameter), the corresponding

ratios in gear-inches and the resulting speed at 80 rpm are given in Table 0302.

What grades could our standard rider climb at these speeds? First, let us consider the amount of long-term power that a typical rider can develop. Table 0303 indicates three such power levels, and the corresponding speed our standard rider would attain on a flat, windless course.

Now we can determine what grades our rider could climb. For example, if he can produce a maximum of 171 watts, he can climb any grade up to a certain maximum at which he is exerting 171 watts of power while moving at the speed corresponding to 80 rpm in his minimum gear. Table 0304 lists these maxima. (Note: Riders who together with their bikes weigh less than our standard rider will be able to climb somewhat steeper grades.)

As you can see, quite a few hills in rolling country will be steeper than most of these maximum grades. Only the fittest (or lightest) riders can expect to be able to climb most of the grades in a hilly course by spinning their lowest gear at 80 rpm. Fitting a 39/26 certainly helps, but not a great deal. Even the fittest (or lightest) riders will be under-geared if an exceptionally steep hill comes along.

Of course, riders are in fact able to climb such steep grades in these gears. Competitive riders have two possible ways to do so. One is to increase power output temporarily, for however long the steep grade lasts. This method assumes that the rider is capable of such a short-term burst of power, which may or may not be the case. Increasing effort will certainly be tiring, leaving less power to apply when the road levels out. The second way is to reduce cadence, and along with it

Table 0302. Typical low racing gears

gear	gear-inches	speed at 80 rpm
42/24	46.0	4.9 m/s (11.0 mph)
39/26	39.5	4.2 m/s (9.4 mph)

Table 0303. Typical power levels and speeds on level roads

power	171 W (.23 hp)	228 W (.31 hp)	297 W (.40 hp)
speed on level ground	9 m/s (20.1 mph)	10 m/s (22.4 mph)	11 m/s (24.6 mph)

Table 0304. Maximum grades that can be climbed at 80 rpm

speed m/s	gear at 80 rpm	max grade at 171 W	max grade at 228 W	max grade at 297 W
4.9	42/24	3.1%	4.4%	6.0%
4.2	39/26	3.9%	5.5%	7.3%

the speed. To avoid excess strain on the knees and leg muscles at lowered cadences, the rider often climbs such grades "out of the saddle," i.e. standing. Climbing out of the saddle is not as efficient, either physiologically or aerodynamically, as pedaling while seated; that is, the rider spends more energy standing than he would seated at the same speed, making this technique suitable only for relatively short climbs. Of course the rider can apply a combination of the two methods. Non-competitive riders have a third option: walking. (A friend of the author's calls this option the "24-inch gear," i.e. one's own two feet.) Taking small steps is equivalent to having a very low gear — much lower, in fact, than 24 gear-inches. Not that pushing a bike up a steep hill is fun, but on the steepest slopes, walking and riding the bike both use about the same amount of energy.

To sum up: the standard low gear on a racing bike is too high for all but the strongest and lightest riders to maintain a rapid steady cadence, unless the terrain is not very hilly. Such gearing is a particularly questionable choice for a recreational rider. For genuine competitors, however, there is more to the subject; Chapter 6 supplies some justification.

Minimum Recommended Gear

Tables 0305 through 0307 expand on the above discussion by listing the gear ratio in gear-inches needed to climb a particular grade, depending on weight, for three different power output levels.

Each table assumes that 60 rpm is the practical minimum cadence, even though 80 or more may be preferable. The weights are for rider plus bicycle, including all clothing and accessories. They range from that of a lightweight woman or adolescent on a pure racing bike to that of a fairly large man on a heavily loaded touring bike. The table also assumes that the rider is upright, not crouched like our standard rider, and therefore has a drag coefficient of 1.1 and a frontal area of 0.51 square meters. It assumes the rider is on a bicycle with narrow tires; gearing should of course be a little lower with wide touring tires and lower yet for mountain bike tires, which have more

rolling resistance. It also assumes that there is no wind; while wind is not usually a big factor at low climbing speeds, riders who expect to battle uphill headwinds should adopt even lower gears.

The grades vary from very moderate slopes to the steepest hills one is ever likely to encounter on paved roads. The three power levels are 75 watts, about what a healthy non-athlete or an average tourist can maintain for several hours; 300 watts, the level a good athlete can maintain for several hours; and 150 watts, something in between. Any rider can exceed his average level for a short period of time, but not necessarily long enough to make it up the last steep hill on a long ride.

The values in the table are gear-inches, rounded to the nearest inch. As a reminder, a 42/24 gear with a 700C wheel is about 46 gear-inches; a 39/26 is about 39 gear-inches; a 28/28 is about 26 gear-inches; and a 24/32 (practically the lowest gear obtainable with a triple crankset) is about 20 gear-inches. Good thing the steepest grades are rare, because a lot of the ratios in the table are well below these commonly available low gears. A brisk walking pace is about 3 mph; 2 mph is more typical, especially uphill. Because at 60 rpm these speeds correspond to 17 and 11 gear-inches respectively, there is little point in devising even lower gears unless walking is out of the question. Besides, most riders find it difficult to balance on the bike at speeds below about 2.5 mph.

Table 0305. Minimum gear, based on maximum grade to be climbed and weight of rider plus bicycle at 75 W power output (about 0.1 hp)

weight (lb) / grade	100	125	150	175	200	225	250	275
3%	47	42	37	33	30	27	25	23
6%	31	26	22	19	17	15	13	12
9%	22	18	15	13	11	10	9	8
12%	17	14	11	10	9	8	7	6
15%	14	11	9	8	7	6	6	5

Table 0306. Minimum gear, based on maximum grade to be climbed and weight of rider plus bicycle at 150 W power output (about 0.2 hp)

weight (lb) / grade	100	125	150	175	200	225	250	275
3%	71	66	61	57	52	49	45	42
6%	54	47	41	36	32	29	26	24
9%	41	34	29	25	22	20	18	16
12%	33	27	23	19	17	15	14	12
15%	27	23	18	16	14	12	11	10

Table 0307. Minimum gear, based on maximum grade to be climbed and weight of rider plus bicycle at 300 W power output (about 0.4 hp)

weight (lb) / grade	100	125	150	175	200	225	250	275
3%	99	95	91	87	83	79	75	72
6%	84	77	70	64	59	54	50	46
9%	71	62	54	48	43	39	35	32
12%	60	51	43	38	34	30	27	25
15%	51	42	36	31	27	24	22	20

Benefits of Extra-High Gears

The trend is to still higher gearing. How useful is a gear higher than the once-standard 52–13? Let's do some calculations to find out. The diameter of a 700C wheel is about 26.3 inches. 52/13 x 26.3 = 105.2 gear-inches, the equivalent of a wheel 105.2 inches in diameter. Each revolution of the pedals advances the bike π (3.1416) times that. At 100 rpm, the bike would be going (after one does the arithmetic and unit conversions) 31.3 mph. The same cadence with a 52/12 gives 33.9 mph; with a 53/11, 37.7 mph. These differences at first glance look significant.

Of course, yet higher cadences could produce any speed one likes, but suppose 100 rpm is our rider's practical maximum, and that he can still apply 100 watts of power at that speed, while anything faster would be impossible; he would have to coast. (This is probably pessimistic; a cyclist could probably still apply some reduced amounts of power at higher cadences if necessary, but we're making this assumption to accentuate the benefits of the higher gear.) For our standard rider, the grades corresponding to that power and the maximum speeds for those three gear combinations would be 4.0%, 4.8%, and 6.1%; these are all fairly steep downhills. That is, our standard rider would go 31.3 mph spinning his 52/13 gear at 100 rpm down a 4.0% grade; any steeper drop would require coasting. With higher gears, he could take advantage of somewhat steeper downhills. (Note: a heavier rider would need somewhat less steep grades to reach his maximum cadence, while a light rider would need still steeper slopes.)

Only in a narrow range of downgrades would the extra-high gear be preferable to the standard high gear. On gentler downgrades, it would provide no advantage, because the speed would be within the range of the standard high gear. On steeper downgrades, the rider would have to coast even with the extra-high gear. In our example, that range is 4.0–4.8% for the 52/12, and 4.0–6.1% for the 53/11, both compared to the standard 52/13.

These grades are fairly steep, but not unusual in hilly country. It would, however, be unusual to encounter such a downgrade for a long distance, particularly one with a combination of good visibility, only gentle curves, and a smooth paved surface conducive to continued pedaling as opposed to cautious coasting (freewheeling to our English readers) or braking. Let us suppose that such a slope 1,000 meters long (.62 mile) is the most one would ever encounter in an event; that is probably being generous except perhaps in mountains such as the Alps or the Rockies.

Our rider equipped with the 52/12 and pedaling all the time would fly down the 1,000-meter 4.8% grade in 66 seconds. If he coasted, however, he'd still get down in 71 seconds, only 5 seconds behind. With the 53/11 down the 6.1% grade, he'd rocket down in 59 seconds, while coasting would take 63 seconds, only 4 seconds worse. (Note: these times do not account for any initial acceleration or deceleration. If prior to the grade the course was more level, the bike will take a few extra seconds to accelerate to the sustained speed for the grade, adding a little time; if however the course was even steeper prior to the grade, the time spent decelerating from the higher speed will reduce the indicated times somewhat.)

As you can see, it seemingly takes unusual conditions for an extra-high gear to be useful, and even then it provides only a small benefit. But these conclusions are based on a rider who can still put out useful power at 100 rpm. Suppose however our rider favors a low cadence, say 60 rpm. Then no gear, even the 53/11, would seem high enough. At 60 rpm, 53/11 gives only 22.6 mph, not the kind of speed that wins many races. He might be able to find a 60-tooth chainwheel, but even then he had better hope the course has no downhills. Or he could work on his spin.

In between these two extremes may be a rider whose useful maximum is 80 rpm, which gives 25.0 mph in a 52/13, 30.2 mph in a 53/11. Downgrades in the gap between these two gears ought to be common. However, it seems unlikely that a rider's power output would really drop to zero if he had to spin faster than such a relatively low cadence as 80 rpm. If he could still supply useful power for another 10 or 20 rpm, the performance advantage of the extra-high gear would be slighter yet.

A mostly unused high gear is of course small and weighs little, so it is not a major drawback, but a lower gear used intelligently is more likely to be useful more of the time.

Despite their limitations, which are shared to some extent by any particular gear we happen to pick on, there are conditions under which extra-high gears can be useful: Riders who prefer (but are not limited to) lower cadences; courses that have long, moderately steep downhills; heavy riders who might be able to use an extra-high gear on even a moderate downhill; light riders who want to try to cancel the one advantage heavy riders have.

A couple of cautions are in order, however. A high gear, even a 52/13, is useless in flatlands unless there is an exceptionally strong tailwind or the rider is drafting within a fast pack. Riders are advised to avoid low cadences in any gear — not just the highest gear — unless their knees are particularly strong, such as well into the racing season or as a result of weight training. However, see Chapter 5 for more on optimum cadence.

Gear Charts

It is useful to draw up a gear chart, listing the number of gear-inches for each combination of gears, in order to learn how the gears of a particular bike relate to each other, and to plan changes. First there is some nomenclature to get out of the way. We will call the cluster of gears ("cogs") centered on the rear hub a "freewheel," even if it is really a freehub (a freewheel mechanism built into a hub body) with a removable cassette of cogs. The discussion will also be applicable to internally geared hubs with only a few modifications.

Table 0308. Gear inches for gear combinations

number of teeth on chainwheel

number of teeth on cog	42	52
12	92	114
13	85	105
14	79	98
15	74	91
16	69	86
17	65	80
19	58	72
21	53	65
23	48	59

gear inches for gear combination

Table 0308 is a gear chart for a road bike with 700C wheels, a double chainwheel with 42 and 52 teeth, and a freewheel with 9 cogs, 12 to 23 teeth.

(Appendix C contains a gear chart program making such a chart easy to produce with a computer.) The chart seems just a couple of columns of numbers at first glance. Of course the gear-inch values decrease from top to bottom, and they are higher for the big chainwheel than for the small chainwheel. Now look closer. Notice that the number 65 appears twice. Notice that some of the others are also very close, such as 92 and 91, 85 and 86, 79 and 80, 58 and 59, and perhaps 72 and 74. Out of the 18 combinations, only about 12 are really distinct. This may be an "18-speed" bicycle, but it has only 12 useful distinct "speeds," or gear ratios.

Figure 0304 may help you visualize how the ratios are distributed. In the illustration, the top line shows the relative positions of each of the gear ratios using the big chainwheel, "A" representing the lowest cog, "B" the next lowest, and so on. The next line does the same thing for the small chainwheel. The bottom line is the scale in gear-inches. The reason the scale shrinks toward the high end will be explained later.

Using Typical Gearing

Let us see how this typical gearing works in a common situation, the beginning of a hill. The rider of course downshifts, that is, changes to a lower gear ratio. Why does downshifting help? Suppose the cyclist's optimum cadence range is a relatively wide 60–90 rpm. He has the setup of Table 0308 above and is in his 42–15 gear combination (74 gear-inches). The road is becoming

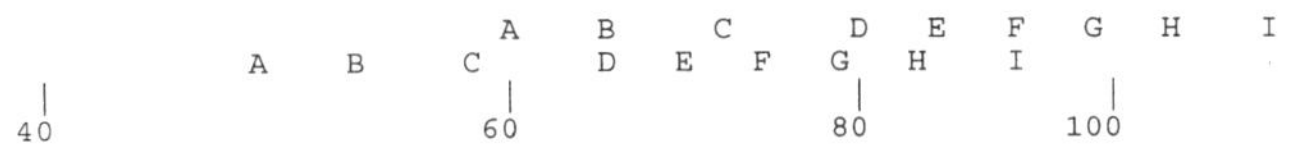

Fig. 0304. Graph of typical 18-speed gearing.

steeper; as it does, his speed is dropping, and along with it his cadence: 65, 63, 60. By immediately downshifting one gear to his 42–16, he obtains a gear combination of 69 gear-inches. We have already seen the relationship of speed to gear-inches and cadence; because speed has not yet had a chance to drop further, the product of gear-inches and rpm stays constant. Changing from 74 to 69 gear-inches must therefore increase cadence by the same ratio: $60 \times 74/69 = 64$, his new cadence, back inside the optimum range. (Go back to the speed equation and try an example if this is not clear.) He could also have downshifted twice, to a 42–17 at 65 gear-inches, giving a cadence of 68. In fact, he could have shifted even further and still have stayed well within his optimum range, which indicates that this gearing is probably more closely spaced than this particular rider needs. (Incidentally, whenever we say gearing is closely, widely, or evenly spaced, we are talking about the ratios between successive gear ratios, not the physical distance between the cogs.)

In fact, freewheels with 8 or more cogs have more than enough gears for almost every rider. Most cyclists are content with them as is. If you are one of the many satisfied customers, skip ahead to the next chapter. Cyclists intent on extracting the most from their gears, however, will want to read on.

Now suppose instead that the cyclist, through extensive training, has determined that his power peak is between 88 and 92 rpm, or he just feels best in that narrow range of cadences. His cadence has dropped to 88 in the 42–15 (74 gear-inch) combination, so he downshifts to the 42–16 (69 gear-inch) combination. His new cadence is now 44, unfortunately outside his optimum range. What does he do? If he has memorized his complicated shift pattern or has a gear chart taped to his handlebars, he may see that there is an intermediate gear available in this case, the 52–19 at 72 gear-inches. A few quick shifts later he could be in this gear with a cadence of 90 and everything would be fine for the time being. Most riders, however, do not even consider the possibility that there may be a better gear available with a shift to the other chainwheel. Instead, they stay on one chainwheel, shifting the rear derailleur only, until conditions change enough to force a shift to the other. Then they hunt for a suitable gear on the freewheel and, having found one, stay on this new chainwheel until conditions change significantly again. So it is far more likely that our rider would just stay in the 42–16 and gradually slow down until his cadence fell back into his optimum range.

Upshifts have the same potential problems. The next highest gear may be too high, making the cyclist shift back to the one he just came from, or making him waste energy trying to pedal at a sub-optimum speed. Either way he slows down. Additionally, if he does use the other chainwheel to fine-tune his selection, sometimes the gear he wants will be there and sometimes it won't, because of the duplication and uneven spacing we mentioned. Again, loss of speed is the result.

No one who has read this far will be content with having to lose speed. Nor is consulting a gear chart before every shift very appealing, and even that is no guarantee of finding the perfect gear in a system such as the one in our example above. The question is whether there is a better way.

Finding the Perfect Gear

The answer is yes, there may be a better way. The first idea that may occur to a rider is more gears. With enough closely spaced cogs on the freewheel, a gear close to what the rider wants has to be there. This is surely the facile thinking that has led manufacturers and consumers from five, to six, to seven, to eight, to nine, to ten cogs on a freewheel (and perhaps to even more by the time you read this). But compare our example 18-speed setup as compared to the old 12-speed alongside it, as shown in Table 0309.

With only 12 gear combinations to work with, the 12-speed in this example really has 12 distinct ratios: no duplicates nor near-duplicates. That is at most one fewer useful ratio than the 18-speed has. (If one also disregards the small-small and large-large gear combinations, the 18-speed has 12 useful ratios, the 12-speed has 10.) Moreover, ratios in the 12-speed are comparably close, except at the very top and bottom. (Figure 0305 helps make this clear.) In addition, the 12-speed's shift pattern is consistent, if not necessarily convenient. From the small chainwheel, the next higher gear is always one front upshift and one rear downshift away, if it is possible to make that downshift. From the large chainwheel, the next higher gear is always one front downshift and two rear upshifts away, again if both those upshifts are possible.

It should be clear that this old, nearly obsolete 12-speed is capable of very nearly the same performance as the 18-speed. Its range of gears is almost identical. It can still be used in the same way as the 18-speed, sticking to one chainwheel or the other and making a front shift only when conditions require. Upshifts and downshifts provide a gear that is usually just as close as (and more consistent than) the 18-speed provides. When

Table 0309. Comparison of 18-speed and 12-speed setups

"18-speed"

	42	52
12	92	114
13	85	105
14	79	98
15	74	91
16	69	86
17	65	80
19	58	72
21	53	65
23	48	59

"12-speed"

	42	52
12	92	114
14	79	98
16	69	85
18	61	76
21	53	65
24	46	57

Fig. 0305. Graph of 12-speed alpine gearing.

fine-tuning to the very next higher or lower gear is needed, the rider ought to know just where to find it without reference to a gear chart. True, there is a relatively big jump to the topmost and bottommost ratios; these are therefore best reserved for hammering down, or grinding up, a hill. To top it off, a 6-speed freewheel, were it still available, might also be lighter and cheaper than a 9-speed.

Earlier, the reader saw the statement that more gears did not necessarily mean more performance. The evidence has been a long time in coming, but this example has provided it. None of this is to suggest that riders should discard their present freehubs and go combing the parts bins for antique freewheels. However, with a little intelligent planning and understanding during use, the gearing on a stock bicycle can be improved.

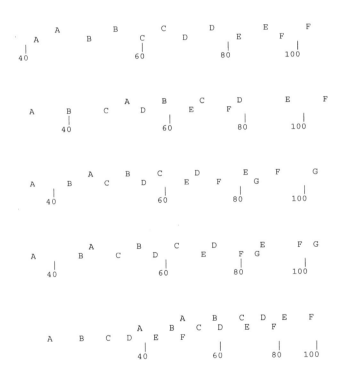

Fig. 0306 through 0310. Graphs of various gearing set-ups. From top to bottom:
0306: 12-speed half-step;
0307: 12-speed extreme crossover;
0308: 14-speed alpine;
0309: 14-speed modified alpine;
0310: 18-speed alpine with granny.

Unfortunately, gear availability is much poorer than it once was, and most cyclists are ignorant about gearing — many do not even realize that individual gears on their bikes can be replaced with others of different sizes. The author, a product of the idealistic 1960s, hopes this will change. If enough cyclists become more knowledgeable about gearing, manufacturers and dealers will have to yield to their demands. In the meantime, the savvy cyclist can at least do the best he can with the available materials.

The 12-speed above was not an isolated, contrived example in which the ratios just happened to come out right. It was an example of the alpine system of gearing: a pattern of gears with certain properties, equally applicable to 14-speeds, 20-speeds, etc. In the following paragraphs, we will talk about the alpine and other gearing systems, noting the characteristics of each, including their advantages and disadvantages. Unfortunately, no system does everything right, but given enough information, the rider should be able to choose gearing that appeals to his own preferences.

In most of the gearing systems the number of teeth on the cogs follows an orderly progression from smallest to largest, but it is what mathematicians call a geometric progression, not an arithmetic one. To illustrate the distinction, the sequence 3, 5, 7, 9, 11, … is arithmetic: it has a constant difference (in this case 2) between the numbers. However, the sequence 5, 10, 20, 40, 80, … is geometric: it has a constant ratio (in this case again 2) between successive numbers. For gearing systems, the constant ratio in the geometric progression is usually only a little larger than 1, such as 1.12, and because the number of teeth on a gear has to be an integer, the ratio between successive gears is really only approximately constant. For example, the ratios between the successive gears 13, 15, 17, 20, 23, 26 are 1.15, 1.13, 1.18, 1.15, 1.13; ideally we may have wanted the ratio to be exactly 1.149, but this is about the best approximation available if any one of the gears is the size we want. We will call the ideal or average ratio between cogs on a particular freewheel a "step," or a "full step." If you shift from the 20-tooth to the 17-tooth cog on the above freewheel, you have shifted up one step; if you shift back down to the 23, you have shifted down two steps, etc. The gears (chainwheels or chainrings), which are part of the crankset (the pedals, the crank, and the gear assembly centered on the bottom bracket) also have a specific size relationship, but it is seldom an integral number of steps. Recognizing the geometric progression, the graphical plots in Figures 0306 through 0310 manage to depict equal steps with equal horizontal distances by using a logarithmic scale. Just as on a slide rule, the position of each number plotted (including the scale indexes) is based on the logarithm of the number.

The Alpine System

The alpine system is most often found on sport and touring bikes, but is also suitable for racing bikes. Usually the chainwheels are widely spaced, with maybe a 10-tooth difference between them, which allows a fairly wide range of gear ratios: low, hill-climbing gears using the small chainwheel, and high, cruising gears on the large chainwheel. But what distinguishes the alpine system is that the ratio between the chainwheels is 1.5 steps; that is, one and a half times the ratio between the cogs. For this reason, the alpine is also known as the one-and-a-half-step system. An example gear chart with 700C wheels is shown in Table 0310 below.

(This and the following examples will show 6- or 7-cog systems for simplicity, and because typical narrow-range clusters for 8 or more cogs do not readily lend themselves to these systems; but wider-range ones could, so don't give up hope.

In this example, one step is about 1.149. Because these are geometric progressions, not arithmetic ones, half a step is not half of 1.149. A full step equals the product, not the sum, of two half steps. Therefore a half step is the square root of a full step. The square root of 1.149 is about 1.072. One and one half steps would therefore be the cube of 1.072, or 1.232, which is close to the ratio of 52 to 42, 1.238.

We already mentioned the fairly wide range possible; for a wider range, increase the step ratio, which means both increasing the range of the freewheel gears and widening the ratio between the two chainwheels. For example, Table 0311 shows two 14-speed alpines with 700C wheels, one with the step ratio equal to 1.12, the other with the step ratio 1.15.

As you can see from the charts, the alpine system has no duplicate gear ratios, and the ratios in the middle are evenly spaced. There is, however, a gap or missing ratio just below the top and just above the bottom ratios. It is easy to see why. In the middle of the range, the ratios from one chainwheel are interleaved with those from the other. For each ratio on the small chainring, there is another one half step higher and another one half step lower: just shift to the large chainwheel

Table 0310. Alpine gearing system

number off teeth on cog	number of teeth on chainwheel: 42	52
13	85	105
15	74	91
17	65	80
20	55	68
23	48	59
26	42	53

ger inches for gear combinaticn

Table 0311. Two different 14-speed alpine gearing systems

	44	52
12	96	114
13	89	105
15	77	91
17	68	80
19	61	72
21	55	65
23	50	59

	42	52
12	92	114
14	79	89
16	69	85
18	61	76
21	53	65
24	46	57
28	39	49

(+1.5) and downshift one (–1) or two (–2) steps to get +.5 or –.5. Likewise from the large chainring, shift to the small (-1.5) and upshift twice (+2) or once (+1) to get +.5 or –.5. But at the top and bottom end the freewheel runs out of gears, leaving only a full step available.

Because the shift pattern (though consistent) requires double shifts to get to the next higher or lower gear, the alpine is most often used with the "crossover" method of shifting: see "Gear Progressions" below. It is therefore sometimes loosely called the crossover system. (There are other crossover systems, but the alpine is the only one in common use in which the relationships of the gears have been well thought out.)

The Half-Step System

Half-step gearing is seldom found any more, especially on bikes with double chainwheels, but it is still worth discussing. As the name implies, the ratio between the chainwheel sizes is only half a step compared with the ratio between the cogs. This usually means that the chainwheels are close in size, generally only 3 to 5 teeth apart. An example with 27" wheels is shown in Table 0312.

In this example, one step is about 1.182; one half step, the square root of that, or 1.087, is close to 50/46.

As you can see, especially with the help of Figure 0306, there are still no duplicate gear ratios, the ratios are well spaced, and there are no gaps. The shift pattern is relatively simple, with half the nearest ratios available with just one (front) shift. However, that still leaves many double shifts necessary. Shifting the front derailleur has always been a little slower and more precarious than shifting the rear one, and that distinction has become even more pronounced with the adoption of indexed shifting and the discontinuation of front derailleurs optimized for close-ratio chainwheels.

Perhaps the biggest drawback of half-step gearing is the limited range of ratios. It seems best suited for use in gently rolling terrain or windy flatlands, and for riders who are both technically aware and who need to keep their cadence within a narrow range: perhaps the perfect system for time trialists. Half-step gearing does not lend itself to crossover shifting (see Gear Progressions, below) because speed is not the criterion for shifting the front derailleur; only fine tuning is.

Extreme Crossover

Just as it is possible to have half- and one-and-a-half-step shifting, systems with two and a half or three and a half steps are possible. The chainwheels differ greatly in size. Table 0313 shows a couple of examples with 27-in. wheels.

In the first, the step ratio is about 1.166; 1.166 to the 2.5 power (or the square root of 1.166, 1.080, raised to the fifth power) is 1.468; 52/36 is 1.444, fairly close. You can see from the chart and Figure 0307 that the chainwheels are 2.5 steps apart; for example, the 54 gear-inch ratio is two and a half steps below the 78, between the 59 and 50. (Some

Table 0312. Half-step system

	46	50
13	96	104
15	83	90
18	69	75
21	59	64
25	50	54
30	41	45

Table 0313. Extreme crossover systems

	42	52
13	75	108
15	65	94
18	54	78
21	46	67
24	41	59
28	35	50

	34	52
12	77	117
13	71	108
15	61	94
17	54	83
19	48	74
24	38	59

ratios seem a little off because of course cogs must have an integer number of teeth.) In the second, a 3.5 step example, the step ratio is about 1.122; raised to the 3.5 power, it is 1.498; 52/34 is 1.529. A 35-tooth chainring, if there were such a thing, would have worked a little better.

Extreme crossovers are not every rider's cup of tea. There is such a big, awkward jump between the chainwheels that many front derailleurs have difficulty making the shift cleanly; large shifts are frankly beyond the capacity of some derailleurs. The rear derailleur, even though it is not making the large shifts, also needs extra capacity to wrap the excess chain. Besides, few double cranksets these days can accommodate a small inner chainring. Still, the range of gears possible is very wide, and there are no duplicates. Ratios one half step apart are available only in the middle of the range, where perhaps riders will use them most often, but getting to the nearest ratio in those cases requires a doozy of a double shift. Because the crossover method of shifting (see Gear Progressions below) almost has to be used with such a system, few double shifts are in fact required. This system seems best for hilly terrain and riders who are unwilling to fit a triple crankset to their bikes; with a close-ratio freewheel, an extreme crossover system may actually be fine for a racing bike in hilly terrain.

We have given examples of 0.5, 1.5, 2.5, and 3.5 step systems. Might other numbers be practical? Not really. A system with 4.5 or more steps between chainwheels would aggravate the shifting problems mentioned above. Small integers, such as a 2 or 3 step system, would guarantee several duplicate gears. Large integers, such as a 6 step system with no overlap between the gear ratio ranges of the two chainwheels, would require a double crankset that accepts both a very small inner and very large outer chainwheel — difficult if not impossible to find. Intermediate fractions (for example, one and a third) would give uneven spacing, with the possible exception of an awkward one-third step system using a triple crankset. However, it is conceivable that a future bicycle transmission without derailleurs may adopt something like one of these.

Modified Alpines

One of the drawbacks of the alpine system is the full-step gap at the top and bottom of the range, where there is no intermediate gear to fill in. In fact, if riders observe the stricture that they must avoid the small-small and large-large gear combinations because of the extreme chain angle and possible derailleur capacity problem, there is also a gap just below that top gap, and just above that bottom gap.

The gaps at the bottom may not be perceived as a problem. Many, if not most, bicyclists use their lowest gear for a wide range of climbing situations, partly because it is really not low enough for the steeper hills they encounter. With such a gear, they are mainly concerned with being able to make it up the hill, never mind that their cadence is not in the optimum range. Such riders may do as well, if not better, with a particularly low "bail-out" gear. They are not likely to be concerned that the gap down to their lowest gear ratio is larger than the half step available between most of their other gear ratios, nor will they worry about having to pass up using the large-large gear combination. Besides, if they lose ground on a steep climb, they are likely to blame the hill or their conditioning rather than their gearing. (Despite this perception, any gap between gears that prevents a rider from staying in his optimum cadence range is undesirable when power output is critical.)

The gaps at the top may be a different story. There the lack of an intermediate gear may be

Table 0314. Standard alpine 14-speed system

	42	52
13	85	105
15	74	91
17	65	80
20	55	68
23	48	59
26	42	53
30	37	46

perceived as hindering efforts to stay with a pack, escape, chase a breakaway group, or take full advantage of a downgrade. In this case, riders may be more likely to blame their equipment, and they may be right.

If the rider views such gaps as a serious drawback, he can alleviate them with a modification to the alpine system. Instead of evenly spaced gear ratios, the top and (if desired) bottom gaps can be compressed. The very smallest and (if desired) very lowest cogs can be chosen to be closer than one step to their adjacent cog(s). For example, Table 0314 shows a standard alpine 14-speed with 700C wheels.

Notice the top gap, 91 to 105. By either replacing the smallest cog with one slightly larger, or all the cogs but the smallest with slightly smaller

ones, the top gap can be cut to about half a step while leaving most of the ratios nearly intact, though in different places (see Table 0315).

The bottom gap could also be cut in a similar way by replacing the largest cog, in this case substituting a 28 for the 30, or a 26 for the 28. However, merely replacing gears with larger or smaller ones changes the overall range. For best results, we would need to recalculate all the gears. Table 0316 shows the result (This and the original alpine are plotted in Figures 0309 and 0308 respectively). The changes here are subtle enough that the same size chainwheels are retained. The duplicate 85 gear-inch ratio is a consequence of narrowing the top gap, but the 42/13 (small-small) combination is not one most riders would use anyway. We will call this arrangement of gears the modified alpine system: alpine with only the top gap modified. If both top and bottom gaps are modified, we will call it the doubly modified alpine system.

Cyclists interested in trying one of these systems for themselves should be aware that the cog sizes on stock freewheels seldom match what these systems call for. They will need to build a custom freewheel from cogs they select. If the cogs are available, building a custom freewheel is not difficult; but if the cyclist does not wish to do it himself, he will have to find a dealer which caters to discerning customers. Many dealers are more interested in high-volume sales than in providing custom service to a small segment of their clientele.

Table 0315. Modified alpines with narrower range of rear cogs

	42	52			42	52
14	79	98		13	85	105
15	74	91		14	79	98
17	65	80		16	69	85
20	55	68		19	58	72
23	48	59		21	53	65
26	42	53		24	46	57
30	37	46		28	39	49

Table 0316. Modified alpine with gears recalculated

	42	52
13	85	105
14	79	98
16	69	85
19	58	72
22	50	62
25	44	55
30	37	46

Triple Chainwheel Systems

Rather than attempt to integrate all three chainwheels into the same general range in the manner of double cranksets, a triple is almost always regarded as two distinct subsystems:

❐ A double crankset consisting of the middle and large outer chainwheel for "normal" riding.

❐ The small inner chainwheel for steep climbs only.

Consequently, the middle and outer chainwheel are set up according to one of the above systems, usually the alpine, half-step, or modified alpine, with a range suitable for the sort of conditions the rider normally encounters. The inner chainwheel is chosen to extend the range downward, not to overlap with it significantly. The resulting system is called alpine plus granny, half-step plus granny, etc., a "granny" being the popular deprecating term for an extremely low gear, one suitable for use by little old ladies. (The author, however, has encountered some genuine bicycling grandmothers capable of running most fit young whippersnappers into the ground. So beware.)

Because with a very small chainwheel it is easy to exceed the ability of the rear derailleur to wrap excess chain, the rider should avoid using the smallest two or three cogs with the inner chainwheel; doing so also avoids the extreme chain angles which are naturally more severe with a triple chainwheel setup.

The remaining three or four relatively large cogs can be used with the inner chainwheel. The size of the inner chainwheel is chosen to leave no great gap between the lowest gear ratio on the middle chainwheel and the highest usable one on the inner chainwheel.

Table 0317 shows three examples of an alpine plus granny with only the inner chainwheel varying. (Unusable combinations are represented by dashes.) The first merely extends the range of single steps available on the middle chainwheel by a couple of steps, leaving some overlap in range to avoid possibly having to shift off the inner chainwheel at an awkward time. The second and third

decrease the amount of overlap. Because inner chainwheels with an odd number of teeth are not generally available as of this writing, it is unfortunately not possible to fine-tune these examples to extend the range of available half steps. The examples are calculated for 26.3-in. wheels, which may be a little smaller than a 700C touring tire and a little larger than a mountain bike tire, but not much different from either. The last of these is shown in Figure 0310.

If the gear ratios on the inner chainwheel are not low enough for the intended use, the first thought may be just to use a smaller inner chainring. Finding one smaller than 24 teeth may be a challenge, however, and leaving a big gap to the lowest gear on the middle chainring would be undesirable. The alternative is to extend the range of the middle-and-outer portion, by fitting a wider-range freewheel and probably reducing the size of the middle chainwheel.

The reader may have received the impression that the inner chainwheel on a triple crankset is less than ideally suited for the job of keeping cadence within its optimum range. That impression is correct. For example, because the inner and middle chainwheels do not interleave to provide half steps between ratios, only full steps are available. The limited choice in small chainwheel sizes reduces the likelihood of a seamless match between the ratios available on the inner chainwheel and those on the outer double. Although long-distance tourists and performance-oriented mountain bikers have the same needs for efficiency that other riders do, their special requirement for

Table 0317. Three different triple chainwheel systems

	28	39	48
13	–	79	97
15	–	68	84
17	43	60	74
19	39	54	66
22	33	47	57
26	28	39	–

	26	39	48
13	–	79	97
15	–	68	84
17	40	60	74
19	36	54	66
22	31	47	57
26	26	39	–

	24	39	48
13	–	79	97
15	–	68	84
17	37	60	74
19	33	54	66
22	29	47	57
26	24	39	–

ultra-low gears compromises efficiency at the low end of the range.

However, the situation is not as bad as it may appear. Tourists do not usually have a time constraint; they are free to slow down slightly to compensate for a missing gear ratio. Even more than tourists, mountain bikers face terrain in which grades vary from instant to instant; there is seldom a need to fine-tune the gear selection because it will usually need to change within seconds. Even if closer low gears were available, mountain bikers would seldom encounter conditions that might allow them to use close gearing effectively. In addition, selecting the middle chainwheel frees the rider from any worries about chain angle. The ability to use any freewheel cog with the middle chainwheel imparts a flexibility denied to double chainwheel users. The great range of gear ratios is of course also a great advantage. Eventually close-ratio triple cranksets will become common in even such a tradition-bound segment of bicycling as road racing, but it will take a daring and skillful rider to overcome his macho bias and lead the gearing revolution.

Gear Progressions

Everyone knows that when you drive a car, you start off in first gear, then shift to second, third, and so on as soon as your speed permits. Besides temporarily downshifting one gear for a steep hill or sharp curve and dropping back down to first after you come to a stop, there isn't much else to know about when to shift a car.

It should not come as a complete surprise that shifting a bicycle is considerably different: more gears, certainly; a much different physical arrangement, of course; but the most important difference is that a bicyclist seldom has the need to shift from the lowest gear upward in absolute sequence. First of all, a bicyclist practically never starts in "first gear" (the very lowest gear ratio). Most starts are nearly level, after all, and unless the bike is geared only for flat criteriums, the lowest gear is just too low for level conditions. In the lowest gear there is so little resistance to pedaling

that it is actually difficult to start up without wobbling. Next, speeds increase so rapidly just after the start that it would be impossible to keep shifting to match. (From a stoplight, an alert bicyclist almost always out-accelerates motor vehicles — for the first few feet.) Once up to speed, both driver and bicyclist find that conditions stay nearly constant most of the time. When they do change, however, they seem to change more rapidly for the bicyclist, whose momentum (speed times mass) is only a small fraction of the car's. Rolling country requires such frequent gear changes that skipping intermediate gears is not only possible but usually necessary. It is only when conditions change gradually that bicyclists find it to their advantage to fine-tune their gearing. Then they can shift to the next higher or lower gear in absolute sequence, if they know how to do that.

The fact that many bicyclists do not know how to find the closest gear indicates both how seldom shifting in absolute sequence is required and how little attention most bicyclists pay to their gearing. When conditions permit, however, the knowledgeable rider can find the gear he needs quickly and either turn his knowledge into a competitive advantage or just save energy and frustration during the final hours of a non-competitive endurance event.

The gear chart for a particular system indicates the shift pattern for going through the gears in absolute sequence. Create a gear chart for yourself and draw in arrows from each gear to the next. Yes, the pattern looks scary. Fortunately, the rider almost never needs to use the whole pattern, merely to get to the closest gears from any given one. That simple task is easy to learn. All it takes is understanding the principle behind the gearing system in use. (If there is no rational system in use, then it takes either a gear chart taped to the handlebars or a very good memory.)

The alternative to shifting in absolute sequence is called crossover shifting. Crossover shifting is best used with an alpine or similar gearing system with widely different chainwheel sizes, including the typical gearing with which most bikes are sold. It is probably how you already shift. The steps are simple. Usually you start with the chain on the inside chainwheel, or the middle one if you have a triple crankset. Once you are moving, you shift the rear derailleur up or down as required, staying on that same chainwheel. When you are moving fast enough, and see that you will probably continue to be moving fast for a while, "cross over:" shift the front derailleur so that the chain is on the large chainwheel. Shift the rear derailleur up or down as required, staying on that same chainwheel. If you slow down enough, "cross over" again: shift back to the smaller chainwheel, etc. (The front derailleur shifts are called "crossovers.") Use your knowledge of the shift pattern in use to fine-tune the gear ratio when you need a slightly higher or lower ratio for an extended period of time.

Gearing Equations

For convenience, let us call the ratio between two gears half a step apart h. The full step ratio is therefore h times h, or h^2.

Let us also call the number of teeth on the smallest cog r and the number of teeth on the largest chainwheel f. ® and f stand for rear and front, respectively.)

Additionally let us name two other variables: w, the diameter of the driven wheel in inches, and n, the number of cogs on the freewheel. Then for any gearing system:

highest gear ratio in gear-inches = f w/r

The following will give the expressions for calculating the remaining gears and ratios for the various gearing systems. Note that all the calculations involve what mathematicians call real numbers, numbers with an arbitrary number of decimal places. The number of teeth on a gear, however, is always an integer, a whole number. The final results for gear sizes must always be rounded to the nearest integer; for example, 14.333 becomes 14, 21.801 becomes 22. Rounding to the nearest integer may not be enough, however; for example, a 25-tooth cog may not be available for a particular

freewheel, or the bolt pattern on a particular crankset may not permit a chainring smaller than 39 teeth. If after doing the calculations and roundings you notice that the ideal gears are not available, try substituting ones that are.

The expressions for gear ratios (gear-inches) are for ideal, real number gear sizes. After you substitute gear sizes which are both integers and available, you should recalculate the gear ratios. As usual, the ratio in gear-inches equals the chainwheel size times the wheel diameter divided by cog size. Only then can you see whether the result is acceptable.

Alpine System

- ❏ cog sizes: r, h^2r, h^4r,...., $h^{(2n-2)}$r
- ❏ chainwheel sizes: f, f/h^3
- ❏ gear ratios on large chainwheel (gear-inches): fw/r, fw/(h^2r), fw/(h^4r),..., fw/($h^{(2n-2)}$r)
- ❏ gear ratios on small chainwheel: fw/(h^3r), fw/(h^5r), fw/(h^7r), ..., fw/($h^{(2n+1)}$r)
- ❏ ratio of highest to smallest gear ratio: $(fw/r)/(fw/h^{(2n+1)}r) = h^{(2n+1)}$

Half-Step System

- ❏ cog sizes: r, h^2r, h^4r, ..., $h^{(2n-2)}$r
- ❏ chainwheel sizes: f, f/h
- ❏ gear ratios on large chainwheel (gear-inches): fw/r, fw/(h^2r), fw/(h^4r), ..., fw/($h^{(2n-2)}$r)
- ❏ gear ratios on small chainwheel: fw/(hr), fw/(h^3r), fw/(h^5r), ..., fw/($h^{(2n-1)}$r)
- ❏ ratio of highest to smallest gear ratio: $(fw/r)/(fw/h^{(2n-1)}r) = h^{(2n-1)}$

Extreme Crossover Systems

- ❏ If number of steps between chainwheels is s (s = 2.5, 3.5, etc.),

- cog sizes: $r, h^2r, h^4r, \ldots, h^{(2n-2)}r$
- chainwheel sizes: $f, f/h^{(2s)}$
- gear ratios on large chainwheel (gear-inches): $fw/r, fw/(h^2r), fw/(h^4r), \ldots, fw/(h^{(2n-2)}r)$
- gear ratios on small chainwheel: $fw/(h^{(2s)}r)$, $fw/(h^{(2s+2)}r), fw/(h^{(2s+4)}r), \ldots, fw/(h^{(2n+2s-2)}r)$
- ratio of highest to smallest gear ratio: $h^{(2n+2s-2)}$

Modified Alpine System

- cog sizes: $r, hr, h^3r, h^5r, \ldots, h^{(2n-3)}r$
- chainwheel sizes: $f, f/h^3$
- gear ratios on large chainwheel (gear-inches): $fw/r, fw/(hr), fw/(h^3r), \ldots, fw/(h^{(2n-3)}r)$
- gear ratios on small chainwheel: $fw/(h^3r)$, $fw/(h^4r), fw/(h^6r), \ldots, fw/(h^{(2n)}r)$
- ratio of highest to smallest gear ratio: $h^{(2n)}$

Doubly Modified Alpine System

- cog sizes: $r, hr, h^3r, \ldots, h^{(2n-5)}r, h^{(2n-4)}r$
- chainwheel sizes: $f, f/h^3$
- gear ratios on large chainwheel (gear-inches): $fw/r, fw/(hr), fw/(h^3r), \ldots, fw/(h^{(2n-5)}r), fw/(h^{(2n-4)}r)$
- gear ratios on small chainwheel: $fw/(h^3r)$, $fw/(h^4r), fw/(h^6r), \ldots, fw/(h^{(2n-2)}r), fw/(h^{(2n-1)}r)$
- ratio of highest to smallest gear ratio: $h^{(2n-1)}$

Triple Crankset Systems

Choose one of the double crankset systems above. Decide which one of the middle cogs is the smallest one to be used with the inner chainwheel; say that cog has s teeth. Call the number of teeth the inner chainwheel will have I, the number of teeth on the middle chainwheel m, and the number of teeth on the biggest cog b. As a starting point for determining a suitable inner chainwheel size (the value of I), the ratio produced by the s-tooth cog and the inner chainwheel will be about the same as the lowest ratio on the middle chainwheel; that is, $I w / s = m w / b$. So:

$$I = s m / b$$

Vary I according to gear availability and the amount of overlap you prefer to have between the gear ratios on the inner and remaining chainwheels.

Final Reminder

Gearing is only a tool to aid the bicyclist's performance. Good tools do not necessarily make good craftsmen. The best, most rational, most carefully thought-out gearing system does little for the cyclist unless he uses it to maintain a nearly optimum cadence. For a cyclist intent on maximum performance, even optimum cadence is not enough. After all, if one can spin, say, 80 rpm in a certain gear, then one can also spin 80 rpm in any lower gear — at reduced speed. The optimum cadence must be used in combination with an appropriate gear and a suitably high, sustainable power output level.

4
Fit and Power Transmission

Proper fit of the bicycle to the rider is vitally important for injury prevention and comfort. It is almost as important for performance, both to allow the rider's full power to be transmitted to the bicycle and to delay the onset of rider fatigue. Most general bicycling books do a reasonable job of covering the subject; so do the magazines, every few months. With so much good information available, the majority of serious riders seem to have little problem buying and adjusting a bicycle to fit them well, and there may be little need for a rehash here.

But casual and beginning cyclists still often remain in the dark, and a book that discusses the minuscule performance consequences of derailleur jockey wheels can hardly ignore a topic that makes a real difference. Unfortunately, fit is a topic that does not always lend itself to precise, definitive conclusions based on math, physics, and human physiology. One cannot take a few rider measurements, then set up a bike with the certain knowledge that it will henceforth be perfectly adjusted for maximum power output, or maximum comfort. The reader should look on the following as guidelines for arriving near the correct adjustment points, then feel free to fine-tune afterwards. For more details, and to obtain different perspectives on the subject, see one of those other sources.

Frame size

The first requirement is to obtain a bicycle that can be made to fit the rider. Sounds simple enough, doesn't it? To make the task simpler yet, the dimensions of a standard, diamond frame bicycle are often boiled down to a single number, the frame size. Frame size is indeed a good place to begin, but it is by no means all one needs to know about fit — no matter what a dealer trying to make a quick sale may imply.

The frame size is the distance from the center of the bottom bracket spindle (the pedaling axis), along the seat tube (the frame tube that runs directly up toward the saddle) to the top tube (the uppermost part of the frame, below the saddle). Exactly where on the top tube does the measurement end? When given in inches, it usually means the distance to the top of the tube, or the top of the seat lug, the adjustable fitting that clamps the seatpost. When given in centimeters, it usually means the distance to the center of the top tube. Yes, this measurement *is* annoyingly vague. It gets worse.

Different types of bicycles have different wheel diameters, which of course would cause two frames of the same nominal size to sit higher or lower above the ground. Likewise, the bottom brackets on different frames may sit higher or lower relative to the wheel axles, according to the frame builder's preferences. The seat tube angle (the amount it slants relative to horizontal) also varies between different bikes of the same nominal size, causing their overall height to vary. The particular components fitted to the frame, especially the crankarms and pedals, have a similar effect. Besides, the measurement does not correspond precisely to the length of any part of the rider's body; in fact, there is usually a range of sizes that can be made to fit a particular person, though different people will have different preferences within that range. The upshot of all these variables is that the frame size is a fine number for reference, but by itself is inadequate for choosing a bicycle that fits.

If a person already has a bicycle, or has borrowed a bicycle, one that either fits or nearly fits, he has a head start toward determining what size he needs. Or if, lucky fellow, he is ordering a custom-built frame based on his measurements, there is no problem — an experienced frame builder will see to it that he gets a bike that fits him to a T. But a person buying a complete, quality bicycle for the first time should always select a frame size based on an actual fitting at the dealer, preferably using the very same model of bicycle that interests him.

There are two coarse constraints on the frame size: it must not be so tall that the rider cannot straddle it with both feet on the ground; but it must also be tall enough that when the saddle is properly adjusted (see below), safe lengths of seat post and stem are inserted into the frame. Allowing for sudden stops on sloped or uneven ground, the first constraint demands a minimum of roughly one-half inch (about 1 cm) straddling clearance for a road bike, about double that to be safer, and at least double that again for a mountain bike. The majority of people, except those whose legs are very short, will have no trouble finding at least one frame size that meets that criterion. The next couple of sizes smaller (if any) should easily meet the second constraint, though the smallest may require an extra-long seatpost and extra-tall stem, especially if the rider is also very tall. Very short and tall riders may have difficulty finding a model with even one size that fits without resorting to a non-standard or custom frame — but if that is what it takes, a good fit is well worth the inconvenience or expense.

Suppose the rider has found at least one size that meets the height criteria. Before purchasing it, he should also determine whether it is too long or short, that is, if it would stretch him out too far or scrunch him up too much. Again, he may judge based on an existing bike that fits, but otherwise he must go through the next steps before he can find out. (Because these are steps that must be taken to get any bicycle, even a perfectly sized one, to fit, they are not by any means a waste of time.)

Pedaling position

Pedaling is what makes the bicycle go. Except on the shortest, most casual ride, the bicyclist spends a lot of time on the saddle pedaling, transmitting a great deal of power from his muscles through his legs, knees, and feet to the pedals. The potential for discomfort and injury (not to mention reduced power output) is high — unless the bike is precisely adjusted to achieve the best position for pedaling. The primary bicycle adjustment is therefore saddle height. There are many rules, and even formulas, for doing this, all of which put the saddle height in the ball park and leave the final adjustment up to the rider. The goal is to use almost all of the leg's extension, but definitely no more than that. The author prefers the following technique:

First the saddle angle must be set. When a straightedge, such as a yardstick, is placed atop the saddle, front to rear, it should have only a slight upward tilt, i.e. just higher in front than at the rear, or level. Adjust and tighten the top of the seatpost accordingly. The precise angle depends somewhat on the construction of the saddle itself and on the rider's physiology. A female rider, for instance, may at first find an upward or even level angle uncomfortable. In that case, the saddle can be tilted down slightly; but later, after the appropriate muscles develop, it can be leveled and perhaps finally tilted upward a little. While it never makes sense to be uncomfortable based only on blindly following supposedly expert advice, a downward-tilting saddle, or one that tilts sharply upward, is a sign that the rider has not paid enough attention to proper fit.

The rider then sits on the bike with a supporting helper or an adjacent wall or rail. He places his heels on the pedals, and pedals slowly backward. (Obviously this method is not intended for a bike with a coaster brake or a fixed wheel. On those bikes, riding forward, pedaling with the heels is also possible, if awkward. Also, because apparently not all riders can tell which part of their foot is on the pedal, a helper is doubly useful.) If with heels on the pedals the knees are still bent at the bottom of the pedal strokes, the saddle is too low. If the rider must rock sideways on the saddle to keep his heels on the pedals, the saddle is too high. At the right saddle height, each knee should fully extend and "lock" at the bottom of its stroke, but without requiring the rider to make any special effort to stretch to that side. Once the rider then tries the bike with feet on the pedals in the normal way, the leg should be nearly fully extended, without locking.

The next adjustment is foot fore-aft position. The ball of the foot must be very nearly directly over the pedal axle. Some sources caution not to set the foot too far forward, which is no doubt good advice; but in the author's experience, if the ball of the foot is even slightly behind the axle, within just a few miles severe knee and calf pain will call attention to the poor position. Casual riders and mountain bikers are often uncomfortable with the idea of locking their feet to the pedals in case they need to make a quick exit. Fair enough; but some method of positioning the foot properly and consistently is essential.

Cleats require very careful adjustment that is critical to the well-being of the rider's knees, but which does not affect performance per se. The author suggests seeking help with this adjustment from either experienced riders or a dealer with one of the kits designed for this purpose. There will be more on cleats later in this chapter.

Alternatively, it may be possible to find what used to be called standard pedals with toeclips from a long-time dealer or experienced rider. The author recommends starting out with just the right foot secured, via cleat or clip, leaving the left foot free to set down. Once the rider realizes how easy it is to manage one secured foot, "locking in" both feet won't be so intimidating.

Back to the saddle: it must also be adjusted for fore-aft position. Set it such that when the crankarm is pointed straight ahead, the knee is over the pedal spindle. What part of the knee? Try the lump of bone just below it, and use a plumb line or some other vertical line, along with a helper. Low gear spinners may eventually like a slightly more forward position, big gear pushers a position slightly to the rear, but vertical is a good starting point. Note that this adjustment merely accounts for thigh length. It is emphatically not the way to adjust reach; read on.

Reach

It is now time to check the reach to the handlebars. First set the stem height to, say, an inch below the level of the saddle, or according to the guidance in Chapter 11. When the rider has his hands on the forward portion of the drops of bent road bars, his elbows slightly bent, a plumb line dropped from the rider's nose should fall about an inch behind the handlebars. With hands atop the brake hoods, or at the ends of a straight bar, again with elbows slightly bent, his nose should be about three inches behind the bars. Racers who spend most of the time on the drops may not mind being stretched out a little more, but tourists who spend most of the time looking at the scenery definitely will mind.

If the results are much different, then the combination of the top tube length and the stem extension (its horizontal dimension) are wrong. Most mismatches can be corrected with a different stem; if the switch is made before purchase, there should be no additional expense. Some handlebars also give slightly different reaches. But if no component substitution is enough to make up the difference, then the frame top tube length is frankly wrong for that rider. Rejecting the frame in favor of one with measurements better suited to the rider is the only option that makes sense. (See also the discussion of the contribution of stem extension in Chapter 9.)

Now is a good time to dispel a cycling myth. One often hears that if the stem adjustment is correct, then when the rider looks toward the front hub, it will be obscured by the handlebars. This effect does indeed happen for many riders mounted on steep-angled road bikes, especially if they cheat by bending their elbows a little more or less. But if it happens at all, it is only by accident. A rider who fits perfectly on a different sort of bike, one with more relaxed angles or greater rake, will probably be able to see the hub just fine, thank you. Don't adjust your bike based on this irrelevant effect.

As the rider gains experience, he will probably want to make position adjustments to improve comfort, aerodynamics, or subjective feel. These are best made gradually, only a couple of millimeters at a time. Each time one makes an adjustment to height or fore-aft position, including the first time, one should go back and recheck each of the positions again, in the same order, adjusting and repeating as necessary until there are no further changes. Riders with multiple bikes will want to set them all up to give nearly identical riding positions. It is also a good idea to measure and record the baseline positions in case they are inadvertently changed during service or transport.

Crankarm Length

The crankarms transmit the rider's pedaling force to the chainrings, and this force along a circular path prompts us to revisit physics terminology. The product of the force and the length of the arm that causes rotation about an axis is called torque. The units of torque are therefore meter-newtons or pound-feet, expressed in that backward order to distinguish them from the energy units newton-meters (i.e. joules) and foot-pounds. When talking about bicycles, we usually call the rotational speed "cadence" and measure it in revolutions per minute (rpm), but we could also view it as angular velocity, some angle per some unit of time. The natural mathematical unit for angle is the radian. There are 2π radians in a complete circle or revolution (360 degrees), which makes one radian about 57.3 degrees — at first glance not such a natural unit, but let's not jump to conclusions. Given angles in radians, the natural physics unit of angular velocity is radians per second, so 1 rpm is 2π radians per 60 seconds, or 0.10472 radians per second.

The product of torque and angular velocity is power. Power has its usual mks unit, namely watts, or (equivalently) joules per second, or newton-meters per second, or in this case meter-newtons per second. Multiply the units out yourself: torque is meters times newtons; angular velocity is radians per second, so the product should be meter-newton-radians per second. Hmm, watts are only meter-newtons per second. What happened to the radians? They disappeared. Angles measured in radians essentially have no unit at all. The definition of a radian is the angle subtended at the center of a circle by an arc of that circle whose length is the same as the radius. Any radian angle is an arc length, expressed in some unit, divided by a radius length, expressed in that same unit. The units cancel out, leaving a "pure" unitless number. The fact that the radian unit can be ignored helps make it such a natural one for mathematicians and physicists to use.

This power, which is the product of torque and angular velocity, is the same power that we saw earlier as work per unit of time, or force times distance per unit of time. For example, suppose a rider exerts 1 newton of force on the pedals for one second, moving the 170-millimeter crankarms one complete revolution during that second. Force is 1 newton and the lever arm is 0.17 meters, so torque is 0.17 meter-newtons. Angular velocity is 2π radians (one complete revolution) per second. Power must therefore be torque times angular velocity, 0.34π watts. Now compute power the other way. Force is 1 newton; the distance over which the force is applied is the circumference of a circle with radius 0.17 meters, namely 2π times 0.17. Work must be force times distance, 0.34π newton-meters or joules. Elapsed time is 1 second, so power is 0.34π joules per second, or 0.34π watts. *Voilà!* The amounts are identical.

Just to be complete, the English unit of power derived from torque would be pound-feet per second, or foot-pounds per second. There are 550 foot-pounds per second in one horsepower — not as tidy as using mks units.

Back to bicycling and the problem of generating more speed. A longer crankarm means more torque, more torque means more power, and more power means more speed. A lot of bicyclists have figured out that much of the problem, because the trend is to longer crankarms for the extra torque they provide. The ticket to winning the Tour de France must therefore be obvious: just install the world's longest crankarms. When the solution to a problem is put into such ridiculous terms, it is easier to see the logical flaw. One never gets something for nothing. In this case we are forced to recall that power is proportional not only to torque but also to angular velocity, cadence. To maximize power, what matters is the product of those two quantities, not either one by itself. The extra torque of longer crankarms won't help if the rider is not able to spin them fast enough — and

once the crankarms exceed a certain length, clearly the rider will not be able to spin them well.

Let's take a simple but realistic example. Suppose a rider can apply an average of 210.6 newtons of force to the pedals at 80 rpm with 170 mm crankarms. The power he generates is therefore 210.6 x 0.17 x 80 x 0.10472 = 300 watts. Now suppose he decides to swap his 170 mm cranks for 180 mm ones. There's no reason to suppose that he could apply any more force using these, because he has the same old legs. If, applying the same force, he can still spin these longer cranks at 80 rpm, he does generate more power, 318 watts. But 180 mm cranks are pretty long, and it is more likely that he will be able to rotate them at only, say, 75 rpm. In that case, the power he generates is only 298 watts, a bit less than he produced with 170 mm cranks. (He would need 80 x 170/180 or 75.56 rpm for the same power.) Or perhaps he can still spin them at 80 rpm but the extra reach feels awkward, and as a consequence he can't quite manage the same force on average. If that force is less than 210.6 x 170/180 or 198.9 newtons, he has lost power.

Ah, but (so goes another argument) the crankarm is also like a lever arm. A longer arm provides more leverage. Under any particular conditions, it takes less force to push the longer lever. The prospect of less pedaling force persuades many riders to opt for longer crankarms, particularly on mountain bikes. On the face of it, this seems to be convincing, but it is another something-for-nothing solution. Does reduced pedaling force ring a bell? It should — it is what happens when one shifts to a lower gear. In fact, the perceived reduction in force from switching from 170 to 180 mm cranks is identical to the reduction felt when shifting from a 17-tooth cog to an 18-tooth cog, or between any two gear ratios with that same proportion. (It is also worth noting that the difference is nearly imperceptible.) Needless to say, shifting is easier and cheaper than swapping crankarms. So is fitting slightly lower gears.

All the above arguments can also be turned around to produce equally convincing, or equally unconvincing, reasons for choosing shorter crankarms instead of longer ones. There is nothing inherent in the physics that makes any particular length best, but when we consider physiology, it's a different story. It should be obvious that short-legged people will have a more difficult time spinning long crankarms than will long-legged people. Many experts sensibly recommend choosing crankarm length based on the rider's inseam (crotch to floor measurement). The formula for adult riders usually comes out something like this:

"recommended" crankarm length in mm = inseam in inches + 139.5

For example, a rider with a 30.5-inch inseam would, according to this rather unscientific formula, find 170 mm cranks perfect; a rider with a 27.5-inch inseam should select 165 mm, probably the closest available size to what the formula suggests.

Unfortunately, physiology is far more complex than a single inseam measurement. Musculature, bone length, flexibility, and other factors vary considerably from individual to individual. A definitive physiological study on the topic of optimum crankarm length may never be performed. Meanwhile, the tests that have been conducted are inconclusive, showing no significant correlation between crankarm length and performance. Most riders who have tried different sizes concur. If (while they weren't looking) someone were to swap their cranksets for ones with 5 mm longer or shorter arms, the chances are good that they would notice no difference whatsoever, the possible exception being if their old cranks were nearly as long as they could handle and the new ones are longer yet.

From all this nebulous data we can draw some relatively clear conclusions. First, the basic crankarm length is 170 mm, but tall, leggy riders may wish to choose one of the longer lengths, tiny riders one of the short lengths. With few choices available and the knowledge that the length isn't critical, this task shouldn't be difficult. Perhaps in case a knee injury or some other condition has made one or both of the legs less flexible, the prospective buyer should reduce this initial choice of

length, on the advice of a qualified therapist. Riders who like to pedal gears at high rpm's ("spinners") may opt for something a little shorter; riders who prefer a lower cadence and higher gears ("pushers") may like something longer.

There may be two additional concerns. On bikes with low bottom brackets, long toeclips often drag annoyingly on the ground when the cyclist is walking the bike somewhere — though it obviously is no problem at all with clipless pedals. And on racing bikes or very small frames, sometimes the rider's toe overlaps the front wheel. As long as the rider is aware of the possibility, it really isn't a serious safety hazard, despite what some lawsuits have contended; the effect shows up only when pedaling through a sharp, low-speed turn, something cyclists rarely do except perhaps in a cyclo-cross. Both of these minor problems may show up or become worse with longer cranks, but once aware of such problems, it is easy to check for them before buying. A longer crankarm is of course also marginally heavier. An extra 5 mm length of aluminum alloy on each arm adds a whopping 7 or 8 extra grams to the bike — can you stand it?

Finally, remember that a longer crankarm is not a sensible substitute for lower gears, and that most coaches advise their riders to develop a fast, smooth spin, something that (though never easy) is at least a little less difficult with shorter crankarms.

Pedaling Circles

The great majority of cyclists handicap themselves by pedaling as if they were a mere two-cylinder piston engine. They push down alternately with each foot, applying force during only a fraction of each pedal revolution. The rest of the revolution produces no power. Ideally, the rider should push both pedals all the way around their circles, continually applying tangential force (tangential to the circle, or perpendicular to the crankarm) regardless of what position the pedals are in. Because humans unfortunately evolved some time before the invention of the bicycle, our muscles and joints are built not for pedaling but for walking. None of us has the innate ability to move our feet in a natural circular path. Pedaling circles is something that must be painstakingly learned. Not an easy skill to master, it requires continual self-correction. Long after the rider thinks he has completely absorbed the correct way to pedal, he will find himself reverting to his former lazier style whenever his attention lapses. But pedaling circles is the only way to obtain full power output.

The peak force the rider can apply is naturally about the same as his weight. For our standard rider, who weighs perhaps 175 pounds, that's about 778 newtons when the crankarm is pointed forward and he stands on the pedal. Alas, once the crankarm rotates away from level, standing on the pedal is less effective. By the time the crankarm reaches the 5 o'clock position, only half the rider's weight goes into rotational force, and at the 6 o'clock (bottom) position, standing produces no rotational force at all. In normal pedaling the rider simultaneously pushes on one pedal while pulling on the other, and he may therefore be able to apply more peak force than by standing on the pedals — or he may not. Likewise, during a climb he can pull on the handlebars and supplement the amount of peak force he can apply. It should still be clear that there is a physical limit to peak force, and that amount of force can be applied only when the pedals are ideally positioned. The remainder of the time, muscle strength is of course important, but high average tangential force depends on more than strength. Good technique — pedaling circles — is essential if the average applied force is to amount to much.

Studies conducted on various types of trained cyclists (cited in Whitt and Wilson's *Bicycling Science*) have estimated that motor-paced track cyclists produce an average pedaling force of 155–165 N, a very narrow range, probably because of the specialized conditions and duration. Other types of cyclists commonly produce a wider range of average pedaling forces, depending on the type and duration of the effort: tourists, 70–145 N; road racing cyclists under time trial conditions (25 to 100 miles), 200–240 N; track cyclists in 200- to 400-meter time trials, 370–535 N. These amounts are well under the peak force available, hardly surprising considering that these numbers represent the average force the studied cyclists applied all the way around the pedal circle, often for an hour or more of effort. Though the track cyclist numbers apply to sprints of only a few seconds, they may be even more impressive, considering that they were achieved at cadences of 136 to 182 rpm. Clearly these cyclists knew how to pedal circles. All the racing cyclists tested, in fact, averaged at least 84 rpm.

That fact reminds us that force is just one factor in power output; the other is pedal speed. With 170-mm crankarms and a cadence of 60 rpm, pedal speed is 1.07 meters per second. A time trialist who can apply 240 N of average pedaling force would attain only 256 watts of power at that cadence, enough to propel our standard rider at 10.6 m/s (23.7 mph) on a flat, windless course — somewhat short of competitive time trial speed. A track cyclist who could somehow maintain an average pedaling force of 600 N at that cadence would produce only 641 watts of power; the tested subjects produced at least one and a half times that, and they were a couple of seconds off record pace. Good average tangential force is insufficient; it must be combined with good cadence for competitive power.

Ankling

Ankling is a technique that used to be mentioned in discussions of pedaling; it is no longer much in favor. It probably originated from the idea of keeping pedaling force perpendicular to the crankarms. The rider who employs ankling flexes his ankle as the pedal rotates. At the top of the pedal stroke, his toe is higher than his heel, to apply force forward. When the crankarm is forward and level, his toe and heel have also become level, with force applied downward. At the bottom of the stroke, the toe has aimed down and the heel has pulled up, to apply force backward. The heel and toe level out again on the way up, and so on. Ankling may be a useful technique for someone pedaling slowly in sneakers without toeclips, but not for a high-performance cyclist. Though the motion superficially resembles walking, it bears little similarity to the way the walking foot applies force. Pedaling circles is unnatural enough; ankling is even more so. How long do you suppose a cyclist could maintain a good spin while trying to fit all that foot flexing into the brief time span of a pedal revolution?

Fortunately, with the foot secured to the pedal, ankling is not necessary. The foot can remain approximately level while applying force to the pedal throughout its revolution. Even with this equipment, pedaling circles is still necessary, however — forward, down, back, up, and everything in between. Otherwise, much of the energy stored in the rider's muscles never emerges to propel the bike. Good equipment is no substitute for good technique.

Cleats and Related Systems

Bicycle designers have long recognized that the force a rider applies to the pedals varies within the pedaling circle. During most of the downstroke, the rider can apply relatively high force. At the top and bottom, where the pedal direction is perpendicular to the natural motion of the leg, the force he can apply drops nearly to zero. On the upstroke, if he must push down to keep his foot from flying off the pedal, or if he just presses down out of habit, the force is negative and counterproductive.

Various inventions have enabled the rider to harness force throughout more of the pedaling circle and thus increase the total available power. Most effective has been the combination of a cleated shoe and a pedal designed to accept the cleat and secure the shoe to the pedal during pedaling. A cleat (if properly adjusted) positions the foot correctly on the pedal. In a modern clipless pedal system, the cleat also holds the foot onto the pedal and allows force to be applied throughout the circle. (So did the older slotted cleat, if used with a tightened toestrap.) Riding a bicycle without such an aid is of course still possible.

Touring cyclists and mountain bikers, who need to be able to walk at various times during a ride, often prefer to forgo cleats, though many are finding that clipless designs with recessed cleats address this particular need. These riders can still attain high performance using clips and tightened straps without cleated shoes, but for ultimate performance, cleats are a necessity.

If performance were the only goal, the only consideration in choosing a cleat system would be to ensure that the foot is held fast to the pedal, a criterion easily met by older slotted cleats and straps, all types of clipless systems, and for that matter, tape wrapped around the foot and pedal as in the movie *Breaking Away*. Practically speaking, however, there are additional considerations, including avoidance of stress on the knees whether the rider is seated or standing, ease of entry and release (intentional, unintentional, and in the event of a crash), compatibility with other shoes and other bicycles the rider may use, reliability in muddy conditions, shoe fit, style, and cost. Knees easily eclipse Achilles's legendary tendon as a human body design weakness. Particularly because the knees are such a notorious trouble area, a bicyclist should take great pains both in selecting a cleat system and subsequently adjusting it to perfection. Any setup pains sidestepped now may easily return manifold when permanent knee problems set in a few years later. Some people have such sensitive knees that they cannot seem to find any comfortable cleat position. If that is the case, uncleated shoes with clips and tightened straps incur only a modest loss of potential power, a small price to pay for healthy knees; however, most riders and their knees readily adapt to the clipless pedal designs that allow a bit of angular play.

Any motion that does not help the bicycle move forward can be considered a waste of energy. If, for example, the shoe does not fit snugly, the rider will spend energy to move his foot around inside the shoe, energy that could have gone into pedaling. For the same reason the play in certain clipless pedal designs (not to mention shoes without cleats) has sometimes been criticized as a power drain, at least by riders and coaches accustomed to fixed cleats. While it may be true that sideways foot motion diverts a small amount of power from the pedaling motion, even minor discomfort during pedaling is certain to rob power. If discomfort occurs while using fixed cleats but not while using cleats with built-in play, the choice should be clear.

Oval Chainwheels

For a gear to mesh with another gear, it must have a constant radius (not counting the profile of the teeth), but when the gear needs only to mesh with a flexible chain, it no longer needs to be circular. Of course there would be no advantage in making the freewheel cogs anything but circular, but it may be a different story at the other end, where the rider drives the chainwheels of the crankset. We have already commented on the different amounts of force available to the rider as he pedals in a circle. For many years designers have dabbled with non-circular chainwheels in an attempt to extract more power from the pedaling cycle. The principle is to increase the radius of the chainwheel, and thus the effective gear ratio, during the portion of the pedal circle when high force is available, and to decrease the radius during the remainder of the circle. For example, because maximum force is possible during most of the top portion of the downstroke, the radius at the top of the chainwheel (where it meets the chain) should perhaps be greater from the 1 o'clock to 4 o'clock crankarm positions. This principle is compromised by the fact that there is only one chainwheel in use, while there are two pedals spaced 180 degrees apart. A large radius during the downstroke of one pedal will be a large radius during the upstroke of the other. Even with cleats, upstroke force cannot match downstroke force.

Nonetheless, some riders favor oval chainwheels. The shapes of these gears have ranged from near-circles to ellipses nearly as eccentric as American footballs. Research by Shimano in the mid-1980s resulted in Biopace™ chainwheels with an irregular shape that was supposed to match a rider's available force well; these chainwheels were nearly universal for a time, but have since declined in popularity. Studies have shown that most riders produce the same amount of power whether they use circular or oval chainwheels, although certain riders who have taken the time to accustom themselves to the different feel are able to increase power output slightly. Every serious rider knows that it is difficult to cultivate a perfectly smooth pedaling motion. A smooth pedal circle in which the foot speed varies throughout the circle may be even more difficult to become used to and master: with an oval chainwheel it must be relatively slow during the portion of the downstroke in which the radius and gear ratio are high, then fast, then slow again on the upstroke, etc. Mechanically, the main flaw of non-circular chainwheels is that the chain bounces as it tries to follow the varying radius, possibly interfering with shifting and increasing the likelihood of derailment. A fast cadence exaggerates this problem. As a result, experienced riders with a good spin often find oval chainwheels annoying, while at least with the milder oval shapes, many other riders often cannot notice any difference, either in feel or in power.

5
Uniform Conditions

Despite the fact that the environment in which we live is ever-changing, often the changes are so slow as to be imperceptible. In a bicycle race or ride, there are usually long periods of time during which the road is level or uniformly tilted, the wind steady, and the speed constant, or nearly so.

When conditions change, they usually change quickly and assume a new set of nearly constant conditions. It is not only rare but almost physically impossible to spend minutes at a time increasing power gradually or braking to a stop. Conditions may differ considerably from time to time during a ride, but during most of those times they stay fairly steady. Because they make up the largest share of the ride, uniform conditions are of great importance to overall performance. Fortunately, they are also relatively easy to study.

Cadence

A derailleur bicycle has several gear ratios. The rider is free to choose from any of them, but not all of those choices give a usable cadence. If the chosen gear (expressed in gear inches) is too high, and therefore the cadence is too low, pedaling force will be jerky and erratic around the pedal circle, and high force may cause knee injury. With too low a gear (too high a cadence), the rider will be bouncing in the saddle and again unable to maintain steady force in a circle. Either of these extremes reduces power output.

In between is a wide range of usable cadences. Whitt and Wilson, in *Bicycling Science*, report a study at Dartmouth that showed that students (not trained athletes) could maintain a steady low power output of 0.05 hp (about 37 watts) for prolonged periods at cadences of 20 to 60 rpm — a wide range, if considerably lower than trained cyclists would use. Interestingly, the same study showed that when the students were required to produce more power for given periods of time, they did so using higher cadences. Their power curves (remember power curves in Chapter 3?) were very broad, like the bottom curve in Figure 0301; but the higher the peak of this curve, the higher the cadence at which the peak occurred — like the other curves in Figure 0301. The peaks ranged from about 65 rpm, for a power level they could sustain indefinitely, to about 95 rpm, for a high output they needed to put out for only 15 seconds. The students obtained power levels very nearly as high as the peak power at cadences both well below and well above these peak-power cadences. Although the study showed that with these subjects cadence was not critical, it did suggest that moderately high cadences may yield higher power output, and hence higher speed, if perhaps only for a short time.

The studies of trained racing cyclists cited in that same book (and already mentioned in Chapter 4) also support high cadences. The track cyclists, for instance, using cadences of 136 to 182 rpm for short distances, were able to achieve power outputs of something like 900 to 1200 watts of power, depending on the particular conditions. Likewise, the studies of road racing cyclists, whose estimated power outputs were in the 300 to 460 watt range for long distances, showed average cadences in the range of 93–102 rpm.

The same book, however, also reports other studies that indicate that maximum power is obtained with high gears and relatively low cadences. Except for short distances on the order of 200 meters, where a wide range of cadences produced identical results, the racing cyclists in these studies achieved maximum speed and efficiency at 60 to 70 rpm, using gears as high as 111 gear-inches on a presumably flat course. Not surprisingly, these subjects complained of leg strain, which suggests that any gains in power using low cadences may be bought with injury or shortened longevity.

Some time trialists do advocate cadences as low as 60 rpm, and can apparently tolerate them throughout a lifetime of competition. It is hard to argue with the success of these riders. However, coaches traditionally recommend higher cadences — 80, 90, even 100 rpm or more. The reasons

usually have to do with injury prevention, the ability to respond quickly to opponents' moves, and the flexibility needed for a single–gear track bike, rather than maximum speed under time trial conditions; but there are other physical justifications for high cadences.

Recall that work is force over a distance. In particular, a joule is a newton–meter, the product of force in newtons and distance in meters. Picture a cyclist who is applying a combined 100 newtons of force (about 22 pounds) to the pedals, using a cadence of 60 rpm. Suppose the pedals travel one meter per revolution. (With typical cranks it's actually a little more.) In one minute, the cyclist does 100 x 60 x 1 = 6,000 joules of work. Because a watt is one joule per second, that is an average output of 100 watts, about 0.13 horsepower. To put these numbers into perspective, if our standard rider did this, he would go about 16.8 mph along a level windless road, or climb a 2.5% grade at 8.2 mph. Suppose that the cyclist now increases his cadence to 80 rpm, but at that higher speed naturally is able to apply less pedaling force, say 90 newtons. After a minute he has done 7,200 joules of work (90 x 80 x 1), an average of 120 watts. He significantly increased power output even though he applied less force to the pedals.

Obviously the above numbers were made up, but it is generally true that with practice, working on smooth, uniform pedal circles, a rider can increase his maximum useful cadence without seriously decreasing the amount of force he can apply. The result is extra power, and therefore extra speed. For another argument in favor of higher cadences, see Chapter 12.

A lower cadence may have aerodynamic benefits. Why may this be so? At the top of the pedal circle, the feet are traveling faster through the air than the bike as a whole; at the bottom, they are traveling slower than the bike. Because aerodynamic drag is proportional to the square of the airspeed, the top portion of the circle adds more drag than the bottom portion can subtract, an effect that worsens with higher speeds. Let's do some rough calculations to estimate whether cadence is a real factor. The calculations have to be rough, because aerodynamic data for individual legs and feet is hard to come by.

Suppose we call the assemblage consisting of a pedal, shoe, and the nearby portions of leg and crankarm a "foot." At 60 rpm with 170 mm crankarms, the foot travels in a circle at 1.07 m/s, but what matters to the aerodynamics is only the component of that speed in the direction the bicycle is traveling. If the bicycle is moving into still air at 11.5 m/s (25.7 mph), the foot travels at 11.5 + 1.07 m/s at the top of the pedal stroke, 11.5 m/s at the middle of the downstroke and upstroke, and 11.5 – 1.07 m/s at the bottom of the stroke. In general, the foot's airspeed is the bicycle's overall airspeed, plus the speed at which the foot is moving around the circle times the cosine of the angle of the crank relative to vertical. See Figure 0501.

The aerodynamic drag force is proportional to the square of that speed. While 11.5 squared is 132.25, the average of the square of the foot's airspeed at each point around the circle is 132.82 for 60 rpm; similar calculations for 90 rpm give 133.53. The foot has a frontal area of about 0.02 square meters (twice that for a pair) and a coefficient of aerodynamic drag of perhaps 0.4. Calculating total drag shows that a 90 rpm cadence requires about 0.0068 newtons (about 1/40 of an ounce) more force than a 60 rpm cadence at that same speed. If the rider applied identical power in both cases, the extra drag would reduce his speed from 11.5 to 11.4990 m/s. In a 40-kilometer (25-mile) time trial, that would cost the rider 0.3

seconds. At lower speeds, the aerodynamic cost of a high cadence is even less significant. It should be clear that aerodynamics need not be a factor in choosing a cadence.

Limits to Sustained Power

How much power should the rider put out at various times during the event? At first glance, such a question may appear stupid. Doesn't a racer go flat-out all the time? No, definitely not. There is no race so short that a cyclist, no matter how fit, could pedal at maximum power for the entire distance. Even in match sprints, at 1,000 meters usually the shortest competitive events, riders save maximum effort for the final 200 meters or less.

It is a characteristic of humans that they can put out their maximum power (whatever it might be) for only a few seconds, somewhat less power for a somewhat longer time, less power yet for a yet longer time, and so on, down to some power level that they can sustain almost indefinitely. See Figure 0502.

The amount of power a cyclist can sustain naturally varies considerably from individual to individual. Whitt and Wilson, quoting the same Dartmouth study mentioned above, report the amount of power that students could maintain for varying periods of time; these are summarized in Table 0501.

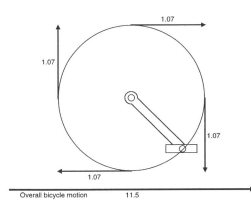

Fig. 0501. Foot and pedal motions. Airpseed vectors of the overall bike and the foot at various points around the pedaling circle, for the above example.

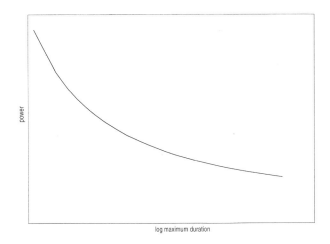

Fig. 0502. Power v. maximum time it can be sustained.

Table 0502 (based on numbers quoted in the December 1983 *Scientific American* article by Gross, Kyle, and Malewicki) gives typical figures for good, trained athletes and ordinary, healthy non-athletes. (These non-athletes are clearly in better shape than the students tested above, but the numbers are still similar.)

A male sprint cyclist of world championship caliber can sustain an average of almost 2 hp for about 10 seconds. To supplement these generalities, Tables 0503 and 0504 list the record times as of 1999 for flying-start and standing-start (time trial or pursuit) distances at a single track racing facility, the Lehigh Valley Velodrome in Trexlertown, Pennsylvania.

The 1,609- and 16,093-meter distances are one mile and ten miles, respectively; the 629,720-meter distance is the record at that track for distance covered in 24 hours. With one exception in the standing-start events, the speeds decrease smoothly with increasing distance. The exception is no doubt due partly to the extra variable introduced by the standing start, and partly to the normal variations one may expect in different records set by different people at different times.

Of course no single rider would be equally capable at 200 meters and ten miles, let alone 24 hours. But the fact that the records were all set at one facility under what were probably very similar conditions, and the fact that they represent a sort of pinnacle of achievement for highly capable competitors of similar stature, allows us to compare them with each other as an index of what is humanly possible.

Table 0501. Sustained power outputs for non-athletes

Power, watts	Duration, seconds
37	indefinitely
71	60–120
142	30
283	15
373	5

Table 0502. Limits to sustained power

	Athletes	Non-athletes
Maximum time one can sustain 750 W (1 hp)	30 seconds	12 seconds
Maximum sustained power for 8 hours	300 W (0.4 hp)	75 W (0.1 hp)

Table 0503. Flying start records, Lehigh Valley Velodrome, 1999

	Distance, m	Average speed, m/s	Holder, year
men	200	19.33	Nothstein, 1996
men	333.3	18.85	Nothstein, 1994
men	500	18.31	Nothstein, 1994
men	1,000	16.13	Wallace, 1986
women	200	17.29	Paraskevin-Young
women	333.3	16.03	Tyler

Table 0504. Standing start records, Lehigh Valley Velodrome, 1999

	Distance, m	Average speed, m/s	Holder, year
men	1,000	15.51	Hartwell, 1996
men	1609.3	15.73	Pate, 1996
men	4,000	14.68	Friedick, 1996
men	5,000	14.36	Anderson, 1992
men	16,093.4	14.08	Anderson, 1990
men	629,720	7.29	Bond, 1980
women	500	13.94	Ballanger, 1997
women	1,000	13.83	Quigley, 1991
women	3,000	13.55	Twigg, 1996

Reaching Your Sustained Power Limit

If a cyclist has been exerting more power than he can sustain, he eventually "hits the wall," "bonks," or "blows up"— waste products such as lactic acid collect in his muscles, he feels terrible, and his power output drops off dramatically. Not necessarily to zero, however; he doesn't die, but generally continues on at a much easier pace, and while he does so, he rests, his muscles begin to get rid of the waste products, and after a while he has partially or completely recovered and is able to exert more power again. The particular power levels in question, the corresponding maximum durations the person can sustain those levels, and the recovery times from various intervals of overexertion must also vary tremendously from individual to individual. The author is not aware of any published study that lists extensive, repeatable data for even one known athlete, let alone the very person who could use it most: you, dear reader.

It will help, however, if we pretend we know such data. Let us assume that our standard rider is about to compete in a flat, windless time trial, and (perhaps based on past performance) expects its total duration to be, say, 30 minutes. Let us also assume that he knows he can sustain, say, a maximum of 225 watts (about 0.3 horsepower) for 30

minutes. If he maintained that level and the time trial were to last 31 minutes, he'd blow up a minute from the end, which would probably give him a less-than-optimum time. If it lasted only 29 minutes, he'd finish with energy to spare, which means he might have been able to use that excess energy to go faster. Ideally he wants to run out of energy just as he crosses the finish line.

The following discussion will be easier if we change the time trial to one based on maximum distance covered in 30 minutes rather than minimum time to cover some fixed distance that the cyclist expects to finish in 30 minutes. The strategy for the rider hardly differs.

If we plot power vs. time, we see that a constant 225 watts for 30 minutes (1,800 seconds) looks like a rectangle (see Figure 0503). The total energy expended is the area of that rectangle, 225 x 1800 = 405,000 joules. Because we made this a simple flat, windless time trial, we know that a particular power level should correspond to a particular speed, as long as our rider maintains his crouched position, stays near his optimum cadence, etc. (We will ignore the brief time he is accelerating at the start and not yet up to speed; pretend it is a flying start event.) It is possible to calculate speed from power using the data for our standard rider. Data such as frontal area and drag coefficients are not very precisely known, but let us suppose they are, just to obtain a precise speed

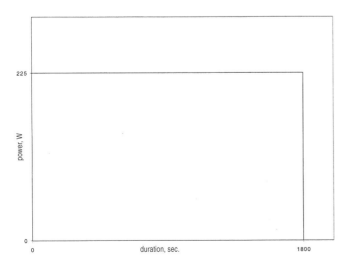

Fig. 0503. Constant power for a fixed length of time.

Fig. 0504. Constant speed for a fixed length of time.

value. The speed corresponding to 225 watts would then be 10.1264 m/s (meters per second), about 22.7 mph. So the plot of speed vs. time is also a rectangle. See Figure 0504. The area of this rectangle is the distance covered, 10.1264 x 1,800 = 18,227.5 meters (11.3 miles).

But is that necessarily the solution to our problem? Does constant power (and speed) really give maximum distance? Is the rectangle the best shape? Or is there some other shape for the power plot that has the same area (i.e. spends the same amount of energy) yet yields a speed plot with greater area (i.e. more distance)? For example, take this different strategy, depicted in Figure 0505: The rider knows that he can sustain a higher output, say 260 watts, for 10 minutes (600 seconds). So he'll ride relatively easily for the first 20 minutes, putting out a constant 207.5 watts, then kick up to 260 watts for the final 10 minutes. Total energy expenditure is 207.5 x 1,200 + 260 x 600 = 405,000 joules, exactly the same as before. Using the same kind of overly precise calculations as before, his speeds would be 9.8332 and 10.6685 m/s (we will ignore the acceleration in between), for a total distance of 18,200.9 meters. This distance is 26.6 meters less than the constant-speed effort, so this strategy is slightly less effective.

It is difficult to prove mathematically that the constant-speed rectangle is in fact the optimum,

because the relationship of power to speed is so complicated. However, anyone who does the calculations for a few different combinations of power, rider weight, and drag factors, should soon be convinced that they give similar results. In fact, the greater the fluctuation in power during the event, the slower the results.

One additional assumption we have been making is that the total amount of energy a rider has available is the same, regardless of what strategy he employs. For example, in the "stepped" strategy above, we adjusted the power so that the total energy consumed was identical to that in the constant-power strategy, figuring that in both cases the rider would run out of steam just as he crossed the finish line.

While for most events this assumption seems reasonable, it may not be true in general. We know, for example, that with sufficient rest, a rider can recover completely and expend a large amount of energy day after day indefinitely; perhaps something similar happens in a shorter time span also. Perhaps riding part of the time slightly slower, part of the time slightly faster, actually increases the amount of power a rider has available. If so, the conclusion might be invalid — but only if the slight amount of rest obtained is enough to enable a speed so fast that it offsets the time lost going slower. (It doesn't seem likely. Suppose you reduce your speed by 1 mph for a mile. Just to gain back exactly the time you lost, you must increase your speed above the original speed by more than 1 mph for another mile.) It is also possible that a short burst of intense effort may exceed the rider's capacity and have long-reaching effects, decreasing the amount of power he can apply in the future. This effect would reinforce rather than cast doubt on the conclusion. Because cyclists are not simple pieces of machinery that we can test and retest and expect to get identical results, it is not surprising that hard data for a question like this is unavailable. We can accept the assumption and conclusion, but leave open the possibility that future research may contradict them.

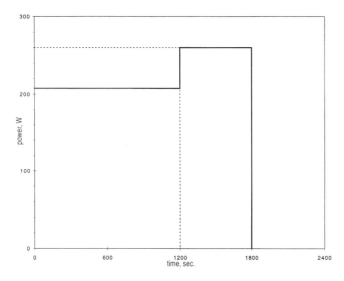

Fig. 0505. A stepped power output strategy. Is it as effective as constant power?

Maximum Power vs. Maximum Efficiency

We have been discussing the effect on speed of power output and energy expenditure, with the goal of maximizing the efficiency of the cycling effort, that is, obtaining the greatest speed from a given amount of energy, or expending the least amount of energy to maintain a given speed. Near the end of a long, exhausting ride, the cyclist's maximum speed may be very low, barely enough to get him home without spending any more energy than necessary. With a little more energy, greater speeds and more ways to spend that energy become available, but the fastest strategy is still synonymous with the one that maximizes efficiency: most speed for the amount of energy to be spent.

Suppose a cyclist has "excess" energy. For example, he may be capable of riding a fast 100 solo miles, but the event at hand is a 1-kilometer time trial. Or in a road race or a criterium, he has been resting in a pack, taking only an occasional pull; only a short distance remains, with a sprint finish inevitable. In such a case, the problem appears to be not how much total energy the rider has, but how quickly he can spend it, that is, the maximum power he has available. Isn't the best strategy in that case different?

Take a look at Figure 0506, for example, which shows for some hypothetical cyclist a power vs. time strategy and the maximum power the cyclist can develop as a function of time. The cyclist attempts to apply a relatively high, constant amount of power (dotted line), but before the time for the event is over, he runs up against the power limit. He simply cannot continue putting out that level of power, and despite trying his hardest, his power output drops. A corner of his power-vs.-time rectangle has unavoidably been lopped off. That corner represents energy he is unable to spend. The ideal shape of the power-time plot no longer seems to be a rectangle, because isn't it true that merely maintaining a lower power output (dashed line) would have slowed him down?

But this argument is based on a misconception. Our hypothetical rider never really had all

that energy to spend in that much time; he had only the amount under the dashed line. When we talk about energy available, we mean not total energy the cyclist can spend today, this week, or in his lifetime, but the total he can spend within some allotted time. That total may be radically different if the allotted time is also very different. In setting a record, the one-lap record holder at the Lehigh Valley Velodrome spent a certain amount of energy in about 18 seconds, no doubt very nearly the maximum amount he could possibly have spent in that time; but that amount is only a fraction of what he routinely spent in, say, a 100-lap madison. Total energy divided by time is of course average power, and though he spent more energy in long events, his average power output during them was less. We can compare different power output strategies, and different total energy expenditures, only if the durations are very similar.

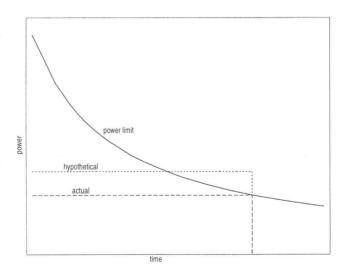

Fig. 0506. Hypothetical power-time plot.
The solid line represents how much power the rider has to spend for a given duration of event.
The upper dotted line may be the power he'd like to spend, but when that line hits the limit, he runs out of power. Only the lower dashed line represents the power he can realistically spend for that length of time.

Efficiency of the Human Body

There is another side to efficiency, and it is the amount of energy the human body consumes compared to the amount of useful work it performs. It is well known that the bodies of athletes operate at a higher efficiency than those of non-athletes. This statement does not mean that athletes are capable of more power (although that is usually also true), but that in performing the same task as a non-athlete, they consume fewer food calories. As used in nutrition, a calorie (properly called a kilocalorie) is a unit of energy equal to 4,186.8 joules. If the human body were 100% efficient, a person could eat a particle of food with a nutritional value of one calorie and subsequently burn it up doing 4,186.8 joules of work. For example, our standard rider does that much work pedaling at 20 mph on a level windless road (which requires a power level of 160 watts) for a little over 26 seconds.

Alas, the human body is nowhere near 100% efficient. The average fit person may have a body that operates at only 24% efficiency, which means he would need to consume not 1 calorie, but a little over 4 calories to perform the above task. Touring cyclists tested at power outputs in the 75- to 220-watt range routinely show efficiencies of about 27%. An athlete at the apex of conditioning may increase his body's efficiency to 30%; a couch potato could well operate at under 10%, if he operates at all. (For more on this topic, refer to "Calories and Power" by David Gordon Wilson, in *The Bicycling Book* by John Krausz and Vera van der Reis Krausz.)

The immediate consequences of the efficiency of the human body have much to do with nutrition; for example, to plan a diet for a racing or touring cyclist, or to explain why it is so difficult to lose weight only bicycling, once one is already in decent shape. But these consequences have little to do with performance. Just as a body has a particular mass, a body is only so efficient, and there is little or nothing one can do to improve that efficiency in the short term. However, that a body is capable of, say, 24% efficiency does not imply that it is actually operating at that level. For example, if the cyclist is thrashing about, attempting to pedal at 200 rpm in a very low gear, he is consuming a lot of energy compared to the effect it is having on his motion. His efficiency drops, perhaps even to zero if he derails the chain or falls off the bike. Likewise, if he is in a high gear attempting to climb a steep hill, his cadence will falter and his efficiency will plummet. Somewhere in between there is a range of cadences at which his efficiency is about as high as it can be; above or below that range efficiency drops off as some of his pedaling force is wasted.

Understand that the cyclist cannot necessarily develop the same amount of power throughout that maximum-efficiency range. His power at 120 rpm may be just as high as at 80 rpm, but his efficiency may be below par, or his power at 50 rpm may be 10% down but his efficiency may still be exactly as high. We know that for most cyclists, the cadence range allowing peak (or near-peak) efficiency is fairly wide, and that training can usually extend that range to higher cadences. It is obviously difficult to measure the efficiency of a particular cyclist's body at a particular cadence, though it has been done. One such study was mentioned earlier, the one in which racing cyclists were most efficient at 60 to 70 rpm, though possibly to the detriment of their legs.

Automobiles also provide a clue. The engine speed that produces the most power is usually high, so auto racers keep the engine revving close to the redline (maximum). In an economy run, however, competitors keep the engine barely ticking over in high gears. (Though seldom seen any more, an economy run is an event in which the winner is the driver whose car achieves the greatest fuel economy — i.e. miles per gallon — or sometimes the greatest fuel economy per weight. More later.) Although the human body certainly does not gulp fuel each rev like an auto engine, it seems likely that a moderate cadence may be more efficient.

Many cyclists feel they obtain a better workout by pedaling slowly with a relatively high pedaling force than they do by spinning the pedals against little resistance. Is that true? It depends on what "better" means, of course. If the idea is merely to expend a great deal of energy, then efficiency is hardly a consideration. Because one never sees cyclists towing sledges or parachutes in an effort to get an even better workout, expending energy does not seem to be what they have in mind; it is more likely they are trying to find a shortcut, to obtain some benefit without expending more effort than necessary. It may be better to ask what the goal of the workout is. Is it to build power, to be able to go faster? (It usually is.) If so, then does a lower cadence increase the cyclist's speed, or equivalently, does shifting to a lower gear and faster cadence slow the cyclist down? No, it probably doesn't — try it yourself. Therefore the energy being expended is practically the same either way, and neither cadence is preferable to the other from the standpoint of a total body workout. The sure way to expend more energy and obtain a better workout is obvious: speed up. (Of course it's more work. That's what a workout is.)

It is also possible to distribute the effort of a workout unevenly among different muscle groups, which may be what some cyclists are thinking when they feel that low cadences give their legs a better workout, compared to … compared to what? The sets of muscles used in pedaling at different cadences are the same, unless the cyclist radically alters his position or the adjustment of the bicycle. The perceived effect is quite different, of course. It may help to remember a trick some time trialists use to settle on a proper cadence. If the cadence is too high, the lungs will start to hurt before the legs do; if the cadence is too low, the legs begin to hurt first. This gives only a rough guide, because at the power required to be competitive in a time trial, both the lungs and legs will simultaneously be screaming for relief, even for some time after the rider stops pedaling. In any case, there is no evidence to suggest that low cadences provide a better workout, either for the body as a whole or for the muscles used in pedaling. Even if the cyclist is one of those whose efficiency is somewhat higher at relatively low cadences, there is no reason to suppose that a workout will be "better" at those cadences as well.

Other factors may also affect efficiency. For example, if the cyclist is especially cold or hot, more than usual of his body's energy will probably be diverted to maintaining his normal body temperature, leaving less for output. A cyclist who has not yet warmed up his muscles prior to intensive activity is undoubtedly sub-par in efficiency. A cyclist whose bike does not fit perfectly may waste energy sitting up, stretching, and stopping, may be distracted by discomfort, or may simply be unable to apply power well. Perhaps one who is comfortable expending 100 watts of power may operate more efficiently at that output than when he is forced to crank out 300 watts; but perhaps more likely, the higher output level may be inherently more efficient if the body spends relatively little energy on non-productive efforts such as digestion and circulation, and more on motoring down the road.

Little is in fact known about the efficiency of the human body under various conditions, yet it is a topic of great importance to the conclusions we reach in this book. We often compare two different power output schemes and pick the one with less total energy expenditure, implicitly assuming that the body's efficiency is the same in either case. Under most conditions, it is a reasonable assumption. We know that riders can pedal in a wide range of cadences and power output levels without major effects on stamina. Yet the reader is advised to keep this assumption in mind when weighing the conclusions; and while riding on his own, he should keep an eye open for possible conditions that may adversely affect his own body's efficiency.

Like the human body and other machines, bicycles are not 100% efficient, either: some of the power applied at the pedals is wasted, not converted into forward motion. As a working simplification, this book assumes that all such power drains are included in the figure for rolling resistance, and that we do not need to worry about bicycle efficiency separately.

Optimum Strategy for Flat, Windless Conditions

It should be reasonable to conclude that for a flat, windless time trial, constant power is best; not just any constant power, of course, but the highest level one can sustain for the duration of the event. While that conclusion is very simple, actually determining and achieving that precise power level is very difficult. No one knows in advance precisely how long he can sustain a particular speed, nor precisely how long it will take to cover a particular distance. The best one can do is to estimate based on training and experience, and make small adjustments during the course of the event based on how one feels and how much distance remains. As we saw above, small differences in speed do matter, but not much: the 26.6 meter difference we saw is equivalent to less than 3 seconds. The principle of trying to maintain a high, steady level still seems the best strategy.

An analogy with automobile competition may support our conclusion. Auto races seldom have serious limits on the total fuel the vehicle may consume during the race. (In cases in which fuel limits were tried, fans understandingly became upset when either the leading cars expired on the track, out of fuel, or the racing evaporated when drivers tooled slowly around the track in order to increase fuel mileage enough to finish the race.) Instead, races usually limit the size of the fuel tank and the displacement of the engine, which (if the race is long enough) forces the cars to stop periodically to refuel. Car designs that can somehow manage to eke out a bit more fuel economy without sacrificing speed might be able to get by with one less pit stop, gaining several seconds on the competition.

Caution periods at lowered speeds also increase fuel economy and enter into the strategy. So do periods when a driver's closest competitors have either dropped out or have built too substantial a lead; with little to be gained by charging, the driver may sensibly back off the throttle, save fuel, and await further developments. Otherwise, though, there is no reason not to use maximum throttle, consuming as much fuel as possible, because fuel is the source of power, and power the source of speed.

Such a strategy is completely alien to a bicycle race. The "engine" of a bike just doesn't work that way. A much more applicable form of automotive competition is the economy run. Competitors prepare their cars to the extent allowed by the rules: high tire pressures, trim removed to reduce aerodynamic drag and weight (except for formulas that compensate for weight), solid disk wheel covers, etc. If allowed, they retune the engine by altering its cam profile and timing for more efficiency at low rpm, even if it reduces overall power. They alter the car's gearing (usually via the final drive ratio) to keep the engine ticking over at the lowest possible rpm consistent with being able to develop enough power to negotiate the hills and to avoid engine bearing damage. They drive at the lowest speeds allowed, to keep airspeed and aerodynamic drag low. They shut off the engine, or at least take the car out of gear and idle the engine, to coast down sufficiently steep hills. And they adopt a very smooth, constant-throttle driving style. They know that even minor accelerations will cost them fuel, and each deceleration must be offset by an acceleration.

As you have observed, most of these economy run techniques are the very same ones employed by a bicycle time trialist. The only difference in goals is that the bicyclist still needs to finish in minimum time. Human "engine" modifications, beyond such universal preparation as training and diet, are impossible. So the time trialist tries to stay at the most efficient (not the lowest) cadence (rpm), and to judge his power output (throttle) to squeeze from his available energy (fuel quantity) the greatest average speed over the course, not merely the maximum distance. Saving energy by coasting is acceptable as long as it doesn't cost too much in speed, but otherwise nearly constant power output is the way to go.

Switchbacks

In mountainous country, roads on long, steep hillsides often employ switchbacks to reduce the grade

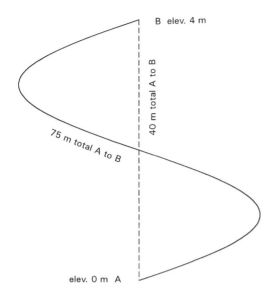

Fig. 0507. Switchback versus straight-line course. Steeper, more direct route takes less time and energy than easier longer route.

vehicles must climb and descend. The principle behind switchbacks is simple: for a given change in elevation, the greater the distance the vehicle travels, the less steep the average grade becomes. A cyclist who while climbing cuts the corner of a switchback curve, staying close to its inside, will notice that the grade becomes noticeably steeper. That's usually enough to satisfy his curiosity — it's the outside of the curve for him thereafter. Some cyclists, particularly those lacking a low enough gear, even manufacture their own switchbacks on a steep hill by zigzagging as they climb, a perfectly valid technique for reducing the grade.

The less steep the grade, the faster a cyclist can ascend it using a given amount of power. But staying to the outside (or zigzagging) increases the distance to be traveled. Which route takes longer? Or, equivalently, which route uses less energy? The answer is apparent with a simple extreme case: reduce the grade to zero by zigzagging an infinite distance up the hill. Will the speed then also be infinite? Of course not; the cyclist would be expending energy indefinitely as he "climbs" the level switchbacks. Need a more realistic example? Take a switchback such as that shown in Figure 0507. From point A to point B there is an elevation gain of 4 m. The direct, straight line route measures 40 m, making it a steep 10% grade. Riding along the edge of the sinusoidal curve, however, extends the distance to 75 m, a much easier 5.33% grade. Climbing strongly with a power output of 300 watts, our standard rider manages a speed of 3.2 m/s on the direct route, giving an elapsed time of 12.4 s. On the roundabout route, his speed would be higher, 5.4 m/s, but because of the extra distance his time would be 1.4 s slower. Energy spent, the product of power and time, would of course also be greater on the longer-distance route.

The conclusion is obvious. Unless the grade is so steep that it would bring the cyclist and his poorly geared bicycle to a halt, the fastest, most efficient way up is the shortest, most direct, and (unfortunately) steepest route. Downhill the conclusion is basically the same, with the added advantage that the curves on the direct route are less sharp and may require less braking. (But see Chapter 8 for more on the best line through a curve.)

6
Nonuniform Conditions

So far we have talked only about ideal, uniform conditions. Wind and hills complicate matters. They are rarely uniform. Days with absolutely still air are unusual. Even if the wind is blowing steadily from one direction, the cyclist's heading almost always changes during the ride. Few courses are entirely flat. Grades vary in steepness, and except in hillclimbs, they both ascend and descend.

Effect of Wind and Hills

At the very least, these nonuniformities change the relationship of power to speed, but of more interest to the competitor is the effect they may have upon equipment and strategy. Uphills and headwinds of course require lower gears; downhills and tailwinds allow higher gears. See Chapter 3, especially the discussion of the range of gearing, if you need a refresher.

Should the presence of hills or wind change the cyclist's power output strategy? Is it possible, for example, to achieve a better time by resting when blessed with a downhill or tailwind, applying the energy saved toward going faster on an uphill or into a headwind? Might the opposite

strategy be better? Or is the highest possible level of constant output power still the fastest way? Suppose we try a variety of examples to find out.

We will need a small selection of time trial courses. Keeping things simple, suppose Course A is a straight out-and-back course, level, 5 km in each direction, but with a steady 3 m/s headwind in one direction (section "u," for upwind) and a steady 3 m/s tailwind in the other (section "d," downwind). Course B is only slightly more complicated: 15 km in total length, windless and flat except for a significant hill somewhere in the middle; the hill is 100 m in height and its slopes are 5% grades, so each slope is 2,002.5 m long. (A right triangle with base 2,000 and height 100 has a hypotenuse of 2,002.5.) We will label all the flat portions, no matter where they are, section "f" and the up and down portions sections "u" and "d." Finally, Course C has a variety of slopes: up a 2% grade for 4 km (section "u"), up a stiff 10% grade for 1 km (section "us," uphill and steep), down a 3% grade for 4 km (section "d"), and down a 6% grade for the final 1 km (section "ds"), 10 km in all. See Figures 0601 through 0603 for depictions of these three courses.

Our standard rider will first ride each of these courses twice with a constant power output strategy. The first time he will apply 168 watts; the

Fig. 0601. Course A: a flat, out-and-back course with a steady wind.

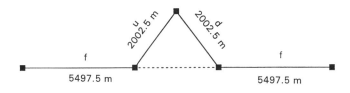

Fig. 0602. Course B: no wind but a hill.

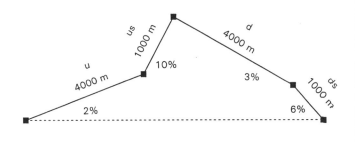

Fig. 0603. Course C: a variety of grades.

Table 0601.
Results, constant power output

Power (W)	Section	Speed (m/s)	Time (s)	Energy (J)
(Course A)				
168	u	6.10	820	137,760
168	d	11.79	424	71,232
Total		**8.04**	**1,244**	**208,992**
313	u	8.30	602	188,426
313	d	14.10	355	111,115
Total		**10.45**	**957**	**299,541**
(Course B)				
168	f	8.95	1,228	206,304
168	u	3.42	586	98,448
168	d	16.05	125	21,000
Total		**7.74**	**1,939**	**325,752**
313	f	11.20	982	307,366
313	u	5.84	343	107,359
313	d	17.21	116	36,308
Total		**10.41**	**1,441**	**451,033**
(Course C)				
168	u	6.07	659	110,712
168	us	1.84	543	91,224
168	d	13.43	298	50,064
168	ds	12.26	58	9,744
Total		**6.42**	**1,558**	**261,744**
313	u	8.76	457	143,041
313	us	3.36	298	93,274
313	d	14.91	268	83,884
313	ds	18.29	55	17,215
Total		**9.28**	**1,078**	**337,414**

second, 313 watts: both reasonable values for long-term power output, depending on the rider's fitness. We will note the speeds, elapsed times, and energy consumption for each section, then total the times and energy and figure the average speed for the total course. Later we'll vary the strategy to see how the times or speeds are affected. In all cases, we will ignore complications that have no effect on the result, such as acceleration, deceleration, and turn-around time; these would be the same, or very nearly the same, regardless of the strategy. Likewise, we will sometimes pretend our numbers have more significant figures than is justified. The exact values of the results are unimportant; discovering the underlying principles and trends is our real interest. Table 0601 has the results of the constant power output strategy, our baseline case.

For those who are not yet comfortable with metric units, the two power levels equal 0.225 and

Table 0602. Results, power output increased 10% on uphills and in headwinds, decreased on downhills and in tailwinds

Power (W)	Section	Speed (m/s)	Time (s)	Energy (J)
(Course A)				
185	u	6.41	780	144,330
146	d	11.32	442	64,532
Total		8.18	1,222	208,832
Improvement			22 s = 1.7%	
344	u	8.68	576	198,144
275	d	13.59	368	101,200
Total		10.59	944	299,344
Improvement			1.3 s = 1.3%	
(Course B)				
168	f	8.95	1,228	206,304
185	u	3.73	537	99,345
160	d	15.98	125	20,000
Total		7.94	1,890	325,649
Improvement			49 s = 2.6%	
313	f	11.20	982	307,366
344	u	6.29	318	109,392
291	d	17.04	118	34,338
Total		10.58	1,418	451,096
Improvement			23 s = 1.6%	

Power (W)	Section	Speed (m/s)	Time (s)	Energy (J)
(Course C)				
185	u	6.45	620	114,700
185	us	2.02	495	91,575
154	d	13.26	302	46,508
154	ds	17.15	58	8,932
Total		6.78	1,475	261,715
Improvement			83 s = 5.6%	
(Course C)				
344	u	9.21	434	149,296
344	us	3.68	272	93,568
289	d	14.69	272	78,608
289	ds	18.13	55	15,895
Total		9.68	1,033	337,367
Improvement			45 s = 4.4%	

0.420 hp. The average speeds our rider achieved during these baseline runs were 18.0 and 23.4 mph for Course A, 17.3 and 23.3 mph for Course B, and 14.4 and 20.8 mph for Course C.

Now our rider will vary his power output strategy. Into the wind or uphill, he will increase his power output by 10%. In flat, windless sections, he will revert back to the baseline power level. With the wind at his back or downhill, he will reduce his power output just enough so that his total energy expenditure is practically the same as during the baseline runs. The precise amount of that power reduction is different for each of the examples. Yes, these examples are artificial. Just as a rider has only a vague idea of his output power and the total time for which he can sustain that power, he can hardly know precisely how far to back off after an extra exertion yet still consume the same amount of energy by the end of the time trial. Again, it is the principle rather than the precise numerical data that we are seeking. Table 0602 has the results.

The results for these various courses and power levels are consistent. When winds or grades vary, the strategy of constant power output is no longer the fastest. It is better instead to increase power output slightly during the more difficult uphill or headwind portions and make up for the extra energy expenditure by decreasing power output slightly during the easier downhill or tailwind portions.

We have assumed that our rider is just capable of sustaining a certain power level (in our examples, 168 watts or 313 watts) for the duration of the time trial. When we ask him to increase his power output for part of that time, we also assume he can meet that request. Ten percent seems a modest power increase. It increases speed only slightly. Yet it may be the straw that breaks the camel's back. Still, if a rider can achieve a certain power output level for a given extended length of time, there must be some greater level (possibly only very slightly greater) that he can achieve for a shorter length of time. Earlier we also mentioned the possibility that a short burst of intense effort may have long-reaching effects, perhaps enough to reduce the total amount of energy the

rider will have available. It is easy to picture a rider overdoing it, pouring everything he has into a brief but steep climb, and then being spent and useless for the rest of the event. Obviously, a rider must avoid such an extreme. It nevertheless seems likely that a rider will be able to recover sufficiently from some lower level of extra exertion. These examples indicate that this extra exertion is worthwhile as long as it is applied during the low-speed portions of the course and as long as the rider reduces his exertion a corresponding amount — but no more than that — during the high-speed portions of the course.

Effect of Greater Power Increases

So far these examples have all increased power by 10% during uphills. Is a greater increase (if it can be achieved) desirable? We'll use Course C with baseline 313 W to find out. Table 0603 has the results with 5%, 10%, and 20% increases during the uphills, and reductions during the downhills to compensate.

Clearly the greater the increase the rider can manage, the greater the improvement in his time. But it should also be clear that there will be some percentage of power increase beyond which improvement is no longer possible. For example, if the rider increases his output power so much that he uses his total allotment of energy during the uphill or headwind portion, he is left with no energy to finish the course. In our Course C example, the rider is climbing more than half the time. It is unlikely that a real rider who is just able to sustain a certain output level for, say, 15 minutes would be able to increase that output greatly for 10 minutes regardless of how much he backed off for the remaining 5 minutes. Probably only a slight increase is possible, but that slight increase is worthwhile.

We have already seen that it is best to apply a little extra to climbs and headwinds and rest a little when the course gets easier. Can we be more specific? After all, most courses have a variety of hills and a variety of wind conditions. Is it better to allot more to especially steep climbs, or to relatively gentle climbs that last longer? Naturally it depends on the specifics of the course. While ideally we should analyze the actual situation, Table 0604 should give a hint. In both examples, the maximum power applied is the same and the total energy expended is about the same. In the first, the rider used his maximum on the long 2%

upgrade; in the second, he saved it for the much shorter 10% upgrade and came out slightly ahead. As a rule of thumb, therefore, the steeper the slope or the more severe the headwind, the more it will pay to apply a little extra effort.

The Downhill

What rider doesn't love to coast down a hill? The sensation of speed is so enjoyable that many of us try extra hard to scrunch into an aerodynamic tuck, squeezing as much speed out of the hill as we can. It is obvious that the highest speed comes from maintaining that extra-low tuck during the entire downhill, if not throughout the entire ride, but the fact that we don't do it implies that such a low tuck is too uncomfortable (or perhaps too unsafe) for more than short periods of time. Given

Table 0603. Results, variable power increases and decreases

Power (W)	Section	Speed (m/s)	Time (s)	Energy (J)
Course C 5% increase				
329	u	8.99	445	146,405
329	us	3.52	284	93,436
300	d	14.79	270	81,000
300	ds	18.20	55	16,500
Total		**9.49**	**1,054**	**337,341**
Improvement			**24 s = 2.2%**	
Course C 10% increase				
344	u	9.21	434	149,296
344	us	3.68	272	93,568
289	d	14.69	272	78,608
289	ds	18.13	55	15,895
Total		**9.68**	**1,033**	**337,367**
Improvement			**45 s = 4.4%**	
Course C 20% increase				
376	a	9.64	414	155,664
376	b	4.00	250	94,000
263	c	14.44	277	72,851
263	d	17.95	56	14,728
Total		**10.03**	**997**	**337,243**
Improvement			**81 s = 7.5%**	

Table 0604. Results, power increase dependent on steepness of climb

Course C, maximum power used on longer but less steep climb

Power (W)	Section	Speed (m/s)	Time (s)	Energy (J)
344	u	9.21	434	149,296
329	us	3.52	284	93,436
289	d	14.69	272	78,608
289	ds	18.13	55	15,895
Total		**9.57**	**1,045**	**337,235**

Course C, maximum power reserved for steep climb

Power (W)	Section	Speed (m/s)	Time (s)	Energy (J)
329	u	8.99	445	146,405
344	us	3.68	272	93,568
298	d	14.78	271	80,758
298	ds	18.20	55	16,390
Total		**9.60**	**1,043**	**337,121**

that constraint, when is the best time to do it? At the end of the downhill, when speed and drag are highest? At the beginning, to set up faster speeds later? Or perhaps somewhere else? Let's try some examples to find out.

Suppose our standard rider finds a somewhat-less-than-ideally aerodynamic position more comfortable for general riding; that position may have a frontal area of 0.38 m^2 and a C_D of 0.90. (These numbers fall somewhere in between the 0.40 and 1.0, respectively, of a straight-elbowed, more upright touring position, and the corresponding numbers for our standard rider's usual tuck.) Suppose there is a downhill with a 5% grade (that is, a –5% grade) lasting 750 meters. Let's divide the hill into thirds, 250 m each, called 1, 2, and 3 — 1 beginning at the top, 3 finishing at the bottom. Our standard rider approaches the downhill at 7 m/s and coasts. He will be in his comfortable position (call it position C) for two of the thirds, but has the choice of any one in which to do his tuck (position T). In which third should he substitute position T for position C, in order to

obtain the highest speed? Table 0605 summarizes the speeds and times.

In the example represented in Table 0605, our rider obtains his fastest time down the hill when he adopts his tuck early and resumes his comfortable position for the remainder of the hill. Doing the tuck in the middle is only marginally worse. Leaving the tuck until the end gives the worst time, though the final speed in that case is highest.

Perhaps these are atypical conditions, though. What if the hill is steeper and the entry speed is slower, to give a pronounced difference in drag between the first and last thirds of the hill? Table 0606 gives results with a –10% grade and an initial speed of 4.5 m/s.

These results are consistent with the earlier ones, except that here doing the tuck in the middle third is even better than in the first third. This finding suggests we can refine the earlier results. Because at low speeds, drag makes relatively little difference, one might suspect that a rider could obtain an even better time by delaying the tuck a little. Readers who take the trouble to go through the calculations will find that to be correct. Of

Table 0605. Coasting on 750 m 5% downgrade with different positions

Position scheme	Speed at end of third				Elapsed time in third			Total time
	1	2	3		1	2	3	
C-C-C	12.36	13.63	14.01		24.565	19.061	18.041	61.67
C-C-T	12.36	13.63	14.37		24.565	19.061	17.778	61.40
C-T-C	12.36	13.46	14.12		24.565	18.795	17.790	61.15
T-C-C	12.61	13.71	14.03		24.302	18.854	17.985	61.14

Table 0606. Coasting on 750 m 10% downgrade with different positions

Position scheme	Speed at end of third				Elapsed time in third			Total time
	1	2	3		1	2	3	
C-C-T	17.02	19.38	20.57		20.997	13.572	12.452	47.02
C-T-C	17.02	19.84	20.21		20.997	13.387	12.464	46.85
T-C-C	17.33	19.46	20.04		20.823	13.444	12.603	46.87

course, the very best time still depends on maintaining the tuck as long as possible.

All the results indicate that for the best time down a constant grade, the rider should pay particular attention to his aerodynamic position near the beginning of the downhill, as his speed begins to increase. Not only his position, of course: anything he can do to increase speed at that point will help his overall time, including drafting, applying power, and choosing a line that starts him off more steeply downhill.

On the other hand, for the highest final speed, he should reserve the all-out anti-drag and other speed-amplifying measures for near the end of the downhill. How important is the speed differential at the end of the hill? Is it enough to offset the time differential down the hill? The answer must depend on the layout of the particular course. If the finish line is at the bottom of the hill, only the elapsed time matters; the speed crossing it makes no difference. If the finish line is some distance away, the rider has the opportunity to use a higher exit speed off the hill to offset some or all of the time he may have lost on the downhill. With the 5% downgrade examples above, if the final run to the finish line is a level 100 m, the total elapsed time to the finish is slightly less when the rider goes for minimum time down the hill rather than maximum speed, assuming equal power. With a longer run to the finish line, higher exit speed may be the deciding factor.

The Dell

Take another example, familiar to recreational cyclists who ride in hilly country: a downhill followed immediately by an uphill. Let us call this sequence a "dell," even if the surroundings may not be as wooded and pastoral as the word suggests. Seemingly every cyclist would love to build up enough speed on the downhill portion of the dell to be able to coast all the way up to the crest of the hill at the exit of the dell. Alas, it seldom happens; the uphill scrubs off speed too quickly, usually forcing the cyclist to pedal.

Such a dell lies a few miles from the author's home. Figure 0604 shows its profile, slightly simplified. Starting at an altitude of 157 m (point A), the road drops 20 m in the first 624 m (a gentle 3.2% downgrade to point B), then drops more steeply 36 m in the next 360 m (a 10% downgrade to point C); leveling out for 120 m to point D, the road then ascends 9 m in 192 m (a 4.7% upgrade) to the next crest, point E. With no side roads, plenty of trees providing shelter from the wind, and a total of 56 m of altitude loss but just 9 m of altitude gain, this dell ought to be perfect: lots of speed at the bottom to carry the cyclist over the top.

Well, though many are the cyclists who have tried, rare is the one who makes it over the top without pedaling. If he just coasts down the hill, the rider does indeed go quite fast at the bottom, but somewhere before the summit his choice is simple: pedal or topple. Naturally, the next time by, the rider tries to increase his speed: he pedals hard at the beginning of the downhill, trying to go supersonic by the bottom, but the ensuing climb is usually more than a match. Of course the goal may only be to attain the highest maximum speed during the downhill; if so, that's a good way to go about it. But suppose the goal is just to crest the next hill without having to expend much energy. It may seem easier to pedal on the downhill rather

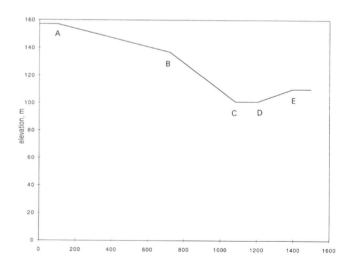

Fig. 0604. A dell. Intermediate points are labeled for the discussion of energy output strategy in the text.

than the uphill, but by now we should suspect that it doesn't work that way in reality.

We'll go through example numbers for our standard cyclist. Suppose he begins at 6.7 m/s (15 mph) and wishes to crest the next hill at that same speed. Coasting all the way, he is up to 11.3 m/s by point B, 19.5 m/s by point C; by point D his speed is down to 14.9 m/s. If he were to continue to coast, he would come to a halt 158 m later, well short of the crest. Well, our standard rider may be only a test dummy, but he's not dumb enough to fall over. Instead throughout the uphill, beginning at point D, he applies a steady 243 W and arrives at point E 19.5 seconds later, matching his original speed of 6.7 m/s. Total energy expenditure is 243 x 19.5 or about 4740 J.

Next time, he starts at the same speed and resolves to expend that energy during the initial gentle downhill. So he pedals from point A to point B, applying 84 W, and arrives at point B 56.5 seconds later, expending almost the same amount of energy as he did during the uphill the last time. Can he coast the rest of the way? Dream on. His speed at point B is 12.7 m/s; at point C, 19.7 m/s; at point D, 15.0 m/s; and were he to continue to coast, he would make it just 161 m farther. To make it over the crest, he would need to go considerably faster. In this real dell, on the real road, strong riders have sometimes reached a maximum of 51 mph (22.8 m/s) — at least according to their cycle computers. Undoubtedly they burned up a lot of energy to do so. Our rider, for example, might apply 600 W to point B and then 540 W to point C to hit 22.8 m/s. To do so, he'd need a pretty big gear, not to mention muscles, and he would expend over 34,000 J. Coasting the rest of the way, he would slow to 17.5 m/s at point D and still be rolling at 2.6 m/s when he reached point E: no, it's not his original speed, but at least he wouldn't fall over. Still, he spent over 7 times as much energy as he did when he not only pedaled up to the top but was going faster when he got there.

Our rider's best effort at saving energy so far cost 4,740 J, when he coasted to the beginning of the uphill, then pedaled the rest of the way, gradually slowing to his target speed. There are better schemes yet. Suppose he coasts part way up the hill until his speed drops to the target speed, 6.7 m/s, then pedals just hard enough to maintain that speed. Similar calculations show him expending 3,960 J. And if he coasts still farther until his speed drops to 2.0 m/s, then accelerates hard back up to 6.7 m/s by the crest, he expends just 3,680 J. For minimum energy expenditure on a dell, the best strategy seems to be to coast as long as possible, almost to the point of toppling over, then power over the top with an intense burst. As before, this strategy assumes that a rider has a certain total amount of energy to expend, that excess power does not reduce that total nor rest increase that total. It also assumes that accelerating over the top does not require more power than he has in his legs. If it does, he will need to start pedaling sooner, expending a little more total energy, but less of it at any given instant.

There are infinitely many ways to expend energy, but relatively few ways to expend only a little of it and still get the job done. Most of the latter involve pedaling hard on uphills.

Making Up Time

Cyclists often have a need to make up time. Momentary delays in traffic, pauses for impromptu repairs, being "dropped" on a climb — the reasons for lost time are endless. Plus in a race there is often a need to gain time — to preempt an anticipated move by a rival or to force one's competitors to try to make up time themselves. Gaining time and making up for lost time are the same problem, and they have the same solution: go faster. By going even only slightly faster, any amount of time can be made up … eventually. Because all rides are finite, however, any discussion of making up time makes sense only if there is some time or distance limit; for example, that a certain amount of time be made up by one lap from the finish of the race.

When is the best time to make up time? Is it less work to make up time on downhills, when the grade isn't adding to the effort, or on uphills, when the speeds are low, or on the flats, or doesn't it make any difference? Again we will call upon our standard rider, giving him the task of making up ten seconds within one kilometer as an example. We'll say that his normal power output is 150 W, enough for a brisk speed on a level road but well short of race pace. The calculations are easy using the programs in Appendix C. First determine the speed at his "normal" power output under the given conditions: call it v_1. Divide 1,000 m (the specified distance) by v_1 to get the "normal" elapsed time, t_1. Divide 1,000 m by t_1-10 (that is, the normal time less the amount of time that must be made up) to get the required speed, v_2. Finally, determine how much power that speed would require under the same conditions. Table 0607 has the results for windless conditions up a 6% grade, level, and down a 6% grade.

Up the grade, it's relatively easy to make up time: our standard ride needs only a modest power increase above his normal 150 W. On the flats, he needs a considerable boost in output. Why? Because he not only has to fight relatively higher wind resistance, but has less time in which to make up his 10 seconds. Downhill, forget it: he needs such a whopping power increase that he would need superhuman effort (for someone who normally puts out a couple of tenths of a horsepower, anyway). Even if the downhill were a gentle −2%, he would need 279.7 W, almost double his usual power output. But though he has to apply much more power downhill, isn't it for a much shorter time? Indeed it is. If, however, you take the trouble to multiple his power increase (that is, the power in the table minus 150) times the elapsed time (t1 minus 10), you will see that the resulting extra energy spent is much less under the uphill conditions. Once again, slow speeds are

where it pays to spend extra energy. If you are unconvinced, try doing the calculations for a high normal output, say 400 W, or with headwinds versus tailwinds.

Nor is power output the whole story. Even if he has the power at his disposal, a rider might not be able to apply all that power downhill. He may be spun out — gears only go so high, after all. Or the high speed may be far too risky. In the example above, the downhill speed of 21.295 m/s translates to 47.6 mph and a cadence approaching 150 rpm in a 108-inch gear. These are probably well beyond the safe limit for most hills and beyond the capability of most riders, never mind the still higher speeds that would be required under racing conditions. It is just not practical to gain significant time by increasing power downhill.

Intervals

Most competitive riders are familiar with "intervals" (or "interval training," i.e. periods of hard effort alternating with rest periods. As a means to build strength, interval training applies to any period of time from a few seconds to full days. It may also be that a cycle of alternating periods of exertion and recovery allows somewhat greater total energy expenditure than constant effort. As usual with human performance, precise data is unknown, but let us take a hypothetical example. Suppose that in the course of the final 10 minutes of an event our standard rider could exert a steady 292 watts of power: a total of 175,200 joules of energy. Suppose also that if (instead of constant output) he pedaled 15 seconds, coasted 15 seconds, pedaled 15 seconds, etc. then he could manage not merely double 292 (i.e. 584), but 595 watts during the pedaling phases. He would expend 178,500 joules. The trouble with the latter plan is that despite the greater total output, he would go slower on average. Accelerating to 13 m/s and coasting down to 8.9 m/s, he would average 11.08 m/s on a flat, windless course vs. 11.12 m/s with the constant 292-watt effort. Of course the reason for the lower speed is that in a 1:1 duty cycle of exertion and recovery he's coasting half the time.

Table 0607. Making up 10 seconds in 1 kilometer

Grade	v_1 (m/s)	t_1 (s)	v_2 (m/s)	power (W)
+6%	2.636	379.35	2.707	154.2
0%	8.728	114.57	9.563	192.2
−6%	17.556	56.96	21.295	772.4

If he were to coast only a third of the time (a 2:1 duty cycle), he would cut his coasting losses, but with less rest his power output would certainly also be less. Greater duty cycles, 3:1, 4:1, etc. would approach the constant output plan in both energy output and speed. If our hypothetical data is realistic, a solo effort under constant conditions demands constant power output if maximum average speed is the goal. Alternating exertion and recovery would have to boost power significantly before such a strategy paid off in terms of speed.

Conditions are not always constant, of course, occasionally affording the chance for partial recovery. Downhills and tailwinds sometimes present themselves. (Never often enough.) Recreational riders on a century encounter occasional rest stops. Because these stops are essential for replenishment of food and drink and are expected of the participants, there is no reason not to take advantage of them. Nevertheless, for the fastest overall time, stops are best kept brief. In other words, whenever rest or partial recovery is available, the rider should take advantage of it — or have a good reason not to, such as to take advantage of the fact that rivals have let their guard down. Otherwise he should use nearly constant effort and postpone rest until after the event.

Drafting

Drafting, or pacing, as it is called in Britain, is probably the best example of a non-constant condition that allows cyclists to rest. The opportunity to draft, in events that allow it, raises overall speeds well beyond what individual riders would be able to manage on their own. In a team time trial, for example, each rider on the team takes approximately his share of pulls at the front while the other riders draft and rest, relatively speaking. In other events, stronger riders may be at the front more than their share of the time in order to help out weaker riders and keep a group together. In competition with rival teams, when to draft, how much to draft, and when not to draft are essential parts of a team's strategy.

We can obtain a clue as to how much drafting can increase speed by comparing individual and team pursuit records. Steve Hegg set a record at the Lehigh Valley Velodrome in 1990 for the 4,000 meter individual pursuit at 4:40.35; two years later, the New Zealand national team set a 4,000 meter team pursuit record of 4:23.02. (Meanwhile, both these records have been superseded, though Gary Anderson, the New Zealand team's leader, set a 5,000 meter record that year that was still intact as of 1999 — See Table 0504.)

The 4-man team in this case is therefore 6.6% faster than a comparable individual. Even if every man on the New Zealand team were equally as fast as Hegg, the team could not be expected to be faster than an individual unless the riders took advantage of those recovery periods to go faster during their turns at the front, because it is still the rider at the front who determines the pace.

We can make some educated guesses to calculate the amount of power the riders develop for these events, in an attempt to determine whether alternating exertion and recovery allows greater overall energy expenditure. Suppose each rider and his bicycle together have a mass of 80 kg, that the coefficient of aerodynamic drag for the lead rider (or the individual pursuit rider) is 0.85, and that the moments of inertia of the wheels are 0.0530 and 0.0536 kg m^2. (Moment of inertia will be covered in Chapter 12.) These figures concede that the record holders are probably both lighter and more aerodynamic than our standard rider, and are mounted on low-mass track equipment. Each rider drafting behind the lead rider essentially has a lower drag coefficient, about 0.50. The riders farthest to the rear may have even slightly lower drag, but in a paceline one rider wide this figure should be close enough.

We'll take the individual pursuit rider first. Starting at a speed of 0, he applies constant power P_s, accelerating the bike up to a speed v; at that point, the elapsed time is t_s and the distance covered is d_s. Then he maintains speed v to the finish. To do so, he applies constant power P_f, which is less than P_s because he no longer needs power to accelerate. The duration of this constant-speed segment is t_f. Total energy expended is $P_s t_s + P_f t_f$. See Figure 0605 for a graphical illustration of the power profile. Table 0608 has some examples with different split distances (d_s) but which all obtain very nearly the target time of 4:40.35. (The energy figures are overly precise, given the precision of the other numbers.)

Clearly the split distance — to the point at which the rider stops accelerating and begins steady speed — is important. On the one hand, rapid acceleration requires much more power during its relatively brief interval. On the other hand, it pays to accelerate up to speed quickly, because the more quickly he reaches the constant speed segment, the less energy he expends by the finish. As usual, any excess energy can always be used to increase speed still further. For comparison purposes, we will use the 333.3-meter split example.

Now we'll look at the team pursuit. All four riders accelerate from a standing start, quickly settling into a tight paceline in which the front wheel of each following bike is very close behind the rear wheel of the bike immediately ahead. Periodically the rider at the front peels off to the side and falls into line at the rear with all the grace and precision of a ballet leap. Each lap at the Lehigh Valley Velodrome is, conveniently, 333.3 meters. If team pursuit riders each take about half-lap pulls, then the position of the team is set back just over one bike length 24 times during the event, a total

of about 40 meters. The elapsed time for the event is as though the total distance were 4,040 meters. To determine the total energy being spent, notice that there is always one rider at the front and three behind. We can calculate the amount of energy the front rider expends as if it were always the same rider, traveling at the team record pace; then calculate the energy spent by the riders behind him matching his pace. Again, the split distance is important, because not only does the lead rider need to accelerate up to a faster speed, but the other three do, too, and they need almost as much power to accelerate as he does. Using the same sort of calculations as above, we obtain the numbers in Table 0609 for the lead rider. (Again the energy numbers are overly precise.) We'll pick the 500-meter split distance this time, to keep the needed power from getting too high.

Because the forces on the trailing riders in the slipstream are much different, their power requirements vary considerably during the event. We need to break down the first 500 meters into shorter segments. Table 0610 shows the speed and elapsed time of the lead rider during that lap, and the amount of power a drafting rider would need to match his numbers closely.

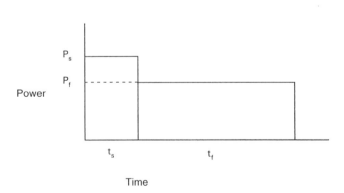

Fig. 0605. Power profile for an individual pursuit. High power to accelerate up to speed, then reduced power to maintain the speed. Total energy is the area under the profile.

Table 0608. An individual 4,000 m TT in 4:40.35

d_s (m)	P_s (W)	T_s (s)	v (m/s)	P_f (W)	Total E (J)
200	780.5	18.6	14.52	596.4	170,625
333.3	666.2	29.0	14.59	606.0	171,638
500	628.2	41.0	14.62	610.7	171,927
1,000	614.4	75.5	14.65	613.9	172,145
1,500	614.1	170.7	14.65	614.1	172,163

Table 0609. An individual 4,040 m TT in 4:23.02

d_s (m)	P_s (W)	t_s (s)	v (m/s)	P_f (W)	Total E (J)
333.3	826.0	27.0	15.70	750.2	199,364
500	778.5	38.2	15.75	756.6	199,838
1,000	761.3	192.7	15.77	760.7	200,195

The 125,724 J applies to each of the three trailing riders. The average of the four is 144,253 J, which is about 16% less than we calculated for the rider setting the individual pursuit record spent.

What can we learn from these numbers? First of all, it is no surprise that riders go faster in a paceline than individually. On his pulls, the lead rider of the team can develop more power than the individual pursuiter can on his one long pull. Yet in this example, each team rider on average spent less energy overall despite setting a record time. It may be that alternating exertion and recovery allows greater total energy expenditure than constant effort, but one couldn't prove it from these numbers. With the riders resting part of the time, we would like to think that they would have more to give, so why is the energy less? There are probably several reasons. One is simple: because of their greater speed, they spent 6% less time applying power; that amounts to a lot of energy that did not get spent. In addition, though the actual New Zealand team riders were obviously very capable, not all of them were of equal strength at that distance, nor was each necessarily as strong as Hegg, the individual pursuit record holder. Plus in playing follow-the-leader, the trailing riders could not apply as much power as they may have had available.

We can also pick up some pointers for team pursuits and team time trials. During acceleration from a standing start (or in similar situations), all the riders need to be closely matched, because most of the power goes into acceleration, and drafting helps only a little. Still, the strongest member, the one who can accelerate the fastest, should be at the front at those times, but it will not help if he pulls away from the rider behind him and upsets his drafting or forces later speed adjustments. Because the power savings from drafting increases with speed, the weakest members should take their pulls last in a flat event, so that when they are not at the front the team is at its highest speed (or nearly so) and they get the most benefit from resting in the slipstream. In a more varied time trial, planning the order of the riders, keeping these principles in mind, may be complex.

When Drafting is Ruled Out

Not all events permit drafting. Notably, time trials and their cousins — pursuits, the bicycling portions of triathlons, and some ultra-marathon events — expressly forbid drafting. When a rider in one of these events comes up on a competitor, he is supposed to pull to the side and overtake him quickly, to benefit from the draft as little as possible. In the same spirit, the overtaken rider is not supposed to try to hang on and benefit from the passing rider's slipstream — not that there is much advantage in doing so. In a pursuit, for example, the overtaken rider is immediately eliminated. In a time trial, with individual starts a minute or so apart, being overtaken is usually equivalent to being uncompetitive: if you are already a minute down, what good will a few seconds do you? In some time trials, such as regular club events on the same course, the goal of the riders may be not so much to compete against each other as to obtain periodic snapshots of their individual fitness levels, or possibly to evaluate new equipment or a new riding position. During such an event, drafting, or doing anything else uncharacteristic or inconsistent, would distort the resulting time. As an evaluation, the time trial

Table 0610. Breakdown of team pursuit into segments

elapsed distance (m)	elapsed time (s)	speed (m/s)	drafting power (W)	cum. energy spent (J)
0	0.0	0.00	0	0
15.3	3.3	7.47	770	2,541
31.3	5.2	9.32	740	3,947
63.7	8.3	11.37	701	6,120
124.6	13.2	13.32	632	9,217
250.2	22.0	14.95	556	14,110
500	38.2	15.75	495	22,127
4,040	263.0	15.75	461	125,724

would be merely wasted effort — not a smart way to spend one's time.

Even in a non-drafting event, however, it is sometimes possible to gain some of the benefits of drafting while remaining legal, ethical, and consistent. Large, stationary objects, such as trees, walls, hedges, embankments, buildings, parked vehicles, and even clumps of spectators, have their own wind "shadow." If there is a prevailing wind and these objects are close to the course, the smart rider can possibly gain a little time by recognizing their effect on local wind patterns. The principle is first to note the prevailing wind direction, then if the wind is even partially a headwind, ride as close to the shielding objects as practicable, but if the wind is mostly a tailwind, then ride as far away from them as possible. The prevailing wind direction can be assessed at the start by noticing the way flags or banners are blowing, or using the golfer's trick of tossing a few bits of grass into the air; the speed of the wind is relatively unimportant, except that the stronger the wind, the more reason there is to try to avoid it or make use of it. If the course runs through a valley, a city street flanked by buildings, or a similar channel, the wind may change direction somewhat to flow along the path of least resistance. During the event, the rider should maintain a mental picture of the course, so he knows which way he is currently going, and therefore the relative direction the wind must be blowing. Because (apart from gale conditions) it is nearly impossible to assess wind direction by feel while moving in one direction, he should also be alert for other clues that may indicate possible changes in wind direction, such as leaves on trees, jackets and skirts on spectators, and blowing dust. Courses that change direction provide much more information; the rider can often deduce the wind direction as he turns into or away from it.

Winds and the objects capable of blocking them are very variable, and it is impossible to specify the precise effect of, say, one parked car on a rider's time. But to give the general idea, suppose that the prevailing wind is 8 mph from the northeast and that the course is a level 10 miles straight north. A rider who can manage 24 mph on that course will of course come in at a time of 25 minutes flat. If he is able to shield himself from the wind just enough that for only one half mile of that distance the wind is reduced by a mere 1 mph, he will save about 2 seconds overall. That is, the increased speed from applying the same amount of power to battle a wind from the northeast of only 7 mph instead of 8 mph nets him a 2-second gain during that half mile.

Needless to say, determining the prevailing wind direction is useful in any event, not only time trials. A drafting rider should also take the wind into account, noting that the wind shadow of the rider(s) ahead will shift sideways in a strong side wind and will also be affected by objects or gaps to the side of the course. A rider being drafted can also use his knowledge of the prevailing wind to make drafting easier for his teammates, or more difficult for his rivals. For example, with a known wind from the left, the lead rider can ride well left of the right edge of the road (traffic permitting) to allow his companions to form an echelon behind and to the right — or he can hug the right curb and make drafting him no easier than necessary.

A hill along the course may also shield the wind. During the climb, unless the wind is unusually strong, it is of little importance; the rider is mainly fighting gravity. On the descent, however, the wind may reassert itself, with implications for competitive strategy. A downhill tailwind may allow the first rider over the top to disappear from sight more quickly than usual, making speed during the preceding climb more important than ever. A downhill headwind or a side wind strong enough to force a cautious descent reduces the value of being able to escape during the climb, because following riders will be able to catch up relatively easily.

Strategy in Nonuniform Conditions

Strategy will almost certainly be different when a rider is racing against one opponent, against multiple opponents, or racing against the clock, and is made more complex by the presence of teammates. Most races, of course, pit many riders against each other. Practically speaking, it is impossible to deal individually with each rider in a pack. Better, perhaps, to think of a pack as one large opponent, at least at first. Because the primary force acting on a bicyclist is aerodynamic, the most important characteristic of an opponent, regardless of size, is the opportunity to draft. See the discussion of drafting in the Chapter 11 for more on the strategic implications.

Opponents also send out signals. They may show signs of tiring or losing interest, or conversely may appear impossibly fresh and strong. These signals (which may be deceptive) can form the basis for a rider's own power output strategy, for example whether to let up and save energy for later or try to make a break now. Opponents may intentionally block or attack; they may also unintentionally upset a rider's momentum or the line he might have taken through a corner or to avoid a rough patch of road. These actions force flexibility and permit volatility, both attributes usually more characteristic of younger riders. Opponents may distract a rider from matters he ought to be monitoring carefully, such as the amount of power he can sustain for long periods; in this case, experience is more helpful than youth. Opponents may both teach and learn, affording a rider a chance to improve his technique and possibly forcing him to guard against revealing his hand too soon.

Racing against opponents is sure to involve alternating periods of effort and rest, a cycle which benefits a young sprinter more than a seasoned endurance rider. In such situations, sub-maximum performance is often acceptable. For example, well-planned gearing and optimum cadence are less important in a pack or break group than being able to grab a gear quickly and respond to whatever is happening. A mediocre line through a corner or an ill-advised burst of energy may not matter as long as one maintains contact with the pack and has time to recover from such mistakes.

A time trial, racing against the clock rather than against nearby opponents, is less forgiving of mistakes. Even in mass-start events, though, most riders at some time or other must perform well on their own, for example in making a breakaway and staying away, chasing a break group, or trying to keep from being dropped. Against-the-clock factors then take on great importance, and a rider needs to use every technique in his arsenal. A time trial favors steady, high-level effort, restraint, and precision; these attributes are often the province of a stoic, experienced, older rider.

With a minimum of logistical worries, training for a solo effort is relatively easy. A time trial is ideal for a rider without a team or for one who is not yet comfortable with wheel-to-wheel racing. The clock by itself cannot be deceptive or intimidating. It lets a rider concentrate on his own effort; in fact, it demands such concentration. Many time trials allow certain aero equipment that is banned in mass start events, which in effect means that for a rider to be competitive, such equipment is almost mandatory. In any case, racing against the clock demands carefully planned components, including gearing.

Especially in a race against opponents, a rider should play to his own strengths. A light rider should try to escape up hills, a heavy rider on downhills. A rider with (to give three more examples) confidence in his ability to negotiate narrow lanes or paths, or the technique and sturdy equipment to skim over rough surfaces, or a combination of low profile and grim determination into headwinds should try to escape under those conditions. The principle of "out of sight, out of mind" comes into play. If you are far enough ahead that your opponents can no longer see you, they tend to forget about you or give up on you. More generally, any show of strength or skill that opponents cannot match may be enough to demoralize them. In addition, a sprinter (together with his teammates) should try to set up a final sprint, by resting in the draft at every opportunity and trying to keep breakaways from succeeding. Conversely, a non-sprinter should try to break earlier to avoid a final field sprint, and force opposing sprinters to work.

Racing Objectives

Many people, including some racers, think that the objective of the racer is to go as fast as possible. They are mistaken. The primary objective of the racer is to finish the race. The secondary objective, valid only if the primary objective can be achieved, is to win, to go faster than the competition.

Why are these objectives not the same as going as fast as possible? As a means of satisfying the primary objective, going as fast as possible is counterproductive. An examination of automobile competition may illustrate this. In a motor race, mistakes such as over-revving the engine or taking a turn too fast risk taking the car out of the race, or worse. The successful auto racer must learn to stay within the limits of his ability and the limits of his vehicle; the closer he comes to those limits (which are never precisely known, and change during the course of the race), the greater the probability of disaster. Most races do not reward the racer for a "DNF" (Did Not Finish). When a car is seriously damaged during a race, or a driver achieves nothing better than a string of DNF's, the team owner is likely to start looking for another driver. All drivers are happier racing than trying to find another "ride," let alone recovering in the hospital from crash-related injuries. The analogies for a bicycle racer are obvious.

The secondary objective is more subtle and more difficult. A racer receives the same credit for a win whether he beats his closest competitor by one thousandth of a second or by several minutes. Ironically, to the racer (not to mention to the spectators) a close victory is often more satisfying than a runaway. It keeps everyone guessing about whether the results might have been different if…, and heightens interest in the next encounter. By attempting to go as fast as possible, to win by the greatest possible margin, the racer risks violating the primary objective, being able to finish. But by holding back and attempting to keep the margin of victory small, he may increase the risk of losing.

While it is difficult to know one's own limits, it is even more difficult to know the limits of one's competitors. In head-to-head racing, familiarity with the strengths and riding characteristics of one's competitors is a great asset; for example, knowing whether a particular rival has a big kick in the final sprint may induce a rider to attempt to escape from the pack early, make repeated attacks, or bide his time until the finish. The ability to size up unfamiliar competitors before or early in the race is almost as important, but one's ability to do so is imperfect. A racer going strongly now may fade later; another may be sandbagging; a third may excel in some situation which has yet to occur in the race. Basing one's own efforts on indistinct impressions is risky, but it may be the best one can do, at first. During the course of the race, as those impressions gradually clarify, one's efforts can be continually updated. Only late in the race (perhaps too late) may the true picture become clear. In a time trial, one has even fewer clues about the competition: possibly encounters in previous events, a greeting at the start, perhaps one glimpse during the event. Lack of information forces the time trialist to compete at close to his limits for the duration of the race: no deception, no pacing oneself based on what the competition is doing, and no drafting, which is why some call it the Race of Truth.

Using Your Physical Attributes to Advantage

It is common knowledge that different body types are better under different conditions. Small, lightweight cyclists have an innate advantage climbing hills. No matter how carefully a large-framed cyclist watches his diet, no matter how assiduously he trains, he will always be fighting an uphill battle (pardon the pun) when he competes with born hill climbers. But big cyclists have their own advantage descending hills, because there they can achieve higher speeds with less effort than their diminutive colleagues. Unfortunately for them, downhill races are rare, if not completely unknown; but in fact, large cyclists may also have a slight advantage under flat, steady speed conditions: their larger muscles should be able to develop a little more power, the level course cancels most of their weight penalty, and their greater momentum helps them maintain their speed. There is no question that low-weight cyclists have an advantage whenever speeds fluctuate, however; with less mass, they can wait a little later to brake and need less power to come back up to speed. It is usually acknowledged that young cyclists have an advantage in sprinting, while older cyclists often excel in endurance events.

Most of the heavy-vs.-light assertions are easy to verify. (The ones that attribute power, sprinting ability, and endurance to different body types depend on individual physiology; their verification may be impossible in general.) Suppose we compare our standard rider, who together with his bike weighs 198 lb, with a lightweight rider just like him except that he and his bike weigh 154 lb; that is, the two masses are 90 kg and 70 kg, respectively. Each putting out 400 watts (0.54 hp) up various grades, their speed varies considerably. Figure 0606 shows their speeds in meters per second for a range of grades; Figure 0607 shows how far behind, in seconds, our standard rider would be after a typical half mile climb. Downhill the tables are turned. Figure 0608 shows coasting speeds for the same riders and grades, ignoring

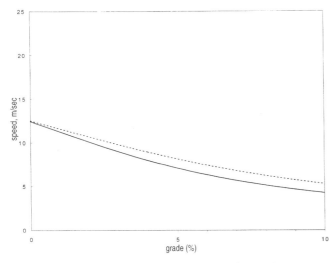

Fig. 0606. Speed riding up a grade. Speed vs. grade for a heavy (solid line) and a light rider (dashed line), each applying 400 W.

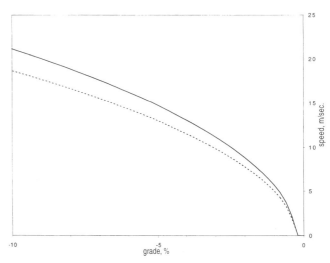

Fig. 0608. Speed coasting down a grade. Speed vs. grade for a heavy and a light rider, each coasting.

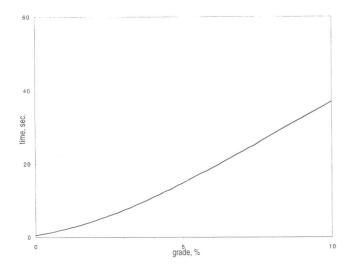

Fig. 0607 Time behind. How far behind the heavier rider of Fig. 0606 would be after a half-mile climb.

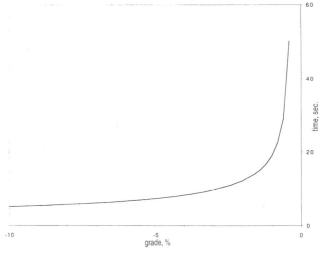

Fig. 0609. Time ahead. How far ahead the heavier rider of Fig. 0608 would be after a half-mile descent.

any initial acceleration or deceleration, and Figure 0609 how far our standard rider would be ahead after a half mile descent. (Though it looks like the heavier rider has a big advantage in time on gentle downslopes, these conditions — competitive coasting at speeds under 10 miles per hour — are a trifle artificial.)

To change from one body type to another is currently well beyond the capabilities of cosmetic surgery. That being the case, most of us shrug, resign ourselves to our fate, and give such differences no further thought. The smart competitive cyclist can use his attributes more wisely, however. While continuing to work on improving his abilities, he can often accentuate his strengths and de-emphasize his weaknesses.

Most obviously, the cyclist can often be selective about the events he attends. If he is looking for

Table 0611. Competitive events and attributes emphasized

solo time trial:	maintaining aerodynamic position for extended period, pacing oneself without being able to view competitors, tolerance for steady high effort
team time trial:	like solo time trial plus precision bike handling, drafting
hill climb:	like solo time trial except climbing rather than aerodynamic position is emphasized
criterium:	bike handling in close quarters, drafting, sprinting, cornering, quick reactions, plus solo time trial attributes for breakaways
road race:	endurance, hill climbing, drafting, anticipating conditions (for example, for a fast descent on an unfamiliar road), plus either solo time trial attributes for breakaways or sprinting for field sprints
stage race:	attributes of its components (road race, usually solo time trial, sometimes criterium, team time trial, hill climb) plus individual and team versatility, ability to recover overnight
cross-country mountain bike race:	like road race (except that drafting is not involved), plus trail riding skills
trials:	trail riding skills, very low speed bike handling skills
cyclo-cross:	like mountain bike events plus running with bike on shoulder, quick dismount/mount
track pursuit:	like solo time trial
track sprint:	sprinting, quick reactions, bike handling in both close quarters and at very low speeds, drafting, both very low and very high cadence
track points:	drafting, sprinting (high cadence), mental calculation, plus solo time trial attributes
track madison:	slinging technique, bike handling in close quarters, plus track points attributes (and a suitable partner)
track keirin:	hard acceleration from start in a high gear, high-speed drafting, sprinting, bike handling in close quarters, intimidation
track miss-and-out:	drafting, sprinting, bike handling in close quarters

an opportunity to train or to widen his experiences, he can pick events with aspects that address those particular needs; if he is looking for good showings or high placings, he can pick events at which he is likely to excel, or at which his usual nemeses will be absent. Many riders find that by developing a specialty at which they can consistently do well, they derive more personal satisfaction from competition. Specialists may also become more valuable to their team. In events that cater to their strengths, they can assume a leadership role; in other events they can let other specialists take charge. Knowing each other's roles in an event helps the riders on a team to work together, to avoid destructive rivalries within the team, and to save their energy for events and situations when they will have a better chance of winning.

Nothing is black and white. Most events call for more than one type of skill, and most riders have several strengths to call upon. In general terms, however, certain types of events emphasize certain attributes more than others. See Table 0611.

The rider's personal experiences and knowledge will supplement the characteristics in Table 0611. Knowledge of the specific course, or at least the general terrain, is invaluable in selecting gearing and planning strategy. Knowledge of the road surfaces may influence one's selection of wheels or even frames. And any information that is not general knowledge can be the germ of a strategy.

7 Braking

If you were handed three still photographs of a moving car, one photo taken while it was moving in a straight line at steady speed, one while accelerating, and the other while braking, the chances are you would be able to tell which was which.

Braking and Moment of Force

Most people know that during braking a car pitches forward: its nose dips lower than its tail. During acceleration, the reverse is true: it rears back, nose higher than tail. These attitudes are known to automotive engineers as "dive" and "squat," respectively. Bicycles do not have such compliant suspension that dive and squat are readily visible, but the underlying cause, the transfer of weight forward or backward, can be a serious concern. Hard braking can transfer enough weight off the rear wheel to cause it to lift off the ground, possibly enough to vault the rider over the handlebars — every cyclist's nightmare. It is almost as unnerving when, as the cyclist powers up a very steep hill, the front wheel lifts off the ground. (What, it has never happened to you? Come ride in Pennsylvania some time.)

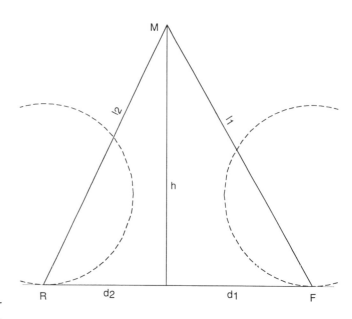

Fig. 0701. Geometry of the bicycle with rider center of mass. Center of mass (M) relative to front (F) and rear (R) wheel contact points.

Both of these phenomena are effects of what physicists call the moment of force, which is another term for torque. Take a look at Figure 0701, which shows three points on the bicycle: F, the point at which the front wheel touches the ground; R, the corresponding point for the rear wheel; and M, the center of mass or center of gravity, the point at which all the mass of the rider and bicycle can be considered to be concentrated. When the bicycle is rolling at constant speed on level ground, gravity is acting on the mass, pulling it vertically downward. From the perspective of point F, gravity exerts a torque or moment of force, just as if line FM were a lever (like a crankarm) and someone were pushing down at point M with a force of m times g, the mass of the rider and bicycle times the acceleration due to gravity — in other words, the total weight. The moment of force is the product of the length of that lever arm and the force perpendicular to it — not all of the weight, but instead the weight times the cosine of the angle between level and the line FM. (See Figure 0702.) Call that angle α. If the lever arm — the line FM — is called l_1, and the distance between F and the vertical below M is called d_1, then the moment of force about F caused by gravity is:

$$L_{gF} = l_1\, m\, g\, \cos\alpha = l_1\, m\, g\, d_1\, /\, l_1 = m\, g\, d_1$$

As shown in the figure, with the bike rolling to the right, that moment is positive in a counterclockwise direction.

Now suppose the bicycle is also changing speed in a straight line. Physicists call change of speed acceleration regardless of whether the change is an increase — what everybody calls acceleration — or a decrease, popularly known as deceleration. Increase of speed will have a positive value of acceleration, say 1 meter per second per second; decrease of speed, a negative value, say –2.5 meters per second per second. Linear acceleration (acceleration in a straight line) produces a force at M just as gravity does, except that the direction of force is horizontal: see Figure 0703, where the acceleration a is shown as positive in a forward direction. Again, just as with gravity, linear acceleration exerts a torque or moment of force. Call h the height of M above the line FR. With the help of Figure 0703 and very similar math to what we did above, we can see that the moment of force about F caused by linear acceleration is:

$$L_{aF} = m\, a\, h$$

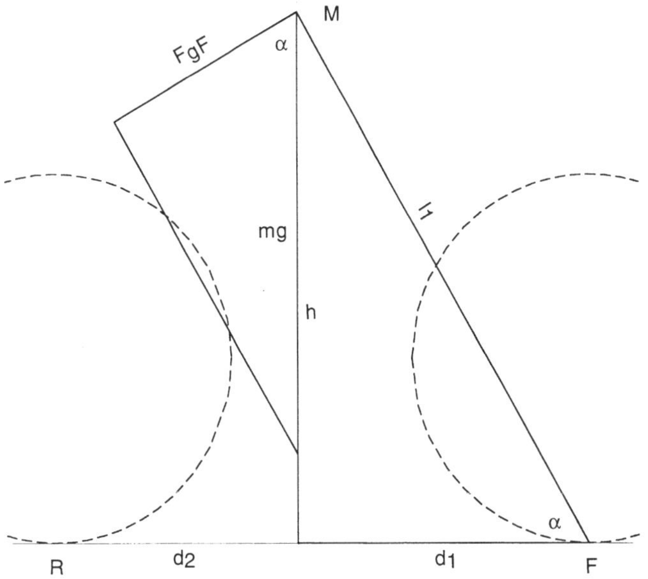

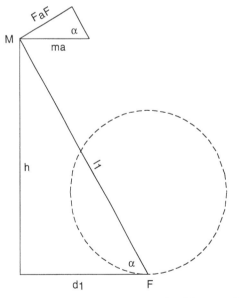

Fig. 0702. Geometry of moment of force about F caused by gravity. Force of gravity (mg) acts like a force (F_{gF}) perpendicular to a lever arm l_1.

Fig. 0703. Geometry of moment of force about F caused by linear acceleration. Accelerating force (ma) acts like a force (F_{aF}) perpendicular to a lever arm (l_1).

Adopting the same convention as we did with gravity, we will call the moment caused by a positive (forward) acceleration positive and show it as counterclockwise. The total moment of force about F is:

$$L_F = L_{gF} + L_{aF} = m \, g \, d_1 + m \, a \, h = m \, (g \, d_1 + a \, h)$$

Pause for a moment (so to speak) to examine the above equation and understand what it means. In the absence of linear acceleration ($a = 0$), gravity produces a positive, counterclockwise moment about the front wheel contact point. Because the bicycle is essentially rigid, it is as though that counterclockwise moment is pushing the center of mass down and pressing the rear wheel onto the ground. When the bicycle is slowing, a is less than zero; the moment of force about F is reduced. With hard enough braking, the magnitude or absolute value of the product of a and h could exceed the product of g and d_1. If that were to happen, the moment of force would become negative, clockwise, lifting the rear wheel upward off the ground, taking with it the center of mass (including the rider) upward and forward: just what we don't want to happen.

How do we make that condition less likely? We want to increase the product of g and d_1, or decrease the magnitude of the product of a and h, or both. In the first product, the acceleration due to gravity is a constant; we can't alter that. We can, however, alter d_1: we can increase it by moving the center of mass back, i.e. sliding back on the saddle, even completely off the back of it, supported by the legs. (Some saddles have a backrest that prevents this: not a wise choice on a standard bicycle if hard braking may be needed.) In the second product, we can reduce the magnitude of a by braking less hard — perhaps not the answer a rider already going too fast wants to hear, but still valid. We can also reduce h, the height of the center of mass, by crouching way down. Mass does not figure in the above discussion at all, which seems to indicate that it is not a factor in whether the rider goes over the handlebars. We will discuss the role of mass a little later.

We could do similar math to find the moment of force at the rear wheel point of contact, but on level ground the conditions causing the front wheel to lift would be of interest only to riders attempting a wheelie — surely not to the mature and sophisticated readers of this chapter.

Most braking is done when the bicycle is going downhill. When the front wheel of the bicycle is lower than the rear, there is an additional moment, clockwise or negative by our conventions, which makes the rear wheel even more likely to lift. Suppose the angle of the downhill grade relative to level is called γ (gamma); then the geometry looks like that in Figure 0704. If γ is positive — and it is unclear how to depict a negative angle — because we have adopted the convention in this book that downgrades are negative, the quantity we call the grade is the negative of the tangent of that angle, $-\tan \gamma$. We won't use up space by going into the math here, but the reader won't find it difficult if he followed the level ground case, as long as he pays attention to the signs and remembers his trigonometric formulas. The resulting equations for moment of force at the front wheel contact point are:

$$L_{gF} = m \, g \, (d_1 \, J + h \, G)$$

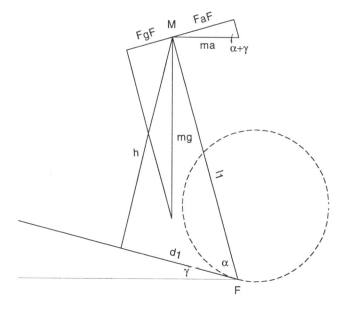

Fig.0704. Geometry of moments of force about F on a slope. Force must take grade (tan γ) into account.

$L_{aF} = m\,a\,(h\,J - d_1\,G)$

$L_F = L_{gF} + L_{aF}$

where G is the grade (percent grade divided by 100), and:

$J = (1 - G^2)^{0.5}$

(The 0.5 power is the square root: $J^2 = 1 - G^2$).

Similarly, the equations for the moment of force around the rear wheel contact point are:

$L_{gR} = -m\,g\,(d_2\,J - h\,G)$

$L_{aR} = m\,a\,(h\,J + d_2\,G)$

$L_R = L_{aR} + L_{gR}$

We had better pause to work some examples. Suppose our standard rider is seated on the bike, hands on the drops, elbows slightly bent. We already know that he and the bike together have a mass of 90 kg; suppose the center of mass is 0.96 m above the ground and 0.55 m behind the front wheel contact point, and that the bike's wheelbase is 1.008 m. The values of m, h, d_1, and d_2 are therefore 90, 0.960, 0.550, and 0.458 respectively. The acceleration due to gravity is its usual 9.8 m/s². On level ground (G = 0) with no speed change (a = 0), the moment of force around the front wheel contact point due to gravity is 90 x 9.8 x (.550 x 1 + .960 x 0) = 485 meter-newtons, the equivalent of about 358 pound-feet of torque. The moment around the same point due to acceleration is of course zero, because a is zero, so 485 m-N is the total moment about the front wheel contact point. Around the rear wheel contact point, the total moment is −90 x 9.8 x (.458 x 1 − .960 x 0) = −404 m-N, negative because it is in a clockwise direction. The magnitude of the moment about the rear wheel is less than that about the front because the center of mass is behind the center of the wheelbase.

Now suppose the bicycle is descending a 10% grade; that makes G = −0.1 and J = 0.995. And

suppose also that it is being braked hard, losing speed at 4 meters per second per second; that is, a = −4.0 m/s². This time about the front wheel contact point, the moment is 90 x 9.8 x [.550 x .995 + .960 x (−.1)] = 398 m-N (from gravity) plus 90 x (−4.0) x [(.960 x .995 − .550 x (−.1)] = −364 m-N (from acceleration), a total of 34 m-N. Notice that not only does the steep slope reduce the moment moderately, but the deceleration reduces it greatly. However, it is still a positive, counterclockwise moment; the rear wheel is not lifting. The corresponding numbers for the rear wheel contact point are −487 + (−327) = −814 m-N: the slope and deceleration have increased the magnitude of the moment there.

From these moment of force equations we can also determine the normal force at F and R, that is, the force pressing the front and rear tires onto the ground. The vertical force at one contact point is the moment of force around the opposite wheel contact point divided by the distance between them, namely the wheelbase or $d_1 + d_2$. But if the ground is not level, the vertical force is not quite normal, that is, it is not perpendicular to the ground. It must be multiplied by the cosine of the angle of the grade, the quantity we called J above. Accounting for whether the moment is clockwise or counterclockwise, the normal forces at the front and rear wheels are therefore:

$F_F = -L_R\,J\,/\,(d_1 + d_2)$

$F_R = L_F\,J\,/\,(d_1 + d_2)$

Let's use the same numbers as in the moment of force examples above. On level ground, the front tire is being pressed to the surface with a force of 404 x 1 / 1.008 = 401 N, about 90 pounds; the corresponding normal force at the rear tire is 485 x 1 / 1.008 = 481 N, about 108 pounds. As a double check, note that 90 + 108 = 198 pounds, the total weight of our standard bike and rider, and the ratio is about 45%/55% front/rear, considered the ideal weight distribution when the rider is on the drops. While braking on the steep downhill, the normal forces at front and rear are −(−814) x .995 / 1.008 = 804 N and 34 x .995 / 1.008 = 34 N, respectively: the front tire is being pressed very firmly to the surface, as though the rider and bicycle had doubled in weight; the rear tire is being held against the surface much more lightly, almost as though the rider had jumped off the bicycle. If the normal force at either wheel were to drop to below zero, that wheel would lift.

When does wheel lift occur? It depends, of course, on the steepness of the slope, the rider's position, and many other variables. It may be useful to look at how much deceleration is sufficient to lift the rear wheel at various downgrades, and the effect that position changes and a few other variables might have on that critical number. Making some assumptions about rider position, bicycle dimensions, and the mass of each, Table 0701 lists the amount of decelerating force sufficient to lift the rear wheel at various downgrades. (Although we dealt with acceleration previously, this table lists force instead of acceleration to account for the effect of bicycle and rider mass. It is easy to calculate the corresponding deceleration if needed.) The decelerating force is mostly due to braking. Although gravity hinders braking, aerodynamic drag aids it; these two forces approximately cancel each other out at the high speeds attainable on a downhill. The column labeled "Std." is our standard rider in his usual racing crouch. "Tops" shows the effect of moving his hands from the drops to the top of the handlebars. "Scrunch" estimates the effect of his crouching way down and shifting a few inches off the back of the saddle. "−1 cm ht." gives the effect of a position 1 centimeter lower, such as from a lower bottom bracket, a slightly lowered saddle on a

mountain bike, or just shorter legs on the same rider. "+5 cm WB" gives the effect of our standard rider on a bike with a wheelbase that is 5 centimeters longer (such as a touring bike), sitting about 3 cm farther back. "−20 kg" gives the effect of a much lighter rider, one who weighs about 130 pounds instead of 174 pounds, but in the standard drops position on the same 24-pound bike our standard rider usually rides.

What does this table tell us? First of all, the steeper the grade, the less force is needed to lift the rear wheel. The "Tops" column indicates that braking from the top of the handlebars instead of the drops is only slightly more likely to lift the rear wheel: in that more upright position, the center of gravity is higher but also farther back. The "Scrunch" column however shows that shifting weight back and down gives a big improvement — significantly more force is required to lift the rear wheel. A lower bottom bracket or slightly lowered saddle, and correspondingly lower rider center of gravity, gives only a slight improvement. (If lowering the saddle on a mountain bike before a descent facilitates shifting one's weight down and back, then it could be valuable, but merely lowering the saddle and sitting normally is hardly worth the bother.) A longer wheelbase, which moves the center of mass back, gives a significant improvement — good news for tourists, mountain bikers, and especially tandem riders.

The final column needs some interpretation. At first, it seems to indicate that a light rider is at a disadvantage, because he can lift the rear wheel with less deceleration force. However, the light rider also needs less force to achieve the same deceleration. For example, on level ground a force of −506 N decelerates the standard rider and bike (total 90 kg) at −506/90 = −5.62 m/s^2; a rider 20 kg lighter needs only 70 x (−5.62) = −393 N to slow at the same rate. The figure given in the table (−399) is actually a little better than this. So although a light rider can lift the rear wheel applying less force, he is slowing a bit more rapidly when he does so and perhaps will not reach the level of deceleration needed to lift the rear wheel. Besides, there is no guarantee that the rider can even supply as much decelerating force as the numbers in

Table 0701. Deceleration force sufficient to lift rear wheel, N

% grade	Std.	Tops	Scrunch	−1 cm ht.	+5 cm WB	-20 kg
0	506	500	−615	−510	−573	−399
−5	−449	−444	−551	−453	−512	−355
−10	−394	−390	−491	−399	−455	−312
−15	−342	−338	−425	−346	−400	−271

the table indicate is needed; the actual force a rider can achieve depends on his hand strength, experience (or courage), brake lever mechanical advantage, brake cable elasticity, brake arm rigidity, pad material, rim surface, wheel trueness, etc. (For the record, the author has found that in low-speed trials, he obtains a maximum deceleration force between –409 and –430 N.) Nor is there any guarantee that the road surface conditions will allow all of the braking force to be applied to slowing the bike; on ice or loose gravel, for example, the tires would surely begin to skid at much lower deceleration values than the ones in this table. (Some consolation.)

In addition to the conclusions from the above table, we can draw a few more. As is so often the case in bicycling, small riders have an advantage in braking, too, not just because of their lower mass but because they sit lower on the bike, lowering the center of gravity. Women, besides often being small, have an additional advantage in that their center of gravity is usually lower than a man's: a man usually has a heavier upper chest. Tourists with heavy loads in front and rear panniers may take longer to slow down, but at least the additional rear load makes lifting the rear wheel during a hard stop unlikely; the same goes double for tandems with front and rear riders. Bikes with smaller-than-standard wheels lower the mass and the center of gravity of at least the bike, if not the rider, giving them a braking advantage. Finally, recumbent bikes have all the advantages: very low rider center of gravity, usually small wheels, and usually very long wheelbase; their riders can screech to a stop worry-free.

Braking Force and Rear Wheel Lockup

We have already seen the approximate deceleration forces that would cause the rear wheel to lift. Although other forces such as aerodynamic drag and gravity up a hill can decelerate the bike, applying the brake levers is the usual way to decelerate the bike quickly. Fortunately the levers are not on-off switches. They allow (in fact, require)

braking force to be applied gradually, from no force at all, through moderate force, up to whatever maximum the rider's hand strength and the brake design can manage. If the rider uses both levers, squeezing both gradually harder, then well before he reaches the decelerating force needed to lift the rear wheel, he will reach the force needed to skid or lock the rear wheel up.

Initially the thought of lockup is alarming — the rider is in trouble sooner than we thought. Alarming may be the right word, but it's a beneficial alarm. Rear wheel lockup is an early warning of impending rear wheel lift. If it happens, the rider knows he had better not try to decelerate any more quickly; it's time to let up a little on the brakes. At the point of lockup, however, both wheels are still solidly on the ground, the rider is still upright, and though the bike may be "fishtailing" as the rear wheel slides around, it is usually not difficult to keep under control. Certainly, skidding the rear wheel is not good for tire life or peace of mind; the rider wants to keep the tires rolling as much as possible. But in an emergency situation requiring the heaviest possible braking, or perhaps during an all-out late-braking effort in competition, bringing the rear wheel to the point of lockup is the only means a rider has of knowing just how much braking force he can safely apply.

When does the rear wheel begin to skid or lock? To find out, we need to go into the physics of frictional forces at the rim and tire. We are all familiar with friction. It is a force that resists sliding; it opposes motion between two surfaces in contact, and is considered "tangential" or parallel to those two surfaces. It is equal in magnitude to the product of two factors:

❑ the "normal" or perpendicular force pressing those two surfaces together, and

❑ the coefficient of friction, a number which describes just how reluctant to slide those surfaces are.

Think of a brake pad being pressed against the rim of a rotating wheel. The first factor is obvious from the way a brake operates: the greater the force pressing the pad onto the rim, the greater the magnitude of the frictional force; or, because we usually consider a force that slows the bicycle to be negative, the greater the positive force that must be applied (by gravity, for example) to balance that frictional force, to keep the wheel from slowing. The other factor is also obvious: the combination of a clean, fresh rubber brake pad and a clean, dry aluminum rim has a relatively high coefficient of friction and is much more effective at slowing the rotation than a grease-covered, age-hardened pad on a wet steel rim, to take an extreme example.

There are really two different coefficients of friction. Each is a pure number, the ratio between the force needed to balance the friction and the normal force between the surfaces. The coefficient we have been implicitly discussing is the kinetic coefficient; it applies to two surfaces in contact that are sliding at a constant speed. The other, the static coefficient, applies if the two surfaces are initially not in motion relative to each other. It always takes more force to break that initial grip than it does just to keep the surfaces sliding at constant speed; therefore, for any pair of surfaces, the static coefficient is always higher than the kinetic coefficient.

Torque again comes into the picture. The product of the frictional force and the radius at which it is applied is called the frictional torque. That radius for a conventional caliper brake is the distance from the center of the wheel axle to the point where the brake pad contacts the rim. Angular acceleration is proportional to torque (more on this in Chapter 12). Because torque is proportional to radius, we can easily see why the brake pads contact the wheel way out at the rim rather than at the hub, where they would be much less effective at slowing the spinning wheel.

Doesn't that mean that a caliper brake on, say, a 24-inch wheel would be less effective than on a 27-inch wheel? Yes, it does. If a brake's only job were to slow the spinning wheel, the answer would be different: a brake on the smaller wheel would work better. Angular acceleration equals torque divided by moment of inertia, which in turn is the product of mass and the square of the

radius of gyration. (We will cover moment of inertia and radius of gyration in Chapter 12). A smaller wheel probably has less mass, and certainly a smaller radius, more than offsetting the decreased torque. But in practice the brake must also slow the bike and the rider, not only the wheels. Smaller wheels may be easier to slow, but riders do not automatically shrink when they mount small-wheeled bikes. To be equally effective, a brake on a small wheel would either need to apply more pressure or use pads with a greater coefficient of friction.

Down at the point at which the tire contacts the ground (it's larger than a point, but never mind for now), the radius from the axle is larger: it's the radius of the wheel. If we divide the frictional torque by that radius, what do we get? Force — the decelerating force the tire exerts on the ground helping to slow the entire bike. Add the decelerating force from the front tire to that of the rear tire to get the total decelerating force from braking. Just to collect everything from the last few paragraphs into one equation:

$$F_d = L_b / r_w = F_f\, r_b / r_w = -F_b\, \mu_b\, r_b / r_w$$

where F_d is the decelerating force contributed by a particular tire, L_b is the frictional torque for its wheel, r_w is the radius of that wheel (including the tire), F_f is the force of kinetic friction at the brake pads, r_b is the radius of the rim at which braking is applied, F_b is the braking force that is applied normal to the rim, and μ_b is the coefficient of kinetic friction between the brake pad and the rim. Note the minus sign; decelerating force, frictional force and frictional torque are negative, while the force of the brake pads on the rim is positive.

While we have so far been discussing only the kinetic friction between brake pads and rim, there is another place where friction is essential: between the tire and the ground. There the type of friction is static as long as the tire is rolling, because at the tire contact point the tire and ground are not moving relative to each other. The tire and the ground have their own coefficient of static friction (call it μ_t) and are pressed together with a normal force (call it F_n) which, as we saw earlier, depends on weight, slope, the bicycle's deceleration, the center of gravity, etc. The maximum force of static friction at the tire is F_n times μ_t.

Now we can combine the two kinds of forces. If at a particular wheel the magnitude of the decelerating force at the tire exceeds the maximum force of static friction, that is, if:

$$F_n \mu_t + F_d <= 0$$

then the tire begins to skid, or the wheel begins to lock.

Time for some examples. Let us assume that the coefficient of kinetic friction between the brake pads and the rim is 0.70, probably a typical number — not that it matters here because in our example we can apply as much force to the brake pads as we like. The coefficient of static friction between tire and a paved surface may be as high as 1.0. Obviously, this can vary a great deal depending on the rubber compound of the tire, and even more on the type of road surface, whether it is dry, wet or icy, and whether it is asphalt, dirt, mud, gravel, or sand. A 700C wheel has a radius of about 0.344 m; the radius of the rim center is about 0.308 m. Suppose while descending a 5% grade our standard rider squeezes the front brake lever hard enough to press the pads to the front rim with 250 N of force, and does the same for the rear brake. Suppose the center of gravity of the combination of our standard rider (in his usual crouch) and his bike is 0.96 m above level ground, 0.55 m behind the front wheel dropout and 0.458 m ahead of the rear wheel dropout. The decelerating force at either tire is –250 N x 0.70 x 0.308 / 0.334 = –161 N, a total of –323 N for the two combined. That was the easy part; now to calculate the moments about the wheel-to-ground contact points, using the formulas we developed for determining when the wheel would lift. For the front, the moment due to gravity is 90 kg x 9.8 m/s^2 x (0.55 m x [(1 – (–0.05)2) + 0.96 m x (–0.05)] = 442 m-N. Due to acceleration, it is –323 N x [(0.96 m x 0.9975 – 0.55 m x (–0.05)] = –318 m-N, giving a total of 124 m-N. For the rear, the moment due to gravity is –90 x 9.8 x [(0.458 x 0.9975 –

0.96 x (–0.05)] = –446 m-N; due to acceleration, –323 x [(0.96 x 0.9975 + 0.458 x (–0.05)] = –302 m-N. a total of –748 m-N. The normal force pressing the front tire to the road is –(–748 m-N) x 0.9975 / (0.55 m + 0.458 m) = 740 N; the corresponding normal force for the rear tire is 124 x .9975 / 1.008 = 123 N. Both of these numbers are positive, so neither wheel is lifting. Multiply them by the static friction coefficient, in our example conveniently 1, to obtain the maximum forces of static friction at each tire. For the front tire, 740 N + (–161 N) is well above zero. But — aha! — at the rear, 123 N + (–161 N) is less than 0. The rear wheel has locked, although it is well short of liftoff. It is easy to make the rear wheel roll again: merely decelerate less, such as by letting up a little on both front and rear brakes. (We will discuss this further a little later.)

Avoiding Rear Wheel Lockup

Was rear wheel lockup avoidable in this case? Yes. In our discussion of rear wheel lift we already saw one easy countermeasure, shifting the rider's center of gravity down and back. Here is another. From the numbers above, it is evident that the front wheel was nowhere near lockup when the rear one began to skid. Why not just have braked harder at the front, less hard at the rear? Let's see. Suppose that instead of applying 250 N to both front and rear rims the rider had applied 375 N to the front but only 125 N to the rear. You can do the math this time, but fortunately almost all of it is identical to last time. The decelerating force at the front tire is –242 N, while at the rear it is –81 N, a total of –323 N, the same as in the previous case. The moments are also the same as last time, as are the maximum forces of static friction. Again, the front wheel is rolling merrily: 740 + (–242) > 0. This time the rear wheel is also some way from lockup: 123 + (–81) > 0. Same conditions, same deceleration, and only the proportion of front-to-rear braking force has changed, yet this time the rear wheel does not lock.

The fact that there is still some margin available before the rear wheel locks up suggests that by applying the front brake harder than the rear, a rider should be able to decelerate more rapidly than with equal braking forces. Tables 0702 through 0704 bear this out. Using the same conditions as in Table 0701 (the deceleration forces at which the rear wheel lifts) but varying proportions of front-to-rear braking, they show the force at which the rear wheel begins to lock or skid. (Compare the numbers in these tables with each other and with those in Table 0701 with the same column label and grade, but remember that the numbers are highly dependent on conditions. Even though trends will be the same, the actual forces on different bikes with different tires, riders, and surfaces will almost certainly be different.)

It looks like the greater the ratio of front-to-rear braking force, the more rapidly the bike can decelerate without reaching the point of rear wheel lockup. Even though even higher ratios have slightly greater deceleration potential, there is little point in exploring 10:1, 50:1, and so on because there is a practical limit to how much force a rider can apply to the front brake lever, and because the rear brake is still needed to warn of imminent lift.

Table 0702. Deceleration force at rear wheel lockup, 1:1 front-to-rear braking force

% grade	Std	Scrunch	+5 cm WB	–20 kg
0	–332	–397	–376	–260
–5	–297	–359	–340	–233
–10	–263	–323	–304	–207
–15	–229	–288	–269	–181

Table 0703. Deceleration force at rear wheel lockup, 3:1 front-to-rear braking force

% grade	Std	Scrunch	+5 cm WB	–20 kg
0	–401	–483	–454	–315
–5	–258	–436	–409	–281
–10	–316	–391	–365	–249
–15	–275	–347	–322	–217

Also notice that the best decelerations achieved are only about 0.5 g's: for example, –432 N divided by the 90 kg of our standard rider and bike gives 4.8 m/s^2. Because 1 g is 9.8 m/s^2, that's 0.49 g's, not very impressive compared to a car. (Tandems, due to their long wheelbase and different weight distribution, can do much better.)

Front Wheel Lockup

Is there a danger of front wheel lockup? This is a serious concern, because unlike rear wheel lockup, front wheel lockup is disastrous. A skidding front wheel means no directional control. No directional control means no ability to balance. No balance means that the rider will shortly meet the ground. On a dry, level paved surface or downhill, however, there is so much normal force on the front wheel during deceleration that it is almost impossible to lock it by means of ordinary braking. We can use similar calculations, for example, to determine how close our standard rider in his standard position is to locking the front wheel. On level ground with a 10:1 front-to-rear proportion of braking forces, when the rear tire begins to skid, the maximum force of static friction at the front tire is 655 N while the deceleration force at the front tire is only –322 N: a large margin of safety. On a downhill the margin of safety is even greater, and who needs to brake hard on a steep uphill?

Don't count on this margin of safety, however, if the rim is warped, damaged, dirty, or otherwise irregular, or if the ground is rough; these conditions may cause rapid fluctuations in deceleration, possibly enough to bring on premature wheel

Table 0704. Deceleration force at rear wheel lockup, 5:1 front-to-rear braking force

% grade	Std	Scrunch	+5 cm WB	–20 kg
0	–432	–520	–488	–339
–5	–383	–468	–439	–302
–10	–339	–420	–391	–267
–15	–294	–372	–345	–232

lockup. If the rims are wet, it often takes appallingly long for the brakes to begin to work at all, and then they suddenly start to grab — another condition to beware of. Nor is there much margin if the road is slick. On a slippery surface, little deceleration may be possible before wheel lockup, so little that the rear wheel will remain more heavily loaded than the front. If so, the front wheel will begin to lock before the rear. On level ground, if the coefficient of friction between the tire and the ground is as low as 0.2, for example — perhaps wet snow or ice — the front wheel will lock before the rear with a front-to-rear braking force ratio as low as 1.8. Under such conditions, however, staying upright is a challenge even when the rider is not braking at all.

With a properly operating bike under all but the most slippery traction conditions, it is clear that the rider should use both brake levers, applying force progressively, squeezing the front one significantly harder than the rear one. For maximum deceleration, he should keep his weight low and to the rear, and squeeze hard enough to make the rear wheel begin to lock. Then what should he do? Let up on the pressure, certainly, but on which brake(s)? If he reduces only the rear braking force, he reduces the total deceleration relatively little, perhaps not enough to make the rear wheel start rolling again until it is released completely. Then he gives up his rear lift early warning system. Releasing only the rear brake is therefore not a good idea. If he reduces only the front braking force, he significantly affects the deceleration of the bike, which ought to be enough to increase the normal force on the rear wheel and get it rolling again; then he can restore force to the front brake and try again. This is an acceptable approach, but perhaps still not ideal. While he reduces the force on only the front brake, the front-to-rear force ratio drops, which as we have seen also reduces his deceleration capability. Although he must indeed reduce his deceleration (that is, slow less), he should not have to reduce it quite that much in order to start the rear wheel rolling. Reducing pressure on both the front and rear brake levers, maintaining the ratio between them, should be a slightly better approach; once the rear wheel is rolling freely, the

rider can restore force to both brakes, again in proportion, beginning the cycle again.

Either way, he should try to make the correction just when the rear wheel begins to skid, not wait until it has completely locked. Aside from control and tire wear considerations, early correction is valuable because less braking force reduction is needed. Because the coefficient of static friction (when the brake pads press against the stationary rim) is higher than the coefficient of kinetic friction (when the rim is still rotating), the rear tire needs more normal force to overcome static friction and resume rolling. Until the rear wheel is again rotating, the bike is not slowing as rapidly as it could be. The most effective braking is just shy of the lockup point. Rapid, controlled deceleration is not only safer, but faster.

For consistently quicker stops or more effective speed control on downhill roads, it would make sense to adopt a brake design that automatically exerts more braking force on the front wheel than on the rear when the levers are squeezed with equal force. (This already happens to a slight extent, because the cable run to the rear brake is longer and loses more to internal friction, but certainly nothing approaching 2:1.) Unequal braking force could be achieved, for example, by using a softer, stickier pad compound in front, or by relocating the pivot at one of the brake levers to give the front brake more leverage. Unfortunately, if the paved surface were to end, or rain or snow were to fall, such a design would turn from more effective to less safe, from an advantage to a liability. (That last word, "liability," virtually guarantees that such a differential braking system will never be commercially available in the lawsuit-happy United States.) Perhaps eventually someone will figure out how to make an anti-lock braking system both lightweight and inexpensive enough to be used on a bicycle, and thereby revolutionize the way bicycles brake. Such a revolution is long overdue.

Types of Brakes

Bicycle brakes come in several varieties. Coaster brakes, operated by backpedaling, are suitable for only the least demanding use, such as by children who ride at low speeds, who do not have to make long, sustained decelerations, and who lack the hand strength necessary to operate a brake lever. They are difficult to apply hard without skidding the wheel, they operate only on the relatively ineffective rear wheel, and they can burn out during a long descent. On the plus side, they are not bothered by wet weather.

Rim brakes, lightweight and good overall performers, are by far the most common sort on quality bikes. They work by clamping small blocks or pads against the surface of the rim, far out near the edge of the wheel where torque amplifies their stopping power. The effectiveness of rim brakes is unfortunately greatly compromised in the wet, because the coefficient of friction of rubber against wet metal is only a fraction of the dry coefficient. A wet rim requires several revolutions under hard braking before it begins to dry and both the coefficient of friction and the terrified rider begin to recover. (One of the main advantages of an aluminum rim versus steel is that when wet its coefficient of friction drops less severely.) Some rims with ceramic coatings have a coefficient of friction that is even higher.

Various types of rim brakes have been successfully used on high-performance bicycles. For a bike on a road with generally good traction on reasonably smooth surfaces and grades that can only be so steep, the main function of the brakes is precise modulation of force, rather than maximum stopping power. The trend over the years has been to improve control by reducing the flexibility of brake designs. For that reason, centerpull brakes with a relatively flexible yoke of cable operating the brake arms have given way first to the stiffer, more direct acting conventional sidepull brakes, which in turn have given way to double-pivot designs with even shorter, more rigid brake arms. (All these types are collectively known as caliper brakes.) The differences in effectiveness are subtle, to be sure, but the main trade-off has been that the short-reach designs that dominate the market are incompatible with fenders and larger-section touring or cyclo-cross tires.

For a bike that needs great stopping power on steep downhills — mountain bikes on dirt, loaded touring bikes, and tandems — the brakes of choice are usually of a cantilever design. Just as you can push harder when your back is against a wall, these designs can provide more force than caliper brakes because they push against the bike frame. Some also use an extra arch to boost the stiffness of the relatively flexible fork blades and seatstays they are pushing against. The newer cantilevers, called V- or direct-pull brakes, reduce flexibility and improve control in the same way as sidepulls do compared to centerpulls. Even so, many riders find them too sensitive and powerful for use on unloaded road bikes.

Used and maintained properly, any of these types of rim brakes can provide perfectly adequate stopping power. It is far more important that the rider can vary the amount of braking pressure smoothly up to the maximum, and such control depends not only on brake design but on compatible lever reach and proper adjustment. Brakes that have only two settings — on and off — are dangerous and should be repaired or replaced immediately. Individual riders will of course have additional criteria, such as "feel," maintenance, and side clearance. Note that a bicycle frame needs particular fittings ("braze-ons") for a particular type of brake; the types cannot be readily interchanged.

Expensive, high-quality disc brakes are sometimes fitted to the rear wheels of tandems and touring bikes, where they are used to supplement the main brakes on major descents. Disc brakes are also fitted to both ends of downhill mountain bikes. Unlike rim brakes, disc brakes remain effective in wet weather, though because of their small diameter they require more pressure. For additional considerations, see below.

Heat During Braking

Braking friction transforms kinetic energy, the energy of the bicycle's motion, into heat. Application of a rim brake heats both the brake pad and the wheel rim. The small pad, usually rubber, is not a good conductor of heat. The pad's braking surface becomes hot but the pad as a whole absorbs and dissipates little of the heat, regardless of whether it has cooling fins, as some brands do. The much larger rim is an excellent heat sink. It absorbs most of the heat of braking and gradually conducts it to the surrounding air — but also to the tire, causing air pressure in the tire to increase. High braking force for an extended period of time, such as that required by high speeds, steep downgrades, or heavy touring or tandem loads, generates a great deal of heat. In an extreme case, such as a mountain descent, the heat may increase pressure enough to cause a blowout, to melt the glue that holds a tubular tire onto its rim, or to liquefy the brake pad surface, all of which have potentially disastrous consequences. One solution is the disc brake; its separate disc adds weight but frees the rim from heat absorption duty.

Although we can expect eventual small improvements with rim brakes due to improved tire, tube, glue, and pad materials, with existing materials there are only two solutions to heat buildup: generate less heat, and allow the rims more time to cool. In descending from one elevation to another, the bicycle unavoidably spends a certain amount of potential energy; but not all of that energy must be dissipated by the brakes. It could instead go into increased speed, which would be the ideal choice, if not always a practical one. A hairpin switchback curve that can be taken a few miles per hour faster not only increases overall speed but reduces the amount of braking heat generated and gives the rims additional cooling time. On a long descent, where the need to reduce heat is more important than maximum average speed, riders who sit up and become less aerodynamic take a little of the burden off the brakes and rims. The most effective technique, however, is to anticipate the corner and begin braking early, alternately applying and releasing the brakes — much like sipping hot soup a spoonful at a time rather than pouring the bowl down the throat all at once. The total amount of heat generated will be about the same, but the rims will have a longer time in which to dissipate that heat and thus stay cooler. A tourist worried about a severe mountain descent may even plan to make a few vista stops to allow his rims and tires to cool and his aching hands to recover … but it is important to plan such a stop well in advance. If speed is not kept under control, stopping may not be possible.

Late Braking

In qualifying for an auto race, or when trying to establish a substantial lead, a good racing driver does not merely try to corner near the limit. He also practices late braking: delaying application of the brakes until the last possible instant. This practice keeps speed as high as possible for as long as possible, resulting in the very best times as long as the driver does not lose control. On a circuit course, the driver will establish braking points, landmarks to guide his late braking. If on one lap he brakes for a corner at a signpost and has control to spare when he gets to the corner, the next lap he'll try braking a few meters past the signpost, eventually homing in on the best braking point. During the race, as road and tire conditions change, he may have to revise his braking points, but they remain the best way to achieve consistently fast laps.

Why do few bicyclists use a similar technique? The probable reason, aside from ignorance, is that it is much more difficult to judge how close one is to the cornering limit on a bike, and a crash is not a desirable way to find out. But as long as one maintains a reasonable margin of safety, the basic idea is still sound: keep speed up as long as possible, brake at a known safe spot, and then corner. The technique is best applied on a circuit, where the same corners come up again and again, or on a course one has the opportunity to ride beforehand. If it is not practical to learn the entire course, one should concentrate on just those curves that are likely to disrupt one's speed the most, or on those that look the most intimidating to riders who haven't had the benefit of practice. Confidently braking and tracking through a known corner is both faster and safer than approaching it tentatively.

Cornering

We are all familiar with gravity as a downward vertical force, pulling objects toward the center of the earth. In actuality, the force of gravity exists between all objects, varying in strength with the mass of the objects and the distance between them. (See Gravitational Force in Appendix B to learn more about the law of universal gravitation.)

Vertical Acceleration

Most of us also know that gravity accelerates a falling object. A rock falling from a cliff gradually picks up speed; so does a bicyclist rolling down a hill. In the absence of any other forces, such as friction, gravity produces uniform acceleration, that is, a constant increase in speed per unit of time. The acceleration due to gravity is usually regarded to be constant, even though (as we saw in Chapter 2) it varies slightly at different latitudes of the earth and at different elevations above sea level. We call the constant g, or refer to g's as units of acceleration, giving g a value of about 9.8 m/s^2, 32 feet per second squared, or 22 mph per second.

A rock about to be dropped from the top of a cliff is initially stationary; 1 second after it is dropped, its speed has increased to 9.8 m/s; in another second its speed has increased by another 9.8 m/s to 19.6 m/s, and so on. Gravity acts on the rock even if it isn't initially stationary. If it has been thrown horizontally at 5 m/s, it continues to move horizontally at 5 m/s while increasing its vertical speed 9.8 m/s per second. If it is fired from a cannon straight up at 100 m/s, after one second it will be going upward at 90.2 m/s (100 minus 9.8), undergoing deceleration, which is the same as acceleration but in the opposite or negative direction. In two seconds the rock will have decelerated to 80.4 m/s, and so on, until at 10.2 seconds gravity has canceled all of the initial upward motion and the rock begins to fall. But another way of looking at the rock's motion is that it continues in its original direction, but the negative acceleration (deceleration) has now given it a negative speed whose magnitude continues to increase. (In all of these simple examples, we have been pretending the rock is extremely slippery so that we can ignore the effect of friction between it and the air. Would that bicyclists could be so slippery.) We refer to acceleration due to gravity even when no object appears to be accelerating, such as when we are standing still on the ground.

Now is a good time to review some equations involving constant or uniform acceleration, and to abandon rocks in favor of bicycles. If v_0 is the initial speed of the bicycle in meters per second, a is the constant acceleration in meters per second per second, t is an interval of time in seconds, v_1 is the speed at the end of that interval (again m/s), and d the distance covered in meters, then:

$$v_1 = v_0 + a\,t$$

$$d = 0.5\,(v_0 + v_1)\,t$$

$$d = v_0\,t + 0.5\,a\,t^2$$

$$v_1^2 = v_0^2 + 2\,a\,d$$

For example, if a bicycle initially going 5 m/s is accelerating down a hill at a constant 2 m/s^2, 3 seconds later it is going 5 + 2 x 3 = 11 m/s. The distance it travels during that time is the average speed times the time, 0.5 x (5+11) x 3 = 8 m/s x 3 s = 24 m. If the bicycle is undergoing constant deceleration into a headwind, say an acceleration of –1.5 m/s^2, from an initial speed of 12 m/s, in 4 seconds it travels 12 x 4 + 0.5 x (–1.5) x 16 = 36 m. Its speed at the end of that time is the square root of [144 + 2x(–1.5) x 36] = 6 m/s.

Lateral Acceleration

Most of us are also familiar with the notion of centrifugal force: it feels like sideways gravity. It tries to pull us off our horse on the merry-go-round, and off the road when we are driving or bicycling through a curve. Physicists decline to discuss centrifugal force, because they recognize that nothing actually pulls outward. Instead, they point out that an object in motion tries to follow a straight line; in order to coerce it into a circular path, there must be an *inward*-pulling force, which they call centripetal force. This idea should be easy for us cyclists to accept, because to ride on a curved path we lean in, pulling against the tendency of the bicycle to continue rolling straight forward.

Just as gravity causes a vertical acceleration, centripetal force causes a lateral (side-to-side) acceleration. Again it may not be apparent that any object is accelerating, but any time velocity changes, in either speed or direction, then acceleration is at work. The appropriate equation in this case is:

$$a = v^2 / r$$

where a is the lateral (centripetal) acceleration, v is the constant speed along a circle, and r is the radius of the circle. Thus if a cyclist rides at 6 m/s along an arc of a circle 20 m in diameter (radius equals 10 m), his lateral acceleration is 6 x 6 / 10 = 3.6 m/s^2; this is about 37% of the acceleration due to gravity (9.8 m/s^2), or 0.37 g.

Importance of Cornering

Cornering is very important in car design. Even modest sedans sport sophisticated independent suspensions with wide wheels and tires. Racing cars regularly corner with a lateral acceleration in excess of 1 g: the sideways force on the racing car exceeds the car's own weight. (Aerodynamic downforce, i.e. negative lift, may play a part.)

Cornering is on the whole far less important to the bicyclist. At the cyclist's relatively low speed, few curves are sharp enough to require braking, and indeed bicycles are not designed to withstand significant lateral accelerations while upright. Instead they lean over to balance the lateral and vertical accelerations — or the lateral and vertical forces, because we could talk of either acceleration or force. Force is the product of acceleration and mass, that of the bicycle and rider in this case.

The exceptions, when a rider really does care about cornering, are mostly during downhill curves. Having to brake from high speed in order to corner gently through a sharp curve and then having to accelerate back to speed could lose the cyclist a lot of time.

How much time? Let's take an example. Suppose there is a fairly steep downgrade with a moderately sharp curve in the middle. The sharpness of the curve is indicated by its radius of curvature — see Figure 0801. This example curve has a radius of 44 meters and is 60 meters in length. Let's also suppose there is no wind and our standard rider coasts down the hill at 15.8 m/s, which is about how fast he would go if the grade were about 5.7% (that is, minus 5.7%). If he could take the curve at that speed, representing a lateral acceleration of 0.58 g's, he would lose no time. See

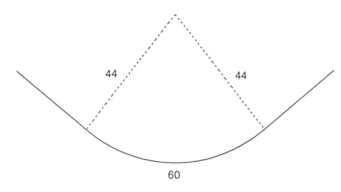

Fig. 0801. Curve example. Curve with radius of 44 meters and total length 60 meters.

Figure 0802, where points B and C represent the times when the cyclist enters and exits the curve.

If however he had to brake to 10 m/s, limiting his lateral acceleration to 0.23 g's, not only would he be going slower in the curve, but he would have to decelerate before he reached the curve and accelerate after it. See Figure 0803. Moderate braking at 200 newtons (time A through time B in the illustration), would bring him down to the required speed in 36 meters. Because this deceleration is nearly uniform, his average speed for that time period would be 12.9 m/s, a loss of 0.5 seconds compared with doing that distance at 15.8 m/s. (See "Calculating Deceleration" in Chapter 2, however.) Harder braking could cut this small loss to almost nothing. In the curve itself (time B through time C in the illustration), he would be moving at 10 m/s instead of 15.8 m/s, an additional loss of 2.2 seconds. Acceleration by continued coasting up to, say, 15.5 m/s would take about 47 seconds (time C through time D in the illustration) and 651.5 meters, assuming the remainder of the grade lasts at least that long, a further loss of 5.8 seconds.

Notice that by coasting and allowing gravity to provide his acceleration, our rider doesn't quite reach the original speed of 15.8 m/s. That's

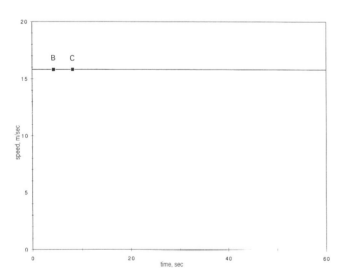

Fig. 0802. Speed profile through the example curve in Fig. 0801 if the cyclist did not have to brake. Points B and C represent curve entry and exit.

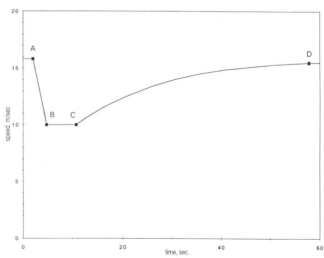

Fig. 0803. Speed profile through the example curve in Fig. 0802 if the cyclist must brake. Point A represents the start of braking, B through C negotiating the curve at reduced speed, C through D accelerating back to speed.

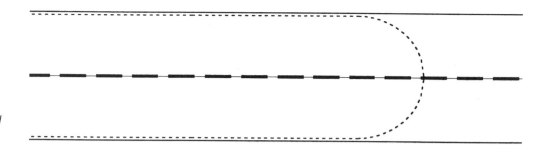

Fig. 0804. Turnaround on an out-and-back course.

because 15.8 m/s is the terminal velocity for the 5.7% grade, where gravity and drag exactly balance. As his speed nears the terminal velocity, the net force accelerating him nears zero. He could cut this loss by pedaling if he could manage a sufficiently high cadence; for example, applying 150 W would bring him back to 15.8 m/s in 20 seconds and 267 meters; in this case, the loss would be only 3 seconds.

In total, our rider lost up to 8.5 seconds in this example of a single downhill curve. Perhaps the road conditions fully justified his caution, in which case his competitors probably lost similar amounts … or crashed. But perhaps conditions would have permitted cornering closer to the bike's limit, reducing the loss significantly.

It clearly pays to work on cornering technique to avoid losing more time than necessary, particularly during fast downhills. Unfortunately, high-speed downhill curves are a dangerous place to practice. Whenever speeds are high, the consequences of misjudgment, or of an encounter with wet leaves or gravel, can be severe. Compounding these hazards are the cyclist's inability to swerve while already cornering hard, and the sharp drop-offs that often flank such curves.

Any curve that severely disrupts speed is costly to performance. Time trialists and triathletes often encounter another example of a curve that potentially loses them a lot of time: the turn-around point on an out-and-back course. (See Figure 0804.) They typically approach at full speed along a level road, then must brake and turn sharply 180 degrees within the width of the roadway, and finally accelerate back up to full speed. Since this kind of turn is seldom encountered in normal riding, practice is essential. Again,

the ticket to a good time is a high cornering speed. Carefully judged braking (to avoid overshooting) is also important, as are the best techniques below.

Using All the Road

One technique that can improve both speed and safety is to use all of the road — all the available road, that is, because if the rider is sharing the road with other riders or motor traffic, or if visibility is limited, perhaps only a single lane or less may be safely available. The idea of using all the road is to begin the turn at the outside of the lane, smoothly sweep fully to the inside, reaching it at a point (the "apex") halfway through the curve; then sweep back out again to finish the turn at the outside. All the while steering corrections should be kept to an absolute minimum during the curve. The resulting path should be as close as possible to an arc of a circle; see Figure 0805.

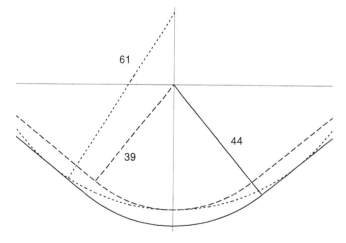

Fig 0805. Using all the road. By beginning the curve early and sweeping from outside to apex, the cyclist increases the effective radius.

This technique has several benefits. First, it increases the effective radius of curvature of the curve, permitting a higher speed, or if a higher speed is not practical, then reduced lateral force and a greater margin of safety. Second, it slightly reduces the distance to be traveled. And third, reducing steering corrections minimizes the chance that they will dislodge grip and induce a skid.

As an example, suppose the curve is the one in the previous example, except that the road is 5 meters wide and the 44-meter radius of curvature applies to the outermost edge. The innermost edge therefore has a radius of 39 meters. For this particular example, it is possible to ride along an arc with radius 61 meters, beginning 14 meters before the road curves and ending 14 meters after it straightens again. (Again, see Figure 0805.) Traveling along this wider arc instead of along the outer edge saves about 4.5 meters. What is more important is that the potential cornering speed, that is proportional to the square root of the radius, goes up. If the rider could corner at 10 m/s before, he could now corner at 11.8 m/s, saving almost 2 seconds, not counting additional savings in braking and acceleration. This gain is with no increase in lateral force, merely a better line through the corner.

Not all corners benefit fully from this technique. Most corners, after all, are taken well below their limit, simply because the cyclist cannot go fast enough to reach that limit. In our example above, if the cyclist previously got through the corner coasting at the terminal velocity of 15.8 m/s at 0.58 g, the improved line would increase the potential cornering speed to 18.7 m/s at the same lateral acceleration. But he would have to apply 357 W power to achieve that higher speed; not only may that be more power than he can muster, but he would be leaning too far over to leave clearance for pedaling.

If speed is sufficiently below the limit, reduced distance may be the only benefit of keeping to a perfect arc. Distance in such cases may be reduced further by adopting a tangential (straight line) approach and exit, hugging the inside edge of the curve. The turn will be sharper but slightly shorter. See Figure 0806.

Also, the apex does not have to be halfway through the corner. By beginning the turn later and more sharply, exiting the corner less sharply, a vehicle shifts the apex of the turn nearer the exit — a "late apex" in the terminology of auto racing, where the technique is commonly used to begin acceleration for the following straightaway a fraction of a second earlier. Though less favored in auto racing, because it often results from misjudging the curve, an "early apex" is also possible, i.e. coming into the corner in almost a straight line at

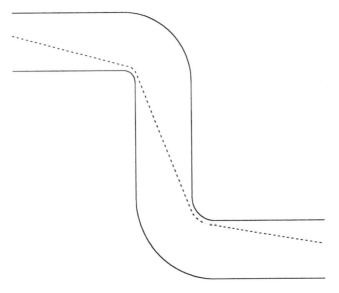

Fig. 0806. Straight-line cornering when speeds are too low to justify a full arc.

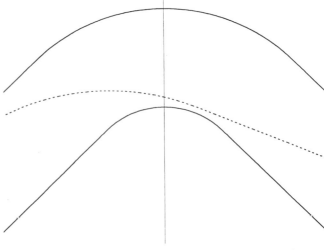

Fig. 0807. Late and early apex. Late apex (past center) if approaching from the left, early if from the right (see text for when these approaches may be suitable).

high speed, usually in conjunction with braking as late as possible. See Figure 0807 for examples. (If the vehicle approaches the curve in the figure from the left, the dotted line gives an example of a late apex. In the reverse direction, it's an early apex.) When might a late or early apex be favorable to the cyclist? It depends on whether it is more important to have extra speed at the exit or the entrance of the corner. Then when is extra speed most valuable? For a cyclist, a small difference in speed during low-speed conditions (such as uphill) results in a greater time difference than during high-speed conditions. Therefore, if either the exit or the entrance of the corner is steeper uphill (or less steep downhill), the cyclist should consider shifting the apex toward that end. All this assumes that the corner is not so long or sharp as to require cornering at the maximum possible speed, and that the cyclist will take advantage of the straightened-out portion with earlier acceleration or later braking. The same sort of logic applies to a rough or slippery section just before or after the corner, where it is important to have the bike as nearly upright as possible.

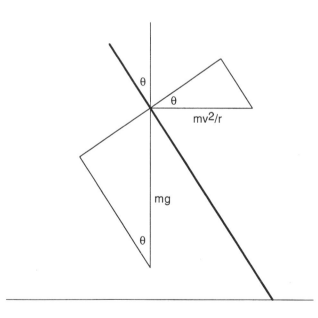

Fig. 0808. Forces on a leaning bicycle. For bike leaning at angle θ, (heavy line), forces perpendicular to bike (due to gravity and centripetal force) must balance.

Lean Angles and Lateral Acceleration

The rider and bicycle lean over to balance vertical and lateral forces. Figure 0808 depicts a leaning bicycle and the forces involved. Call the lean angle from vertical the angle θ (theta). We will assume the bike and rider lean as a unit, so θ is the angle from vertical to the line that is normally the vertical axis of the bike, the line that passes through the center of mass of the bike and rider. The vertical force is weight, the product of the mass of the bike and rider (call it m) and the acceleration due to gravity, g. The horizontal force is centripetal force, $m\,v^2/r$, where v is the speed along a circular arc and r is the radius of that arc. From Figure 0808 one can see that the component of gravity perceived as being lateral, that is perpendicular to the bike axis, is $m\,g\sin\theta$. Likewise the component of centripetal force in that same direction is $(m\,v^2\cos\theta)/r$. The magnitude of these two components must be equal, otherwise the bicycle would either fall over or right itself.

$$g\,m\,\sin\theta = (m\,v^2\cos\theta)/r$$

$$\sin\theta\,/\,\cos\theta = m\,v^2/(g\,m\,r)$$

Because the sine of an angle divided by the cosine of the same angle is the tangent of that angle, and because the masses cancel out, we are left with:

$$\tan\theta = v^2/(g\,r)$$

But v^2/r is the lateral acceleration, just as g is the vertical acceleration. So lateral acceleration in g's = tangent of lean angle.

Table 0801 gives a few values of lean angles and corresponding lateral accelerations. There is of course no assurance that a bicycle will actually be able to corner at, say, 0.84 g's, nor is there any reason why with sticky enough tires and road surface the lateral acceleration could not exceed 1 g.

The lean angle also provides an easy way to check your cornering technique. As you exit a sharp corner, do you gradually return to upright over a period of a few seconds? Then if

Table 0801. Lean angle vs. lateral acceleration

Lean angle, degrees	Lateral acceleration, g's
0	0.00
5	0.09
10	0.18
15	0.27
20	0.36
25	0.47
30	0.58
35	0.70
40	0.84
45	1.00

performance is your goal, your technique leaves something to be desired. Your cornering radius must have been smaller near the apex of the turn, larger near the exit: that is no circular arc, and consequently your speed is not all it could have been. A perfectly executed corner will have a constant lean angle and a quick transition to upright. A similar argument applies to the entry into the corner.

Road Holding

One of the practical limits to cornering speed for a bicycle, or any wheeled vehicle, is the ability of its tires to grip the road surface. This ability is expressed by the coefficient of friction between the two surfaces in contact, in this case the rubber of the tire and the road, or whatever surface the bicycle may be riding on. Even on a paved surface, the coefficient of friction varies widely depending on the composition and tread pattern of the rubber and the composition and roughness of the road surface, not to mention extraneous matter that may be on the road, such as water, ice, leaves, sand, gravel, paper litter, and manhole covers. There is little point in trying to determine cornering limits from a coefficient of friction that

changes radically from one surface to another. The bicyclist must discover them for himself, or stay well on the side of safety.

Incidentally, it is the static coefficient of friction that is of interest in cornering. (We call it static because the tire contact point and road are not moving with respect to each other. Rolling coefficient may be a better term.) The kinetic coefficient of friction applies when surfaces are sliding with respect to each other. If a bicycle wheel is sliding, it is usually too late to do anything about it. The bicyclist must take care not to exceed the maximum force implied by the static coefficient.

We should not leave the subject of road-holding without discussing the effect of weight. Everyone knows that friction increases with weight: a bicycle is much easier to drag sideways all by itself than with a rider sitting on it. The coefficient of friction, though, takes weight into account; it is the force needed to slide one object over another at a constant speed, divided by the force pressing the objects together. If the objects are stacked vertically, as a bicycle tire on a road, that latter force is weight, the weight of the bicycle and rider. As we have already seen, weight is mass times acceleration due to gravity, and the lateral force in a corner is mass times lateral acceleration. At some maximum lateral acceleration, the bike will begin sliding sideways. The quotient of the two (maximum lateral force divided by weight) is the coefficient of friction between the tire and the road. Notice that mass is in both the numerator and denominator of that quotient. It cancels out. Therefore, it makes no difference what the mass is; in a given corner, with the same kind of tire and thus the same coefficient of friction between tire and road, the maximum lateral acceleration and cornering speed will be the same for a 250-pound rider as for a 100-pound rider. Even though the heavier rider is pressing his tires more firmly onto the road, centrifugal force is also trying that much harder to push him off the road.

Perhaps you have heard the old saying "A heavy car holds the road"? As far as cornering is concerned, the saying was only a myth, perhaps intended to help sell heavy cars. More accurately, the saying should be "A heavy car holds the road

… but no better than a light car does" — not nearly as catchy, but then catchy slogans have never been known for their accuracy. (To be fair, a heavy car may hold the road better when not cornering — for example, when accelerating in a straight line. If that was the original intent of the slogan, it was lost through decades of misuse.)

Cornering Force and Tire Width and Pressure

"Muscle" cars and sports cars have wide tires for fast cornering. Racing cars have wider tires yet, and corner at phenomenal speeds. As a consequence, many people naturally assume, without giving it much thought, that wide tires on a bicycle provide more grip. Yet these same people also know that road racing bicyclists use skinny tires, but corner at least as fast as other cyclists. Something must be amiss. We also know that automobile tires have a recommended inflation pressure. Exceed that pressure and the sides of the tread start to lift off the paved surface, leading to increased wear; and with less rubber on the road, so the obvious thinking goes, poor cornering results. Yet autocrossers, weekend auto racers who compete on parking lot courses and drive a whole lot faster than almost anyone else, routinely pump their tires up to roughly double the "recommended" pressure, much harder than anyone would tolerate for normal driving. How could this possibly make sense? And what should it tell us, if anything, about bicycle tires? There are a few misconceptions at work here, both about cars and bicycles. Let us try to straighten them out.

Each tire on a vehicle supports a fraction of the vehicle's weight; all of them together support all the weight, and as usual the weight includes that of the human rider, or the driver and passengers. Ignoring kiddie cars and the like, all these vehicles have pneumatic tires, approximately toroidal (ring- or doughnut-shaped) rubber vessels containing pressurized air. The bottom of the tire, the part touching the road, deforms under the load it is carrying, flattening out into what is called a "contact patch." How large is this contact patch? It

should be easy to see that the size depends on the tire pressure and the load. No load, or rock-hard pressure, and the tire doesn't deform at all: the contact patch is just a tiny point. Heavy loads and less pressure increase the size of the patch. In fact, if the tire really is like a flexible doughnut, it is easy to calculate the area of the patch. We'll depart from the metric system for a while: if the tire is supporting, say, 120 pounds, and the pressure in the tire is 100 pounds per square inch, then the contact patch providing that support must be 120 / 100 or 1.2 square inches in area.

Many tires really are like uniform, flexible toruses (doughnuts). Others depart from a perfect torus in various ways. Automobile tires, for instance, have stiff sidewalls that inhibit flexing, plus a stiff, flattened tread area designed to lie against the road surface; at least these tire parts seem stiff at the relatively low pressures used in automobile tires. Some bicycle tires, too, have stiff portions of tread — a central raised ridge, or lugs and knobs on mountain bike tires — which do not flatten out and conform to the road. These tires may be comparable only to others of a similar type. But it is still true that for tires of similar construction, two tires with the same load and pressure will have the same contact area. Notice that we have not mentioned tire width at all. The omission is intentional, because the area of the contact patch does not depend on the width of the tire. Inflated to 90 psi and fitted to a bike under the same rider, a super-narrow 700C x 19 clincher (wired-on tire to my British readers) would have the same contact patch area as a medium-width 700C x 25 or a 700C x 32 loaded touring tire. Only the shape of their contact patches would be different.

Now remember our earlier discussion of friction. For two surfaces in contact, perhaps rolling but not sliding, the coefficient of static friction is the ratio of the force parallel to those surfaces needed to break that contact and the normal force pressing those two surfaces together. The pair of surfaces that concern us here are of course the tire and the road, which together have a particular coefficient of static friction. The friction equation tells us that given a certain coefficient of friction, the maximum lateral force the tire will withstand before it loses grip with the road is proportional to the force pressing the tire to the ground. Period. Nothing about contact patch area or shape. This news actually fits very well with what we know about bicycles. Cornering grip is basically independent of tire width — at least we never see racers trading in their tubulars for fat commuting tires before they ride a criterium, nor tourists fitting skinnier tires before tackling the switchbacks on a mountain descent: there's no need. Cornering grip is also basically independent of tire pressure and thus contact patch area. And we already saw that it is basically independent of mass or weight.

The reader will perhaps have noticed the word "basically" in the above sentences. Yes, the word does indicate a bit of hedging, and that calls for an explanation, one that will also attempt to explain why automobile tires do not at first seem to follow these principles. Wide tires do enable a car to corner faster. The complex interaction of the rubber with the road at microscopic levels essentially produces a higher coefficient of friction under a lateral load with a wide (though foreshortened) tire patch than with a narrow but longer patch. A similar sort of interaction happens on a much larger scale as the knobs and tread blocks of a mountain bike tire dig into a soft surface. Coefficients of friction are calculated for smooth, flat surfaces. Real surfaces are not ideally smooth and uniform and do not always behave as neatly as a simplistic application of the laws of physics says they should. A wide tire may contact a portion of the ground that gives more grip, improving the overall coefficient of friction compared with a skinny tire that missed that high-grip portion. More bits of tread in a wide tire may dig obliquely into tiny pits in the surface, like miniature rails, resisting side forces and slippage. Because keeping mass low is a more important consideration for road racers than ultimate cornering power, it is no more likely that we will be seeing road racers adopt 32-mm wide tires than that we will be hearing mountain bikers extol the virtues of "slicks" for off-roading.

As for tire pressure, obviously the tire must be inflated at least enough to keep the tire from rolling off the rim, or all of a sudden the coefficient of friction with the road will be that of aluminum, not rubber … not a comforting thought. At extremely low or high pressures, the ability of the tire to conform to the road surface may be compromised, leading to brief intervals in which the tire is pressing less firmly against the paved surface, or leaves it altogether, again effectively reducing the average coefficient of friction. Friction may not depend on contact patch area, but with no contact patch, there is no friction. Autocrossers use high tire pressures not to improve cornering grip but to stiffen the tires, to improve the responsiveness of their vehicles in the quick turns and slaloms typical of the tight courses they run. A stiff tire changes direction more quickly and surely than a soft, gelatinous one. No doubt responsiveness is also a factor in selecting bicycle tire pressures for criteriums. (The first sign of an underinflated or slowly deflating tire is often that the bike's handling has become squirrely.) And finally, the distribution of weight produced by the bike's geometry, the rider's position, and the slope places unequal loads on the tires. In a sharp corner during a steep downhill, for example, though both tires may experience the same lateral force, the front tire will be more heavily loaded, especially if the rider is braking. Therefore at high speeds the chances of the rear tire running out of grip and beginning to skid are increased, compared to a similar corner and speed on level ground. Weight does have something to do with cornering after all.

The construction of the wheel itself has some bearing on roadholding, though it may be small in relation to the tire. Traditional spoked wheels have some built-in "give," which may not be apparent until one tries a much stiffer disc or aero wheel with a few wide composite blades for spokes. With high tire pressures, such aero wheels can be so stiff that they are skittish on anything but the smoothest roads. (When split-second-conscious racers deliberately trade away an aerodynamic advantage for more secure handling, you know the problem can be serious.) Among traditional wheels, the fewer the number of crosses in the spoking pattern, the stiffer the wheel; i.e. radial (0-cross) wheels are stiffest, 4-cross patterns the most yielding. The greater the number of crosses, however, the longer the spokes and thus the heavier the wheel. The practical difference in ride or roadholding between a 2-cross and 3-cross, or between a 3-cross and 4-cross, is subtle.

Physical Obstacles to Leaning

The width of the bicycle may also restrict its ability to lean over, and thus limit its maximum cornering speed. Suppose we ignore exceptionally wide panniers, other wide carried objects, and the wide seats or other peculiarities of some recumbent designs. When a standard bicycle leans over, the first part (other than the tires) to touch the ground will be the inside pedal. Figures 0809 and 0810 show how the geometry of the inside pedal affect the ability of the bicycle to lean. In the figures, h is the height from the ground to the bottom bracket center when the bicycle is vertical; b is the width of the bottom bracket and crankset from the center line of the bicycle to the outer face of the crankarm; a is the crankarm length and p is the pedal width. Note that b is not the same as half the width of the bottom bracket itself or half the length of its axle; it must also include the width of the crankarm. Also, p is not just the width of the pedal body, but must include the ex-

posed portion of its axle and any projecting part of the rider's shoe.

If θ (theta) is the maximum lean angle from vertical, one can see from the figures that when the pedal is down:

$$\tan \theta = (h - a)/(b + p)$$

and when the pedal is up:

$$\tan \theta = (h + a)/(b + p)$$

These two equations define two different maximum lean angles. The smaller of the two, from the pedal down position, indicates the maximum lean while the bike is being pedaled. The larger indicates the maximum lean, period.

The values of these dimensions are not completely standardized. Bottom bracket heights vary according to the preferences of the bicycle designer and the intended use of the bike. Typically, road racing and road touring bicycles will have a relatively low bottom bracket height, perhaps 267 mm, giving a low center of gravity and good stability. Criterium bikes may sacrifice a bit of stability to be able to lean further, and often have higher bottom brackets. (Mountain bikes of course have high bottom brackets, but only for obstacle clearance.) We will take 270 mm as a typical value for h. As the bike leans and moves from the relatively high center of the tread toward the tire

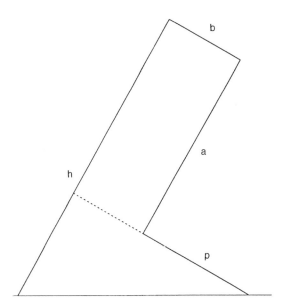

Fig. 0809. Geometry of leaning bicycle, pedal down.

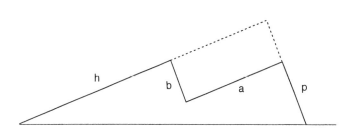

Fig. 0809. Geometry of leaning bicycle, pedal up.

edge, h will decrease a little, but we will ignore this effect.

The value of b depends on which way the bike is turning, the model of crankset, and whether it is a double or triple. For the left side (left turns), b is typically 65 mm; for the right side (right turns), b is typically 70 mm for a double crankset and 75 mm for a triple because of the space taken up by the chainwheels. Pedal width varies with brand and model, with some designs touting their narrow width and thus greater cornering abilities. Pedals are also not simple horizontal lines but three-dimensional objects. A boxy pedal shape may effectively make it wider when the bicycle is leaning. We will take 105 mm as a typical value of p.

Finally, as we saw earlier, crankarm length also varies, usually based on the length of the rider's legs and his cadence preferences. The usual range is nonetheless rather narrow, with 170 being the typical value we will take for a.

Table 0802 summarizes maximum lean angles for the typical dimensions given above, on a level road. (Banked roads must of course include the angle of banking.) The table also gives the corresponding values of lateral acceleration and the speed through a fairly sharp curve of 10-meter (32.8-foot) radius.

The table does not give further details for the "pedal up" case, because obviously no bicycle is going to be able to corner at 2.5 times gravity without some sort of extra help to keep it from flying off the road — a set of curved rails, perhaps? Bicycles are never in danger of hitting a raised inside pedal on the roadway, unless they are already skidding off.

The other numbers are remarkably close to each other, which shows what little difference even a 5–10 mm variation in pedal or bottom bracket width makes. With 165 mm crankarms, the angles increase by about 1.3 degrees; with both 165 mm cranks and a high 276 mm bottom bracket, the angles increase about 2.7 degrees.

Racing cyclists can certainly take advantage of these numbers, but the only events likely to show any benefit are criteriums. There a careful rider may be able to approach his maximum cornering speed consistently on repeated corners. Fitting shorter crankarms and narrow pedals and shoes may help any criterium bike a little. A criterium specialist may also wish to test ride a bike with a high bottom bracket, evaluating its stability before deciding whether to order one for himself. Other sorts of riders need not lose any sleep about whether their bike is able to lean far enough. Nothing they can do to it will make much difference.

Table 0802. Typical maximum lean angles and corresponding lateral accelerations and cornering speeds

	lean angle (degrees)	lateral acceleration (g's)	speed through curve of radius 10 m
pedal down, left turn	30.5	0.59	7.6 m/s (17.0 mph)
pedal down, right turn, double chainring crank	29.7	0.57	7.5 m/s (16.7 mph)
pedal down, right turn, double chainring crank	29.1	0.56	7.4 m/s (16.5 mph)
pedal up	68.3	2.51	15.7 m/s (35.1 mph)

Cornering Techniques

Much of the literature on cycling discusses cornering techniques, to which the following brief comments apply.

Usually cyclists are taught to stop pedaling and to lift the inside pedal in a sharp curve. The main object is of course to avoid hitting the pedal on the road surface while leaning over; clearly a good idea, as anyone who has experienced the jolt and resulting skid from hitting a pedal will attest. Nevertheless, coasting longer than necessary means that power is not being applied and speed is therefore lower than what it could be.

This discussion does not apply to track cyclists, whose fixed-gear bicycles cannot coast and do not permit lifting the inside pedal. Fortunately, track curves are wide and steeply banked, obviating problems. A well-designed velodrome banks its curves enough that at some typical cornering speed the bicycle will lean as much as the angle of banking, and thus stay perpendicular to the track.

In order to allow pedaling at more extreme lean angles, the industry has been quick to develop narrower pedals and shoes. (Or — more cynically — in order to sell shoes and pedals, the industry has been quick to develop advertising claims about the extreme lean angles possible with their products.) Assuming these products do not sacrifice other desirable properties, a greater maximum lean angle is beneficial. It allows pedaling deeper into the curve and resuming pedaling sooner, and in some curves the rider may not need to stop pedaling at all.

However, it is difficult to take advantage of an improved maximum lean angle, which after all is improved by only a few degrees. First of all, unlike racing cars, racing cyclists seldom corner at the maximum lateral acceleration of which their equipment is capable, that is, right on the verge of skidding. Compared with the four wide tires of a racing car, the bicycle's two narrow tires are much more susceptible to a skid caused by minor road irregularities. Whereas most skids can be controlled by a racing car driver and amount to no more than a small change in position or direction, a bicycle skid usually results in a crash. So cyclists must leave more margin for safety, which means lower speeds, less lateral acceleration, less lean, and thus less chance of hitting a pedal. Practice drills can help reduce this margin safely.

A sharp curve on level ground or downhill requires slowing rather than acceleration, so pedaling into the curve is not important under those conditions. Pedaling into a curve becomes important, however, in a sharp uphill curve, because the cyclist will want to keep applying power as long as possible. In addition, the relatively low speed inspires confidence and induces the cyclist to corner harder and lean over more. Hitting the inside pedal on the road surface is therefore more likely. Fortunately the consequences of a brief jolt and skid under those conditions are less serious.

Except during steep downhills, resuming pedaling upon exiting a curve is important to keeping up speed, but it is difficult to judge the precise lean angle at which pedaling is again safe. Practice and a margin of safety seem the best bets for now. Perhaps the industry will develop an instrument that measures lean or (preferably) pedal-to-ground clearance, and that informs the cyclist as soon as a preset limit is reached.

Hitting a pedal is not the only drawback to pedaling in a corner. A tire can supply only so much force, and it does not matter whether that force is due to cornering, braking, or acceleration. If the rear tire is already near its cornering limit, the application of additional force from pedaling may be enough to cause a skid. Likewise, all hard braking should be completed before the bike begins to corner, because the combination of hard braking and hard cornering may also induce a skid.

Cycling literature advises the rider to transfer his weight to the outside pedal while coasting through a corner; that is, not only lift the inside pedal, but apply force to the lowered outside pedal. Though this is the most natural thing to do, it is unlikely to have any real benefits other than keeping the pedals in position. It does not change the center of gravity.

A racing motorcyclist typically moves his inside leg to the side during a corner, either pointing the knee in the direction of the turn or moving his foot so that it grazes the ground. Many bicycle racers also point the knee, probably consciously or unconsciously imitating motorcyclists and imagining it to be the fast way through the corner. However, the motorcyclist (whose leg is protected by a heavy leather suit and whose shoe has a steel skid plate) probably does it to gauge how far over he is leaning and thus how close he is to the maximum safe cornering speed. With less rubber on the road and less protection, bicyclists do not generally lean that far, and there has been no evidence to indicate that pointing the knee is of any practical benefit to a bicyclist. It is clearly less aerodynamic.

Some coaches advocate a cornering technique in which the rider lifts himself off the saddle and leans into the corner while keeping the bike more upright. While there is not general agreement on the effectiveness of this technique, it does have some advantages, at least in theory. For one, it decouples the bike from the rider. In effect, the rider becomes sprung mass (his arms and legs are the springs) and the much lighter bike becomes unsprung mass. Keeping unsprung mass low is a tenet of racing car design, the same principle behind the use of light alloy wheels and certain types of independent suspension; it is (or perhaps we should say "was") also the principle behind high-compliance phonograph cartridges. A low-mass portion of an assembly is able to track undulations in a surface better than the mass of the complete assembly can. (Chapter 9 will also discuss sprung and unsprung mass.)

We would expect this technique to allow the bicycle to corner more surely (and therefore faster) in a rough or bumpy curve, and possibly have a better chance of recovering from a momentary skid, once the cyclist gains practice in controlling the bike from this position.

There are also arguments against this technique, however. One is that the side area of the tread of some tires has a softer, stickier rubber compound or a tread pattern designed for cornering, whereas the center strip is harder or designed for low rolling resistance and extended wear rather than high traction. These tires may work better with more traditional leaning of the bike and rider as a unit. Another argument is that though bicycles, especially bicycle wheels, are designed to withstand considerable compression force along their vertical axis, they can tolerate much less lateral (shear) force. Leaning the bike less under the same cornering conditions means increasing the lateral component of the cornering force borne by the wheels. Most riders have seen a wheel that after a side impact has collapsed into the shape of a potato chip. It is also possible to collapse a wheel by excessive lateral force with no impact, such as by suddenly jumping onto the pedals during a climb while the bike is leaning under the rider. The author suspects that only a wheel of marginal strength — for example, one with a loose or broken spoke, or one with spokes not up to proper tension, or one with too few

spokes for the rider's weight — would be in danger of collapse. But riders considering this technique with ultralight time trial wheels may do well to keep the possibility of wheel failure in mind. A final drawback is that pedaling in this attitude is impossible; acceleration out of the curve may be delayed.

Slopes and Banking

So far, the corners we have been discussing have been level ones, in every direction: i.e. the cyclist enters and leaves the corner at the same elevation, plus the inside and outside of the curve are also at that same elevation. Corners on slopes are seldom so neat. A sloped uphill corner is of little concern, because uphill speeds are rarely so high as to approach the cornering limit. Downhill corners are another matter. There a cyclist can often be near the ragged edge even if he is not trying to be.

Most of the reason a downhill corner is trickier than a level one is simply the increased speed. The downhill slope, however, does reduce the normal force pressing the tires onto the road. (As an extreme example, a vertical road surface would leave zero roadholding force for cornering.) However, even a –15% grade retains almost 99% of the normal force on level ground, that is, the cosine of the slope angle, where the slope angle is arctan (grade in percent divided by 100).

The banking of the corner may also be significant. In a banked corner, the outside of the curve is above the inside. Velodromes, for instance, even though they may be level in the direction of travel, are usually steeply banked, permitting very high cornering speeds. Roads are sometimes also banked by design. However, some roads, and perhaps most trails, are reverse banked: the outside of the curve is below the inside. A cyclist's cornering ability is changed in a banked or reverse banked corner, compared to an unbanked corner. We'll discuss only the worst case, the reverse banked corner, because there the cyclist is hit with a double whammy:

□ In addition to the lateral acceleration due to cornering, the cyclist must also cope with an additional lateral acceleration, namely the component of gravity parallel to the sloped surface (and perpendicular to the direction of travel). If α is the slope angle, that extra acceleration is g times the sine of α.

□ At the same time, the force perpendicular to the road surface is reduced. Instead of what on a level surface would be the full weight of the rider and bicycle, m times g, the force is only m g times the cosine of α. This is same reduction as for a downhill slope, but banking is often steeper than slope.

It's time for some numerical examples to show the magnitude of the effects of reverse banking. Suppose our standard rider sweeps through a level, unbanked corner at 0.5 g. As a simplification, we'll pretend that the force pressing the wheels onto the road is the same for each wheel, for a total of 90 kg times 9.8017 m/s^2, or 882 N. (Refer to Chapter 7 if you wish to break the calculations down by individual wheel.) The lateral force is therefore 0.5 times that, or 441 N. If the coefficient of static friction between the tires and road is, say, 0.8, the force that it would take to start his tires sliding would be 0.8 times 882, or 706 N — plenty of margin.

Now suppose his speed is the same except that this time the corner has a reverse banking of 10 degrees. The reverse banking contributes an extra 153 N (90 x 9.8017 x sin 10 degrees) of lateral force, bringing his total to 594 N. At the same time, the force pressing his tires onto the road is just 868 N (factoring in the cosine of 10 degrees), which brings the force it would take to initiate a skid down to 694 N. His safety margin is less than half what it was in the level corner.

One might also think a third factor is at work: Isn't the road also dropping out from under the bicycle, lightening its contact with the road still further? No, not if we are talking about the road and its overall slope rather than the occasional local dip or pothole. Because the cyclist propels the bicycle in the same direction as that of the road surface, not necessarily horizontally, the road is not really dropping away from the tires. For that to be a problem, he would need wings.

We have already seen that in a level corner, at least when the cyclist is able to achieve a sufficiently high speed, the optimum path through the corner is the arc of a circle. More generally, regardless of whether a corner is banked, level (unbanked), or reverse banked, the optimum path is the line of constant lateral acceleration. Suppose the cyclist is entering a reverse banked corner and starts at the outside, upright, at the full speed the radius of the corner, if it were level, would allow. As he begins to turn in toward the apex, he begins to experience some of the reverse banking, which forces him to reduce speed. At the apex, he is traveling perpendicular to the banking, forcing him to reduce speed further.

Because tires are not capable of undergoing both a full cornering load and additional force from braking, unless the cyclist has some other form of brake that doesn't act through the tires (such as a parachute drag), braking during the corner is not a good idea — it would cause a skid. Because the lateral acceleration in a reverse banked curve is greatest at the apex, if the cyclist were following the usual arc of a circle, he would have to slow to the speed needed at the apex well before then, namely by the time he enters the corner.

Except at the apex, he would be going more slowly than necessary, which doesn't seem quite right, but what's he to do? Well, ideally what he should do is enter the corner with a relatively sharp turn (small radius of curvature) and approach the apex with a relatively gentle turn (large radius of curvature). This would be a more elliptical path. That said, it is probably not humanly possible to judge such a curve perfectly. The principle for the cyclist to keep in mind is not to allow reverse banking to push him over the cornering limit. If he can offset the increasing lateral acceleration by gradually turning in less sharply, then bravo!

9 Handling

Handling is a complex subject, made the more so by the fact that there is no single standard of performance. Speed is simple and unequivocal, easily measured with a stopwatch; good handling, in contrast, is a matter of vague "feel" and personal preference. A bicycle that for one rider is ideally responsive may seem too twitchy and unstable for another. For this reason, it is best to avoid value judgments; instead, this chapter will attempt to describe the way in which a particular attribute affects the handling characteristics of the bicycle, a task that is difficult enough.

Fork Rake and Trail

The concepts of fork rake and trail are closely related. Indeed, the terms are often confused even in books by cycling experts. (Some references also confusingly call trail "tail" or "caster." The potential for misunderstanding a reference to "tail" are obvious. In automobiles, caster is an angle, the angle the wheel steering axis makes with the ground.) At least as used in this book, rake and trail are entirely distinct. Rake is the amount of bend or offset in the fork. Picture a fork blade that has not been bent (raked) at all. Viewed from the side, the blade would simply extend the center line of the headset (the steering axis); the dropout, which receives the wheel axle, would lie along that same line. A raked fork blade moves the dropout forward of the steering axis line. Rake is the perpendicular distance from that line to the center of the dropout. See Figure 0901.

Now again picture an unraked fork and the imaginary line of the steering axis extended until it hits the level ground. The point at which the axis meets the ground will be ahead of the point at which the tire touches the ground. (The latter point — the center of the contact patch, if you prefer — is directly below the dropout.) The distance between these two points is called the trail, because the tire contact point trails behind the steering axis. It is easy to see that the amount of trail varies depending on the angle between the steering axis and the ground. This angle, corresponding to caster in automobiles, is called the head tube angle. If the head tube angle is steep, that is, approaching 90 degrees or nearly perpendicular to the ground, the amount of trail will be very short. If the head tube angle is relaxed, numerically smaller and laid back like a chopper motorcycle, the amount of trail could be very long indeed. Now introduce rake into the picture. Rake moves the dropout and the tire contact point forward. Because the steering axis is not altered, rake shortens the amount of trail. See Figure 0902 for the geometry of head tube angle, rake, and trail.

Before discussing the functions of rake and trail, we need to place them in the context of the suspension of a bicycle. The suspension of any vehicle is whatever devices support the vehicle upon its wheel axles. At first glance, most road bikes do not seem to have a suspension at all, because the wheel axles seem to support only a rigid, unyielding frame. Let us pretend at first that a bicycle's suspension really is completely inflexible, and that the entire bicycle is therefore "unsprung mass."

A wheel rides up each bump it encounters. With a completely solid, rigid suspension, such vertical travel at one end of the bicycle would cause the rest of the bicycle to pitch, that is, to rotate backward or forward around the center of the opposite wheel. The change in direction amounts to a change in velocity, which is an acceleration. Acceleration times whatever mass is involved produces a force, the force of impact the rider feels when the wheel hits the bump. After the bump, the momentum of the bicycle would keep carrying it in the same, upward direction until gravity is able to overcome that momentum and return the bicycle wheel to the ground. With high speeds, large mass, or large bumps, and thus high momentum, there could be quite a delay before the wheel again hits the ground. Consequently, the wheels of a completely rigid bicycle would spend a lot of time bouncing off the ground on a bumpy road. A wheel that is not contacting the ground obviously cannot provide traction or apply power.

With a supple, flexible suspension, the bicycle behaves quite differently. As the tire climbs the bump, the suspension compresses like a spring; in fact the suspension *is* a spring. By compressing, the suspension imparts much less vertical travel to the rest of the bicycle; it is now "sprung mass." It also imparts much less shock force to the rider. After the bump is past, the spring rebounds, accelerating the relatively light wheel (the only

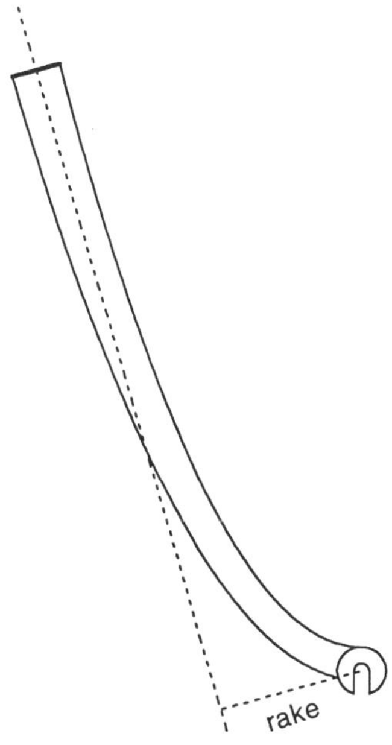

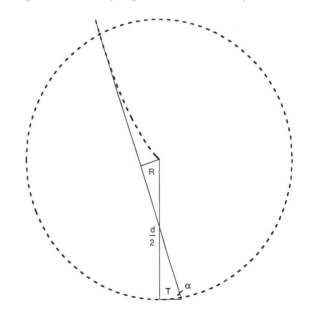

Fig. 0901. Definition of rake: offset of the wheel center perpendicular to the steering axis.

Fig. 0902. Geometry of rake and trail. Trail (T) is determined by rake (R), wheel diameter (d), and head tube angle (α).

remaining unsprung mass) downward faster than gravity could alone, helping to keep the tire in contact with the road and thus aiding traction.

Even though a standard bicycle may seem completely rigid all by itself, its relatively thin fork blades and stays flex enough to act as a suspension when the bicycle is supporting a rider. The characteristics of the fork and stays (or other suspension components on some bicycles) are chosen with the expected weight of the rider and the intended use of the bicycle in mind. A supple suspension is particularly necessary for vehicles that are to operate at high speeds or on bumpy surfaces, but not at low speeds or smooth surfaces, hence the rigid designs of children's tricycles and track bicycles, the particularly flexible suspensions of mountain bikes, and the intermediate designs of road bicycles.

Wheel mass also plays a part. A lower-mass wheel is able to accelerate more quickly in any direction, and thus is better able to follow the irregularities of the road and to be controlled by the suspension. This fact would seem to put mountain bike wheels at a traction disadvantage compared to road bike wheels, except for two ameliorating properties.

❑ Mountain bike tires enclose a high volume of air, which acts as an almost ideal spring.

❑ While all tires act as part of the bike's suspension, mountain bike tires make a very significant contribution.

Plus mountain bikes usually have slightly smaller-diameter wheels than road bikes, which (if all else were equal) would lead to lower mass. For the very best roadholding, a bicycle would have small, lightweight wheels but not necessarily narrow tires, controlled by a very supple suspension — a description that not coincidentally fits Alex Moulton's radical bicycle designs to a T.

One of the functions of rake is to make the fork more flexible, to assist the fork in its role as most or all of the bicycle's front suspension. The bend or offset from the rake increases the length of the fork blades (compared to a straight line

between the headset and dropout), reducing their rigidity. (See the section on frame stiffness in Chapter 10 for more on the topic of rigidity.) The bend also changes the angle of incidence between the road shocks and the axis of the fork blade, so that most of their force causes the fork blade to flex and relatively little is transmitted directly up the blade toward the rider. Obviously, the more rake, the more supple and flexible the fork. Many mountain bikes and a few road bikes augment the basic suspension capabilities of the fork with an automobile-like suspension consisting of additional springs and shock absorbers (or "dampers," the more accurate British term). For reasonably smooth roads, however, most riders find that a standard, raked fork provides the same functions adequately with less of a weight penalty.

The other function of rake is to provide about the right amount of trail, given the head tube angle. Trail directly affects the amount of self-centering action in the steering and hence the stability of the bicycle at medium and high speeds. Remember pushing a grocery cart or a chair with casters? Notice anything about its directional stability? Right, it needs a couple of firm hands to keep it from wandering all over the place. Those little casters provide very little trail. Small sideways forces from steering corrections are dwarfed by the random forces from the bumpy wheels, floor, and carpet, so the wheels point every which way. With more trail — a longer lever arm between the wheel and its pivot — forward motion would pull the wheels firmly into line. So it is with a bicycle. A bicycle is designed to have more trail, and (let us hope) much less friction and play in its steering that might interfere with the self-centering action. Of course, it may be possible to have so much trail that the bicycle would be reluctant to change direction at all; in practice, however, too much self-centering at normal speeds is not a problem. More noticeable is "wheel flop," the tendency of the front wheel to turn too far on its own when the bike is leaning at very low speeds, a characteristic made more pronounced by greater trail. Although a rider can control bicycles with a wide range of trail values, most bicycles have between 3 and 7.5 cm of trail. Some frame builders recommend a relatively short trail — 3 or 3.5 cm — for bicycles that are to be used for climbing, and a relatively long trail — 7 or 7.5 cm — for descending. Because few events are all uphill or down, and even fewer riders have the luxury of being able to swap bikes at the top of a hill, the intermediate trail on most bicycles is a perfectly acceptable compromise.

From Figure 0902 and the application of a little trigonometry and algebra, it is possible to derive formulas or equations relating trail to rake. If d is the front wheel diameter, α is the head tube angle (the acute angle from horizontal to the steering axis), R is the rake and T the trail, then:

$$T = (d \cos \alpha - 2R) / (2 \sin \alpha)$$

$$R = (d \cos \alpha - 2T \sin \alpha) / 2$$

(There are other equivalent equations, for example using tangents instead of sines. Do not be concerned if you encounter one of these elsewhere — unless it gives a different answer.) Suppose one has a bike with 73 degree angles, 700C wheels of about 66.8 cm diameter, and 5 cm rake. Then the trail is (66.8 x 0.29237 – 2 x 5)/(2 x 0.95630) = 4.98 cm. To achieve the same trail with a bike that has 75 degree angles, the rake would have to be (66.8 x 0.25882 – 2 x 4.98 x 0.96593)/2 = 3.83 cm.

In a head-on crash, often the fork sacrifices itself, bending permanently backward and leaving the remainder of the frame relatively unscathed. Once the unfortunate rider has recovered and is satisfied that the rest of the frame is not seriously damaged, it is a relatively simple matter to replace the fork. Ideally the replacement fork should be identical to the original, or perhaps an upgrade from the same factory that built the bicycle. If an exact replacement is not available, before purchasing an aftermarket replacement, the prospective buyer should try to ensure that it will make no serious changes to the bike's geometry. The first criterion is length. One might think that forks built for the same wheel size would not vary in length, but in fact differences do exist, partly because some forks are built for large tire or fender clearance and others are not. A new fork that is longer than the original will tilt the bike backward, relaxing the frame angles; one that is shorter will steepen them. With a racing frame that has a typical 99-cm wheelbase (the distance between the points at which the tires contact the ground), an 8 millimeter greater fork length effectively reduces the frame angles by about one-half degree. Even such a small angular difference will necessitate a saddle position change; the stem and handlebar position, the quickness of the steering, and the trail will also be affected slightly. The second criterion is rake, which in replacement forks is more variable. As we have seen above, less rake than the original increases the amount of trail; more rake decreases trail. Once the new angles and rake are known, the buyer can use the formula above to assess whether the new trail will still be about the same as the old or uncomfortably close to the limit for acceptable handling. Changes in the geometry or in the material of the fork (for example, replacing a steel fork with a carbon fiber one) will also change its spring rate, which may lead to (or cure) shimmy — see the discussion of oscillation below.

Effect of Wheelbase on Handling

Most riders are familiar with the visual differences in geometry between road racing bicycles and touring bicycles (or, because the latter are relatively rare these days, between road bikes and mountain bikes or hybrids). The road racing bike has steep frame angles and a fork that is barely raked at all. Its front wheel is so far back that it may overlap the rider's toe when the crankarm is forward. Its chainstays are so short that there may be barely enough room behind the seat tube to permit changing the rear wheel. In fact, some radical designs use an indented or split seat tube to allow the rear wheel to be moved even farther forward. The seat tube angle is steep, moving the rear wheel a bit farther forward yet. The combination of steep angles, little rake, and short chainstays make the wheelbase relatively short for a road racing bike. (Incidentally, the wheelbase is most easily measured between the centers of the front and rear dropouts.)

But why do road racing bikes have short wheelbases? Is there a performance advantage? After all, all bikes are capable of turning sharply, and rarely encounter a corner that remotely taxes their capabilities. Even tandems have no problems negotiating ordinary roads — nor should this be surprising, because even the most compact car has a much longer wheelbase and turning radius than a bicycle.

A short wheelbase, of course, affords a vehicle quicker handling, which can be a competitive advantage. In autocrosses (automobile time trials with many tight turns), Mini Coopers, Sprites, and Miatas consistently outperform larger, more powerful cars. There is no bicycle event on the road or the track that puts a comparable premium on handling, nor are the wheelbases of single bicycles quite as variable as those of cars. Nonetheless, most racers and performance-oriented riders favor quick handling, especially in criteriums and track events. To clarify what is meant by quick handling, imagine that the front of the bicycle is steered a certain amount to the right. The entire bicycle then turns or rotates a certain angle clockwise about its vertical axis. This angle of rotation (called yaw) is greater for a short wheelbase than for a long wheelbase. Naturally, any bicycle can turn any amount; but with a particular steering angle, a short-wheelbase bicycle will turn (yaw) more in a specified length of time than a long-wheelbase bicycle could, hence the idea of quicker handling. For a given steering angle, the turning radius is also tighter for a short wheelbase. Referring to Fig. 0903, if θ (theta) is the steering angle measured in the plane of the ground and expressed in radians, and W is the wheelbase, the turning circle radius is approximately W /θ.

Effect of Head Tube Angle and Rake on Handling

A road racing bike handles quickly by virtue of its relatively short wheelbase, and that short wheelbase is achieved not only by shorter chainstays but by steeper frame angles and shorter fork rake. It is therefore natural to assume that any bike with steeper angles or shorter rake will handle more quickly. Surprisingly, neither of these assumptions is the case; in fact, the opposite is true. The figures and equations that follow will illustrate these points.

Figure 0903 shows a top view of the steering geometry. The distance labeled f is the horizontal length of the fork (projected onto the ground) as it rotates through a steering angle θ. The distance c is the constant portion of the wheelbase, back to the rear wheel; W is the actual wheelbase, equal to f + c when θ is zero but a little less when θ is greater than zero. The angle between the two wheelbase lines is labeled φ (phi), the yaw. Figure

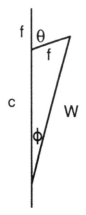

Fig. 0903. Steering geometry, top view. Bike of wheelbase W is steered through an angle θ: it yaws an angle of φ. Distance f is horizontal length of fork, c is remainder of wheelbase.

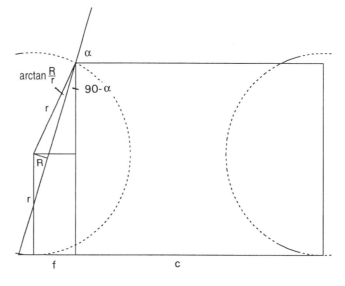

Fig. 0904. Steering geometry, side view. Enables calculation of f from rake R, wheel radius r and head tube angle α.

0904 shows the side view. Here α is the head tube angle, R is the fork rake, and r is the wheel (and tire) radius. R (rake) is shown as a short line perpendicular to the steering axis and ending at the fork dropout. The radius r is of course the vertical distance from that dropout to the ground, and also the distance from the dropout to the point at which the steering axis and the circumference of the tire meet. Those who wish to go through the trigonometry will find that with angles expressed in degrees:

$$f = r \sin (\arctan R/r + 90 - a)$$

$$\phi = \arcsin [(f \sin \theta) / W]$$

Given these equations and a little serious calculator work, it is easy to determine that yaw decreases as head tube angle steepens. For example, given 700C wheels, a constant trail of 5 cm, a steering angle of 10 degrees, and a constant wheelbase of 99 cm measured when the front wheel is pointing straight ahead, yaw is about half a degree more (over 40% greater) with a 70-degree head tube angle than with a 75-degree angle. (The reader should be cautioned that it would be difficult if not impossible to achieve a wheelbase as short as 99 cm with shallow frame angles and a long rake.)

Similarly, with a constant head tube angle, say 73 degrees, if everything else is held constant except for the rake (and the corresponding trail), yaw decreases with decreasing rake: it's almost 30% greater with 7 cm rake than with 3 cm. Even if we allow the wheelbase to shorten solely on account of the steepening frame angle and shortening rake, keeping the quantity c (as used in the figures and equation above) constant, yaw decreases as head tube angle steepens. The quick handling of the road bike is thus the result of the short wheelbase only. While steep angles and short rake contribute to that short wheelbase, they slow the steering more the short wheelbase quickens it. Shallower angles win the quickness contest.

Do these results mean that riders interested in quick handling should order bikes with shallow frame angles? Not necessarily. For one thing, a

wheelbase can be only so short. If the top tube is correctly sized for the rider, once the chainstays are at their minimum length and the seat tube angle is as steep as tolerable, the only remaining ways to shorten the wheelbase are to steepen the head tube angle and reduce the rake, both of which (as we have seen) make the handling slower. A short wheelbase may be physically impossible to achieve with shallow angles without a radical design change, such as smaller wheels or a seat tube that is bowed forward. The front-to-rear balance must also be considered. An experienced frame builder would likely balk at producing a frame that places the rear wheel almost directly under the rider yet extends the front one forward due to a shallow head tube angle. Many builders adopt steeper angles for large frames for that very reason.

It would be counterproductive to pursue quick handling by adopting ever-steeper frame angles. Considering that roads are not likely to get much smoother, that should be good news. Despite its longer wheelbase, a comfortable touring bike is not necessarily more sluggish a handler than a racing bike, though it may not be quite as efficient at transforming the rider's power into speed (as discussed in Chapter 10). Finally, because many a performance-oriented cyclist loves the way his road racing bike handles just the way it is, the results also hint that ultra-quickness may not figure strongly in the subjective "feel" of a good-handling bike.

Effect of Stem Extension on Handling

Proper stem extension (that is, forward length, not height) places the handlebars at the correct distance in front of the rider. (See Chapter 4.) But because the distance depends on the sum of the top tube length and stem extension, any given distance can be achieved with a variety of combinations. After purchase there is of course no further choice in frame dimensions. However, someone about to buy a new bike or order a custom frame should be aware of the tradeoffs. A shorter top tube gives a shorter wheelbase, the effects of which were discussed above; but (for a given size of rider, to retain good fit) it must be counteracted with a longer stem. A longer stem extension increases the length of the lever arm effecting steering corrections, which makes the steering more stable, or (viewed another way) more sluggish. Minor road jitters transmitted to a long stem cause only small changes to the steering angle, and a given steering angle change requires a physically longer sweep of the hands. Conversely, a long top tube may require a short stem extension, which could seem either responsive or nervous, depending on one's point of view. Stem extension should not be a serious handling concern unless the rider is forced to use a very short or very long stem. In that case, if his physical dimensions and the models available permit, he should consider a different frame, that is, a model of the same size with a different top tube length, or perhaps a slightly bigger or smaller version of the same model. Good fit should override all other considerations.

Fork Oscillation

Occasionally a rider will discover that his bicycle shimmies or vibrates alarmingly, especially during a fast bumpy downhill. In some cases, the vibration may be severe enough to provoke loss of control. The cause is usually the fork's natural frequency of oscillation when loaded with a particular mass and induced to vibrate. Possible sources of the vibration include a particular road surface, a wheel that is out of true or damaged, a tire that is out of round, improperly mounted, or defective, or a headset that binds or has excessive play. Regardless of the source, however, it is the fork itself that oscillates.

We will go into the subject of fork oscillation in some detail. The fork is of course a spring. The stiffness of any spring is quantified by a number called the spring constant. (The spring constant is also called the force constant to distinguish it from the analogous torque constant, which does not interest us.) Starting with one end of the spring fixed and the spring in equilibrium, the spring constant is the quotient of two quantities: the force

needed to move the opposite end of the spring away from the equilibrium position, and the displacement resulting from that force. For example, picture a bicycle fork rotated backward and facing upward so that it is nearly horizontal, its crown level with its dropouts. Now picture its crown clamped securely in a vise, leaving the remainder of the fork free to flex. Ignoring the weight of the fork itself, which is not enough to flex the fork noticeably, we can say that the fork is in equilibrium. Suppose we hang a heavy weight from the dropouts — not heavy enough to bend the fork permanently, of course. Once any vibrations die down, we measure how far the dropouts have moved. (See Figure 0905.) The quotient of the weight (force) and the displacement is what we will call the "pure" spring constant for the fork. (The word "pure" will be explained a little later.) In algebraic terms:

$$k_p = F / s$$

where k_p is the "pure" spring constant, F is the force, and s is the displacement. For example, suppose the weight is 200 newtons (45 pounds) and the dropouts are displaced 7 millimeters (about $^9/_{32}$ inch). The "pure" spring constant is 200 N / .007 m, about 29,000 N/m; or in English units, 45 lb / $^9/_{32}$ in. = 160 lb/in. (Chapter 10 will cover an alternative method for calculating the spring constant.)

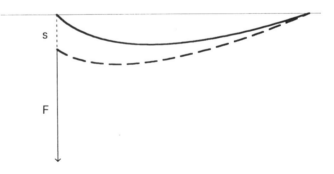

Fig. 0905. Determining the pure spring constant of the fork. Clamp crown (right), hang weight F from dropouts. Pure spring constant is the quotient of force F and displacement s.

Of course a bicycle does not operate with its fork horizontal. In fact, because it holds the front end of the bike up, its vertical flexing ("flection") interests us the most. Imagine a fork with straight blades. When horizontal, it is relatively flexible; it takes only moderate force to displace the dropouts vertically a given distance. Now, still using your imagination, rotate it forward. As it becomes more nearly vertical, the fork becomes stiffer in the vertical direction: it takes more force to move the dropouts the same vertical distance. If it were rotated to perfectly vertical, it would become so rigid that it would be practically useless as a vertical spring.

On a real fork, a straight line between the crown and the dropouts tilts at an angle (relative to horizontal) of 75 degrees or less, depending on the head tube angle of the frame and the amount of rake in the fork itself. Figure 0906 depicts the idealized straight fork, tilting at an angle θ when at equilibrium. When a perpendicular force is applied, the dropout moves a perpendicular distance s; but vertically the displacement is a smaller amount, y. From the figure, one can see that:

$$s = y / \cos \theta$$

Figure 0907 gives the corresponding geometry for the forces involved. W is a vertical force, such as the weight of the rider bearing down on the fork; F is the component of W perpendicular to the fork, the force that produces the displacement s in Figure 0906. From Figure 0907, one can see that:

$$F = W \cos \theta$$

Since $k_p = F/s$:

$$k_p = W \cos \theta / (y/\cos \theta) = (W/y) \cos^2 \theta$$

Let us call the quotient W/y (that is, vertical force divided by vertical displacement) the vertical spring constant, k_v. While k_p describes the stiffness of the fork considered purely as a spring, independent of its position, k_v describes its stiffness in the vertical direction only, as though the fork were a vertically aligned coil spring extending from the fork crown down to the dropouts. The relationship of the two spring constants is:

$$k_v = k_p / \cos^2 \theta$$

Suppose the line between the fork crown and the dropouts is 65 degrees from horizontal, which is about what it would be if the head tube angle were 73 degrees and the fork rake 5 cm. The square of the cosine of 65 degrees is 0.179. If the "pure" spring constant is 29,000 N/m as before, the vertical spring constant would be about 160,000 N/m, indicating a much stiffer spring. Accordingly, a vertical load of 250 N (about 56 lb) on the front of the bike would flex the fork enough to lower the front of the bike 250/160,000 = 0.0016 m — that is, 1.6 millimeters.

Again, think of the fork as a vertical coil spring. Mentally clamp its top, where the fork crown would be, securely in a vise; let the rest of it hang freely. Attach a mass to the opposite end, where the dropouts would be. Give the mass a vertical rap; it will vibrate vertically with a predetermined frequency, depending on the amount of mass and how stiff the spring is. The time of one

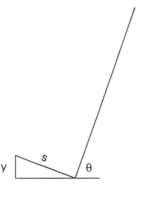

Fig. 0906. Relationship of perpendicular and vertical fork displacement. For fork with tilt θ, perpendicular force giving displacement s gives only vertical displacement y.

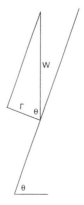

Fig. 0907. Vertical force (weight) W on the fork is equivalent to a perpendicular force F = W cos θ.

complete cycle, for example from the mass's lowest point to its highest point and back, is called the period of the spring-mass combination. The period is given by the equation:

$$T = 2 \pi (m/k)^{\frac{1}{2}}$$

where T is the period in seconds, m is the mass in kilograms, and k is the spring constant in newtons per meter. If a 25.5 kg mass is attached to the end of a spring whose constant is 160,000 N/m, the period is 2 times π times the square root of the quotient of 25.5 and 160,000, or 0.079 seconds.

Now mentally flip the spring over. It's still vertical, but this time the bottom is clamped and the mass is suspended by the top of the spring — same mass, same spring rate, same period of vibration. It's easy to see that this is very much like the application a bicycle fork handles. Its bottom is held above the road at a (nearly) constant distance; its top suspends a certain portion of the mass of the rider and bicycle, which vibrate accordingly. Granted, it is an oversimplification. The rider, the bicycle frame, and the wheels also flex with their own complex and variable set of spring rates in different directions, partially damping out the vibration of the fork. But when the load on the front of the bike is 250 N (25.5 kg x 9.8 m/s²), a real fork with the above vertical spring rate ought to be inclined to behave in a similar way, to vibrate vertically with a period of 0.079 seconds.

Suppose the front wheel is out of true or unbalanced. All wheels are, to some extent. For example, the rim is not perfectly true; the tire mounted on it is not perfectly circular; or the rim joint is heavier than the rest of the rim and does not perfectly balance the valve stem opposite it. There are doubtless many other minor irregularities, and perhaps some major ones if the bearings are out of adjustment or the wheel needs truing, but let us boil them all down to one small representative bump on the circumference of the wheel. With each revolution of the wheel, the bump imparts to the fork a vertical displacement. Most of the time the small displacement is lost in the noise, just one among thousands of other minor bumps coming up from the road. At some speed,

however, this periodic bump may arrive with nearly the same period as that of the fork's natural vibration. If so, and if large enough, the bump will induce the fork to oscillate; the bike will shimmy.

A 700C wheel is about 2.1 m in circumference, so the critical speed for the above fork and load would be 2.1 m / 0.079 s = 27 m/s, about 60 mph. On a level road, a problem with this particular combination would be very unlikely. (Even "Mile-a-Minute" Murphy was drafting behind a locomotive when he performed the famous feat that earned him his nickname.) But suppose instead that the bike is descending a steep downhill, where the fork carries a much greater load because the rider's weight is shifted forward. A front load of 580 N (about 130 lb) is akin to a vibrating mass of 59 kg. Now the period is 2 x 3.14 x (59 / 160,000)^{½} = 0.12 s; the critical speed is 2.1 m/0.12 s = 17.5 m/s, about 39 mph. This speed is well within the range of possibility on a steep downhill.

The cure for shimmy is to change the conditions. We will first assume that any headset or wheel problems have been corrected. On an unloaded bike, it may be effective to shift position forward or back to change the loading of the fork and thus the period of vibration. One common recommendation is to clamp the top tube between the knees, both to add mass and dampen vibrations. (Obviously this maneuver requires care.) Simply slowing down is also effective, but a severely vibrating front wheel may be difficult to brake. See below for additional measures to take with a loaded bike. If shimmy is a frequent problem, the only permanent cure may be a different model of bicycle, one with a different fork or a different head tube angle. Oscillation does not necessarily indicate a defective or poorly designed bike, but with a well-adjusted bike it does indicate a poor match between rider and bike. (The figures above hint that a heavy rider and a light, flexible fork is a combination to avoid.)

Although it is easier and more accurate to measure the spring constant of a fork empirically, we can also estimate it using the equation for the rigidity of a beam fixed at one end:

$$s = F \, l^3 / 3 \, E \, I$$

where s is the distance by which the unsupported end is deflected, F is the perpendicular force applied to the unsupported end, l is length of the beam, E is Young's modulus of elasticity for the material, and I is the "moment" of the beam cross section. For a tubular beam (i.e. a tube or cylinder):

$$I = \pi \, (D^4 - d^4) \, / \, 64$$

where D is the outside diameter and d is the inside diameter; because a fork has two such beams, we should multiply I by 2. (There will be further discussion of rigidity in Chapter 10.)

We will try one example. Suppose the fork is a simple steel cylinder, 356 mm long and 24 mm in diameter, with a constant wall thickness of 0.4 mm, as illustrated in Figure 0908. Young's modulus for steel is 30 million pounds per square inch; converting that to mks, we get 2.07×10^{11} newtons per square meter. Converting the distances to meters, l = 0.356, D = 0.0240, and d = 0.0236. Suppose the perpendicular force is 29 newtons; if we plug these numbers into the equations, we get the displacement s = 0.000994 m, just under a millimeter. The

pure spring constant is therefore 29 / 0.000994, about 29,200 N/m: very close to the figure for the hypothetical oscillating fork we discussed above.

How realistic is this example? The choice of fork tube gauge (wall thickness) was exceptionally thin; most straight-gauge steel forks have walls at least twice as thick. Otherwise, all the dimensions are in the ballpark. Real forks are usually raked, slightly variable in length partly as a result of that rake, oval in cross section near the crown, tapered in diameter from crown to dropout, and sometimes also tapered in gauge. The mathematical complexities put exact calculation of real fork spring constants outside the scope of this book. Nevertheless, we can see from the third and fourth powers in the equations above that the spring constant of even an idealized cylindrical fork is very sensitive to its precise dimensions. Clearly there may be very little difference between the dimensions of a fork that oscillates with a particular load and those of one that is well-behaved.

Panniers and Other Bags

If increased performance is the motive for reading this book, one might wonder why space is devoted to a discussion of panniers, because most performance-oriented riders would never consider mounting panniers on their precious lightweight road bikes … even if it were possible. Although relatively few in number, long-distance touring cyclists spend on average more time and energy bicycling than any other type of rider. They are often on the road ten hours a day, pedaling a bike that (including its baggage) weighs more than two or three road bikes put together. Though their goals are different, their need to maximize efficiency is just as great as any racer's. While most cyclists do short-distance rides in closed loops, and elite racers are accompanied by a caravan of support vehicles, touring cyclists ride long distances point-to-point and must carry with them almost everything they will need: spare clothing, toiletries, maps, tools, food, and usually camping and cooking gear. Most of these items are stored in bags mounted on the bike.

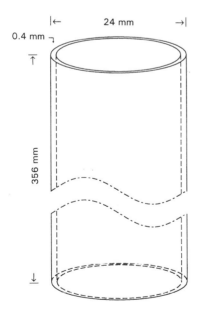

Fig. 0908. A simplified cylindrical "fork" to illustrate calculation of spring constant from dimensions and material.

With the possible exception of trailers, panniers are the overwhelming choice of long-distance touring cyclists. (Trailers add rolling resistance and weight but add little stress to the frame and the wheels, and change the handling of the bike only slightly. Just because they are not discussed here any further, prospective tourists should not dismiss them.) Panniers are bags that are attached on each side of racks mounted at the front, rear, or both ends of the bike. They come in a variety of sizes to satisfy touring needs ranging from a credit-card, luxury motel overnight to a several-month camping expedition to the remote corners of the earth. Besides capacity, the main advantage of panniers is their stability. At the rear, a properly designed and mounted rack and a set of panniers attach rigidly to the bike and do not flap, sway, or shift weight as the bike moves. Many tourists rely on only one set of panniers on a rear rack, with additional items strapped atop the rack, omitting panniers at the front. This arrangement, though serviceable, drastically changes the front-to-rear weight distribution of the bike. The front wheel is more prone to lift on steep uphills, and road curves require careful attention. A "standard" front rack, mounted on the fork and accepting panniers positioned above the hub, restores a more normal weight distribution and is a step in the right direction.

A better choice, as virtually every cyclist who has tried it agrees, is to fit a low-mounted front rack and distribute the weight between front and rear panniers. The low-mount rack also attaches to the fork, either with clamps or brazed-on fittings, with a brace looping across to the other side. It turns with the steering but centers the panniers on either side of the hub, adding inertia but no handling surprises. In fact, with good fore-aft and side-to-side weight distribution, the combination of low front and standard rear racks and panniers actually increases the stability of the bicycle. Loaded with the extra mass, the bicycle reacts and turns more slowly, but maintains a desired line without steering corrections even more easily than an unloaded bike. Additional items, if needed, may be strapped rigidly atop the rear rack without upsetting the handling, as long as at least half

the carried weight is stored in the front panniers. For light touring, an arrangement of just a pair of low-mounted front panniers, with little or no weight carried at the rear, is often perfectly acceptable and upsets the handling less than one might think.

Saddlebags, often used even on racing bikes, mount below the saddle and to the rear of the seatpost. Usually saddlebags carry little weight and are affixed securely to the rails and post so that what weight there is moves with the bike frame. Very large saddlebags, about the size of a pannier, are sometimes used for light touring, especially in Britain. While the lack of a rear rack might be seen as an advantage, a heavily loaded saddlebag compromises weight distribution and stability. A rear "trunk"— usually a bag but sometimes something more rigid — is popular with cyclists who have the rear rack to mount it upon. It is also reasonably stable, but may interfere with mounting panniers on the same rack if more capacity is needed.

Another popular container is the handlebar bag, which mounts to the handlebars and sometimes the fork. This bag turns with the steering, but unlike low-mounted panniers, the added moment of inertia (high up and all on one side of the steering axis) can greatly impair the bike's handling. Some riders refuse to accept the constant steering struggle a handlebar bag imposes; others feel the convenience of a bag immediately in front of them more than makes up for the poorer handling. A handlebar bag should always be only lightly loaded: perhaps a rain jacket, map, tissues, and miniature camera, but no wrenches, water bottles, walking shoes, or watermelons. Kept light and used in conjunction with more heavily loaded low front panniers, a handlebar bag may not even deteriorate handling noticeably.

As we saw earlier, additional mass at the front end of the bicycle may cause the bike to shimmy and vibrate under certain conditions. Handlebar bags, especially when they carry weighty items, are usually the worst culprits, but sometimes loaded panniers can induce shimmy in a bike that otherwise handles perfectly. Securely mounted low front panniers are seldom a problem, though, because most of their mass is supported near the ends of the fork blades, where it loads the wheel axle rather than the whole fork and thus does not significantly change the natural oscillation period. It is also possible for a shifting or bouncing load to induce shimmy or other handling problems. If securing the load does not solve the problem, usually just rearranging it, placing more of it fore or aft, does. In any case, the mass on each side of the bike (left and right) should always be as nearly balanced as possible.

All mass added to the bicycle is of course detrimental to performance. (See Chapter 12 for more on this topic.) Experienced touring cyclists, like experienced backpackers, ruthlessly eliminate unnecessary items from their touring load and insist that the lightweight items they do carry perform multiple functions. Compared with a "normal" bike, the loaded panniers and the necessarily heavier, more rugged wheels of a touring bike impose a speed penalty (except downhill), but lower speed is not incompatible with seeing the countryside. Equipped with low enough gearing and effective riding technique, touring cyclists genuinely enjoy those long hours on the road and look forward to more, day after day and year after year.

10
Minimizing Rolling Resistance

In the next few chapters we will talk about the forces impeding a bicycle's motion and how a bicyclist can minimize them. We'll start with rolling resistance. This book lumps together everything that would absorb energy during constant-speed motion on level ground in a vacuum, and calls the collective force rolling resistance. But the reader should know that not everyone defines rolling resistance in the same way.

Some limit the topic to the wheels, the only parts of a vehicle that actually roll. Some restrict the topic further, by considering only the interaction between the tire and whatever it rolls on, omitting the wheel bearings. Many ignore the road surface, as though it didn't matter. And a few widen the topic to include resistance to climbing (gravity) and resistance to acceleration (inertia). In addition, some sources give the coefficient of rolling resistance (C_R) a unit such as pounds per ton (that is, pounds of resistance per ton of vehicle weight), and label the resulting quantity rolling resistance. Their rolling resistance is merely our C_R times 2,000, or times 2,240 for a long ton. In this book, the coefficient C_R never has a unit, and rolling resistance itself is always a force expressed in such units as newtons or pounds.

As we go into detail, we will try to deal with the consequences of our particular definitions. Almost all efforts to cut rolling resistance involve equipment — the bicycle and its components — and in our discussion of equipment we may range over some related topics.

The Drivetrain

The components of the bicycle that transmit power are called the drivetrain. The chain drive of a bicycle is a very efficient way to deliver power to the wheels. Make that "wheel" — unlike most vehicles, only one wheel of a bicycle is driven. As long as the drivetrain is clean, lubricated, and properly adjusted, further improvements can make very little difference. Nonetheless, the rider seeking that last fraction of an ounce of performance will want to make sure he has attended to all the details. Unfortunately, precise data on the contribution of components to rolling resistance is unavailable, but it is easy to feel by hand which components are the worst offenders and whether a change has made any real improvement.

Bicycles use bearings in the places where parts need to rotate freely: the headset, freewheel, rear derailleur pulleys, pedals, bottom bracket, and hubs. In this context, we can ignore the headset: it is not directly involved in making the bike go, or keeping it from going. (However, it *is* critical to the bike's handling and steering, and must be kept free of play and binding. See Chapter 9 for more on this aspect of performance.)

The freewheel bearings are not usually accessible or adjustable. The best the rider can do is keep the freewheel clean and lubricated. When the rider is applying power, the freewheel is of course locked; it makes no difference then whether it is factory new and freshly lubricated, or choked with internal grit and rust. When the rider is coasting, however, the freewheel moves. Its bearings and ratcheting mechanism (the source of the clickety sound) then contribute a little rolling resistance. Some mechanics prefer to lubricate a freewheel by injecting grease. Others (including some manufacturers) worry that grease may be thick enough, especially in cold weather, to cause one of the pawls in the ratchet to stick, causing the freewheel to lock — to cease to be a freewheel, in other words. They prefer oil, or one of the other liquid or dry lubricants that minimize rolling resistance. These usually provide adequate longevity, considering that the load on the freewheel bearings is light, and that freewheel cogs wear out more rapidly than the internal mechanism.

The rear derailleur pulleys, also called jockey and tension wheels, add a slight amount of resistance to the drivetrain. (Except on a fixed-gear track bike, of course.) The pulleys help the lower cage of the derailleur wrap up whatever length of chain is left over after a particular chainwheel and cog are selected. They are the pivot points for the lower cage, and do not have to counter the rider's pedaling force, merely the force of the derailleur spring and the weight of the chain. Most pulleys have sleeve bearings, which work adequately in this low-load application if kept lubricated. However a few models containing sealed ball bearings are available. The makers of at least one such model claim that by using theirs instead of a sleeve-bearing type, the rider will save energy equivalent to so many feet of climbing at the end of a century ride. Such a claim at first seems incredible. Riders are generally unaware of any drivetrain resistance when pedaling, and what little resistance they notice when just spinning the cranks is difficult to blame on the jockey wheels. How much could sealed ball bearing pulleys help? First, most models do have a little less resistance, noticeable when spinning them detached from the chain. Little savings add up. Second, in the gear combinations that produce more extreme chain angles, sealed bearing pulleys seem hardly affected, whereas sleeve bearing models, especially worn ones, tend to shift laterally and bind slightly. Third, some sealed bearing pulleys have metal rather than plastic teeth, which (though noisier) may deform slightly less when contacting the chain and thus reduce friction a very little bit.

While it is impossible to verify the advertising claims without additional data, it is clear that sealed bearing pulleys should yield a slight improvement, if not necessarily a measurable one. We can, however, work an example to get a feeling for whether the claim is believable. How much energy does our standard rider expend riding a century and climbing a hill? It depends, of course, on his speed, the steepness of the hills, the wind, etc. Suppose he has somehow found 100 miles (160,935 m) of flat, windless terrain, and that he covers them at a speed of 17.9 mph (8 m/s), taking a little over 5 hours and 35 minutes. From our power equation, we know he put out 118.9 watts all along the way. The product of power and time is energy: a total of 2,392,000 joules. If he were to climb, say, a 5% grade 100 feet (30.5 m) high at 5.6 mph (2.5 m/s), he'd put out practically the same power, 119.9 W. This grade would be 30.5/.05 = 610 m long, which would take him 244 seconds at 2.5 m/s. Energy consumed up the hill would be a little over 29,000 J, a tiny fraction of what he spent on the century. If his bike's coefficient of rolling resistance on the century had been just slightly greater, not 0.003 but 0.004, that difference alone would have consumed an extra 142,000 J, quite a bit more energy than that one hill took. None of this verifies the advertising claim, but it does show that the amount of energy under discussion is very modest.

While we are on the subject, note that jockey wheel teeth are much stubbier and more rounded than gear teeth. Their function is only to guide the chain, not to transmit power. Some older models dispensed with teeth entirely, probably reducing friction further in some gear combinations, but without the benefit of personal experience with these, the author wonders how effective they were in keeping the chain from rubbing the derailleur cage in the extreme combinations.

Bearings in the pedals, the bottom bracket, and the hubs are similar in design if not in size. In the conventional "non-sealed" design, ball bearings roll around inside a concave circular race called a cup, confined there by a cone. The cup and cone rotate with respect to each other; for example, in a pedal the cup is part of the pedal body, while the cone is part of the pedal axle or spindle. The cone is adjustable, pressing the ball bearings loosely or tightly onto the surface of the cup. Properly adjusted, there should be absolutely no binding, and extremely little or no play. (One can test the former by twirling the axle in the fingers, the latter by grasping the body while pulling on and wiggling the axle.) A tiny amount of play is desirable in hubs secured by a quick-release skewer, because the quick-release compresses and deforms the axle slightly. Ball bearings are sometimes held within a retaining clip for ease in handling during installation; sticklers for minimum friction may prefer to put up with the inconvenience and omit the clip. Ball bearings should be coated with grease, but for minimum rolling resistance the cup should not be packed solidly with grease. Some hubs used to have a port for lubricating the bearings with oil instead of grease, which reduced resistance still further for time trial applications. Lubrication with oil instead of grease

does not protect the cups as well against wear, however, and most riders prefer not to replace expensive hubs regularly just to obtain a minuscule or imaginary improvement.

Sealed cartridge bearings are increasingly popular in hubs and pedals, and sealed bottom brackets have also earned a reputation for smoothness and reliability. They are also at least as well protected against the intrusion of dust and water as conventional bearings. They require no maintenance during their lifetime and in fact sometimes cannot be adjusted. Most sealed bearings run quite smoothly, and most riders find them an excellent choice, but in the author's experience the best conventional bearings sometimes exhibit even less resistance.

The total frictional drag contributed by the roller bearings of a bicycle has been estimated at one thousandth of the rider's weight, obviously only a ballpark figure. For our standard rider, and we might as well include his bicycle, that means somewhere in the neighborhood of 90 kg x 9.8 m/s^2 x 0.001, or 0.88 newtons (0.20 pounds). By comparison, in riding into still air at just 6.8 m/s (15 mph), our rider fights ten times as much as that in aerodynamic drag. The relative insignificance of ball bearing drag, especially at the higher speeds associated with high performance, is one reason why we have chosen to include it in rolling resistance rather than worry about it separately.

At high speeds, the chain may contribute a little more rolling resistance, but only when the bike is being pedaled, of course. The most noticeable source seems to be the friction of the chain sliding onto and off each gear tooth, and friction in the chain itself as it runs its tortuous route through the rear derailleur. The efficiency of a good, clean chain has been estimated to be as high as 98.5%, but that number may only be attainable with a track bike whose chain is always perfectly aligned and never winds through jockey wheels. The estimated power loss in a derailleur system is less than 5%, which at racing speeds translates to perhaps 1 newton of drag force. Because that is still very low, we again lump it indiscriminately into rolling resistance, though possibly with less justification.

The chain is also the component that requires the most maintenance. Regular lubrication is essential. A newly lubricated chain makes an immediately noticeable difference in noise, shifting performance, and pedaling feel. While the first two of these may not actually affect rolling resistance, they certainly improve the rider's frame of mind and self-confidence. The author recommends lubricating the chain immediately before any event in which performance matters, but at least once every 200 miles. Those who prefer paraffin treatments instead of oil may find they can get by with a longer interval. Different riders and mechanics have their personal chain lubricant preferences, and new miracle products hit the market regularly. Despite advertising claims, there seems to be little to choose between the various products strictly on the basis of performance.

Many mechanics advocate using as short a chain as possible for the set of gears in use, for the best possible shifting. They shorten the chain by removing links until the rear derailleur is stretched forward about 45 degrees from vertical in the large chainwheel-large cog combination. A short chain of course also reduces weight. On the negative side, the increased tension from the rear derailleur cage upon a shortened chain increases the force required to pull it past the jockey wheels. For the least resistance, the chain should be under as little tension as possible, yet the chain must not be so long that the rear derailleur doubles over on itself trying to wrap up excess chain in the small chainwheel-small cog combination. The concerned rider-mechanic, trusty chain tool clutched in his greasy fingers, should be able to find a happy medium in which the chain runs freely but the bike still shifts well. A bike without a derailleur has it simpler, and benefits from less resistance — its chain should have a little slack, but certainly not enough to skip.

During installation of a chain, the mechanic should test the chain for possible stiff links and avoid introducing a new one himself when he joins the end links. All links should flex easily. Riders should also keep tabs on chain wear, which shows itself as stretch under tension. The usual recommendation is to replace a chain when it has stretched about 1%. For a standard derailleur-bicycle chain with half-inch links, this means 24 links pulled tight should measure no greater than 12 and 1/8th inches. As the links of the chain gradually wear to greater than one-half inch, they force the gears to wear in step, eventually leading to shifting or skipping problems and further replacement expense, but also certainly contributing resistance. Heavy riders who climb a lot of steep hills and use small gear combinations (which put more tension on a chain than large gears) will find that their chains wear more quickly than average. While shifting performance may vary between different brands and models of chain, there is nothing to suggest that any one model revolves more easily than another.

Before we leave the subject of chains, note that the chain line on a properly adjusted bicycle should be close to perfect; that is, a straight line from a point midway between the inner and outer chainwheels to a point midway between the inner and outer cogs should be parallel to the planes of the chainwheels and cogs (see Figure 1001). Chain line is more critical than ever with wider freewheels and triple cranksets. Even with a perfect chain line, the performance-oriented rider should avoid extreme chain angles, such as outer chainwheel to inner cog, which increase friction and therefore rob power. In a very critical time trial application along an uninterrupted flat stretch, it may even make sense to choose a gear combination in which the cog is nearly directly behind the chainwheel in preference to one with a similar ratio but a more extreme chain angle. When performance is not an immediate concern, riders may still wish to avoid extreme chain angles because of

Fig. 1001. Ideal chain line: line from center of chainwheels and parallel to them should meet center of freewheel cogs (not to scale).

the greater noise and faster wear. The same goes for chains noisily rubbing on the front derailleur cage or not properly centered on the freewheel cog. The grating sound of a poorly adjusted drivetrain often elicits gruff verbal rolling resistance from one's riding companions.

The Frame

Frame materials and frame designs vary in stiffness or rigidity. A certain amount of stiffness is essential: the bicycle frame must support the rider's weight and pedaling forces without collapsing. A certain amount beyond that is desirable: the frame should absorb little of the rider's pedaling energy itself, but instead allow that energy to be transmitted to the wheel, driving the bike along. Too much stiffness, however, is undesirable: an extremely stiff frame may give such a harsh ride that few riders would tolerate it for long on an ordinary road. In between, there is a wide range of possibilities and rider preferences.

Rigidity can be characterized and measured in various ways. The degree of resistance to bending (against the vertical weight of the rider or the lateral forces of cornering, for example) is clearly important for the fork blades, seat tube, and seatstays, but also important in one way or another for each of the frame tubes. Resistance to twisting, countering the unequal forces of pedaling, is most important to the down tube, but again to a lesser extent to each of the frame tubes. Resistance to stretching may not seem important, but as some tubes bend or twist, others attached to them must sometimes momentarily stretch.

(As a side note, it is important to realize that strength and stiffness, though they often go hand in hand, are not the same thing. Think of grocery bags. An empty brown paper bag stands stiff and tall, while a plastic one collapses in a heap. Yet loaded with soup cans, the paper bag may tear while the plastic bag stays intact.)

Consider a tube such as one that could go into making a bicycle frame. The tube's stiffness depends on a number of its properties. We have already seen an equation relating these properties (in Chapter 9), but here we will expound on them in English and consider the implications of each for bicycle frames. A longer tube bends more easily than a shorter one: think of a full beard versus stubble, or a length of garden hose versus only a short piece. Therefore, a larger frame is more flexible than a shorter frame of the same model. A tall rider may find his size in a particular frame too flexible, whereas a short rider may find the same model in his size too stiff. Likewise, frames with longer chainstays, such as those usually found on touring and mountain bikes, are less stiff than frames with the short chainstays typical of racing bikes. Stiffness depends also on the thickness of the tubing wall. We would therefore expect that frames with heavier gauge tubing will be stiffer. For example, Columbus SP tubing is stiffer (and heavier) than the thinner gauge SL, and is often used in place of SL in larger size frames. Likewise, the internal ribs of SLX tubing make it a little stiffer (and a little heavier) than SL. For the same reason, a straight gauge frame is stiffer (and heavier) than one with butted tubes. Increasing the diameter of the tube also makes it stiffer, even if the wall thickness is reduced to keep the mass constant. Aluminum bicycle frames provide ready examples: the "standard" diameter tubes of the compliant Vitus, the somewhat wider and moderately stiff tubes of the various aluminum Treks, and the "oversize" tubes of the very rigid Klein, to name a few. A few steel frames are now also made with tubes the diameter of which has either been increased overall or are flared at one end for increased stiffness. If the amount of material is kept constant, the diameter of a tube can only be increased so far before its walls become very thin, however. Engineers consider a 50:1 ratio between diameter and wall thickness to be about the limit before a tube is in danger of crumpling.

The material of which the tube is made also affects stiffness. For example, aluminum is only about one-third as rigid as steel, as indicated by its Young's modulus, a measure of a material's resistance to bending or stretching. To achieve similar rigidity, an aluminum tube needs about three times the wall thickness of a steel tube of the same diameter. Because aluminum is only about one-third as dense as steel, however, the weight comes out about even. For more on properties of metals, see the table and discussion in Chapter 12.

In addition to the tubes themselves, frame designs affect rigidity. While most bicycles have a standard diamond frame design, one occasionally sees variations. "Ladies'" frames without a top tube are notorious for being overly compliant. Other frame designs may also permit a short seat tube without sacrificing the strength of the triangulated diamond frame. Frames designed for extra rigidity, such as some tandems plus a few single frames built for sprinters, have stiffening stays in addition to a top tube. In some frames, the seatstays cross the seat tube and attach to the top tube for the same reason. But additional stiffness is not always the goal of either the designer or the rider. For example, Hetchins frames (which were made by one of the many English custom builders) often came with unique "curly" stays for an extra comfortable ride.

A thoughtful frame designer can juggle these various elements to produce a frame with almost any desired characteristics; a steel frame does not have to be rigid, nor an aluminum frame flexible, for instance. In addition, the use of non-metallic frame materials has opened up new avenues. Whereas a cylindrical tube has the same stiffness in both the vertical and lateral directions, composite frames can be molded into untraditional shapes and made with distinctly different properties in different directions: vertically soft and compliant while laterally stiff and resistant to torque, for instance.

Like everything else, prevailing frame stiffness has waxed and waned with fashion. At one time, the trend was to super-light frames, even if it meant a lot of flexibility: very thin-gauged steels and aluminum tubes of about the same diameter. Then increased stiffness came into vogue, with reinforced or large-diameter tubes and mountain bikes designed to withstand battles with rocks and logs. More recently, relatively compliant titanium frames have become increasingly popular.

When a rider applies force to one of the pedals, he flexes the frame. The bottom bracket tilts, the bottom of the seat tube moves sideways, the down tube twists, the chainstays skew, and all these tubes tug at their neighbors. While most of the time the effect is imperceptible, a heavy, powerful rider can cause the frame to flex noticeably. The chain, for instance, may rub on the front derailleur on alternate downstrokes. Flection (this uncommon word is the noun form of the verb "flex") may cause a taut derailleur cable to tug at the shift lever, making the bike shift all by itself. Flection may also cause a poorly glued joint to creak, or it may cause a frame tube to crack, especially if the tube had been overheated and weakened during assembly. It would be nice to be able to quantify such flection. Unfortunately, the complexities of the forces and the structure of the bicycle put the necessary mathematics well outside the scope of this book.

Stiffness is of course only one of many aspects to consider when comparing bicycle frames, but generally speaking, large or powerful riders, especially sprinters and racers who mostly climb out of the saddle, will lean toward stiff frames to minimize such potential problems. Cyclists who live in areas blessed with smoothly paved road surfaces or who favor relatively short rides may also find stiff frames to their liking.

Spending energy to flex the frame rather than make the bike go forward is obviously wasteful. All frames are resilient to some extent: push gently sideways at the bottom bracket and they spring back as soon as you withdraw your foot. Frames of certain materials (particularly the better butted steel alloys and titanium) are regarded as being especially resilient. Some riders believe that most of the energy spent making such frames flex is not lost, but merely stored and subsequently imparted to the pedaling effort during the rebound, just as a trampoline alternately stores energy and releases it for a higher jump. While this is an attractive notion, it is of course very difficult to verify. Anyone worried about energy losses is advised to seek a stiff frame.

Those who favor the rebound theory, or who do not make a frame flex badly, ought to be quite happy with a more comfortable, compliant frame. These include lightweight riders, those who prefer spinning rather than hammering on the pedals, and those who favor steady effort rather than sprinting, such as time trialists. Cyclists who spend a lot of time on the saddle — stage racers, ultra-marathon cyclists, randonneurs, century riders, and tourists — ought to appreciate the comfort benefits of relatively compliant frames.

We already know that a short wheelbase makes a bike more rigid and therefore less comfortable. (See the discussion of stiffness above.) A short wheelbase also accentuates shock transmitted from irregularities in the road to the rider: the angle at which the bike tilts when running over a given bump is very nearly proportional to the wheelbase. The momentary tilt temporarily displaces the handlebars and saddle, the very places where a rider is apt to notice bumps.

Tall riders may notice bumps even more, because their higher bars and saddle will be displaced farther. (Note that this is not an argument for a smaller frame; it is the saddle height, not the frame size, which matters. Nor of course is it an argument for positioning the saddle too low for the rider.) With bicycles traveling at the same speed over the same bump, the displacements happen in the same amount of time, which means that saddle velocity and acceleration are greater on the taller bike. A rider needing a tall frame also usually weighs more than a rider on a small frame. Consequently, the force felt by a tall rider because of a given bump will potentially be greater. Though the longer, more flexible tubes of a tall frame will partly compensate (unless the frame builder uses thicker, stiffer tubing), a tall rider may also want longer chainstays, more relaxed frame angles, wider tires with lower pressure, or other devices to help absorb shock. This is yet another example of how cycling favors small riders. A compact rider may remain blissfully unaware that his road bike is less comfortable than a longer bike.

A mountain biker may need a short wheelbase to help avoid obstacles and negotiate hairpin turns on trails. Ironically, though, few mountain bikes have short wheelbases, a situation that may change as advances in mechanical suspension take the place of relaxed frame geometry, generous fork rake, and long stays. Road racers, particularly criterium specialists, favor a tight geometry for instantaneous response in the close confines of a pack or in a sprint, but time trialists and recreational riders, even high-performance ones, may find that the drawbacks of a short wheelbase outweigh the advantages. See Chapter 9 for more about the effects of wheelbase.

Because this chapter is nominally about rolling resistance, it is only fair to state that any differences in rolling resistance due to frame stiffness are probably negligible; at least, they are very small compared to the contribution by the tires and road surface.

Tire Rolling Resistance

As a wheel rolls, it changes shape. Like the frame, the structural part of a wheel, consisting of the rim, spokes, and hub, changes shape only slightly. Its contribution to rolling resistance is practically negligible. However, the tire changes shape greatly. The portion of its tread that contacts the ground distorts to conform to the surface, providing the grip needed for acceleration, braking, and cornering. The sidewalls flex, especially near that contact area. Pressing against the inner tube (if the tire is a clincher), the sidewalls force the tube to flex more or less in the same way. The local decrease in volume pumps internal air toward the newly expanding portion of the tire.

All these motions, though necessary, do nothing to propel the bicycle in a straight line. Quite the opposite: as surfaces slide and molecules collide against each other, they produce heat, which is lost to the surrounding air. The heat represents energy that might have gone into making the bicycle go faster, but did not. Though it is natural for the bicyclist to want to minimize this energy waste, it should be apparent that, given the above sources, doing so will be difficult or impossible. We will consider the sources of tire rolling resistance one at a time.

Large-diameter wheels roll more easily than small-diameter ones. Have you ever seen farm machinery, earth-moving equipment, horse-drawn carriages, or Conestoga wagons using small wheels? Of course not; small wheels bog down easily in soft ground, and rolling resistance is critically important in low-speed, low-power applications on poor surfaces. Though gears and chain drive eventually rendered the large wheels on early bicycles unnecessary, it took smoothly paved roads to lower rolling resistance enough for the relatively small wheels of the "safety" bicycle to become the standard.

For a given load, wheel rolling resistance is approximately in inverse proportion to radius; that is, a wheel half the size has about double the rolling resistance. Of course, most bicycles built for adults have wheels of nearly the same size, 26 to 27 inches, but there are exceptions. Bicycles designed to disassemble easily for transport often use two small wheels; recumbents and bicycles built for small adults often use at least one small wheel. The fact that these exceptions are not significantly slower than bicycles with full-size wheels shows that on a smoothly paved surface, aerodynamic drag masks all but the most radical variations in rolling resistance.

Off-road, at lower speeds, rolling resistance takes on far greater importance, which makes one wonder why mountain bikes have merely 26-inch wheels. The reasons, of course, are the practical considerations of frame clearance, maneuverability on tightly twisting trails, weight, and (given that falls are common) the distance from the rider to the ground. Tests on agricultural vehicles found that on soft ground, a 35% increase in wheel diameter decreased rolling resistance 20% (a number that probably includes other sources of resistance besides the tire-to-ground contact), while a 35% decrease in tire width decreased rolling resistance only 10%. Cyclists have been quick to adopt narrow tires when surfaces permit, but changing wheel diameter is of course less practical. Still, the potential performance advantage is enticing. Ground conditions fluctuate greatly, but suppose that with 26-inch wheels the coefficient of rolling resistance on a particular unpaved course is a steady 0.03, and that the course consists of four half mile segments: level, 6% grade up, level, and 6% grade down. Imagine a rider similar in size and weight to our standard rider, but in a more

upright mountain biking position. He applies 300 watts of power. On the level, he would move forward at 7.35 m/s; up the 6% grade, 3.62 m/s; and down, 13.54 m/s. If he could somehow switch to 35-inch wheels with a C_R of 0.024, his speeds would increase 4 to 8%, and (ignoring accelerations and decelerations) he would finish a lap over half a minute ahead. The worse the ground surfaces, the greater the role wheel rolling resistance plays in determining speed. For off-road competition in events under which conditions permit, the potential advantage of larger wheels will surely result in future innovative bicycle designs.

To minimize distortion against the road surface, the tire tread needs to be hard. Because a hard rubber compound offers a lower coefficient of friction with a paved surface, tire engineers must trade off low rolling resistance against high cornering grip. In automobile applications, hard rubber compounds are used wherever extended wear is more valuable than ultimate adhesion — namely, on almost all passenger cars and trucks. Most bicycle tires are made of a similar hard compound for the same reason. For those seeking low rolling resistance, long wear is a fringe benefit. There is some variation between models and brands, which should be detectable by feel before purchase; a few models even use a hard compound for the center of the tread and a softer compound on either side. Although bicycles spend relatively little time leaning over and cornering, cyclists that do a lot of high speed cornering may be willing to sacrifice a little tread hardness.

Also to minimize tread distortion, the tire tread needs to be smooth and solid, or nearly so. Knobs, grooves, and ridges weaken the tread structure, allowing it to squirm in contact with the road. In addition, riding a knobby tire on a smoothly paved surface is like having to climb thousands of tiny hills — it uses extra energy. Many tires are now available with a smooth tread (often called "bald" or "slick"), ideal for low rolling resistance. In an automobile tire, a slick tread reduces rolling resistance by as much as 20%. Though slicks are illegal for cars on public roads, there is fortunately no such restriction for bicycles.

On a paved surface, the only drawback of slicks is possible hydroplaning during wet weather, when water can be trapped between the tire and road. Tread grooves can help the water escape and thus restore grip, but most bicycle tires are narrow enough, and most roads rough and porous enough, that hydroplaning is rarely a problem for bicycles even with slick tread. Cyclists who need to ride often on wet smoothly sealed paved surfaces may feel better about choosing a grooved tread pattern, but the rest of us ought to be quite happy with slicks. By the same token, however, there is little value in choosing a slick tread if all the road surfaces are rough. Fine diamond or herringbone patterns, for example, are probably no rougher than the surface of most good roads, and should not distort appreciably more than a slick tread; but neither would they provide appreciably more grip in the wet.

Layers inside the tire contribute to frictional losses. These include the tube in a clincher tire, the accessory liners some cyclists use to help prevent punctures, and the internal belts certain tire models use for the same reason. The tradeoffs to these are obvious.

To minimize sidewall flection, the tire carcass might be made stiff, or the entire tire might be solid rather than air-filled. However, as you may recall, solid rubber tires were abandoned long ago, shortly after Dunlop invented the pneumatic tire. Bicyclists easily did without the extra mass and the shock that solid tires transmitted. The air in a pneumatic tire acts as a nearly perfect spring; attempting to substitute another material, such as more rubber, is practically guaranteed to increase rather than decrease frictional losses. Thinner tire and tube walls, though risky in the face of road hazards, ought to be one way to improve both rolling resistance and mass. Look for future improvements in this area as materials continue to be refined. Despite all this, it is still possible to envision a specially designed wheel and ultra-thin solid tire, perhaps about the diameter of a pencil, for record attempts on very smooth tracks where cornering is unnecessary and rider comfort is not a consideration.

The other way to stiffen the tire is to add more air to increase its pressure. At very low pressures (say, under 30 psi), rolling resistance is high enough to be apparent to a person walking beside the bike and pushing it along. Ever-higher pressures continue to reduce rolling resistance, though at least with a single rider and an unloaded bike, it is nearly impossible to detect improvements to rolling resistance once tire pressures go beyond 90 psi or so. Part of the reason is that there is little difference in the amount of tire distortion at pressures in the 90- to 120-psi range. Another part of the reason is that beyond a certain pressure, tire rolling resistance is masked by other sources of resistance, such as that of the freewheel, the chain, and the road itself.

A value of about 0.003 is often quoted for the coefficient of rolling resistance of a single bike with tubular tires inflated to about 105 psi and (though the sources don't say it explicitly) rolling on a very smooth road surface. The same sources quote figures of 0.004 to 0.0045 for a recreational or sport-touring bike with 90-psi tires and 0.006 to 0.008 for a typical European utility commuting bike with 40-psi tires. Let us suppose that the differences are due mainly to load and tire inflation pressures rather than, say, differing tread patterns, road surfaces, drivetrain lubrication, or state of repair. We can express the load and pressure as one number, the tire contact patch area (see Chapter 8) and plot that area vs. the coefficient of rolling

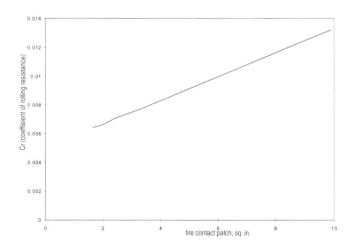

Fig. 1002. Possible relationship between tire contact patch area and rolling resistance.

resistance. Figure 1002, which does this, suggests an approximately linear relationship between C_R and the tire contact patch area. However, the figures sometimes quoted for tandems (0.0045 with 90-psi tires) and for certain other bicycles — such as relatively heavy, streamlined, recumbent human-powered vehicles and machines designed for high-speed motor-paced record attempts — do not fit this curve well. Nor does the curve begin to flatten out at very low C_R values, as it eventually must when non-tire sources of rolling resistance begin to dominate. The figure may suggest a simpler relationship than is actually the case, and the data upon which it is based may reflect the difficulty of making accurate C_R measurements.

Whitt and Wilson (*Bicycling Science*) suggest a speed-dependent formula for the coefficient of rolling resistance of a 27-inch tire:

$$C_R = 0.005 + (0.15 + 0.35 \, (v/100)^2) / p$$

where v is speed in miles per hour, p is inflation pressure in pounds per square inch, and the constants inside the parentheses depend on these units. Despite a definition that restricts the term rolling resistance to the interaction between tire and road (surface unspecified), their formula is very pessimistic compared to estimates in other sources. If we suppose it to be accurate, however, and plug the resulting C_R into our speed-power equations, we can estimate the effect tire pressure would have upon speed. With enough power to do a flat, windless 10-mile time trial at a constant speed in the range of 20 to 25 miles per hour, our standard rider should be able to knock 5 or 6 seconds off his time merely by increasing his tire pressures from 100 to 120 psi, according to this formula. These savings are great enough to make pumping the tires up worth a try even if the formula turns out to exaggerate the effect pressure has on rolling resistance.

What about the inflation pressure number usually printed on the sidewall of a tire? What does it have to do with rolling resistance? In a word, nothing. The number is only a guideline based loosely on the pressure that is likely to blow the tire off the rim. Many tires, if mounted on compatible hook-bead rims, will withstand twice the printed pressure before blowing off. There is no reason why a tire rated at 110 psi cannot be operated at 90 psi, or vice-versa. As a practical matter, however, it is likely that only on a smooth velodrome might one be able to benefit from the extra-low rolling resistance of tire pressures much above 100 psi.

Heat During Inflation

As a tire is inflated, its internal air pressure of course increases. Once the tube has expanded fully against the inside of the tire carcass, the volume of that air stays practically constant. By the general gas law relating pressure, temperature, and volume, as the pressure continues to increase, the air temperature rises. When you inflate a tire fully after repairing a flat, you may notice that the valve stem gets quite hot. The air in the rest of the tire is hot, too, but the metal stem conducts heat to your fingers much better than the rubber tube and sidewalls do. Gradually, however, the tire and stem conduct the excess heat inside the tire to the surrounding air, and the temperature inside the tire drops, eventually matching the ambient air temperature. As that happens, the inflation pressure decreases.

For example, suppose a tire has been rapidly inflated to 100 psi and the internal air temperature at that time is 149° F. When the internal temperature drops to the ambient air temperature, say 77° F, what is the pressure remaining within the tire? The general gas law says:

$$(p_1 \, v_1) / T_1 = (p_2 \, v_2) / T_2$$

where p is pressure, V is volume, and T is absolute temperature in Kelvin. Volume here is the same both before and after the temperate drops. The temperature in degrees Celsius is initially 149 minus 32 times 5/9, or 65 C; to convert to the Kelvin scale, add 273, giving 338 K. Afterwards it is (77–32) x 5/9 + 273 or 298 K. Therefore the new pressure is (298/338) x 100, or just 88 psi, a significant drop.

After rapidly inflating a tire (as opposed to just giving it a few pump strokes to "top it off" or bring its pressure up a few pounds), and especially if the tire is narrow and pressure is relatively critical, it is a good idea to recheck the pressure after a few minutes. It is also a good idea to check the built-in gauge on a floor pump against a reliable hand-held gauge occasionally. Underinflated tires increase rolling resistance. Time spent repairing pinch flats made possible by underinflation robs performance even more.

For a similar reason, some cyclists partially deflate the tires of a bicycle they must keep inside a car parked in the sun on a hot day, because internal temperatures can skyrocket under those conditions. Sound tires and tubes can almost always handle the additional pressure without a blowout, but any slow leaks become faster leaks, and the combination of heat and high pressure can be too much for some patches.

You may have heard that well-heeled automobile racing teams sometimes inflate their tires with gases other than air. Would another gas pay dividends for bicycle tires, too? Sorry, but it is very doubtful. The purpose of the auto racing tire application is to reduce operating temperature. (Nitrogen-filled tires run a little cooler than air-filled ones.) But bicycle tires slide very little and therefore operate at much lower temperatures. About the only potential benefit for bicycles would be reduced mass. Figuring that if low mass is the goal, a 700C x 25 tire is about the largest size one would use, and that a 700C x 25 holds a little less than a liter of air (see Appendix B), Table 1001 gives the mass difference per tire (compared to air) for three common gases.

Even if one could figure out how to fill the tire with helium and keep it from leaking out for the

Table 1001. Mass compared to air, 0.944 l, 25° C, 100 psi

gas	difference, grams
carbon dioxide	+4 (that is, 4 grams heavier)
nitrogen	−0.25
helium	−6.6

duration of the event, the mass savings would be minuscule. And anyone who may have been thinking that filling his tires with helium would buoy him up hills is in for a disappointment. Half an ounce of lift won't get him very far. Perhaps even more disappointed will be the minimum weight fanatics who now realize that the carbon dioxide they have been obtaining from pressurized cartridges is so heavy.

Determining Minimum Adequate Tire Pressure

Harking back to the section on cornering, you will recall that tire pressure has little effect on lateral grip. But low tire pressure does increase susceptibility to pinch flats. The discussion of contact patch and load suggests a method for determining minimum adequate tire pressure.

Deflate a tire enough so that it can be easily compressed by hand. Dip it in water, then press the wet tire down onto a piece of paper — finely ruled graph paper held in place by a paperweight or two would be ideal. Press firmly enough to flatten the tire as far as you would want it to compress during extreme conditions on an actual ride; that is, a realistic flattening, but well short of bottoming out on the rim. (Notice that tire width definitely does make a difference here. Narrow tires have relatively little margin before bottoming out.) Lift the tire cleanly off the paper and measure the area of the wet (and probably dirty) impression. Graph paper makes this easy — just count wet squares and multiply by the area of a square; otherwise, outline the area and divide it into figures such as rectangles and triangles the areas of which are easy to estimate. Now figure the loading. The sum of your weight plus the bike's, times 65%, should be close to the minimum loading on the rear wheel on very smooth, level roads. Under braking on a steep downhill, though, the front tire carries more weight than the rear one ever does, and that's not even considering bumps in the road (see below). Here a factor of 100% times the total weight may be more realistic. (See the discussion of rear wheel lift in

Chapter 7 for more about weight distribution and normal force at the wheels.)

Divide weight in pounds by area in square inches to get pressure in pounds per square inch. Suppose for example that our standard rider goes through this exercise. The tire contact patch he measures is 2.1 square inches, and he and his bike weigh 198 pounds. Maximum expected load is 198 divided by 2.1, which is 94 psi, the minimum recommended pressure for that rider and those tires. He may be able to nurse the bike home on a smooth road with just 65% of that in the rear tire — 61 psi — and even less in the front. The number obtained is of course only an approximate minimum, and says nothing about what pressure is desirable to keep rolling resistance low.

What about those bumps in the road? How do they affect the recommendation? They increase it, of course. A bump imparts a vertical component of velocity to the bike, proportional to the speed of the bike, adding a vertical acceleration to what gravity already supplies. Real bumps are extremely variable in size and shape, making it impossible to characterize the amount of vertical acceleration. However, just as a simplified introduction, suppose that the bumps that concern us have a semicircular cross section. Figure 1003 shows an idealized, inflexible bicycle tire of radius

R that has started to climb over a bump of radius r. The wheel has been lifted a height h and its center trails the bump center by a distance d. From the geometry, one can see that:

$$d^2 + (R + h)^2 = (R + r)^2$$

When h is zero, the value of d is at its maximum: the distance at which the tire first contacts the bump. Naturally, the bigger the bump, the bigger the value of d, that is, the sooner the wheel comes in contact. Perhaps not as immediately obvious, the larger the wheel diameter, the sooner the contact also; this implies that it takes a large wheel a longer horizontal distance to roll over a bump of a given size. This in turn means that the larger the wheel, the lower the vertical acceleration from a given bump at a given speed. For a semicircular bump of radius 1 cm, Table 1002 gives the distance between first contacting the bump and rolling over its center (i.e. half the total contact distance), and at 2 meters per second (4.5 mph) the average vertical acceleration during the first thousandth of a second of contact, for four different wheel diameters. Acceleration is given in g's: 1 g is the acceleration due to gravity, 9.8 m/s^2. Acceleration is proportional to speed, but as you can see, the acceleration numbers for even this modest bump at low speed are alarmingly high.

But the spring characteristics of the bicycle (the tires, the fork, the rear triangle, the rider) affect how much mass is accelerated, and thus how much force is borne by the air pressure in the tires. If the bicyclist spots the bump early, and gently eases over it extremely slowly, vertical

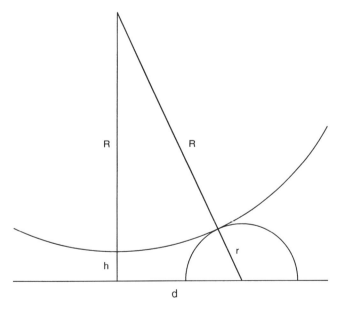

Fig. 1003. Geometry of an idealized, inflexible tire climbing over an idealized bump.

Table 1002. Encountering a 1-cm semicircular bump at 2 m/s

Wheel size (in)	Distance from first contact to bump center (m)	Avg. vertical acceleration during 1/1000 s (g's)
27	.0834	49
26	.0819	50
24	.0787	52
17	.0665	62

acceleration is negligible, the tires and fork hardly flex, and the entire mass of the bicycle and rider is lifted up and over the bump. At very high speed, the reaction is different. The bump deforms the tire and is gone in a flash, merely vibrating the fork and rider; there is no significant lift. At intermediate speeds, the fork and rider may be affected more, the tire less. These complexities, plus the variation in bumps already mentioned, prevent calculation of the increased force borne by a tire during a bump, and thus the corresponding safe minimum inflation pressure. The general recommendation for narrow tires is to avoid large or sharp bumps, run over unavoidable bumps slowly, keep tire pressures up, and remember that small wheels are particularly susceptible.

Rolling Resistance and Ground Surfaces

The surface upon which the tire is rolling makes at least as great a difference to rolling resistance as the tire itself does. In fact, the relationships between resistance, wheel diameter, and inflation pressure discussed above should only be expected to apply when the tire is the dominant contributor to rolling resistance — that is, on a hard, smooth surface. Normally the rider has little choice but to travel the same roads or trails as his competitors or companions. Nevertheless, he can minimize rolling resistance by carefully tailoring his path. Naturally, he should try to stick to a smooth, firm paved surface, avoiding rough, crumbling, sandy, and muddy patches if possible. However, any steering corrections he makes must be begun well ahead, otherwise he will lose a great deal of speed and stability by swerving.

In contrast to the ultra-smooth velodromes where bicycle performance is often evaluated, off-road the coefficient of rolling resistance is much higher. It also fluctuates wildly as the surface changes from gravel to packed dirt, mud, grass, slickrock, and sand, and as each stone becomes a miniature alp to be climbed and descended. For automobile tires, rolling resistance on rolled gravel is roughly 1.5 times that on asphalt; on

loose sand, rolling resistance is roughly 10 to 20 times that on asphalt. Narrow bicycle tires that sink into soft surfaces may be affected even more severely. Deep sand, mud, or water can bring the bike to an abrupt halt while the rider keeps going — the ultimate in performance-robbing rolling resistance.

Tire rolling resistance is one of the off-road biker's main worries, but possibly even more important to him is traction. For that he needs tires with lugs and knobs that can bite into soft surfaces. Manufacturers market an incredible variety of tread designs, each purported to be good for certain specific conditions, just as there are hundreds of automobile tire tread patterns. While advertising hype undoubtedly plays a part in this variety, the predominant size of the rocks and other irregularities encountered probably should bear some vague relationship to the sizes of the chunks of tread and the spaces between them, if not for traction then to prevent excessive stones and mud from clinging to the tire. The best tread design for a particular course is very much a trial-and-error area for the rider to study. So is inflation pressure, beyond the general principle of low pressures (and wide tires) for soft surfaces and higher pressures (and possibly narrower tires) for harder surfaces. (When the surface is soft, it is the dominant source of rolling resistance. Tire pressure then can hardly affect rolling resistance, leaving the rider free to change pressure to improve traction.) Perhaps at least as important are the corners and edges of the tire tread blocks. Experienced mountain bike racers find that they cannot be competitive unless they have fresh tires that retain sharp edges on their lugs. This fact points the way to future tire designs utilizing studs or harder tread materials. Of course, recreational riders who use their mountain bikes mainly on roads and smooth, hard-packed trails will benefit from relatively high pressures, narrow widths, and predominantly smooth treads, just as road cyclists do.

Rough Surfaces and Vibration

We discussed fork oscillation in Chaper 9. The behavior of the bicycle on rough surfaces is related. Roads are never perfectly smooth, but the characteristics of their irregularities vary a great deal, both in amplitude (height and depth) and in wavelength (distance between successive peaks or valleys). All irregular surfaces increase rolling resistance, but not equally. In addition to the obvious differences due to amplitude, usually a bicycle will take the long-wavelength irregularities in stride but will be slowed drastically by short-wavelength washboard surfaces. The reason has to do with the natural vibrational frequency of the unsprung mass of the bicycle, relative to the frequency the surface transmits to the bicycle. If we view the fork as a spring, the rider and the remainder of the bicycle frame are "sprung" mass: they (or at least their forward portions) are supported by the spring. The front wheel, however, is "unsprung." At the rear of the frame, the stays are the spring, and the rear wheel is the unsprung mass.

The natural frequency of vibration of the unsprung mass depends on the amount of that mass and on the spring constant:

$$F_w = (k / m)^{1/2} / 2\pi$$

where k is the spring force constant and m is the mass. This is merely the inverse of the period formula we saw in Chapter 9. Our hypothetical fork in that chapter had a vertical spring constant of 160,000 N/m; with a front wheel whose mass is 1.3 kg, the natural frequency of the wheel would be 56 Hertz. Because the rear triangle is normally much stiffer, even though the rear wheel is heavier than the front, it would have a higher natural frequency. (A word about units is in order. A newton is a kilogram-meter per second squared, that is, kg m / s^2; a newton per meter is therefore kg / s^2. Dividing by mass in kg and taking the square root gives 1 / s, inverse seconds, usually expressed as cycles per second or Hertz, abbreviated Hz. With other units, the formula needs an additional conversion factor.)

The forced frequency of vibration the road surface imposes is:

$$f_f = v / s$$

where v is the speed of the bicycle and s is the wavelength of the roughness. Examples of rough paved surface unfortunately common in the author's state include the concrete slab roadway interrupted every several feet by a seam; the asphalt highway that has buckled by frost heaves or become furrowed by braking truck traffic; potholes and the slapdash asphalt patches that pass for repair; and the secondary road cheaply "oiled" or "tarred and chipped," often making the road rougher than it was prior to repaving. Off-road, the variety of roughness is even greater. With the possible exception of such artificially constructed roughness as speed bumps, rumble strips, and cattle grates, the wavelengths of all these surfaces vary continuously across the spectrum, but in many surfaces a relatively narrow range of wavelengths dominate. Wavelengths of 0.2 to 2 meters may be common on a smooth, paved or hard-packed dirt road, for instance, while a gravel or tarred-and-chipped road may be characterized by wavelengths of 0.1 meter or less. At a leisurely speed of 5 m/s (11.2 mph), the dominant forced vibration frequency ranges would then be 2.5–25 Hz and 50 Hz or greater, respectively.

Mechanical engineers tell us that in order to keep energy losses small, the ratio of the natural frequency of the unsprung mass to the forced frequency of vibration (F_w/f_f) should be high. The picture we should have in mind is of the bicycle frame and rider moving in a straight line, isolated from vibration by the springs (fork and rear triangle) and therefore unruffled by any road imperfections, while the wheels vibrate up and down, busily following each nook and cranny of the surface. Clearly this picture is reasonably accurate only if the wheels are light and the springs are firm enough to keep the wheels planted on the road — that is, if the ratio of frequencies is indeed high. If the numbers above are realistic, then the rather flexible fork we cited above should drain relatively little energy on a smooth road, because the ratio is

56/2.5, and even 56/25 may be considered high. Double the speed to something closer to race conditions, however, and forced frequencies double. The shorter wavelengths of roughness then begin to give the fork trouble. Worse yet, a short-wavelength gravel or chipped road would seemingly sap a lot of energy regardless of the speed.

This example is unsatisfying. In fact, the entire ratio principle is simplistic for a number of reasons. For one thing, the fork vibrates not only vertically but in other directions, most of which have a lower spring constant. The tire is another spring, one with both a much lower spring constant (from its easily compressed air) and even lower unsprung mass (the material at the contact patch); it absorbs some frequencies and passes others on to the suspension. The fork and frame spring constants cannot arbitrarily be increased; the ride would become unacceptably harsh, and the tires would skip over the low spots and shirk their roadholding duties. At some point a spring becomes so stiff that it ceases to act as a suspension but turns itself and its load into unsprung mass instead. Rider mass and weight distribution play a part, because the rider also absorbs vibration, and therefore some of his own energy output. The formulas cope with neither the amplitude of the roughness nor the myriad wavelengths and frequencies present, nor do they attempt to quantify the amount of energy loss. We don't even know what a "high" ratio means.

We are better off putting aside our quibbles and concentrating on the underlying principles. To minimize energy losses at high speeds, we need to minimize unsprung mass and/or use stiff springs. Keep in mind that the principle is concerned only with energy losses, not comfort, durability, traction, or any other practical consideration. Applying the principle foremost to the wheels, it implies relatively lightweight wheels and relatively steep frame angles, such as a traditional road racing bike, or at least relatively stiff fork and stay tubing. Applying the principle to the tires themselves, it implies thin, narrow tires and high pressures, again like those of a traditional road bike. We can also apply the principle to the rider-bicycle combination. If we view the rider as the vehicle chassis and the entire bicycle as the unsprung mass, it implies a lightweight bike and a suspension holding the rider's body off the bike so that it does not add to the unsprung mass. This suspension could be the rider's arms and legs, tensed enough to support the rider but not so rigid that the rider and bicycle become a solid unit; or perhaps the suspension could be an additional mechanism, such as springs in the stem and saddle or seatpost. Most riders lift themselves off the saddle to traverse bumps, but few have considered that the technique may also lower rolling resistance.

Alignment

If a wheel is displaced to one side of the bicycle center line or is not parallel to the direction of travel, its off-center drag causes a moment (like a lever arm), which must be countered by steering, much as momentary imbalances are also corrected by steering as the cyclist rides. While such corrections are small and the effect on rolling resistance almost impossible to estimate, it makes sense to minimize them, to keep as much of the applied power as possible propelling the bike forward rather than sideways. Well-made frames and wheels should not require additional alignment or centering, but it does not hurt to check before purchase. It is common to see a rear wheel inadvertently twisted so that it does not line up with the seat tube; fortunately, it is usually easy to correct this condition by adjusting the axle in the dropouts.

11

Minimizing Aerodynamic Drag

Aerodynamic drag is usually the greatest force the bicyclist faces. The reason is simple. Aerodynamic drag itself is proportional to the square of airspeed; the power needed to overcome aerodynamic drag is proportional to the cube of airspeed. Doubling your speed in still air, say from 10 to 20 mph, takes not twice as much power, but *eight* times as much. As you ride through still air at 20 mph, suppose you turn a corner and meet a gentle 5.2-mph headwind. Wham! You have to double your power output in order to maintain your speed! On a paved surface at all but the most leisurely bicycling speeds, aerodynamic forces dwarf rolling resistance; on everything except steep inclines, aerodynamic forces exceed even the effect of gravity.

Aerodynamic Drag and Stem Height

Because different bicycles and different people all have basically the same shapes, the most important of the aerodynamic drag factors is frontal area. The ideal is a low profile, with the back nearly level and flat, to keep frontal area to a minimum. (As a bonus, this posture also reduces the drag coefficient, C_D.) It can be achieved with hands on the drops and elbows bent, or with arms on aero bars — but only if the bicycle fits the rider adequately and is then specifically set up to allow a low profile. Assuming the combined top tube length and stem extension are sufficiently long for the rider, the stem height determines how low a profile is possible. The usual general-purpose recommendation is to set the stem height so that the top of the handlebar is an inch or two below the level of the saddle. However, a touring or recreational rider, especially a female one, may find the result uncomfortably low even for riding in the typical straight-armed touring position. Such a rider may prefer to set the stem about even with the saddle height, at least at first.

Any cyclist interested in reducing drag, however, will find it advantageous to become accustomed to a lower position, bending the elbows, using the drops periodically, and gradually lowering the stem over a span of months or even years. On the other hand, a time trialist may find that he is robbing himself of speed in the usually recommended position, even with well-bent arms and deep-drop handlebars. He may need to lower the stem still farther, and spend a period of time becoming, if not perfectly comfortable, then at least accustomed to the position and able to tolerate it for the duration of an event. (It is possible to adopt such a low position that adequate vision, safe steering and braking, unencumbered pedaling, and the ability to straighten up after the event may no longer be possible. That's going too far.)

For a simple illustration of the benefits of the improved aerodynamics, consider our standard rider, not in his usual crouched position, but instead riding in a typical touring position with hands atop the bars and straight arms. Now his frontal area is about 0.40 square meters and his coefficient of aerodynamic drag is about 1.0. With 150 watts output (about 0.2 hp), he could do a flat 10-mile time trial in still air at about 8.11 m/s, for a time of about 33:04 in that position. By adopting the optimum crouch, however, with suitable stem height and bent arms, he reduces his frontal area to about 0.36 square meters and his C_D to 0.88. With the identical power output, his speed increases to 8.73 m/s, lopping 2:20 off his 10-mile time trial, a huge improvement achieved with zero expenditure on equipment and no additional fitness. No equipment upgrade, regardless of cost, can make such a dramatic difference. Only with a lengthy, intensive physical conditioning program

could one hope to approach this level of performance improvement. Becoming accustomed to that ideally crouched posture is no easy task, but once accomplished, the bicyclist can attend to the details, which mostly have to do with improving the drag coefficient, C_D.

Before leaving the topic of stem height, however, we should note that not all stems, and not all bicycle frames, are equally amenable to adjustment. To avoid failure or frame damage, at least a certain minimum length (height) of stem must be inserted into the frame, that is, into the steering tube, an internal tube attached to the fork crown and supported by the headset. A high handlebar position or a relatively small frame may call for more exposed stem length than is safe, minding the minimum insertion mark. A low handlebar position may leave a lot of excess stem length and mass buried inside the frame. Consequently, stems are not only adjustable but come in different lengths. Certain conditions make the choice of stem length critical. Small frames, with little steering tube length to work with, are very sensitive to length. If the rider determines that the stem should be raised or lowered, there may be too little length left inside or outside the frame. Instead of a simple adjustment, a new longer or shorter stem may be needed. Mountain-bike-style stems with right-angle or obtuse-angle bends, though potentially lighter because of the nearly direct route from frame to handlebar, cannot be lowered as far as road-style stems with acute-angle bends. If possible the rider should determine the optimum handlebar height with an old, inexpensive stem before investing in a new stem of the ideal length.

Aero Bars

Among new components, aero bars have enjoyed an unusually high adoption rate. The term "aero bars" refers to either an integral bar or a clip-on accessory to standard handlebars, either of which allows a low-profile position with the arms close together and forward. Unlike most aerodynamic components, aero bars do nothing for the aerodynamics of the bicycle, but instead help the rider attain a good aerodynamic posture. The posture achieved, if the bars are positioned correctly, is only slightly better than a standard crouch on the drops: a small reduction in frontal area due to moving the arms inward, and a small reduction in form drag due to the longer, pointier profile. Perhaps an even more important benefit is comfort: many riders find that they can tolerate a good aerodynamic posture for longer periods of time on aero bars than they can on the drops. With that posture unfortunately comes a sacrifice in control. Steering corrections are slower and less precise with outstretched arms; brake levers and shifters are usually not at hand. Most such devices are quite sensibly banned in mass-start events, which already have more than enough accidents. Even in a time trial or triathlon, a sensible rider will use the aero position with caution, reverting to the drops when more control is needed, such as when passing another rider closely, in bumpy conditions, in sharp turns, and during steep downhills; because aero bars are most effective on long, flat or slightly downhill stretches, being safe does not mean being slow.

Some aero bars leave little room for the hands on the tops of the bars for climbing, and all impose a weight penalty (compared to standard bars) of about a pound. In flat and gently rolling terrain, the aerodynamic benefit easily offsets the added weight. Most performance-oriented riders in such areas have already adopted them. Often even long-distance tourists do not object to passing more quickly through flatlands they have supposedly come to see. In hilly country, however, where nearly level, open stretches of road are rare, the aero posture can be used only a small fraction of the time. Many riders in those areas will feel that aero bars are not worth the trouble, and touring cyclists may feel that extra speed under those scenic conditions is counterproductive. Hills and scenery will not stop dedicated time trialists and triathletes from adopting aero bars, however. Cyclists who have a special fondness for high-speed descents may also want them, if they have some places where they can safely put aero bars to use — or are terminally foolhardy.

Less forward alternatives to the usual aero bars also exist. These bars, again either integral units or clip-ons, provide a narrower profile and may afford better control, enabling them to be used in mass-start events. In addition, their weight penalty may be lower, though their aerodynamic advantage is probably also reduced.

All aero bars, and standard drop handlebars for that matter, need careful attention to positioning to achieve a posture that is both aerodynamic and tolerably comfortable for long periods. In addition, riders using them need a long period of time to become accustomed to the posture, to fine tune the position, and to practice being able to control the bike under a variety of conditions. What about straight or upright bars found on mountain bikes, cross bikes, and utility bikes? It goes without saying that they, and most likely the bikes to which they are attached, were not designed with aerodynamics or high speed in mind. Surely anyone who has read this far will not need further prompting to replace them, and will not be taken in by add-on fittings.

Aerodynamic Drag and Clothing

The most common fabrics in use for bicycle clothing are smooth, slick synthetics, mostly for reasons of comfort, insulation, ventilation, absorption, wicking, appearance, and other properties unrelated to performance. The fact that they are slippery to the touch at least gives the impression that they also reduce aerodynamic drag to the minimum. Serious students of fluid dynamics realize that perfect smoothness is not necessarily the path to minimum drag. The skin of a porpoise is covered with tiny bumps; the surface of a golf ball, with tiny depressions. Fortunately for the bicyclist, he never has to ride immersed in water, and fortunately for his dependents, he never approaches the speed of a driven golf ball. A pimpled or dimpled fabric (sure to hit the cycling market any day now) is unlikely to make any significant reduction in drag; even the most competitive cyclists may wish to spend their money on something more effective. Until independently verified tests show otherwise, cyclists who wear cotton, wool, polypropylene or acrylic garments — fabrics that are generally not slick — need not lose much sleep over their imagined aerodynamic shortcomings.

To minimize drag, all garments must be snug against the body. Loose clothing is said to increase drag as much as 30%; that would amount to over two extra minutes in a 10-mile time trial. Clothing should also be reasonably free of wrinkles when the cyclist is in the crouched position on the bike. Some jerseys, in fact, are cut in such a way as to be comfortable only while riding, not standing. The most aerodynamic cycling wear also minimizes seams and borders, especially those perpendicular to the airflow. For example, a skin suit deliberately omits the boundary that is normally between the bottom of the cyclist's jersey and the top of his shorts, and may also extend the shorts into full-leg tights for the same reason.

It is ironic to see a racer with slick cycling wear, a smooth teardrop-shaped helmet, aero rims or a disk wheel … and a hastily pinned-on competitor number flapping in the wind, negating most of the aerodynamic savings. The smart rider will bring additional pins to the race and have a teammate or companion pin the number on so that it is secure and pulls taut against his body when he is in a crouch.

Drag, Helmets, and Hair

Though the primary function of a helmet is head protection in the event of a crash or fall, a helmet can also be an aerodynamic accessory. Some helmets were clearly designed to minimize drag, or at least to create the impression that they do. As with clothing, a smooth surface uninterrupted by openings and seams is the aerodynamic ideal, and some designs go further with a narrowed or pointed tail, giving the helmet a teardrop shape. In Europe, where traditional resistance to helmets is high, the fact that the most competitive riders use helmets in time trials and pursuits, even if they eschew them in mass start events, confirms that helmets are an essential element in achieving

the best aerodynamics. (Ironically, the protective function of a helmet is much more likely to be useful in a mass start event. No one said European cyclists were sensible or safety-conscious, merely competitive.)

Judged in terms of skin drag (surface friction with the air), most helmets are considerably better than a bare head of hair, or even a cloth-capped head. Their form drag still leaves something to be desired, though; certainly helmet designs will continue to make improvements in this area. Compared to a solid surface, ventilation openings, though obviously necessary, disrupt the smooth airflow. However, racing cars, which must also divert air for cooling, are able to do so successfully. Properly designed vents do not add excessive drag, and it has been demonstrated that the slightly higher air temperatures surrounding the head during helmet use do not affect rider power output. Look for ventilation innovations, perhaps utilizing internal fans, in the future. The transition between the bottom edge of the helmet and the side of the head is not always as smooth as it could be; on some helmets, the bottom is virtually a shelf. These helmets, and those with a pronounced tail, may require a level position for maximum performance; adjustment of the fore-aft tilt during fitting may be necessary, as well as attention to one's head position while riding. Finally, the frontal area of the helmeted head is necessarily larger than that of the head alone, another zone where future improvements in materials will undoubtedly help.

While these factors may be considerations in helmet selection, none of them should take priority over the protective function of the helmet, and especially not be an excuse to ride without one. Practically all domestic competitive events in the U.S., Canada, and Australia now require helmets. Most other organized bicycling events do, too. Intelligent riders recognize that it makes good sense not only to protect themselves, but to train using the same equipment they would use in competition. Helmets have managed to become dramatically lighter in weight while simultaneously exceeding previous protection standards. Although many bicycle innovations have been mere frills or fads, helmets have been a genuine success story.

Most racing cyclists already shave their legs, even if the purpose is mostly to facilitate massage, to intimidate competitors, or to please a girlfriend, but there is also a small aerodynamic benefit. For maximum streamlining, the cyclist would need to go even further. Picture a competition swimmer: no mustache or beard, in fact no hair at all that isn't covered by a cap. (Many bikers think looking "cool" is everything; any of them reading this paragraph have by now probably fainted.) Unless perhaps some popular cyclist shaves his head and promptly wins a major race, this particular extreme measure is unlikely to catch on. Granted, the drag reduction due to hairlessness would be slight, but surely greater than, say, the savings from that expensive aerodynamic seatpost.

Drag and Wheels

The usual bicycle wheel is an assemblage of several parts. The ones that are externally visible include the hub; the rim, upon which is mounted the tire; and the spokes, which together with their screw-on nipples hold everything together under tension. Because of its location, the hub makes no significant contribution to wind resistance. Rims are available in "aero" and "non-aero" varieties. The aero models are almost triangular in cross section, giving them (in comparison with non-aero models) extra stiffness and strength in addition to noticeably reduced drag, at the cost of significantly more mass and sensitivity to side winds. Riders who sprint regularly (in points races and criteriums, for example) or whose aerodynamic needs are mostly satisfied by drafting may prefer lower mass to lower drag. Serious climbers will feel the same way. Those who want the streamlining benefits and can tolerate the somewhat harsher ride and touchier handling should go for aero rims. (See Chapter 12 for more on this topic.)

With spokes there are many choices. First is their number, which of course must be compatible with the number of holes in both the hubs and rims. The top spokes of the wheel plough through the air at about double the bike's overall airspeed, more than offsetting the bottom ones, which are almost stationary. Heightened awareness of this principle figures among the reasons that 32-hole hubs and rims are now more common than the formerly standard 36-hole versions. There is always a tradeoff, however; in this case it is that having fewer spokes also means reduced reliability and increased maintenance. Given similar loads and road conditions, the wheel with fewer spokes is more susceptible to spokes loosening (hence the need for more frequent truing), to spoke breakage, and (in extreme cases) to wheel collapse. The usual recommendations are summarized in Table 1101. (The table assumes standard rims of 26 to 27 inch diameter, and may be slightly conservative. Small diameter rims need fewer spokes. Stiff rims with a pronounced aerodynamic cross section may also get by with fewer spokes.)

Table 1101. Number of spokes for various applications

24	Front wheel only, time trials on smooth roads with lightweight rider
28	Front wheel with medium weight rider or rear wheel with lightweight rider, time trials on smooth roads
32	General use on smooth roads or light duty off-road, with light to medium weight rider
36	General use on average roads or off-road, or with heavier rider or touring load; tandems on smooth roads
40	Heavy-duty loaded touring and tandems
48	Heavy-duty loaded touring and tandems, where reliability is paramount

The spoke crossing pattern affects aerodynamics slightly. Only touring and tandem wheels with many spokes have a 4-cross pattern; drag is not their primary concern. More common are 3- and 2-cross patterns, the number of crosses mainly an outgrowth of the number of spokes. The aerodynamic tradeoffs are hardly a reason to lose sleep. Radial spokes (0-cross) give the shortest length between hub and rim and therefore save a bit of drag. However, a radial pattern is usable only on the front wheel and perhaps the non-freewheel side of the rear wheel, because a radial spoke does not transmit torque well. Also, not all hub flanges and rims can withstand the stress a radial spoke applies.

Spokes also come in a number of thicknesses or gauges. Choose these based on application, not aerodynamics. Because spokes almost never break except at their ends, the butted varieties (thicker at the ends than in the center section) save weight while retaining adequate strength; more than that, their increased elasticity allows them to give rather than loosen when the wheel flexes, leading to improved reliability. Table 1202 (in Chapter 12) lists the usual gauges for stainless steel spokes and the appropriate applications.

Oval and bladed spokes are also available, both in steel and more recently in an ultra-lightweight composite material. Their superior aerodynamics make them desirable for time trials and similar uses, but the higher cost and more difficult wheel building (sometimes the hub holes must be modified) reduces their attractiveness. Straight spokes (without the bend) may also be available; however, these require specially designed hubs. Though less likely to break, they do not offer any aerodynamic benefit.

When minimum aerodynamic drag is the goal, however, a solid disc wheel is the prime choice despite its high cost and fairly high weight. (Disc-like wheel covers, not always legal in competition, offer similar aerodynamic performance at a much lower cost.) Because of their extreme sensitivity to crosswinds, discs and covers are usable only on the rear wheel except perhaps in a wind-free velodrome. Composite wheels with three to five airfoil-like spokes are almost as good aerodynamically, are usable on both front and rear wheels, and are comparable in weight to standard spoked wheels. Alas, they too are expensive. With the exception of standard wheels with covers, none of these wheels can be trued or inexpensively repaired or replaced in the event of damage, unless covered under a generous warranty. Consequently, cyclists who must pay their own way may wish to reserve them for important time trials on smooth roads.

The advertising claims for most of these aerodynamic wheels and spokes sound good, but on closer examination are vague enough to be meaningless: "Shaves 10 minutes off a 100-mile time trial"; "can increase your speed up to 5 mph"; "weight savings alone [can cut] 24 seconds in a 50K time trial." By conveniently neglecting to specify speeds and terrain, such ads protect the manufacturers with built-in loopholes, because different riders on different courses are unlikely to realize similar savings. Expect improvement, but take advertised figures with a grain of salt.

"Aero" tires, designed to make as smooth as possible a transition between sidewall and aero rim, can also be expected to help a little on a wheel that is already approaching the limits of how much streamlining is feasible. Fortunately, most high-performance tires are already narrow and nearly smooth.

The Effect of Drag on Other Components

Because rotating feet also move through the air faster than the bike as a whole, specialists favor smooth, laceless shoes, clipless pedals, and perhaps even a reduced cadence (but see the section on aerodynamic benefits of reduced cadence in Chapter 5). Some cranksets have oval "aero" crankarms, but conventional crankarms are also rounded, and either type must travel through turbulent air; any difference must surely be negligible. Hidden cables would make airflow slightly cleaner with a riderless bike, but because riderless bikes do not move and because cables do not add frontal area, any advantage beyond neater appearance is almost certain to be negligible. The effect of streamlined brakes and seatposts is marginal, but as long as they are not much heavier or weaker than the "non-aero" parts they replace, at least they don't hurt.

Oval aero frame tubes, featured in the 1980s by several manufacturers (even on cheap bikes) never really caught on. True, aero tubes can make what is seemingly only a small difference, about a 10% reduction in drag, which equates to about a 3% increase in speed. (Try calculating the speed improvement for yourself using the power equations or the computer program.) Compared with the effects of many other modifications, a 3% improvement is significant. As molded composite frames are gaining in popularity, oval cross sections are coming back, even though they are slightly heavier than circular ones of similar strength. They are already a feature of most specialized time trial bikes.

While there may be little difference between the various types of water bottles and cages by themselves, often a rider breaks his aerodynamic tuck for a few seconds to reach for them. Serious time trialists are right to be concerned about the added drag during that interval. Solutions include improving the reach technique, acquiring a different delivery system, and limiting drinks to low-speed conditions, such as at the beginning of a hill. Similar arguments apply to shift levers. Though the rapid acceptance of shifters combined with the brake levers is undoubtedly due to other reasons, such as trendiness and general laziness, at least they can usually be operated with a minimum disturbance to the rider's aerodynamic position. Regardless of the shifting system, reaches for the shift levers are much more frequent than reaches for the water bottle, except in flat terrain. Fortunately they can become very brief and efficient with practice.

Although Chapter 9 already covered panniers, it did not discuss their effect on aerodynamics. One surprising advantage of low front panniers is that the bicycle may become slightly more aerodynamic. The front panniers are positioned in front of the rider's shins, ankles, and feet, adding little frontal area but diverting air away from the aerodynamically messy pedaling going on behind them. With front panniers that have a smoothly curved exterior, not a lot of bulging pockets and straps, the result of the improved drag coefficient is quite noticeable. Rear panniers, usually larger, extend a bit more into the airstream at the sides, but are partially shielded by the rider's legs. Though they probably have little effect on the drag coefficient, at least rear panniers do not add much to frontal area. Saddlebags and rack trunks are usually completely out of the airstream.

We have already discussed frontal area, the area of the cross section perpendicular to the direction of motion. Actually, our discussion made a slight simplification. As if things were not already complicated enough, with both forward motion and a strong side wind, the cross section of the bicycle and bicyclist the airflow "sees" will be more like that of a quarter view portrait. The larger effective frontal area will increase aerodynamic drag. While there is little the rider can do about it (other than seek shelter or change direction), a side wind also reduces the effectiveness of normal aero equipment designed for head-on winds. As a result, components such as water bottles that were formerly hiding in the wind shadow are now exposed. Normal cylindrical bottles, frame tubes, crankarms, and seatposts may have less drag under such conditions than their flattened aero counterparts. In a strong side wind, not only disc wheels but wheels with aero rims and bladed spokes are likely to affect the bike's steering and handling, and may also lose most of their aerodynamic advantage. The same is true of panniers. The wind is literally heartless.

Even if some improvements have no measurable effect in a wind tunnel, and that has to be the case for most improvements taken individually, their psychological effect on one's competitors and on one's own confidence may justify them. Remember that cycling is as much a mental sport as a physical one!

Aerodynamic Alternatives

There are alternatives to the standard bicycle that greatly reduce drag. One is a partial fairing, such as a Zzipper, which mounts on the handlebars of a standard bicycle and diverts air around the rider's face and chest. Although a fairing adds mass to the steering, still requires a good aerodynamic tuck to be effective, and increases frontal area a little, it improves the drag coefficient greatly. A fairing-equipped bicycle is significantly faster and more efficient than a standard bicycle under most conditions. A fairing also helps against wind chill in cold weather.

Another alternative is a recumbent bicycle. A recumbent is, alas, generally heavier than a standard bicycle. A rider pedaling a recumbent may not be as effective at producing power as he would be in the upright position on a standard bicycle. Both position and control of a recumbent take some getting used to. Despite these drawbacks, a recumbent is so much better aerodynamically that under most conditions it is significantly faster than a standard bicycle — approximately equal to a faired standard bicycle. The recumbent's lowness to the ground may make it less visible in traffic, which of course worries some people; but it also means that in the event of a mishap, the rider falls a much shorter distance and is often better protected. Many riders also appreciate its comfort; in fact, some people with back problems or who for some other reason cannot tolerate the riding position on a standard bicycle find they can take to a recumbent happily.

A tandem is of course also faster than a single bike. Compared to a single rider and bike, a tandem has approximately double the power, yet a little less than double the weight and only slightly more aerodynamic drag. The fastest human-powered land speed vehicles use a combination of a recumbent position, a full fairing that shields the entire rider, and two or more cyclists to provide power.

All the above alternatives are normally excluded from competition against standard bicycles. Faired and recumbent bicycles are eligible in only a few races organized specifically for aerodynamic human-powered vehicles; likewise, there are a few tandem-only events, including track events. A serious competitor who needs a full calendar of races will therefore want a standard bicycle that is eligible for almost all forms of sanctioned competition. However, only a small fraction of cyclists, even among those who think of themselves as performance-oriented, have the inclination (or, admittedly, the talent) to enter even the lowest level competitions. Yet the vast majority continue to use standard, competition-legal bicycles exclusively. Some cyclists may of course be unaware of the alternatives, and some may be deterred by the extra expense, but others spend vastly greater sums to achieve negligible improvements. The facts suggest that most cyclists are more concerned with fashion and image than with actual performance.

Drafting and Related Strategy

Except for time trials, most bicycle competitions allow drafting, or pacing, i.e. riding in the slipstream closely behind another rider, or in a pack of riders. Drafting is also possible and advantageous in many non-competitive situations, but its benefits during competition are so profound that drafting largely determines the characteristics of any type of race. At 20 mph in still air, closely drafting a single rider reduces power requirements by a whopping 39%! Higher speeds and larger groups yield even greater savings. It is no wonder that almost every element of race strategy revolves about the ability to draft. Every move and every plan must consider the potential effect on drafting, whether it concerns getting into or staying in the draft, denying an opponent effective use of the draft, granting an opponent the draft in return for a similar favor, temporary drafting cooperation in order to stay clear of another set of opponents, or gauging how successful a breakaway will be without the benefit of the draft.

A match sprint, a short race with just two riders, offers a microcosm of drafting strategy. Just as a chess player must learn and understand the classic opening moves if he hopes to advance beyond beginner level, a bicycle racer must know how a sprint unfolds if he expects to compete successfully. Most of the tactics to be found in other forms of bicycle racing are present in a match sprint, where they show up with crystal clarity.

One rider is chosen to lead the event initially. The rider ahead both blocks his opponent and controls the pace. Usually that pace is initially slow; why should he burn himself out while the rider behind him gets a free tow to victory? Sometimes, however, a rider will go all out from the start, hoping both to catch his opponent off guard and that his opponent will be the first to tire and become discouraged. For the latter strategy to work, he needs more than just hope. It is best employed by a rider with good high-speed pursuit skills but perhaps a weaker sprint than his opponent, and can be used at any opportune moment during the slow-speed portion of the event. A rider ahead is forced to keep looking back to check on his opponent and (because he can't do this continuously) is vulnerable to sudden moves. Often he will try to make his opponent take the lead, using real or feinted swerves, accelerations and decelerations, and possibly a trackstand, though this last maneuver is declining in popularity. The rider behind tries to stay in his opponent's blind spot, which on a counterclockwise oval is behind and to the right. The rider ahead tries to minimize his blind spot by riding along the right edge of the track. Eventually the remaining distance becomes short enough (perhaps 350 meters) to force the rider ahead to increase his speed, to keep the rider behind from coming around him so quickly that he has no time to counter. To increase speed, the rider usually tries to take advantage of the banking of the track by dropping down as he accelerates. Naturally he also tries to prevent his opponent from following his every movement and benefitting from the draft. But eventually a one-on-one draft is almost inevitable. The rider behind tries to draft and save energy (relatively speaking) up until the point at which he must use the saved energy to come around his opponent and nip ahead by the finish line. That point is perhaps 100 meters before the finish, but (at least between well-matched opponents) timing is critical.

If the move is too early, he will not have saved enough energy drafting and will run out of steam; if too late, there will not be enough time to get around his opponent. Even in this ultra-simple race, the strategy is surprisingly complex, and there are undoubtedly additional nuances and insights that experienced competitors have acquired.

A match sprint is, however, too small-scale to permit certain other drafting strategies. In a long race, opponents often form temporary alliances in an attempt to reduce the number of players who have a chance to win and to reduce the advantage of a particularly strong rider or team. The riders in the temporary alliance will draft each other and attempt to build a lead against their rivals, or will draft their rivals and keep their share of the work as low as possible. They will keep up the cooperation until either the strategy has worked — their rivals are far behind, or at least tired — or the strategy is proving ineffective, at which point the alliance will dissolve.

In a well-rounded baseball team, players are assigned to fielding positions and batting order based on their agility, speed, and throwing and hitting prowess. A bicycle racing team often has similar diversity, with one or more time trialists, climbers, sprinters, and endurance specialists, plus all-round riders. Even the specialists are usually expected to be reasonably accomplished outside of their specialty, because not every event the team enters calls for the same mix of skills. In addition, teams may sometimes send contingents of riders simultaneously to different events, or may need to compensate for team members who are exhausted, injured, or sick. Often the team will formulate a plan for a particular race and assign its members different roles to play in its accomplishment. Such assignments help an individual member stay focused on his responsibilities during the chaos of a race, help prevent wasted effort, try to capitalize on the individual's strengths, and (the bottom line) give the team as a whole a better chance of winning or placing well.

The individual members of a team are seldom equally matched. Its lesser riders may be in training for possible future stardom, may be past their prime, or may just not be star quality but are still capable and willing. These riders may be called upon to play a role similar to that of a pawn in chess: a utility player who assists the stronger players and may be called upon to sacrifice himself for the team, but who may set up the win or even on rare occasions win himself. These riders (often called "domestiques") may, for example, be assigned to stay with a stronger teammate who has a mechanical problem, to relay him back to the pack (while he drafts) and afford him some chance of staying in contention; to relay water and food from the support areas to the remaining riders on the team; to "mark" an opposing team's star rider; to "lead out" a sprint; or to make an early (possibly suicidal) escape to test the field and whittle away the competition.

The most conspicuous team tactic is for one team member (one who at least in the early stages is usually a good time trialist or pursuiter rather than a sprinter) to break away from the pack, while the remainder of the team then try to help the break succeed. Neither task is easy. A solo breakaway rider, of course, has no draft whatever to help him; a small breakaway group, only the draft off each other, and a limited time share even of that. If the break does occur, methods of ensuring its success include riding at the front of the pack and controlling the pace, that is, adopting a speed just slow enough to give the break enough time to get away or stay away, yet fast enough to keep the others in the pack from mounting successful attacks to counter; blocking to reduce the ability of rivals to escape; chasing, but not assisting, any attacks by rivals, making it clear that if they succeed in bridging the gap they would also drag along fresh unwelcome competitors with them; and generally discouraging any chase attempts that, if successful, would damage or destroy the prospects of their teammate's break. The same principles apply to multiple teammates in a smaller group. The tactics of a team that failed to get a rider into the break group are related: try to disrupt the rival team's ability to control the pace, evade the blocking efforts, stage attacks, and mount a full scale team time trial-like effort at the front of the pack to reel in the break. Or hang back and rest while the stronger teams wear each other out: strong teams may concentrate their efforts on their strongest rivals, ignoring teams they do not expect to pose serious threats. Teams can also enlist weaker teams or independent riders, offering them the chance for a good placing in return for their support. Almost every team tactic is in some way related to the ability to draft.

An Airflow Model

The shape of a rider on a bicycle, along with the spinning cranks and wheels, make the airflow past the bicycle difficult or even impossible to study in detail. To get an idea of what is happening when a bicycle moves through the air, we will consider a simplified model: air uniformly moving past a stationary cylinder, perpendicular to its axis. It makes no difference whether air is moving past an object or the object is moving through the air, but as a substitute for the shape of a bicycle and rider, a cylinder is obviously less than ideal. Furthermore, we will assume that the air is an incompressible fluid, more like water, although even water is slightly compressible. And finally, we will examine only a two-dimensional slice in a plane parallel to the direction of airflow and perpendicular to the cylinder axis, as though we were looking down upon the cylinder and airflow. (In this idealized model, all such slices are identical.) Despite these radical simplifications, the model tells us a great deal about what really happens.

Figure 1101 depicts the airflow around the cylinder. The airflow depicted is called laminar,

Fig. 1101 Airflow around a cylinder.

because the air acts as if it were comprised of self-contained layers, parting and bending around the obstacle, then neatly rejoining on the opposite side. Each layer is like a pipe delivering a constant flow of air — that is, a constant volume per unit of time. Far in front of or behind the object, the layers are parallel and the airspeed within them is constant. As the layers are forced to bend around the object, they have farther to go. The extra distance forces the airflow to speed up. The faster speed in turn causes the layers to become narrower in order to keep the flow constant. (The principle of constant flow in an incompressible fluid is a consequence of a tenet of fluid dynamics called the equation of continuity.)

As a side issue, is the airflow really laminar? The type of flow in a particular system depends on a quantity called the Reynolds number. We are told that in systems in which air is flowing past an obstacle, a Reynolds number of 10 or less indicates laminar flow. Reynolds numbers above 10 indicate turbulent flow, in which the layers do not neatly separate and rejoin, but curl, form eddies, and generally become chaotic. The Reynolds number is defined as:

$$N_R = \rho \, v \, L / \eta$$

where N_R is the Reynolds number, ρ (rho) is the density of the fluid, v is the velocity, L is a characteristic length in the particular system (in our case, the diameter of the obstacle, the cylinder), and η (eta) is the viscosity of the fluid, a measure of its resistance to flowing. Let's see, for our case the density of air is about 1.2 kg/m^3, the airspeed of a cyclist may be 10 m/s, the diameter of a cylinder about the size of a cyclist is about 0.86 m, and the viscosity of air at 20 C is about 1.8×10^{-5} poiseuilles [N s/m^2, or kg/(m s)]. The Reynolds number must be on the order of 600,000 — somewhat greater than 10, in other words. Another simplification fails the reality test! Nevertheless, we will continue to pretend the airflow is laminar, because enough characteristics of laminar flow apparently continue at high Reynolds numbers to make this simpler case worth examining.

The theory of aerodynamics uses a concept called the stream function to define the flux, or rate of flow. The value of the stream function is constant along a streamline, such as each of the bulged lines in Figure 1101. For our simple two-dimensional model, the stream function is:

$$\psi(x,y) = v \, y \, \{1 - [a^2 / (x^2 + y^2)]\}$$

where ψ (psi) is the value of the stream function, v is the overall velocity of the air, x and y are the horizontal and vertical coordinates of a particular point, and a is the radius of the cylinder. The cylinder is centered at (x=0, y=0), the wind is moving horizontally (parallel to the x-axis), and all the units are supposed to be consistent. We are more interested in the speed of the air at various points around the cylinder, however, in particular the component of the velocity of the air in what would be the bicycle's direction of motion, parallel to the x-axis. It turns out that the velocity we seek (let's call it v_x) is the partial derivative of the function ψ with respect to x. Without delving into differential calculus, let us just say that:

$$v_x = [\psi(x + \delta x, y) - \psi(x, y)] / \delta x$$

for some small value of δx.

Using calculations based on the above equation, Figure 1102 plots lines of constant v_x, the horizontal component of air velocity, around the cylinder. The circle at right is the cross section of the cylinder, with a radius of 0.43 m to approximate a cyclist. The wind is coming from the right at an overall speed of 10 m/s. The horizontal component of velocity is exactly 10 m/s along the slanted straight lines; that is, they are the boundary between velocities higher than 10 m/s (to the right, on either side of the cylinder, as the air is forced to speed up to get around it) and velocities lower than 10 m/s (to the left, in the slipstream). The leftmost or outermost closed curve is the boundary for 9.5 m/s: the horizontal velocity is between 9.5 and 10 m/s outside it (left or to the sides), less than 9.5 m/s inside it. Moving progressively inward, the other curves are the boundaries for 9.0, 8.5, 8.0, and 7.5 m/s.

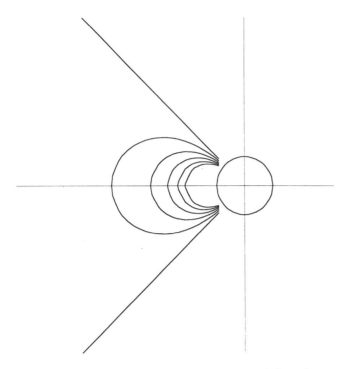

Fig. 1102. Lines of constant velocity as airflow from right passes a cylinder (circle). Lowest velocities (best draft) are small curves immediately behind the cylinder.

A rider attempting to sit in the draft of this cylinder wants to minimize the air velocity he faces. It's no surprise that the closer he can approach the cylinder (the rider ahead) from directly behind, the lower the air velocity he will face, and the greater the drafting benefit he will enjoy. Of course, approaching is possible only up to a point, and overlapping the wheels of the bicycles is dangerous, especially for the drafting rider. These constraints impose a practical limit upon how low the air velocity can drop. Bicycles designed specifically for team time trialing often have small front wheels, not only to permit an ultra-low position but to enable riders to benefit as much as possible from the slipstream of their teammates. There is no reason why a similar design should not give a rider an advantage in road races or other events in which a rider is often drafting; yet so far, very few riders seem to have thought this trick promising enough to try with a pursuit bike or other small-wheeled bike. Even fewer seem to have thought of the reverse trick, that is, using a long-wheelbase bicycle with a rear wheel placed well behind the rider, in order to deny rivals an effective draft!

Notice from Figure 1102 also that well to the rear of the cylinder-bike, there is considerable leeway in the draft on either side, but as one moves forward, staying centered in the slipstream becomes more and more critical. The best draft zone will also skew to one side in a strong side wind, because what matters to drafting is the overall air velocity. Its direction is the direction resulting from the vector sum of wind velocity and bicycle velocity. It is usually close to, but not necessarily the same as, the direction the bicycles are moving. Figure 1102 does not show the area to the right (forward) of the cylinder, which has a symmetric pattern of airflow and speeds. A cyclist unfortunately cannot take advantage of the lowered airspeeds directly ahead of another rider, because he cannot enter that area without becoming the lead rider himself and radically altering the airflow. Nor can he enter the slipstream without radically altering its shape. His presence prevents at least some of the layers of air from rejoining until they are past him, elongating the closed curves in the figure and (fortunately) further reducing the velocity he faces. Turbulent airflow is far too complex to predict even approximately without sophisticated simulation software; but even with our crude model, we can see that the airflow is heavily dependent on the radius of the cylinder. Two or more riders in close proximity effectively increase that radius, enlarge the slipstream area, and push the lower-velocity zones further back, where a drafting rider can make use of them.

12
Maximizing Acceleration

Weight is the force gravity exerts on a mass. It is very important to the cyclist, but mostly when he is climbing. Given equal power and the means to apply it, a heavier cyclist can achieve higher speeds on downhills, but (alas) not enough to offset his lower speeds on uphills. So except in flat terrain, competitive cyclists, perhaps even more than most other athletes, need to keep their weight as low as possible. The small differences in weight between different bicycles and different components are far less important, yet reduced weight is still worthwhile.

Minimizing the Effects of Gravity

The numbers below will illustrate these points. Suppose our standard rider, weighing in at 90 kg with bicycle, is competing in a flat, windless, flying-start 10-mile time trial. If he puts out a constant 150 watts (about 0.2 hp), his completion time should be about 30:43. Now suppose that next week he loses one pound, about half a kilogram. How? It really doesn't matter, as long as it has no effect on either his power or the way the bike works. Perhaps he forgoes his bowl of ice cream for a couple of nights before the event, or he fits a new super-light saddle and leaves his spare tools and tube at home, or he acquires a titanium frame and fits all his old components to it, or he merely empties a pint of water from his water bottle. With power output and all other conditions identical, he rides the same time trial. He finds that his time is a mere 0.5 second better. The changes were hardly worth the trouble, were they?

With hills the story would be a little different. Applying the same power up a long but moderate 4% grade, his 1-pound loss would put him 1.8 seconds ahead after just a mile. Down that same 1-mile grade, being a pound lighter would be a slight disadvantage; it would put him 0.2 second behind. These small savings and losses of course add up in a long ride, but to make a significant difference, the weight loss would have to be rather larger than a pound: i.e. at least by a serious diet, if not a change in heredity. The weight savings from a minor component swap cannot amount to much of a performance increase.

Several manufacturers now make ultra-light components; we see "micro" freewheels with aluminum cogs, minimalist saddles with hollow rails, not-quite-so-quick-release hex key fittings, and the like. For most of these items, lowered mass is their sole *raison d'etre*. It is up to the prospective purchaser to evaluate his needs and determine whether their advantage in mass compensates for their disadvantages, which always include additional expense (of course!), and may also include faster wear, increased discomfort, reduced convenience, etc. It is also possible to buy axles, bolts, screws, and other common parts that have been made from a lighter material and that are intended to replace standard, heavier parts, usually of steel. Before investing, it is wise to investigate some of the metallurgical properties of the materials involved.

Properties of Materials

Though some bicycles also use non-metallic composite materials, most of the structural materials used in bicycle frames and components are metals. Almost all metals used in bicycle manufacture are alloys. An alloy is an amalgam of a metal element — any metal element — with other elements, possibly metal, possibly not. Be on your guard when misinformed sales personnel try to sell you an "alloy frame": even the lowliest department store bike has an alloy frame! But not all alloys are equal. Individual alloys are tailored to provide properties desirable for particular applications. In addition, the way the metal is worked during and after manufacture (for example, if it is cast, rolled, forged, annealed, or drawn) greatly affects its properties, and some alloys also respond to being heat-treated. If a bicycle frame is

the end product, the method used to assemble the tubes — gluing, brazing, or welding — and the expertise and care exercised during assembly have a great deal to do with the ultimate strength and durability of the product. Frames have been known to corrode from chemicals improperly left inside the tubes; steel and titanium tubes overheated during careless assembly become brittle and crack during use; and failures in glued-lug aluminum and carbon fiber frames due to galvanic corrosion were once common. Newly developed alloys occasionally find their way into bicycles, while others that may look good on paper can be totally unsuitable for bicycle use.

Steel is an alloy of iron and various other elements. Aside from the mild steels used throughout the cheapest bikes, the most common steel alloys found in bicycles are carbon steel (also called "hi-tensile steel"), used in relatively inexpensive bicycles; stainless steel, used in high-quality spokes; and chromium-molybdenum (Cr-Mo) steel found in better-quality bicycle frames and such parts as axles and pedal spindles. Chromium-molybdenum steel is in such common use for bicycles that its name is often shortened to "chrome-moly" as though it were not an iron alloy at all. Manganese-molybdenum (Mn-Mo) and other slightly more expensive steel alloys can be even stronger in some applications. Steel is inexpensive, very strong, very stiff, hard, and can be flexed short of its yield point indefinitely. It is unfortunately relatively heavy. Because all steels are almost equally dense, it does not make sense to refer to high-strength alloys as "lightweight steels," but of course the stronger the alloy, the less material needs to be used for adequate strength. Frame tubing made from the strongest steels is already close to the practical limit of how thin its walls can be, however. Most steels need to be coated (painted, chromed, or nickel plated, for instance) to prevent rust.

Aluminum is almost as inexpensive as steel and much lighter. It is however also weaker, softer, and less rigid than steel. It is therefore normally used in applications in which these properties are advantageous or in which a high-enough volume of aluminum can be used to achieve adequate strength and rigidity, yet remain slightly lighter than a thinner steel counterpart would be. For example, as implied above, the extra thickness of a large-diameter aluminum tube compared to a steel one can be used to advantage if a very stiff frame is the goal. (Do not confuse increased stiffness with increased strength, however.) Aluminum alloys are usually designated with a 4-digit code that identifies the principal alloying elements. Codes that begin with 2, 6, or 7 respond to heat-treating: for example 7075, a high-strength alloy with zinc, magnesium, copper, and chromium; and 6061, a lower-strength alloy with magnesium, silicon, copper, and chromium. (The code is no guarantee that the alloy has actually been heat-treated, however.) Unlike steel and titanium, aluminum cannot be flexed indefinitely; it fatigues and eventually cracks. Aluminum frames and parts must therefore be "overbuilt," that is, include enough material to allow for a sufficiently long useful life. Though aluminum is ideal for many bike components, it would be inappropriate for high-stress applications, such as spokes and spindles. Aluminum is also widely used for quality lightweight wheel rims. The reason, however, has less to do with weight than with friction: aluminum provides a braking surface almost as good as steel when dry, but much better than steel when wet. Aluminum does not rust in air but instead forms a coating of aluminum oxide, like a tough clear coat of paint.

Titanium, though also a common metal in the earth's rocks, is more difficult to extract than either iron or aluminum. Titanium burns in air, even in pure nitrogen, and thus requires special procedures to weld. It is these processing difficulties that make titanium expensive. Considerably lighter than steel and very strong, resilient, and hard, it is finding increasing bicycle applications. Although per weight an item made from certain titanium alloys can be stronger than a chrome-moly steel one, per volume chrome-moly usually wins. Therefore a lightweight titanium part that exactly replaces a heavier chrome-moly steel one — an axle or spoke, for instance — is not usually as strong as the original; to allow titanium's strength-to-weight advantage to come into play, the part must be redesigned. Nor can a titanium part be quite as stiff as steel without also being slightly heavier. Titanium nicely combines aluminum's resistance to corrosion with steel's resilience.

Carbon fiber is the popular generic term for a non-metallic composite material increasingly being used in bicycle applications. Several varieties of carbon fibers are used. The purest is graphite, but other types include PAN (polyacrylonitrate), rayon, pitch, and carbon silica. Though soft, fibers of carbon are extremely high in tensile strength and even higher in rigidity. To take advantage of those attributes, the fibers must be aligned or woven into a fabric and embedded in a plastic or resin matrix, just as steel rods are sometimes

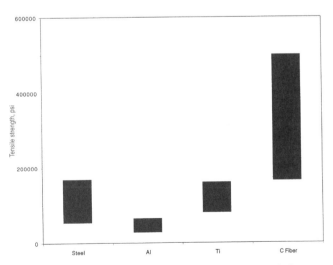

Fig. 1201. Tensile strength of different materials.

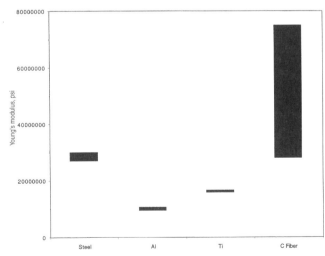

Fig. 1202. Rigidity of materials.

embedded in concrete. The result can be even lighter (that is, less dense) than the fibers themselves, giving these materials a tremendous advantage on a per-mass basis. Composite processing assures that carbon fiber materials are and will continue to be expensive, but the variety of properties attainable, the ways in which carbon fiber can be useful, and (possibly) its limitations are only just beginning to become evident in bicycling applications. One exciting way in which woven carbon fiber can be used is to tailor the alignment of the fibers to the position on the bike, for instance to make a frame that is vertically compliant but laterally stiff, something difficult to achieve with a round tube.

Table 1201 lists properties of materials. It can only be a rough guide for comparisons, and if it omits some super-strong alloy with bicycle applications (which it almost certainly does), or quotes figures for a non-steel material not actually used in bicycles (again likely), it is not through any intention to make a particular material look good or bad. There is more data for steel in the table because steel has been in use a long time and its properties are public knowledge. The composition, manufacturing methods, and properties of some of the other materials used in bicycles are not publicized — trade secrets, you might say. The numbers given for carbon fiber in particular may be optimistic. Other potentially useful data is also not readily available; for example, how welding affects the properties of steel, aluminum, and titanium — an important consideration now that welding rather than brazing is used on almost all metal frames. However, certain new steels from the major tubing manufacturers are claimed to become even stronger when welded.

Pounds per square inch (psi) is admittedly not a neat metric unit like the others we have been using, but it is the one most commonly encountered. One psi equals 6,894.7 newtons per square meter.

Figures 1201 and 1202 show the differences in tensile strength and rigidity more readily, but even more telling are Figures 1203 and 1204, which show the differences on a per-mass basis. Carbon fiber composites have deliberately been omitted from the latter chart because if the density range listed in Table 1201 is accurate for bicycle applications, there is no contest; carbon fiber puts the metals into the shade. Notice that many of the ranges overlap; unless you know more about the particular alloy in your bicycle, you may not be able to assume that its strength ranks with the "best," nor that the "best" would even be suitable in that application; these properties are not the only ones that matter in a practical design.

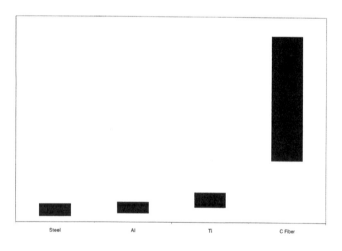

Fig. 1203. Tensile strength per unit mass of different materials.

Table 1201. Properties of materials

alloy or other material	density (g/cm^3)	modulus of elasticity (psi x 10^6)	tensile strength (psi)
mild steel	7.8	30	56,000–60,000
carbon steel	7.8	30	78,400 (53,700 after brazing)
stainless steel	7.8	27	100,000
Cr-Mo steel	7.8	30	116,500 (85,200 after brazing)
Mn-Mo steel	7.8	30	116,500–168,000 (100,800–145,600 after brazing)
aluminum, various	2.7	9.4–10.5	28,000–64,000
titanium, various	4.5	15.8–16.5	60,000–160,000
carbon fiber composites, various	0.91–2.2 (?)	28–75	165,000–500,000

Other light metals, such as beryllium, magnesium, and boron, are seldom used in bicycles at present, but may be in the future. They will have their own special processing difficulties and idiosyncrasies to overcome. Like carbon fiber, steel and aluminum alloys are also occasionally used in super-strong composite materials with bicycling applications. A few other materials are seen now and then. Nylon and certain types of wood, for instance, are very light and on a per-mass basis approach the strength of aluminum, but are very much more flexible. Fiberglass (glass-fiber-reinforced resin) is stronger yet but still too flexible for most bicycle applications. Ceramics are starting to come into use for improved braking surfaces but are not used structurally.

Weight Savings from Tight Frame Geometry

In Chapter 10 we already saw that a short-wheelbase bicycle is stiffer and less comfortable than a longer-wheelbase version. While there is no inherent advantage in having an uncomfortable bike, a tighter, steeper geometry leads to shorter tubing lengths, which ought to save weight. How much? The mass of a portion of frame tubing depends on the density of the material and its volume, which in turn depends on the

length, the thickness of the tube wall, and the diameter:

$$V = L \pi t (D - t)$$

where V is the volume of the material itself (not the volume of air it encloses), L is the length of the section of tubing (measured parallel to its axis), t is its wall thickness, and D is the outside diameter of the tube.

For example, take a frame of Reynolds 531C, a manganese-molybdenum steel that has a density of about 7.8 grams per cubic centimeter. A 531C chainstay is 22 mm in diameter, 0.8 mm in wall thickness. The volume of steel in a 1-cm length is 1 x 3.14 x 0.08 x (2.2 – 0.08) = 0.53 cm^3. A frame lengthened by 1 cm due solely to longer stays would thus weigh an extra 7.8 x 0.53 x 2 or 8.3 grams. (The seatstays would also have to be a bit longer, increasing this total slightly.) For comparison, one swallow of liquid from your water bottle weighs about 11 grams. Suppose instead that the frame angles are relaxed one degree, say from 74 degrees to 73 degrees, but that the bike stays the same size. The seat tube length would not change (by definition); the bottom bracket would essentially rotate forward a little, which would require at most only tiny changes to the lengths of the seatstays and chainstays. Only the fork would become slightly longer because of the shallower angle, about 3 mm longer if the rake is unchanged, perhaps 6 mm longer if a little extra rake is added to keep the trail constant. (See Chapter 9 for a fuller discussion of rake and trail.) The latter amount would add about 6.5 grams to a 531C fork. The down tube would also have to become a bit shorter, because the bottom bracket would rotate farther forward than the bottom of the head tube would, saving a slight amount of mass. Suppose instead that the frame is one centimeter larger (taller). Corresponding masses of 1 cm lengths of 531C seat tube, head tube, steering column, and seatstays are 3.4, 6.8, 9.5, and (2 x) 1.4 g, so we would expect a 1 cm larger frame to weigh 22.5 grams more. Frames made of other high-quality materials should give similar numbers, and none of the differences are anything to lose

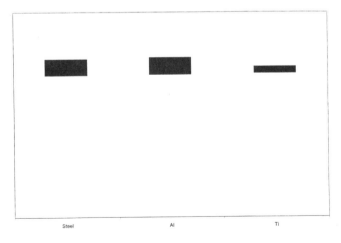

Fig. 1204. Rigidity per unit mass of different materials.

Steel   Al   Ti

sleep over. A cyclist can safely buy a frame with the dimensions and geometry he prefers and forget about any consequences on the weight.

Minimizing Mass

We have seen that weight (if sufficiently large) matters to a cyclist, but mass is important in another way, one that has nothing to do with weight or hills. Mass is a measure of an object's resistance to acceleration. The greater the mass, the longer it takes a given amount of force — whether pedaling force or gravitational force — to bring the bicycle up to speed. And the longer it takes to come up to speed, the slower the average speed. Alternatively, the greater the mass, the more power the cyclist must apply to achieve the same acceleration — power that might not be on tap. The energy spent fighting excess mass is energy that could have been spent to increase speed, or increase the distance the cyclist can cover. Mass is the enemy of performance.

Mass also resists deceleration. Yes, that means that during coasting or braking the bicycle stays at a higher speed longer, but unfortunately, slower deceleration is no speed boon. Suppose our standard rider is matching pace on a flat stretch with another rider who (together with his bike) weighs 10 kg (22 pounds) less; that is, the other rider and his bike have a total mass of 80 rather than 90 kg. Suppose they both pedal in spurts: when either rider reaches a speed of 9 m/s, he coasts a few seconds until his speed drops to 8 m/s, then he applies 200 watts of power to bring his speed back up to 9 m/s. Pedal, then coast, then pedal, then coast: you may know some cyclists with a similar riding style. Our standard rider, the heavier — that is, the more massive — of the two, does indeed spend more time coasting: 5.5 seconds out of each cycle compared to 5.0. However, he needs to apply power for 13.5 seconds to get back up to speed, whereas his lighter companion is back to speed in 2 seconds less. Though both riders average 8.54 m/s, our standard rider spends 2,700 joules during his 19-second cycle, an average power output of 142.1 watts; his companion

spends just 2,300 J in 16.5 seconds, an average of 139.4 W. Sorry, extra mass is not really a benefit to coasting.

Most of us know that tandem bicycles, due to the combined masses of their riders, are capable of scary downhill speeds. Likewise, tandems have a speed advantage on flat roads, due to about double the power with only moderately increased rolling resistance and drag. (In a flat century, a briskly propelled tandem is always a magnet for solo riders seeking a draft. The line of freeloaders that forms to the rear is comical.) Despite these benefits, tandemists sometimes complain that they lose momentum rapidly when the road begins to go uphill. Is it true? In a word, no — at least, no more rapidly than a solo bike. If our standard rider begins a hill at 10 m/s and coasts, his speed drops to 3 m/s in 11.4 s 72 m up a 5% grade. Suppose two riders about the size of our standard rider try the same thing on a tandem: the total mass of the riders and bike is 175 kg, the coefficients C_R and C_D 0.0045 and 1.0, respectively, and the frontal area 0.48 m^2. The tandem speed drops from 10 m/s to 3 m/s in 11.5 s 73 m up the 5% grade. These numbers are almost identical to those for the single bike. Perhaps the lamenting tandemists, accustomed to rolling along the flats at single-bike speeds with relatively little effort, are merely reacting to the sudden need to do as much work as their single-bike companions. Compared to a single rider and bike, the tandem's higher momentum (mass times velocity) is enough to offset the moderate increases in rolling resistance and drag. Here is a case where at least extra mass does not hurt, though it can hardly be said to help, either.

Nor is mass any aid to braking. Braking is, after all, intentional. It is done to slow the bicycle to some particular safe speed, or to adjust the bicycle's position. Given the same amount of braking force, increased mass requires earlier braking: the cyclist needs more time to reduce his speed or adjust his position adequately. While the average speed during the braking period may be the same, maintaining that lowered speed for a longer time results in a lower average speed overall. Fortunately, during braking the cyclist spends little energy of his own — the effort of squeezing the brake levers leaves few cyclists gasping by the roadside. (True, track cyclists, with no brakes and no freewheel, may have to expend energy to slow down rapidly, but track events, by design, seldom require such a maneuver.)

We can afford to concentrate on acceleration, where mass has pronounced performance consequences, confident that any improvements there will benefit braking as well. The acceleration-conscious cyclist needs to be concerned about mass for two different reasons. First, all mass on the bike and on the rider resists linear acceleration, the change of speed in the straight-line direction the bike is moving. Remember that $F = m\,a$. Decrease mass by 1% and you need 1% less pedaling force to achieve the same acceleration. It doesn't matter where that mass is: in the frame, in the accessories, in the rider's clothing, or in the rider's waistline. Mass is mass and least is best, where acceleration in a straight line is concerned.

Rotating Mass

But the second reason is that some of that mass rotates. Rotating mass adds an extra penalty, because in addition to accelerating the bike forward, the cyclist also has to accelerate the wheels and other rotating parts, to spin them faster or slower in their respective circles. Picture yourself standing on smooth ice holding a bicycle wheel motionless up in the air, grasping the opposite ends of its axle with your hands. To set yourself in motion, you must expend energy: you would shove off with your foot against something solid — the shoreline, perhaps, or the blade of a skate dug into the ice. But as you and the wheel glide along, the wheel would not be rotating. If you wanted to make the wheel rotate, you would need to give it a twirl, expending a little more energy. A cyclist has no choice. In order to move the bicycle forward, he must also spin its wheels. The energy needed to make those wheels rotate does not come free of charge.

Just as the bicycle and rider have a property called mass, the wheels have a property called moment of inertia. Back to physics class for a moment (sorry, that word just slipped out), where our first subject is indeed the moment of inertia, a concept analogous to mass in a discussion of linear force and acceleration. The moment of inertia of a rotating object is a measure of its resistance to a change in its angular velocity. It depends not only on the object's mass, but on the distribution of that mass relative to the axis of rotation. If the rotating object is comprised of individual parts, the moment of inertia of the total object is the sum of the moments of the individual parts. For each part, the moment of inertia is the product of its mass and the square of the radius of gyration, that is, its distance from the axis of the whole object.

For example, a bicycle wheel consists of several parts that rotate about a stationary axle: the hub shell, the freewheel (if it's a rear wheel on a derailleur bicycle), spokes and nipples or possibly a solid disc, a rim, a tire, and (if it's a clincher wheel) a tube and probably a protective rim strip. The rim may have a mass of 0.45 kg and be situated 0.308 m from the center of the axle; its contribution to the moment of inertia would therefore be 0.45 x 0.308 x 0.308 or 0.0427 kg-m^2. All the spokes of one wheel together may have a mass of 0.23 kg, roughly half the rim's mass, but the center of each spoke is only about half the rim's distance from the axis, say 0.152 m. The contribution of the spokes to the moment of inertia is therefore only about 0.0053 kg-m^2, roughly one-eighth that of the rim. The moments for the remaining parts are calculated in the same way and summed to obtain the moment of inertia of the entire wheel.

Next we'll talk about torque. Remember torque in our discussion of crankarm length? Torque is the product of two factors: a tangential force that produces rotation, and the distance between the point at which that force is applied and the axis of rotation. In the mks system, torque is measured in meter-newtons. Just as in the linear world force is the product of mass and acceleration, in the rotational world the analogous torque is the product of moment of inertia and angular acceleration. If an object with a moment of inertia of 0.8 kg-m^2 is accelerated 9 radians per second per second, the torque producing that angular acceleration must be 0.72 kg-m^2/s^2, or (because a newton is a kg-m/s^2) 0.72 meter-newtons.

Under any normal conditions, a bicycle wheel is firmly in contact with the ground. Its angular acceleration is precisely determined by the linear acceleration of the entire bicycle, and vice versa. An angular acceleration of 2 π radians per second per second is the same as 1 revolution per second squared. One revolution in linear terms is the circumference of the circle, or 2 π times the radius. So for a bicycle wheel, linear acceleration equals angular acceleration times the radius of the wheel, or angular acceleration equals linear acceleration divided by the radius of the wheel. Because bicycles occasionally have wheels of different sizes and often have wheels with different moments of inertia, we had better use a subscript to distinguish between the two wheels of a bike. Let the subscript i stand for either f (for the front wheel) or r (for the rear wheel). If L_i is the torque on wheel i, I_i is wheel i's moment of inertia, r_i is wheel i's radius, and a is the linear acceleration:

$$L_i = I_i\, a / r_i$$

But we know that torque is force times radius:

$$F_i\, r_i = I_i\, a / r_i$$

$$F_i = I_i\, a / r_i^2$$

Call F (with no subscript) the total force acting on the bike, not only from the forces due to acceleration of its two wheels, but from aerodynamic drag, rolling resistance, gravity, braking, and pedaling. Then if m is the mass of the bike and rider:

$$F = m\, a + (I_f\, a / r_f^2) + (I_r\, a / r_r^2)$$

$$F = (m + I_f / r_f^2 + I_r / r_r^2)\, a$$

(This ignores the forces due to angular acceleration of the feet, pedals, crankset, chain and jockey wheels, which are small to negligible.) The above equation allows us to calculate the effect the moments of inertia and radii of the wheels have upon the bicycle's acceleration.

Wheel Components and Their Effect on Moment of Inertia

Let us start next to the wheel axle and work our way out, examining the contribution of each of the wheel components to the wheel's moment of inertia. The hub shell is first; it is so light and so close to the axis that we need not give it much thought. The freewheel (or the internal mechanism and cogs of the freehub, whichever applies) is considerably heavier, but also so close to the axis that even a heavy touring or mountain bike freewheel with large cogs makes only a small contribution to moment of inertia.

Spokes are next. Most spokes are steel, circular in cross section, either straight gauge (constant in thickness) or butted (thinner in the center than at the ends). See Jobst Brandt's book *The Bicycle Wheel* for a more thorough discussion of types of spokes. Only three gauges are in common use: 14, which has a diameter of 2 mm; 15, 1.8 mm; and 16, 1.6 mm. However, a 16-gauge spoke end would be too weak, so the only varieties commonly seen are 14 straight gauge, 14–15–14 butted, 15 straight gauge, and 15–16–15 butted, the last being recommended only for the front wheel, which does not have to sustain pedaling torque. Table 1202 gives spoke gauges and suitable applications.

Table 1202. Spoke gauge for various applications

gauge	application
14 straight gauge	Low cost, heavier rider or touring load or tandem
14–15–14 butted	Greatest reliability, heavier rider or touring load or tandem
15 straight gauge	Low cost, lightweight rider or smooth roads
15–16–15 butted	General use, lightweight rider or smooth roads, front wheel only

Ignoring the spoke head, which is at the hub and therefore adds little to moment of inertia, the mass of a spoke depends on its diameter and length. Because the thin central section of a butted spoke is much longer than the thicker ends, its mass is closer to that of the next smaller straight gauge than that of the next larger straight gauge. Spoke length depends on the wheel size, with minor variations due to hub and rim design. Spoke length also depends on the cross pattern, which in turn depends on the number of spokes in the wheel and the intended use. Three-cross wheels with 32 or 36 spokes are most common for racing and recreational use; a typical length for 700C wheels is 300 mm; for 26-in. wheels, 265 mm. However, especially for time trials on smooth roads, fewer spokes and fewer crosses (down to zero-cross, a radially spoked wheel) are sometimes used; these spokes will be a little shorter. For heavy touring or tandems, more spokes and more crosses are also sometimes used; these spokes will be a little longer. Table 1203 gives the approximate mass of a typical 300 mm steel spoke.

To estimate the moment of inertia of the spokes, one needs both the mass of the complete set and their radius of gyration. To obtain the mass, either weigh the spokes or estimate in proportion to length from Table 1203, then multiply by the number of spokes. The radius of gyration is approximately the distance from the hub center to the midpoint of any spoke; square that and multiply by mass to obtain the moment. While reducing moment of inertia is desirable, the choice of the number of spokes, the cross pattern, and the spoke gauges should be based on the reliability of the wheel in its intended application.

Oval and bladed spokes vary in design but their moment of inertia should be similar to that of butted spokes of similar gauge. Titanium and carbon fiber spokes are starting to appear on the market; their advantage over steel spokes is reduced mass. A 14-gauge titanium spoke should weigh in at about .0042 kg, with tensile strength comparable to a stainless steel spoke. A bladed carbon fiber spoke should have a mass of about .0039 kg. One ad claims its composite spoke is tested to withstand "over 400 pounds" of tension, but because stainless steel spokes have been tested at 600 pounds or more, that statement is hardly a ringing endorsement. Finally, aerodynamic wheels, with either a solid disc or a few composite blades, are the alternative to standard spokes. The masses of these vary considerably, but so far most seem to be heavier than a standard spoked wheel of similar durability.

The rim is the next major wheel component. Although rims for cheap bikes may be stamped from steel, and in principle a well-designed steel rim could be about the same weight as an aluminum one of the same strength, in practice steel rims are too heavy for high-performance use. Currently almost all quality bikes have aluminum rims, though formerly wooden rims were the ticket for track bikes. Some track racers may still use super-light wood-reinforced aluminum rims, and rims of space-age materials must surely be around the corner.

Rims come in two basic designs, for clincher and tubular tires, respectively. The enclosed structure of a tubular rim is inherently stronger than the projecting flanges of a clincher rim and thus a tubular can be made very light. For decades, racing cyclists used tubulars exclusively, competing with light rims and tires and training with heavier, more durable versions. Clincher rims (together with their tires and tubes) have become ever lighter, to the point that many racers now use them even in races, but it is still not difficult to find a tubular rim that together with its tire easily undercuts the mass of the lightest clincher.

Most road frames are now designed for 700C wheels (either clinchers or tubulars), the slightly larger 27-in. size having fallen into decline, even though there is little practical difference between a 700C and 27-in. wheel in performance, or in any other respect. Mountain bikes are mostly designed for 26-in. wheels, although there are a variety of

Table 1203. Approximate mass of a single 300 mm spoke, kg

gauge	14	14–15–14	15	15–16–15
mass	.0073	.0063	.0059	.0050

incompatible rims with slightly different diameters all purporting to be 26-in. Although 700C and 26-in. are the "standards" for high-performance adult bicycles, there are exceptions. Alex Moulton's road bicycles have had 17-in. wheels for years, and his mountain bike has 20-in. wheels. Georgena Terry has been very successful marketing bikes with a 24-in. front wheel, based on Bill Boston's original 1970s design for women (or men) for whom the smallest standard frame is too tall, and a few other manufacturers have followed suit. It is also possible to find road bicycles that use two wheels of 24 to 26 inches in diameter, including both narrow clinchers and tubulars; 650C is one such size. A smaller-diameter rim is more rigid than a larger one of the same design, and thus small rims can be made even lighter than proportional to their size. Though practical considerations such as availability, susceptibility to flats, and increased road shock have prevented more widespread acceptance, small wheels enjoy an advantage in mass (though, as we have seen, not in rolling resistance).

Depending on intended use and durability, 700C tubular rims vary from about 200 to 450 grams each. The lightest of these are used only on the track, for pursuits and time trials; the middle of the range for other track events and important road events where one-day performance takes priority over extended life; and the heaviest are used for a season or more of day-to-day training and racing. Clincher rims in 700C size vary from about 395 to 590 grams each. The lighter half are used for sport and recreation with narrow tires; the heavier half for commuting, loaded touring and tandems with wide tires. Aerodynamic rims with a pronounced peak necessarily weigh more than their conventional counterparts, both tubular and clincher, but are also particularly stiff, may be more durable, and may be able to get away with fewer spokes.

The spoke nipples are the wheel parts next in line away from the hub. Nipples are usually nickel-plated brass and weigh about 0.99 g apiece, although rims with wood inserts require longer nipples, which weigh a little more. Aluminum nipples are also available to reduce rotating mass. Because the density of aluminum is about 32% that of brass, on a 36-spoke wheel aluminum nipples ought to save about 24 grams. (*Caveat emptor*: if one were to believe some ads, replacing brass nipples with aluminum would yield savings in excess of the total mass of the brass nipples themselves — a good trick.)

Clincher wheels are ordinarily built with a protective plastic or cloth rim strip that adds about 20 grams to the rim. Tubular rims have a layer of glue between the tire and the rim, which should weigh even less.

Finally, the tire is the last contributor, and a significant one, to the wheel's moment of inertia. Tubular tires range between about 200 and 400 grams apiece. Again, road surface and durability are the criteria. The heaviest tubulars are intended for cyclo-cross; about 260 grams is the standard for racing on roads. Clinchers in 700C may weigh anywhere from 165 to 700 grams, an enormous range, encompassing everything from racing to expedition touring. The lightest figures are misleading, however, because clincher tires require tubes, which necessarily add significant mass. Standard butyl tubes vary between 90 and perhaps 200 grams depending on width, although a precise match between tire width and suggested tube width is not sacrosanct. The more expensive but supposedly less puncture-prone latex tubes are lighter, perhaps 49 to 185 grams. For 26-in. mountain bike wheels, the range in tire masses is perhaps 400–750 grams, with most models falling toward the high end of this range because they are designed for traction on soft surfaces and durability in the face of rocks and logs, rather than minimum moment of inertia. Because these tires are also clinchers, the additional mass of the tube must be added: mountain bike tubes run perhaps 130–350 g for butyl, 105–335 g for latex. Table 1204 gives a sampling of typical wheels: mid-range mountain bike 26 x 1.95 clincher, loaded touring 700C x 35 clincher, mid-range sport 700C x 25 clincher, light aero-profile 700C x 20 clincher, mid-range tubular, and ultra-light tubular.

Moment of Inertia and Performance

Because the smaller the moment of inertia of its wheels, the faster the bicycle can accelerate or decelerate, a step taken to reduce the moment of inertia is a step toward improved performance. This step usually entails choosing a lighter tire, a lighter rim, and fewer and thinner spokes. However, this is also a step toward reduced reliability: more frequent truing, shortened useful life, greater likelihood of road damage, probably greater likelihood of flats. The rider must be careful to choose wheels and tires sturdy enough for the load they must carry and the road surfaces they will encounter. He must trade off performance versus maintenance. This is a trial-and-error process, based on one's own experience and the advice of one's riding companions and shop personnel.

Another consideration, however, is aerodynamics. Most wheels are designed for a good strength-to-mass ratio without regard to drag. Though standard wheels are perfectly adequate for most uses, the availability of aero versions raises questions. A rim with a tall parabolic cross section no doubt improves the aerodynamics of the wheels, but it is also heavier than a standard rim, and its extra mass is far from the hub — the worst place to put it as far as moment of inertia is concerned. Do the improved aerodynamics offset the increased mass and inertia? Aerodynamic

carbon-fiber composite wheels with a few blades instead of standard spokes are supposed to be very effective in reducing drag, but they may be heavier yet; so are disc wheels and wheel covers. Under what conditions are aero wheels improvements?

If the conditions are flat, or nearly so, and if the application is time trialing or similar riding at a nearly constant speed, the answer is simple: aero wheels unquestionably improve performance. Mass and moment of inertia under such conditions make little difference, because the bicycle is seldom climbing or accelerating; what matters is a low coefficient of drag. Disc wheels (or wheel covers, if permitted) usually give the lowest C_D, followed by aero composite wheels, then aero rims with fewer-than-usual bladed spokes. Unfortunately, precise coefficient of drag figures for these options are not available, and the best aerodynamic wheels are often very expensive, but at least the qualitative answer is straightforward.

When mass matters, the answer may be different. Here the lack of precise C_D data hurts, and though wheel mass may be known, moment of inertia can only be estimated. But estimation is exactly what we have to do to assess how effective different wheels may be in improving performance. Suppose we take one of the severest tests of acceleration: a 200-meter sprint. We will assume a lighter bike and rider than our standard, beginning at a total of 80 kg, perhaps more typical of sprint conditions. We will also give the rider sprinter horsepower: 1,120 W, about 1.5 hp, to accelerate from an initial 11.2 m/s (25 mph) to whatever speed he can reach by the finish. Our standard wheels will be very light ones, with particularly low-mass tubular rims and tires suitable for a smooth track but strong enough (we hope) to stand up to a sprint — moments of inertia 0.0528 and 0.0534 kg-m^2 at front and rear respectively. Nothing aerodynamic, however; our rider and bike have a C_D of 0.88 with these wheels. When we run them through their paces, we find they complete the 200 meters in 13.54 seconds, accelerating to 16.71 m/s (37.38 mph) by the finish line.

The next option will be very similar, the only difference being aero rims. We will suppose the

Table No. 1204. Moment of inertia of typical wheels

wheel type	number of spokes	rim mass (g)	tire and tube mass (g)	moment of inertia (kg-m^2)
mountain	32	440	835	0.129
touring	36	575	505	0.120
sport	36	450	380	0.094
light aero	28	480	285	0.085
mid tubular	32	360	300	0.074
ultra light	32	260	225	0.053

aero-profile rims add 360 grams to the bike and have moments of inertia of 0.0699 and 0.0705 kg-m^2 respectively. (These numbers are based on actual rims available on the market.) The resulting C_D, however, can only be a guess; we'll try 0.87. The corresponding time for the same sprint is also 13.54 s, the final speed 16.74 m/s: a photo finish against the lightweight standard wheels. If our guess is only a little pessimistic, these wheels could win easily despite their considerable extra mass.

Finally, we'll make some wilder guesses about composite aero bladed wheels, again based on a model actually available. These are very light for such wheels, adding only 160 grams to the bike — better than the aero rims above. Judging from the distribution of carbon fiber and aluminum, their moments of inertia may be about 0.0782 kg-m^2 each, not quite as good as the other wheels in this example, but better than a lot of wheels used by recreational riders. C_D is more problematical. Ads for one model of such composite wheels estimate a certain time savings in a time trial; assuming that their time trial is flat (not downhill!) and that their reference bike and rider are similar to ours, it is easy to calculate the drag coefficient which could produce such savings all by itself. Doing so, however, yields a number near 0.78, a C_D so low it is frankly unbelievable: it's almost recumbent bike territory! Even though the ads are almost certainly exaggerating their product's performance advantage, we will go ahead and use that drag coefficient value. The sprint then takes 13.37 s, ending at 17.10 m/s: not surprisingly, the best by far.

While the results hinge on data that is difficult to come by, it should still be clear that it takes only a modest improvement in aerodynamics to offset a hefty quantity of rotating mass. Already some sprinters are showing up with wheels that were formerly reserved for time trialists and triathletes. Their numbers are bound to increase.

Acceleration and Cadence

Spinning has its advantages. One is the possibility of faster acceleration, though the reasons behind this possibility may not be immediately obvious. We tend to remember F = m a, and deduce that for more acceleration, we need more force. Don't we get more force at low cadences rather than high ones? Not exactly; we *need* more force at low cadences. To maintain a constant speed in the face of rolling resistance, aerodynamic drag, and the other forces acting on a bicycle, a rider needs a certain amount of power. To accelerate, he needs more power yet.

For example, under flat, windless conditions, our standard rider needs to apply a mere 37 watts to maintain a constant 5 m/s (11.2 mph), but to accelerate to 6 m/s within 1 second, he needs much more power: about 537 watts during that second. The amount of pedaling force he needs in order to produce that much power depends on the gear he has selected. With a very low gear, he doesn't need much force at all — but he needs one heck of a spin! With a very high gear, he hardly needs to rotate the cranks, but if he applies the force necessary for that acceleration, his knees may need a series of visits to an orthopedic surgeon. In between, there may be a good compromise allowing both reasonable force and reasonable cadence. The relationship between power and force, if you recall, is:

$$P = L \omega = F s \omega$$

where P is power, L is torque, F is force applied to the pedals, s is the crankarm length, and ω (omega) is angular velocity. Take 537 watts at 60 rpm with 170 mm crankarms, for instance. The angular velocity is 60 x 2 π radians per 60 seconds, or 2 π radians per second; therefore the force which must be applied to the pedals is 537 / (.17 x 2 π) = 503 newtons, about 113 pounds. Using the formula for gear-inches:

$$g.i. = v /(c \text{ rpm})$$

where g.i. is gear-inches, v is speed, rpm is cadence, and c is 0.00133 for speeds in meters per second, we can also determine that 5 m/s is attainable at 60 rpm with a gear ratio of about 63 gear-inches, a medium gear for most bikes.

We have already acknowledged that human beings can supply only so much power over a given span of time. As we saw in Chapter 4, it is also true that humans (and their muscles and joints) can supply only so much force. That force limit — whatever it is — imposes a lower limit on cadence or an upper limit on gear ratio, depending on the current speed and the level of acceleration needed. By keeping cadence high enough, yet not so high that power is compromised, the rider can keep force within manageable limits and still achieve maximum acceleration.

Another advantage spinning offers has to do with crankarm position. Again, the pedaling force available varies throughout the pedaling circle: high during much of the downstroke, low at the top and bottom of the circle, perhaps even lower during the upper part of the upstroke.

Though good riders work hard to pedal circles, some variation remains in the smoothest pedaling style. Probably as a result, most riders prefer a particular pedal position when they shove off from a stop or to begin to accelerate. Suppose a rival rider "jumps" and a rider needs to match his acceleration as quickly as possible. Quite simply, when he is already pedaling at a fast cadence, there is on average less of a delay before his feet move into his favored position. At best a tiny difference, yes, and possibly no advantage at all; but perhaps it is enough to give him the edge more often than not.

Neither of the preceding two arguments applies to constant power applications such as time trialing. There the optimum cadence is based strictly on available power and avoidance of injury.

13

Summary

This book has discussed many areas that potentially affect performance. The most basic among them are the mechanics of the bicycle itself and the forces that act upon it; anyone who expects to use a tool to its fullest needs to understand the details of its design and operation. Less obvious, but equally important, is an understanding of the consequences: how knowledge of the technical aspects of cycling can be applied to advantage in the situations a cyclist routinely faces during a long or fast ride. With luck, some of the principles and analyses in this book may suggest measures the reader can take to come closer to his potential as a high-performance cyclist, both now and in the future.

All measures intended to improve performance should be tempered with common sense. After reading about the evils of mass, for example, anyone would be foolish to lose so much body weight that he loses strength in the process, or to use lightweight components on rougher roads or with heavier loads than those for which they were designed. A thoughtless rider might be tempted to adopt such a low aerodynamic tuck that it interferes with safe control of the bike, or he might fly off the road watching his computer during an all-out downhill record speed attempt. Less harmfully, a person may merely look pretentious and ridiculous going to great expense to tweak his bike for speed when his own athletic abilities are less than top rank. Yet most of us have seen numerous examples of such follies.

Along similar lines, among cyclists it is a common attitude, one certainly fostered by the bicycle industry, that performance can be purchased. While it is true that certain pieces of equipment have performance-enhancing potential, high performance is not available as a plug-in module. It is up to the cyclist to exploit the potential and master the unique characteristics of the upgrades. A softer tire compound will not make the bike corner faster; the cyclist must learn to carry more speed into the corner and lean over farther, a technique that is unlikely to pay off unless he was already using his former tires to their full capability. The smart cyclist knows not to expect any advantage from light wheels under steady-speed conditions, but also that he cannot get away with subjecting them to the sort of abuse he gave his utility wheels. More numerous gears or higher gear ratios may even slow the cyclist down, unless he is savvy enough to use them to maintain a good cadence.

The main danger of thinking of performance as something to be purchased is that by far the most significant source of performance is the cyclist himself. To improve, the cyclist must change, physically and mentally. It is up to him to increase his strength and endurance, to manage his diet and weight, to acquire and hone his skills, to learn how his bike and his body work (separately and together), to formulate riding strategies and refine or revamp them as he gains experience, and to tailor his riding style to the conditions that evolve moment by moment and day by day. It is also up to him to muster the determination and patience needed to make all these changes. Most of us fall somewhat short.

The cyclists who have the most success in competition, and the cyclists who most enjoy riding, are those who have adapted themselves to the sport. No one has lost a race through lack of the latest shift levers or pedals, but many with state-of-the-art equipment have failed to finish a race through neglecting to implement and follow an adequate training program. Many more never even came close to entering their first race. While many touring cyclists have seen breathtaking sights, met wonderful people, and enthusiastically immersed themselves in a different way of life, a far greater number of potential cyclists never made it beyond their immediate neighborhoods because they felt the bike's saddle was uncomfortable, they couldn't get the hang of shifting, they were intimidated when a car brushed by their elbow, or they became discouraged when they couldn't keep up with a more experienced rider. A certain level of physical ability is necessary in order to ride a bicycle at all, and it is no surprise that riding long distances or at brisk speeds requires a much higher level of fitness and technique. Yet the process of improvement is not merely physical. The greatest obstacle to better cycling performance — but also the most satisfying cycling component to upgrade — is one's own mind.

Appendices

Appendix A: Measurement, Calibration, and Test

It is easy to spout generalities — indeed, this book does it often — but more difficult to back them up with hard numbers. Isn't it obvious, for example, that a loose jacket flapping in the wind is less aerodynamic than a snug jersey? Most of us are content to take the obvious for granted, discard the jacket in favor of the jersey, and go for a ride.

Often, however, the choice is not so obvious. Just how bad aerodynamically is that standard water bottle and cage? Will one of those narrow cages and bottles that sit in the wind shadow behind the down tube really save seconds in a time trial? Or perhaps one of those water bags that rests on the back is better? We could simply make a judgment, adopt one of the choices, and continue on; but if we are seriously committed to improving performance, guesswork won't do. We have to test the alternatives, turning the qualitative into the quantitative. Unfortunately, testing is not as simple as hooking up a handy Digital Electronic Perform-O-Meter to the item and glancing at the readout.

Time Measurement

Because bicycle performance is mostly about minimum time or maximum distance, we have to go back to the basics. For time measurements, a stopwatch is the ideal instrument. Many inexpensive wrist watches have a stopwatch built in; so do some cycle computers. Resolution to the tenth of a second is more than adequate; in fact, for measurements of a few minutes or more, an ordinary watch or cycle computer clock that measures only to the second will do.

Distance Measurement and Calibration

Almost everybody riding a bicycle these days has a cycle computer that measures distance traveled on a ride. And at the end of that ride, almost none of the cycle computers agree on what the distance was. The reasons for the discrepancies are numerous, but the most fundamental of them is that few cyclists bother to calibrate their computers after installing them. An approximation may be good enough for a casual ride, and an exaggerated distance is good for the ego, but for serious measurement purposes, the computer must be calibrated, that is, brought into close agreement with a known standard, preferably an accurate one. Merely setting the computer to the number printed in the manual next to the appropriate wheel size is not the same thing as calibration, although many cyclists do not even do that much.

The first step in any kind of distance calibration is to set the bike up exactly the way it will usually be ridden — the usual tires, the usual tire pressures as measured with the usual gauge, the usual accessories — because the accuracy of the cycle computer very much depends on a consistent wheel diameter. The cycle computer itself must also be operating well, not for example periodically zeroing out because of a faulty contact or too-distant pickup. Some models turn themselves off during stops and do not necessarily turn themselves back on

immediately, a feature that may extend battery life but severely limits their usefulness.

The next concern is to find a standard measurement that can be applied to the distances the bike travels. Many states, for instance, erect periodic mileposts, sometimes on roads cyclists may travel on. Unfortunately, mileposts are not necessarily accurate; their purpose is to provide reference points rather than to assist odometer calibration. Individual posts may be placed up to several hundred feet ahead or behind their correct locations, depending on local conditions. Even averaged over extended distances, the posted mile may be considerably different from a "real" mile, as defined by the Bureau of Standards. As an example, the average posted mile on rural Highway 70 in New Jersey is 2% longer than on suburban Interstate 76 in Pennsylvania a short drive away. (Perhaps "a country mile" is more than just an expression?)

Still, if there is a convenient source of standardized mileage, even if it is not absolutely accurate, it may be reasonable to adopt it as the standard rather than be faced with the discrepancy every time one rides by. Given that approach, calibration consists of riding the "known" distance, preferably at least twice, then adjusting the computer to compensate for any discrepancy. For example, suppose you have access to a measured mile. Zero the odometer at the start and ride toward the finish line. Relax while riding so that you don't waver any more or less than usual. Suppose the odometer reads 1.03 miles at the finish line. Don't stop the computer, but turn the bike around on the finish line and ride back to the start. Suppose the odometer now reads 2.07. (If you hadn't ridden that extra mile, you would have thought the odometer read 3% high, but it actually read closer to 3.5% high.) Referring to the computer manual, adjust the constant to compensate; for example, if the current constant set in the computer is 217 (just what this constant represents doesn't matter at this point), multiply it by 2.00 (the real distance), divide by 2.07 (the distance as measured), round off, then input the newly calculated constant, in this case 210. Re-ride the measured distance to make sure the computer is now set correctly. If you wish to be extra precise, you can note where the computer actually ticks the tenths or hundredths digit over, break out a tape measure, and figure these measurement differences into the calculations, but because most computers cannot be set more precisely than to about the nearest 0.5%, there is little point in going to extremes.

If local mileage sources are unavailable or inaccurate, one must turn to the low end of the distance scale. Rulers are reasonably accurate, but difficult and tedious to apply to the distances bicycles travel. A steel tape measure is a better bet. The idea here is to measure precisely how far the bicycle travels in a certain number of wheel revolutions — revolutions of the same wheel the cycle computer sensor is mounted next to, of course. The most accurate method is to put a spot of paint on the tire tread of that wheel, mount the bicycle, ride it in a straight line on the same sort of a paved surface one usually rides, then measure the average distance between spots. If the idea of spotting your silk tubulars does not appeal to you, or if you are stuck indoors with nothing better to do on a frigid winter night, then find a long hallway or basement with a hard (not carpeted) floor. Start the bicycle so that the valve of the wheel to be measured is at the bottom of the wheel; mark that starting place with a piece of tape. (It helps to have an assistant.) Then carefully ride the bicycle forward, counting at least two wheel revolutions, and mark on the floor where the valve again reaches bottom. You must ride in your usual position, not walk the bike, to put the proper amount of weight on the wheel, and it's best to do this process several times to try to cancel out the inevitable errors. Carefully measure the distance between the tapes; it's a good idea to do this a few times, too, in case the tape measure slips or curves. Then divide the distance by the number of revolutions to obtain the average circumference of the wheel.

The constant that must be input to some cycle computers is this number (the circumference) in centimeters; to convert inches to centimeters, multiply by 2.54. If that is the case for your computer, just enter the circumference and you should be done, assuming the computer does its job accurately from there. If the constant is the wheel diameter instead, divide the circumference by π (3.1416) and enter that. If neither of these seems to be the case and you can't deduce from the manual what the constant represents, you may be forced to adopt a different plan, such as adjusting your computer to read what another rider's computer does after the two of you have ridden the same distance. Accuracy is desirable, but usually not crucial. Consistency and agreement are often more valuable.

Elevation Measurement

Unless you happen to be a surveyor, it is difficult to measure the height of a hill directly, but there are other means that ought to be accurate enough. One is to buy (or borrow) one of the cycle computer models that include an altimeter. A barometer can also be used for this purpose (see Elevation in Appendix B), but a good barometer is both more fragile and more expensive than a bicycle altimeter. Besides, one would usually want to adjust it to mean sea level, and for that it is useful to have a topographic map. In addition to roads and other details, topographic maps have contour lines indicating elevations above mean sea level. Given such a map, to determine the elevation of a particular point, first locate the point on the map. Determine the elevations represented by the nearest contour lines, by noting both the labeled lines and the "contour interval," the elevation difference between lines that are not labeled. Estimate the elevation of the point by interpolation. Topographic maps of the U.S. are available for purchase from the U.S. Geological Survey, 1200 South Eads Street, Arlington, VA 22202. To determine which maps you want, ask for the free index to topographic mapping for your state. The most detailed maps, best for this purpose, are the 7.5-minute series at 1:24,000 scale. Topographic maps may also be available from local dealers and can often be found at libraries.

While we are on the subject of measuring elevation, notice that some bike altimeters measure "total climb," an indication of how hilly a ride has been; for example, if we climb three hills each 20 feet in elevation difference from bottom to top, we have climbed 60 feet total. Although this sounds reasonable, it should remind us of the Coastline Problem. Suppose we want to measure the length of the coastline of the eastern United States. The straight-line distance from the tip of Florida to the Maine-New

Brunswick border, estimated from a globe across the room, is about 1,450 miles. Looking at the globe more closely, we see that the coastline undulates; a better estimate would be 1680 miles. Pulling out a map of the United States, however, we see that the coastline is more irregular than the globe could show. The previous measurements grossly underestimated the real length. The more detailed individual state maps in the atlas show still further irregularity; a geological survey map shows more yet. Each level of finer resolution would force us to revise our coastline length upward. A rowboat tour or a shore walk would show that even that number was an underestimate; consider what a magnifying glass or microscope would reveal. Consequently, coastline length is a virtually meaningless quantity; practically any estimate is as good as another. Only when the measurement resolution is defined can the number be estimated well enough to be repeatable; and even then, what's the point? The same is clearly true of total climb measurements. They can probably tell us that one course is hillier than another, if we didn't know that already. The displayed number itself is not very useful, more for entertainment than for information … and for bragging rights, or shouldn't we see "total descent" measured equally often?

Grade Measurement

It is often useful to measure the grade of a hill. Using an altimeter and odometer, note the elevation and distance readings at one end of the hill, ride to the opposite end, note the readings again, and divide the difference in elevation by the difference in distance, converted to the same unit. For example, if the elevations are 350 and 470 feet and the distance covered is 0.38 miles, the grade is $(470 - 350) / (0.38 \times 5280) = 0.06$ or 6%. If you are obtaining the elevation difference from a map, you can also measure the distance between the points directly off the map using a ruler or an "opisometer," a measuring device designed to follow the meanderings of a road on a map. Once you have the distance, multiply by the map scale. Calculate grade as above.

Angle Measurement

A bicyclist may be curious about the frame angles — that is, the head tube angle and seat tube angle — of his bicycle(s). The instrument for measuring angles is of course the protractor, and there is even a specialized frame angle protractor on the market that ought to relieve a lot of squinting and guesswork. Another option is to measure the linear dimensions precisely, perhaps using bits of tape as reference points, and solving for the angles using trigonometry. (Try the law of sines.) Whichever method you try, however, remember that frame angles should be measured with respect to level ground. A bicycle's top tube is not necessarily parallel to the ground.

Weight Measurement and Comparisons

Another instrument the serious performance-seeker may want to use is a scale. The spring bathroom scales people use for keeping track of their weight are not usually very accurate, especially at the low end of their range. To weigh a complete bicycle, for example, do not attempt to put the bicycle on the scale. Instead, holding the bicycle off the floor, step onto the scale, note the reading, then put the bicycle down and weigh only yourself. The weight of the bicycle is the difference of the two readings. For better accuracy, calibrate the scale against a more accurate instrument, such as the sliding-weight balance kind most doctors' offices have. Smaller spring scales marketed for weighing food portions, packages to be mailed, or fish catches can also be calibrated using an object of known weight. You know the adage "A pint's a pound the world around"? It's close: a pint of water at 68 degrees F weighs 1.040 pounds or 471.8 grams, allowing for the buoyancy of air. That should be enough to get you started. But often accurate weight is not as important as merely knowing whether one particular component is lighter or heavier than another. Calibration in that case is unnecessary.

Weight comparisons are simple and unequivocal, perhaps too much so. Either a new component is lighter or it isn't. Lower weight (or mass) can only improve performance, right? Well, perhaps that principle is not completely true. How about a lighter component that breaks because it is not strong enough for the application? Or one that flexes enough to rob power, or creaks annoyingly, or is too uncomfortable to tolerate, or requires a lot of maintenance, or is so expensive that no money is left to buy something that might have improved performance more significantly? Some thought beyond a simple comparison of weights should go into the decision.

Other comparisons are more complex yet. Most require the same sort of subjective considerations, but do not lend themselves to an easy, objective assessment. Not all new components should be expected to make a difference in performance. A new saddle can hardly improve speed even if it weighs next to nothing; the question is whether it will be tolerable to sit on. A new model of tire may have many virtues, but (compared to the old one) noticeable differences in rolling resistance or cornering grip are unlikely to be among them. A new shifting system may (or may not) feel natural; it may improve your confidence in being able to make a quick, reliable shift, but you'd be unwise to look for any consistent speed improvement as a result. Yet many component changes ought to have performance consequences, otherwise there is little point in acquiring them. The same goes for the rider's position on the bike. How do you know whether a change is worthwhile unless you evaluate it?

Performance Evaluation

There are basically two ways to evaluate the performance of a new component or position on the bike: analysis and test. Analysis is much the same procedure we have been using in most of this book. For example, one might measure a reduction in weight and moment of inertia obtained by substituting a different rim, then calculate its effect on speed. Or one could measure a reduction in frontal area caused by a lower stem height, then calculate the difference in aerodynamic drag. If the measurements are accurate, if all relevant factors are considered, and if the reasoning and mathematics are correct, analysis can be very useful, particularly when a test would be difficult to conduct or the results might be too subtle to show up.

Test, i.e. actual on-the-bike speed comparison, is the other way to evaluate performance. The procedure is simple in concept: first ride with the old component or position, measuring time over a fixed distance or distance over a fixed time; then fit the new component or adopt the new position and repeat, comparing the numbers afterwards.

Unfortunately, this procedure is full of potential pitfalls. Variable conditions during the tests can easily account for most or all of the difference in the results. For a test to be successful (that is, for it to give accurate and useful results), all differences not attributable to the items under test must be systematically eliminated or accounted for.

One of the greatest variables is the performance of the rider himself. A human being cannot be expected to produce exactly the same amount of power at any given time during a trial, nor on average in subsequent trials. If possible, the test should be performed without having to depend on consistent power output: the rider should coast. For aerodynamic and most rolling resistance tests, coasting is perfectly adequate. The tester should find a steep downhill with a sufficiently long run-out distance, and take care always to begin the downhill at the same speed on successive trials, either using a standing start (if the hill is very steep) or approaching the start at consistent steady speed. High average speeds help accentuate aerodynamic drag differences that may not be detectable at lower speeds, though they may mask rolling resistance differences. A flat stretch of road, protected from the wind, may be adequate if the tester always uses exactly the same stretch and begins at a high enough speed, because barely perceptible variations in slope can greatly affect the results. Because so much of the bicycle's speed depends on drag, a consistent rider position from run to run is crucial. The bicycle should also always take the same path along the course, keeping any steering corrections as small and gradual as possible. If there is a significant difference in the weights of the items being tested for drag (for example, two radically different handlebars), the rider should carry enough extra

weight while testing the lighter item to assure that the trial tests aerodynamics, not gravity, bearing in mind the fact that any measured advantage will vary up and down hills.

Note that a constant-speed approach, the faster the better, is the only way the computer speed display should be used in a test. Even there it is not ideal. Because there is always a delay, on some models as much as a few seconds, between when the bike attains a particular speed and when the computer displays it, the bike must first settle into a steady speed to ensure that the display has caught up. There are additional uncertainties in the displayed speed. Is actual speed of 19.99 mph displayed as 19 or 20, for instance? Is there hysteresis in the display, so that if the bike is going very nearly 20 mph the display does not flicker annoyingly between 19 and 20 but settles on one or the other until there is a significant change? Momentary "glitches" and "bugs" in computation algorithms, both surprisingly common, can also cause cycle computers to show moderately or wildly inaccurate maximum and average speed readings. Calculating speed from cadence in a known gear is an improvement over using the displayed speed, but the basics — time and distance — give by far the most accurate speed measurements.

In drivetrain tests, such as the use of oval chainrings or different gear ratios, or in tests of the rider himself, such as his ability to supply power in a different position on the bike, coasting is obviously inadequate. The trials must attempt to cancel out inconsistencies. On level ground, an equal number of trials should be run in each direction, to cancel variances in wind and any slight differences in grade. The rider must first warm up, then perform trials according to a strict routine of fixed-duration efforts alternating with fixed-duration rest periods. In each trial, the rider must attempt to maintain the same level of effort, preferably near maximum, because more comfortable lower levels are even more difficult to reproduce.

By measuring the rate of oxygen consumption during exercise, physiologists can deduce the amount of power an athlete is producing; the relationship is a linear one. Needless to say, this precise clinical method is impractical for the average cyclist, whose rides seldom take him through a laboratory. It has been shown, however, that for a given individual there is also an almost linear relationship between heart rate (pulse) and oxygen consumption rate. (See Whitt and Wilson's *Bicycling Science* for details.) The linearity of the relationship is probably less valid at especially high and low heart rates, before one is warmed up, and when one is becoming tired. Individuals also vary greatly in how quickly their bodies respond to changes in effort. These facts suggest that in performing a test that requires the cyclist to provide constant power, a heart rate monitor, used intelligently in maintaining a steady pulse, may help assure nearly constant output.

Deducing power output from pulse is a less reliable undertaking. For instance, just because someone has a rapid pulse does not mean he is currently producing all the useful output of which he is capable. Readers who wish to experiment can try calibrating their own pulses. First, select a hill with a long, constant, and preferably steep grade, to ensure that gravity rather than the less-accurately quantified rolling resistance and aerodynamics plays the major role. Carefully measure the grade and the weight of the rider and bicycle. Ride up the slope at a low constant speed and note the heart rate; repeat for a high constant speed. In subsequent trials, try to maintain that constant heart rate both on the approach to the hill and during the climb, and measure distances and times rather than relying on the computer for speeds. Calculate the power outputs achieved, using the equations or supplied program, and graph power vs. heart rate. Do not, of course, overexert yourself in the name of science, nor attempt to read more into the relationship than is warranted. Low heart rates obviously do not produce negative results, for example, and high rates may be physically impossible, or dangerous.

During any evaluation by test, the tester must conduct several trials for each alternative, recording the results. It is important not to look at the computer display during the trial, lest it influence performance during the remainder of the trial and thus bias the results. After the trials are run, it is not sufficient merely to take the average for each of the alternatives. For example, suppose the times for three trials of alternative A are 20.6, 21.2, and 20.8 seconds, while for alternative B they are 20.4, 20.9, and 21.0 seconds. The mean for A is 20.87; for B, 20.77. B beats A by a tenth of a second on average, but a glance at the original numbers reveals that the average variation between the trials for either alternative is much greater than a tenth of a second.

With so much noise in the data, it is impossible to know whether B is really better, let alone better by a certain amount. One needs more trials, and if possible more care in reducing the variation between trials, before being able to determine whether A or B is the better alternative. The variations between trials in this example were relatively mild; variation in real trials are often both more pronounced and more confusing. Long, tedious, and inconclusive test sessions may be the norm. Though the answer "It really doesn't matter much one way or the other" may be frustrating, perhaps it is really the correct one. For a more thorough treatment of how to deal with variations in data and how to draw conclusions from them, consult a book on statistics; a couple are listed in the Bibliography.

Appendix B: Equations

Equations used throughout this book or otherwise useful in a cycling context are collected here for convenience. The equations are grouped alphabetically by concept (acceleration, energy, force, gearing, etc.), followed by an explanation of the variables, suitable units, and possibly notes.

Acceleration (Linear Acceleration)

$$a = (v_0 + v_1) / t$$

$$v_1 = v_0 + a\,t$$

$$d = 0.5\,(v_0 + v_1)\,t$$

$$d = v_0\,t + 0.5\,a\,t^2$$

$$v_1^2 = v_0^2 + 2\,a\,d$$

where

a is linear acceleration (m/s^2)

v_0 and v_1 are the speeds at either end of an interval of constant acceleration (m/s)

t is elapsed time (s)

d is distance traveled (m)

Note: See also Angular Acceleration and Lateral Acceleration.

Acceleration Due to Gravity

$$g = 9.80616 - 0.025928 \cos(2\,\phi) + 0.000069 \cos^2(2\,\phi) - 0.000003086\,H$$

where

g is acceleration due to gravity (m/s^2)

ϕ is latitude (degrees)

H is altitude (m)

Note: This is known as Helmert's equation. There are also local variations caused, for instance, by massive mineral deposits. See also Gravitational Force Between Two Masses.

Aerodynamic Drag

$$F_D = 0.5\,C_D\,\rho\,v_a^2\,A$$

where

F_D is aerodynamic drag force (N)

C_D is coefficient of aerodynamic drag

ρ is air density (kg/m^3)

v_a is airspeed (m/s)

A is frontal area (normal to direction of v) (m^2)

Air Density

$$\rho = \rho_0\,(T_0 / T)\,(P / P_0)$$

where

ρ is density of dry air (kg/m^3)

T is absolute temperature in K (Kelvin)

P is barometric pressure (see below)

and the 0-subscripts refer to the density at some known absolute temperature and pressure.

Notes: At a temperature of 0 C, the absolute temperature is 273.15 K; when at that temperature the barometric pressure is 760 mm (29.921 inches) of mercury (Hg), the air density is 1.2929 kg/m^3: three useful values for T_0, P_0 and ρ_0, respectively. See also Temperature and Barometric Pressure.

This is the equation for dry air. For moist air, the barometric pressure in mm Hg must be modified by subtracting 0.3783 e, where e is the vapor pressure of the moisture of the air in mm Hg. See the included programs to calculate density of moist air, or consult the tables found in some reference works, such as the *Handbook of Chemistry and Physics*.

Airspeed

$$v_a = v_g + v_w \cos(z_g - z_w)$$

where

v_a is airspeed (m/s), the speed of the air relative to the bicycle, positive if it is apparently a headwind

v_g is ground speed (m/s), the speed of the bicycle relative to the ground

v_w is wind speed (m/s), the absolute speed of the wind relative to the ground, in whatever direction it is blowing

z_g is azimuth of bicycle motion (degrees clockwise from north to the direction the bicycle is headed: 0 = north, 45 = northeast, 90 = east, etc.)

z_w is wind azimuth (degrees clockwise from north to direction from which the wind is coming)

Note: Direction of a moving vehicle is usually expressed in terms of its destination: a bicycle heading east has an azimuth of 90 degrees. However, wind direction is usually expressed in terms of its source: a westerly wind comes from the west and thus has azimuth 270 degrees even though, like the bicycle, it is heading east. In this case, 90 − 270 = −180; cos −180 = −1, so the airspeed is the ground speed minus the wind speed.

This equation applies only to a solo bicyclist, not to one drafting another rider or inside a pack of riders, where the wind conditions would be complex and the airspeed normally less.

Angular Acceleration

$$\alpha = (\omega_1 - \omega_0) / t$$

$$\alpha = a / r$$

where

α is angular acceleration (radians/s^2)

ω_0 and ω_1 are angular velocities at beginning and end of a period of constant angular acceleration (radians/s)

t is duration of that period (s)

a is linear acceleration (m/s^2)

r is wheel radius (m)

Note: The second equation describes the angular acceleration of a bicycle wheel firmly in contact with the ground. See also Torque.

Area of Tire Contact Patch

$$A = F_w / p$$

where

A is area of the tire contact patch (sq. in.)

F_w is normal force or load on the tire (lb.)

p is air pressure inside the tire (psi)

Note: This formula does not account for the reduced volume (and increased pressure) of a partially compressed tire, nor can it account for knobby treads or very irregular road surfaces. Approximate conversions to and from mks units: 1 square inch = .000645 m^2; 1 square meter = 1550 sq. in.; 1 pound = 4.45 N; 1 newton = 0.225 lb.; pound per square inch = 6895 N/m^2 = 0.0680 atmospheres; 1 newton per square meter = 0.000145 psi = 0.00000987 atmospheres; 1 atmosphere = 14.7 psi = 101,325 N/m^2.

Average Speed

$$v = d / (t_2 - t_1)$$

$$v = 0.5 (v_1 + v_2)$$

where

v is average speed (m/s)

d is distance traveled (m)

t_1 is start time (s)

t_2 is finish time (s). The difference $t_2 - t_1$ is called the elapsed time.

v_1 and v_2 are speeds at either end of an interval of constant acceleration (m/s)

Barometric Pressure

$$P = e^{(\ln((145447.2 - A) / 76189.27) / .19025433)}$$

where

P is barometric pressure (inches of Hg [mercury]), given a pressure of 29.92126 inches Hg at mean sea level

e is the base of natural logarithms, 2.718281828

ln is the natural logarithm function (also written $\log_e$)

A is elevation (altitude) (ft)

Note: This gives the standard barometric pressure for a given elevation. Because in all likelihood the current barometric pressure "reduced" to sea level will not be exactly the standard (i.e. 29.92126 inches Hg at sea level), use this equation for correcting barometric pressure for elevation. For example, if the radio broadcast indicates the current barometric pressure is 29.120 (at sea level), you know the pressure is about 0.801 below standard. If you are at 1000 ft elevation (28.856 inches Hg standard by this equation), the true current pressure where you are must be about 28.055 inches Hg.

Calories Consumed

$$C = E \%e / 100 / c$$

where

C is energy consumed in incremental dietetic calories (kcal)

E is energy expended (J)

%e is net metabolic efficiency (percent)

c is a unit conversion constant. For E in joules, c = 4186.

Note: A dietetic calorie is also known as a food calorie, kilocalorie, kilogram calorie, or large calorie. By "incremental," we mean the calories consumed in performing the activity, not those consumed just to stay alive and maintain body temperature. Likewise, "net" metabolic efficiency is the ratio of energy output to this incremental energy consumption. The efficiency of trained athletes has been measured at between 20% and 30%; nonathletes are undoubtedly less efficient. To use this formula in practice, calculate energy as average power output, using a power equation below or the program in the appendix. Multiply power (watts) times duration (seconds) to get energy (joules). If there are different periods when average power is significantly different, multiply each power level by its duration and sum the products to get total energy expended. Choose a suitable percentage of efficiency and apply the above formula.

Centripetal Acceleration

See Lateral Acceleration.

Circumference of a Circle

$$c = \pi d$$

$$c = 2 \pi r$$

where

c is circumference (m)

π is 3.14159…

d is diameter (m)

r is radius (m)

Crankarm Length

See text in Chapter 4. There is no universally agreed-upon formula for crankarm length.

Decelerating Force

$$F_d = -F_b \, \mu_b \, r_b \, / \, r_w$$

where

F_d is decelerating force contributed by a particular tire (N)

F_b is braking force applied normal to the rim (N)

μ_b is coefficient of kinetic friction between brake pad and rim

r_b is radius of the rim at the brake (m)

r_w is radius of wheel including tire (m)

Distance

See Average Speed and Acceleration.

Drag

See Aerodynamic Drag and Rolling Resistance.

Elevation (Altitude)

$$A = 145447.2 - 76189.27 \, e^{(.19025433 \, \ln P)}$$

where

A is elevation (altitude) (ft)

P is barometric pressure (inches of Hg [mercury]), given a pressure of 29.92126 inches Hg at mean sea level

e is the base of natural logarithms, 2.718281828

ln is the natural logarithm function (also written $\log_e$)

Note: Because in all likelihood the current barometric pressure at sea level will not be exactly the standard 29.92126, use this equation only for measuring elevation differences, i.e. elevation from pressure atop a hill minus elevation from pressure a the bottom of a hill.

Also, e raised to the (c ln P) power is equivalent to P raised to the c power; it was phrased this way because not all calculators and programming languages have a y-to-the-x function.

Energy

$$E = P \, t$$

where

E is energy expended, or work done (J)

P is average power (W)

t is time taken to do that work (s)

Note: See also Kinetic Energy and Potential Energy.

Force

$$F = m \, a$$

$$F = (m + I_f \, / \, r_f^2 + I_r \, / \, r_r^2) \, a$$

where

F is force (N)

m is mass (kg)

a is linear acceleration (m/s^2)

I_f is moment of inertia of front wheel (kg m^2)

r_f is radius of front wheel (m)

I_r is moment of inertia of rear wheel (kg m^2)

r_r is radius of rear wheel (m)

Note. The first equation is the general one for force and acceleration in a straight line. The second includes terms for accelerating the wheels of the bicycle. A further refinement could be made for accelerating the other rotating parts of the bicycle also.

See also Decelerating Force, Force Due to Gravity on a Grade, Normal Force, Pedaling Force, and Torque.

Force Due to Gravity on a Grade

$$F_G = g \, m \, \%G/100$$

where

F_G is force due to gravity (N), viewed (like aero-dynamic drag and rolling resistance) as a force opposing pedaling, along the line of the bicycle's motion.

g is acceleration due to gravity (m/s^2)

m is mass of the rider and bicycle (kg)

%G is percent grade, that is, 100 times the vertical increase (m) divided by the horizontal distance (m). %G is negative for downhill slopes.

Notes: This force of gravity is the force affecting the bicycle's motion, viewed as a force along the line of that motion. It is a vector component of weight (the vertical force of gravity); the vector component of weight perpendicular to this force would be the normal force pushing the bicycle against the ground.

A simplification has been made in the above equation. Strictly speaking, the term %G/100 should really be sin s, where s is the angle of inclination of the slope. Because %G/100 is equal to tan s, the expression could be sin [arctan (%G/100)]. But for small angles, such as almost all actual road slopes, the sine and tangent are nearly equal. Omitting the trigonometric functions still retains 3-digit accuracy up to 10% grades, 2-digit accuracy through 20% grades.

Frequency and Period of Vibration

$$F_w = (k \, / \, m)^{1/2} \, / \, 2\pi$$

$$f_f = v \, / \, s$$

$$T = 1/f$$

where

F_w is natural frequency of vibration (Hz)

k is spring force constant (N/m)

m is mass (kg)

π is 3.14159…

f_f is forced frequency of vibration imposed by an external source, such as a road surface (Hz)

v is speed (m/s)

s is wavelength of the external source (m)

f is frequency (of any sort) (Hz)

T is period of vibration (s)

Note: See Chapter 9 for a method of estimating k from the shape and dimensions of a fork and the value of Young's modulus of elasticity for its material. In practice, however, it is easier to determine the spring constant experimentally from the ratio of force to displacement. Also see that text for a fuller discussion of spring constant and load.

Friction

$$\mu = F_f / F_w$$

where μ is coefficient of friction (see below)

F_f is tangential force between two surfaces (see below) (N)

F_w is normal force pressing the surfaces together (N)

Note: When the surfaces in contact are sliding with respect to each other, F_f is the force balancing the friction that maintains constant velocity between the two surfaces; μ is then the coefficient of kinetic friction. When the surfaces in contact are not sliding, F_f is maximum tangential force (called the maximum force of static friction) that can be applied without causing the sur-

faces to slide; μ is then the coefficient of static friction. "Tangential" here means parallel to the two surfaces.

Gearing

$$g.i. = f\,w\,/\,r$$

$$v = c\,g.i.\,rpm$$

$$g.i. = v/(c\,rpm)$$

where

g.i. is gear ratio (gear-inches)

f is number of teeth on (front) chainwheel

w is diameter of driven wheel (inches)

r is number of teeth on (rear) cog

v is speed (units dependent on c)

c is a constant: for v in miles per hour, c = 0.002975; for v in m/s, c = 0.001330.

rpm is cadence (revolutions per minute)

Note: For the speed equations to be valid, bicycle speed must be due entirely to pedaling, not coasting.

The value of gear-inches is equivalent to having a driven wheel with that diameter in inches. Its circumference is π (3.14159…) times that diameter. One crank revolution advances the bicycle that circumference. The rest of c is merely unit conversion. For example, π x (1 meter per 39.37 inches) x (1 minute per 60 seconds) = 0.00133.

For expressions giving gear sizes, ratios, and ranges for various gearing systems, see the section on gearing equations in Chapter 3.

Gravitational Force Between Two Masses

$$F = G\,(m_1\,m_2\,/\,r^2)$$

where

F is force of attraction between masses (N)

G is 6.670×10^{-11} N-m^2/kg^2

m_1 and m_2 are masses (kg)

r is distance separating them (m)

Note: This is known as the law of universal gravitation; the constant G is called the gravitational constant and depends on the units chosen. Because for terrestrial applications one of the masses is usually the earth, the following data may be useful: mass of earth, 5.983×10^{24} kg; radius of earth at equator, 6,378,388 m; radius of earth at poles, 6,356,912 m.

Kinetic Energy

$$K.E. = 0.5\,m\,v^2$$

where

K.E. is kinetic energy (J)

m is mass (kg)

v is velocity the mass is moving (m/s)

Lateral Acceleration (Centripetal Acceleration)

$$a = v^2 / r$$

$$a = g\tan\theta$$

where

a is lateral (centripetal) acceleration (m/s^2)

v is constant speed along a circle (m/s)

r is radius of the circle (m)

g is acceleration due to gravity (m/s^2)

θ is lean angle from vertical (radians)

Lean Angle

$$\theta_d = \arctan[(h - a)/(b + p)]$$

$\theta_u =$ arctan $[(h + a)/(b + p)]$

where

θ_d is the maximum lean angle from vertical when the inside pedal is down (degrees)

θ_u is the maximum lean angle from vertical when the inside pedal is up (degrees)h is bottom bracket height (m)

a is crankarm length (m)

b is distance from center of bottom bracket to outer face of crankarm (m)

p is pedal width (m)

Note: See also Lateral Acceleration.

Moment of Force

See Torque.

Moment of Inertia

$I = m_1 r_1^2 + m_2 r_2^2 + m_3 r_3^2 + \dots$

where

I is moment of inertia ($kg\ m^2$)

m_1, m_2, etc. are the individual masses of the parts that comprise an object (kg)

r_1, r_2, etc. are the corresponding distances between the centers of mass of these parts and the rotational axis of the object (m)

Normal Force

$F_F = -L_R J / W$

$F_R = L_F J / W$

where

F_F is normal force at the front wheel contact point (N)

F_R is normal force at the rear wheel contact point (N)

L_F is moment of force about the front wheel contact point (m-N)

L_R is moment of force about the rear wheel contact point (m-N)

W is wheelbase (m)

$J = (1 - (\%G/100)^2)^{0.5}$

%G is grade (percent)

Note: The equations describe the force pressing the wheels to the ground. See Torque.

Pedaling Force

$F = P / (s\ \omega)$

where

F is combined force applied to pedals (N)

P is power (W)

s is crankarm length (m)

ω is crankarm angular velocity (radians/s)

Note: To convert cadence in rpm to angular velocity in radians per second, multiply by $\pi/30$, or 0.1047. For example, 60 rpm is $2\ \pi$ radians per second, about 6.28.

Potential Energy

$P.E. = m\ g\ h$

where

P.E. is potential energy (J)

m is mass (kg)

g is acceleration due to gravity (m/s^2)

h is vertical distance the mass is lifted (m)

Power

$P = E / t$

$P = F\ v$

$P = L\ \omega$

$P = (FR + FG)\ v_g + FD\ v_a$

where

P is average power (W)

E is energy expended, or work done (J)

t is time taken to do that work (s)

F is force applied (N)

v is velocity of body to which force is applied (m/s)

L is torque (m-N)

ω is angular velocity (radians/s)

FR is rolling resistance (N)

FG is force of gravity (N)

FD is aerodynamic drag (N)

v_g is ground speed (m/s)

v_a is airspeed (m/s)

Note: The equation involving force and velocity implies that these two vector quantities have the same direction. The equation involving rolling resistance, etc. applies to constant speed conditions. It also omits braking force, because a rider does not normally pedal and brake simultaneously; to cover such conditions as braking to maintain constant speed while coasting downhill, a term for braking force could be added inside the parentheses. See also Rolling Resistance, Force Due to Gravity on a Grade, and Pedaling Force.

Pressure, Temperature, and Volume of a Gas

$(p_1\ v_1) / T_1 = (p_2\ v_2) / T_2$

where

p_i is gas pressure under a particular condition (N/m^2)

V_i is gas volume under that same condition (m^3)

T_i is absolute temperature under that same condition (Kelvin)

Note: This is called the general gas law, a generalization of Charles' law or Gay-Lussac's law. Pressure and volume units may be anything suitable, such as psi and cubic centimeters, as long as they are the same on both sides of the equation. See Area of Tire Contact Patch for pressure unit conversions. See Temperature for temperature unit conversions.

Rake

$$R = (d \cos \alpha - 2 T \sin \alpha)/2$$

where

R is rake (m)

d is front wheel diameter (m)

α is head tube angle (degrees)

T is trail (m)

Rigidity of a Beam Supported at One End

$$s = F l^3 / 3 E I$$

where

s is distance the unsupported end is deflected (m)

F is perpendicular force applied to the unsupported end (N)

l is length of beam (m)

E is Young's modulus (N/m^2)

I is moment of beam section (see below) (m^4)

Notes: For a tubular beam (i.e. a tube), $I = \pi (D^4 - d^4) / 64$, where π is 3.14159…, D is the outside diameter of the beam (m), and d is the inside diameter (m). A solid cylindrical beam or bar is the special case of a tubular beam in which d = 0. For a rectangular beam, $I = a^3 b / 12$, where a is the cross-section dimension parallel to the force (e.g. height if the force is vertical) (m) and b is the cross-section dimension perpendicular to a (e.g. width) (m). See Chapter 12 for the Young's modulus (of elasticity) for various materials.

Rolling Resistance

$$F_R = g m C_R$$

where

F_R is rolling resistance force (N)

g is acceleration due to gravity (m/s^2)

m is mass of the rider and bicycle (kg)

C_R is coefficient of rolling resistance

Note: The above equation makes a couple of simplifications. One is that all contributions to rolling resistance are proportional to weight. While this assumption is very plausible for friction within hubs and tires, it is probably incorrect for friction within the chain, freewheel, and other lesser sources. The other is that the coefficient of rolling resistance is basically constant. Obviously, different types of paved surfaces (and unpaved surfaces) greatly affect rolling resistance. To a lesser extent, rolling resistance also varies depending on whether the rider is coasting or pedaling. While coasting, the chain and gears are stationary, adding no resistance, but the freewheel is spinning and its ratcheting mechanism is adding friction; while pedaling, the opposite is true. Other conditions also cause the coefficient of rolling resistance to vary slightly, such as the particular gear combination selected or the rider's weight distribution on the bicycle.

Speed

See Average Speed, Acceleration, and Airspeed.

Temperature

$$C = 5 (F - 32)/9$$

$$F = 9 C/5 + 32$$

$$K = C + 273.15$$

where

C is temperature in degrees Celsius

F is temperature in degrees Fahrenheit

K is absolute temperature in Kelvin

Note: See also Pressure, Temperature, and Volume of a Gas.

Torque (Moment of Force)

$$L = F s$$

$$L = I \alpha$$

$$L_F = m (g (d_1 J + h \%G/100) + a (h J - d_1 \%G/100))$$

$$L_R = m (-g (d_2 J - h \%G/100) + a (h J + d_2 \%G/100))$$

where

L is torque (m-N)

F is force perpendicular to lever arm (N)

s is length of lever arm, i.e. distance between axis and point at which perpendicular force is applied (m)

I is moment of inertia (kg-m^2)

α is angular acceleration (radians/s^2)

L_F is moment of force about the point at which the front wheel touches the ground (m-N)

L_R is moment of force about the point at which the rear wheel touches the ground (m-N)

m is mass (kg)

g is acceleration due to gravity (m/s^2)

d_1 is the portion of the wheelbase forward of the center of gravity (m)

d_2 is the portion of the wheelbase rearward of the center of gravity (m)

h is height of the center of gravity above the ground (m)

%G is grade (percent)

a is linear (i.e. forward) acceleration (m/s^2)

$J = (1 - (\%G/100)^2)^{0.5}$

Note: The equations of moment of force about the front and rear wheel contact points use the conventions that a is positive if the bicycle is increasing speed forward, %G is positive if the bicycle is moving uphill, and LF and LR are positive if the moment is counterclockwise as viewed from the right side of the bicycle. See also Normal Force.

Trail

$T = (d \cos \alpha - 2R) / (2 \sin \alpha)$

where

T is trail (m)

d is front wheel diameter (m)

alpha is head tube angle (degrees)

R is rake (m)

Trigonometric Formulas

See the Trigonometry Review in Chapter 1.

Turning Circle Radius

$r = W/\theta$ (approximately)

where

r is turning circle radius (m)

W is wheelbase (m)

θ is steering angle, measured in radians in ground plane

Note: The formula ignores tire slip and the shortening of the wheelbase as the fork turns and the bike leans.

Volume of a Cylinder

$V = L \pi r^2$

where

V is volume (m^3)

L is length of cylinder, parallel to axis (m)

π is 3.14159…

r is radius (m)

Note: This formula gives the total volume of the cylinder, for example the steel in a straight-gauge spoke or the air within a frame tube. See also Volume of Material in a Cylindrical Tube.

Volume of Air Enclosed by a Tire

$V = 2 \pi^2 R r^2$

where

V is volume (m^3)

π is 3.14159… and thus π^2 is 9.8696…

R is distance from the center of the wheel to the center of the tire (m)

r is radius of the tire, that is, the distance from the center of the tire to its inside wall (m)

Note: This formula assumes the tire is a perfect torus (doughnut), and does not take into account the rim channel of clincher wheels, the valve stem, deformation under load, etc.

Volume of Material in a Cylindrical Tube

$V = L \pi t (D - t)$

where

V is volume (m^3)

L is length of tube, parallel to axis (m)

π is 3.14159…

t is tube wall thickness (m)

D is tube outside diameter (m)

Yaw

$\phi = \arcsin [(f \sin \theta) / W]$

where

ϕ is yaw (angle of rotation about the vertical axis) (degrees)

θ is steering angle, measured in ground plane (degrees)

W is wheelbase (m)

f is the length of the projection of the fork upon the ground; f = r sin (arctan R/r + 90 − α)

R is rake (m)

r is wheel radius (m)

α is head tube angle (degrees)

Note: Angles, including the value of the arctangent function, must be in degrees for the constant 90 to work. For angles in radians, use $\pi/2$ instead.

Appendix C: Programs

A scientific calculator with trigonometric and exponentiation functions is perfectly adequate for all the math in this book. Even pencil and paper will do, if supplemented by some tables. However, because many of the calculations must be repeated over and over, and because many people these days have access to a personal computer, the author has included some short programs to enable the curious reader to do some of the more common tasks easily.

The programs are written in a generic style of BASIC and should run without modification on any computer that has a BASIC interpreter. See your computer manuals for details. Carefully type in the program of interest, correcting any typos as you go, then save it. Run the program first with the data from the included example to make sure you get very nearly the same answer; if not, there are still errors to be corrected. (Between different computers or BASIC interpreters, the results may vary in the least significant digits.)

The included programs are deliberately simple, no-frills versions, devoid of the bells and whistles that often pass for substance in commercial software. Some ambitious readers with software credentials may enjoy adding a graphical user interface replete with colors, help windows, and CD-ROM-based cinematic imagery — while the rest of us are out riding. The bare-bones user interface has little or no error checking. Readers who are acquainted with BASIC can easily modify the programs to suit their needs. Those who know both BASIC and some other software they may own, such as a spreadsheet program or a C compiler, should not find it too difficult to convert the programs into their preferred language if they have been following and understanding the text.

1. Gear Chart, GEARCHRT.BAS

This program produces a gear chart like the ones elsewhere in this book. It is usable for any wheel diameter, any number of chainwheels from 1 to 3, and any number of freewheel cogs from 1 to 10. The displayed chart shows the chainwheel sizes across the top, the cog sizes down the left side, and the corresponding gear-inch values.

```
10   REM DISPLAY A GEAR CHART FOR
     SPECIFIED GEARS
20   DIM CW(3), FW(10)
30   INPUT "DRIVEN WHEEL DIAMETER IN
     INCHES"; WD
40   INPUT "NO. OF CHAINWHEELS"; NC
50   PRINT "NO. OF TEETH ON EACH:"
60   FOR I = 1 TO NC
70   INPUT " "; CW(I)
80   NEXT I
90   INPUT "NO. OF FREEWHEEL COGS"; NF
100  PRINT "NO. OF TEETH ON EACH:"
110  FOR J = 1 TO NF
120  INPUT " "; FW(J)
130  NEXT J
140  PRINT
150  PRINT ,
160  FOR I = 1 TO NC
170  PRINT CW(I),
180  NEXT I
190  PRINT
200  FOR J = 1 TO NF
210  PRINT FW(J),
220  FOR I = 1 TO NC
230  PRINT INT(WD * CW(I) / FW(J) + .5),
240  NEXT I
250  PRINT
260  NEXT J
270  PRINT
280  END
```

Example run (user responses are underlined):

```
DRIVEN WHEEL DIAMETER IN INCHES? 26.3
NO. OF CHAINWHEELS? 2
NO. OF TEETH ON EACH:
? 42
? 52
NO. OF FREEWHEEL COGS? 6
NO. OF TEETH ON EACH:
? 13
? 15
? 17
? 20
? 23
? 26
        42      52
13      85      105
15      74      91
17      65      80
20      55      68
23      48      59
26      42      53
```

Variables:

CW   array of up to 3 chainwheel sizes (in number of teeth)

FW array of up to 10 freewheel cog sizes (in number of teeth) chainwheel number

J cog number

NC number of chainwheels

NF number of cogs

WD diameter of driven wheel, inches

How it works:

Line 20 gives array dimensions. (Change if bikes ever have more than 3 chainwheels or more than 10 cogs.) Lines 30–130 accept user inputs, including loops based on the number of chainwheels and cogs the user inputs. Lines 140–270 display the gear chart: lines 140–180 the top of the chart (the chainwheel sizes), lines 200–180 the remainder, one line per freewheel cog. Within each line is the cog size (line 210) and a rounded value of gear-inches corresponding to that cog and each of the chainwheels (loop, lines 220–240). To obtain a printed gear chart instead of one merely displayed on the computer screen, change the PRINT in line 140 and subsequent lines to LPRINT.

2. Suggested Gearing, GEARANGE.BAS

This program suggests appropriate gear sizes that conform with a particular system of gearing. The user enters the wheel diameter and chooses the system he prefers. For extreme crossover systems, he also selects the number of steps between chainwheels. (See Chapter 3 if you need a refresher.) He enters the range of ratios in gear-inches and the number of teeth on the smallest cog. The program responds with a gear chart including the calculated chainwheel and cog sizes and the corresponding gear-inches.

This program works for double chainwheel systems only. For triples, the user should decide on his normal range, select gearing for that normal range, then extend the low range with an appropriate inner chainwheel size.

Note that the program has no way of knowing what gear sizes are practical, let alone available, so it may often choose odd (though mathematically correct) numbers. In addition, especially at the small-cog end of the chart, the necessity of using integer sizes may produce duplicate ratios or other irregularities. The user will probably wish to rerun the program several times with different ranges in order to find an acceptable selection. The program includes a rerun query; if answered affirmatively, it will loop back without forcing the user to re-enter unchanging data. To try a different wheel size,

number of cogs, or gearing system, however, the user should rerun the program from the start.

```
10   REM SUGGESTED GEARING BASED ON RANGE
     OF GEAR-INCHES
20   REM AND A PARTICULAR GEARING SYSTEM
30   INPUT "DRIVEN WHEEL DIAMETER IN
     INCHES"; WD
40   INPUT "NO. OF FREEWHEEL COGS"; NF
50   PRINT "GEARING SYSTEM (H HALF-STEP,
     A ALPINE,"
60   INPUT "M MODIFIED ALPINE, X EXTREME
     CROSSOVER)"; S$
70   MT = 0
80   IF S$ <> "H" AND S$ <> "h" THEN 110
90   NS = .5
100  GOTO 240
110  IF <> S$ "A" AND S$ <> "a" THEN 140
120  NS = 1.5
130  GOTO 240
140  IF S$ <> "M" AND S$ <> "m" THEN 180
150  NS = 1.5
160  MT = 1
170  GOTO 240
180  IF S$ <> "X" AND S$ <> "x" THEN 220
190  PRINT "NO. OF STEPS BETWEEN
     CHAINWHEELS"
200  INPUT "(FOR EXAMPLE 2.5, 3.5,…)"; NS
210  GOTO 240
220  PRINT "???"
230  GOTO 50
240  INPUT "LOW GEAR-INCHES"; LG
250  INPUT "HIGH GEAR-INCHES"; HG
260  H = (HG / LG) ^ (1 / ((NF + NS) * 2
     - 2 - MT))
270  INPUT "SMALLEST COG (FOR EXAMPLE 11,
     12, 13, ...)"; SC
280  FL = INT(HG * SC / WD + .5)
290  FS = INT(FL / H ^ (NS * 2) + .5)
300  PRINT
310  PRINT , FS, FL
320  GT = SC
330  G = GT
340  FOR I = 1 TO NF
350  PRINT GT, INT(FS * WD / GT + .5),
     INT(FL * WD / GT + .5)
360  G = G * H
370  IF I = 1 AND MT = 1 THEN 390
380  G = G * H
390  GT = INT(G + .5)
400  NEXT I
410  PRINT
420  INPUT "ANOTHER RANGE (Y OR N)"; A$
430  IF A$ = "Y" OR A$ = "y" THEN 240
```

```
440 END
```

Example run (user responses are underlined):

```
DRIVEN WHEEL DIAMETER IN INCHES? 26.3
NO. OF FREEWHEEL COGS? 7
GEARING SYSTEM (H HALF-STEP, A ALPINE,
M MODIFIED ALPINE, X EXTREME CROSSOVER)?
    A
LOW GEAR-INCHES? 50
HIGH GEAR-INCHES? 114
SMALLEST COG (FOR EXAMPLE 11, 12, 13,
    ...)? 12
        44      52
12      96      114
13      89      105
15      77      91
17      68      80
19      61      72
21      55      65
23      50      59
ANOTHER RANGE (Y OR N)? N
```

Variables:

A$ yes or no response

FL   number of teeth on large chainwheel

FS   number of teeth on small chainwheel

G   ideal number of gear teeth (a real number)

GT   rounded number of gear teeth (an integer)

H   half-step ratio

HG   high gear ratio, gear-inches

I   cog number

LG   low gear ratio, gear-inches

MT   flag indicating whether top step is modified

NF   number of freewheel cogs

NS   number of steps between chainwheels

S$ gearing system code (see lines 50 and 60 for values)

SC   number of teeth on smallest cog

WD   diameter of driven wheel, inches

How it works:

Lines 30–60, 240–250, and 270 collect user inputs. Lines 70–230 set the number of steps and a flag to indicate whether the top step must be modified. If the user requests extreme crossover, lines 190–200 obtain the number of steps. Lines 220–230 express dismay if the user enters an unknown code. Line 260 calculates the size of a half step, based on the overall ratio, the number of cogs, and the gearing system. Lines 280–290 calculate the chainwheel sizes and round to the nearest integer. Lines 300–310 display the top of the gear chart. Variables GT and G in lines 320–330 track the current freewheel cog beginning with the smallest. Lines 340–400 loop through each freewheel cog, displaying the cog size and the corresponding gear ratios, rounded to the nearest integer. In a modified alpine, the two smallest cogs are separated by only half a step; hence line 370. In all other systems, the next cog is a full step (H * H) larger. Lines 410–430 give the user the option of trying another range.

3. Velocity to Power, V2P.BAS

This program calculates the amount of power needed to propel a bicycle at a particular speed, given wind and slope conditions. The user enters the wind, grade, and ground speed; the program displays the corresponding power.

The program is set up for our standard rider and normal conditions. Before running the program, the user should inspect the lines of code and change the constants to agree with the particular rider, bike, and conditions he wishes to simulate. For example, another rider will probably have different mass, coefficients of rolling resistance and drag, frontal area, and wheel diameters and moments of inertia. The user may also wish to change the values of acceleration due to gravity and air density to be more representative of the particular conditions being simulated. If any of these values is likely to vary each time the program is run, the user should change the assignment statements to INPUT statements.

Constants and input and output values are in mks units. See the glossary for suitable conversion factors. To change to another unit, the author recommends multiplying by a conversion factor immediately after the value is input (or immediately after the line defining a constant), so that the program continues to operate on mks values. Then, immediately before the PRINT statement, multiply each value to be output by its conversion factor. Finally, test the program to ensure that the values displayed agree with those in the unmodified program allowing for the different units. For example, to input values in this program in miles per hour, change the "M/S" in lines 80 and 100 to "MPH" and insert line 85 VW = VW * .44704 and line 105 VG = VG * .44704; to output a value in horsepower, insert line 125 P = P * .001341 and change the "W" in line 130 to "HP."

"Wind speed toward rider" is the component of the wind velocity directly along the bicycle's line of motion (but opposite the direction the bicycle is moving), relative to a ground speed of zero. For example, a value of 2 means effectively a 2 m/s headwind when the bicycle is stationary, which could be produced by an actual 2 m/s headwind or a somewhat stronger headwind arriving partially from one side. A value of –2 means effectively a 2 m/s tailwind. See the airspeed program to obtain this value if needed.

"% grade" quantifies the slope: 0 is level, 6 a 6% uphill slope, –2.5 a 2.5% downhill.

```
10   REM VELOCITY TO POWER
20   M = 90
30   G = 9.8017
40   CR = .003
50   CD = .88
60   FA = .36
70   RHO = 1.205
80   INPUT "WIND SPEED TOWARD RIDER,
     M/S"; VW
90   INPUT "% GRADE"; GR
100  INPUT "GROUND SPEED, M/S"; VG
110  VA = VG + VW
120  P = G * VG * M * (CR + GR * .01) +
     CD * FA * RHO * .5 * (VA ^ 3)
130  PRINT "POWER "; P; "W"
140  END
```

Example run (user responses are underlined):

```
WIND SPEED TOWARD RIDER, M/S? 2
% GRADE? .54
GROUND SPEED, M/S? 11
POWER 500.8568 W
```

(Pedaling up a 0.54% grade into a 2 meters per second headwind at 11 meters per second requires just over 500 watts of power.)

Variables:

CD   coefficient of aerodynamic drag
CR   coefficient of rolling resistance
FA   frontal area, m^2
G   acceleration due to gravity, m/s^2
GR   grade, percent

M   mass, kg
P   power, W
RHO air density, kg/m^3
VA   airspeed, m/s VG ground speed, m/s
VW   wind speed toward rider, m/s

How it works:

Lines 20–70 set constants, lines 80–100 accept user inputs. Line 120 calculates airspeed. Line 130 calculates power from the speed and the forces of rolling resistance, gravity, and aerodynamic drag. Line 140 displays the result.

4. Power to Velocity, P2V.BAS

This program calculates the ground speed of a bicycle to which a particular amount of power is applied, given wind and slope conditions. The user enters the wind, grade, and power; the program displays the corresponding ground speed.

The program uses an iterative algorithm for determining the speed, and it is possible that unusual inputs will prevent the algorithm from converging to a positive value for speed. Should this condition occur, the program will abort with a message. In this case, the user should recheck the numbers for reasonableness and try again with different inputs.

The program is set up for our standard rider and normal conditions. The notes in the Velocity to Power program apply.

Constants and input and output values are in mks units. The notes in the Velocity to Power program apply here also. For example, to input and output values in this program in miles per hour, change the "M/S" in lines 110 and 320 to "MPH" and insert line 115 VW = VW * .44704 and line 315 VN = VN * 2.2369.

Also see the notes on wind speed and grade in the Velocity to Power program.

```
10   REM POWER TO VELOCITY
20   M = 90
30   G = 9.8017
40   CR = .003
50   CD = .88
60   FA = .36
70   RHO = 1.205
80   EPS = .01
90   A = CD * FA * RHO * .5
100  DC2 = 3 * A
110  INPUT "WIND SPEED TOWARD RIDER,
     M/S"; VW
120  FC2 = DC2 * VW
```

```
130 DC1 = 2 * FC2
140 INPUT "% GRADE"; GR
150 DC0 = (DC2 * VW * VW) + (G * M * (CR
    + GR * .01))
160 FC1 = DC0
170 INPUT "POWER, W"; P
180 VG = 5
190 FC0 = A * VW * VW * VW − P
200 F = VG * (VG * (VG * A + FC2) + FC1)
    + FC0
210 TRY = 0
220 VN = VG − F / (VG * (VG * DC2 + DC1)
    + DC0)
230 IF VN >= 0 THEN 290
240 TRY = TRY + 1
250 VN = 20 * TRY
260 IF TRY < 5 THEN 290
270 PRINT "COULD NOT CONVERGE"
280 STOP
290 VG = VN
300 F = VN * (VN * (VN * A + FC2) + FC1)
    + FC0
310 IF ABS(F) > EPS THEN 220
320 PRINT "GROUND SPEED "; VN; "M/S"
330 END
```

Example run (user responses are underlined):

```
WIND SPEED TOWARD RIDER, M/S? -1.1
% GRADE? -3
POWER, W? 156
GROUND SPEED 15.00763 M/S
```

(Applying 156 watts of power down a 3% grade with a 1.1 meter per second tailwind moves the bike at just over 15 meters per second.)

Variables:

A   product of aerodynamic factors

CD   coefficient of aerodynamic drag

CR   coefficient of rolling resistance

DC0,
DC1,
DC2 coefficients of first derivative of function f

EPS epsilon, a convergence criterion

F   function f to be solved by Newton's Method

FA frontal area, m^2

FC0,
FC1,
FC2 coefficients of function f

G   acceleration due to gravity, m/s^2

GR grade, percent

M   mass, kg

P   power, W

RHO air density, kg/m^3

TRY number of tries in case of convergence problems

VG ground speed, initial or previous guess, m/s

VN ground speed, new guess, m/s

VW wind speed toward rider, m/s

How it works:

The program solves the power equation (the one used in V2P.BAS) for speed using Newton's Method. (See a calculus text for details on Newton's Method for finding roots of an equation.) Lines 20–80 set constants, including epsilon, the convergence criterion. Lines 110, 140, and 170 collect user inputs. Lines 90–190 set up the coefficients for the function f and its derivative f'. Line 180 makes 5 m/s the initial value (guess) for speed. Line 200 computes the value of function f. Line 220 calculates the next guess for speed: the old guess minus the quotient of f and f'. Because the speeds are supposed to be positive, line 200 tests the next guess, and lines 210 and 240–260 keep track of the number of tries the program makes in finding a good starting guess for speed. After five unsuccessful tries, the program will abort with the message in line 270. Otherwise, the program keeps iterating: line 290 replaces the old guess with the new guess, line 300 recalculates f, and control returns to line 220. When eventually the value of f is close enough to zero (line 310, its absolute value less than or equal to epsilon), iteration stops. Line 320 displays the resulting speed.

5. Airspeed, AIRSPEED.BAS

This short program calculates the speed at which a solo bicycle is moving through the air, given the wind velocity (the speed and direction of the wind) and the corresponding data for the bicycle. Direction is specified as azimuth in degrees clockwise from due north. (See table below.) For wind, the azimuth is that of its source: wind coming from due west has an azimuth of 270 degrees. For the bicycle, the azimuth is that of its heading or destination: a bicycle moving due east has an azimuth of 90 degrees, even though it is moving in the same direction as that west wind. After accepting speed and azimuth for both wind and bicycle, the program displays airspeed. Positive values indicate what would be perceived as a headwind; negative values, a tailwind.

See the note in "How it works" regarding units. To determine "wind speed toward rider" as used in V2P.BAS, P2V.BAS, and ACCEL.BAS, enter a ground speed of zero, but the ground azimuth must still indicate the correct direction the bicycle is heading.

Compass direction — azimuth table

N	0	E	90	S	180	W	270
NNE	22.5	ESE	112.5	SSW	202.5	WNW	292.5
NE	45	SE	135	SW	225	NW	315
EME	67.5	SSE	157.5	WSW	247.5	NNW	337.5

```
10   REM AIRSPEED
20   INPUT "WIND SPEED AND SOURCE AZIMUTH
     (M/S, DEGREES)"; VW, ZW
30   INPUT "GROUND SPEED AND HEADING
     AZIMUTH (M/S, DEGREES)"; VG, ZG
40   VA = VG + VW * COS((ZG - ZW) *
     .01745329#)
50   PRINT "AIRSPEED "; VA; "M/S"
60   END
```

Example run (user responses are underlined):

```
WIND SPEED AND SOURCE AZIMUTH (M/S,
     DEGREES)? 12, 292.5
GROUND SPEED AND HEADING AZIMUTH (M/S,
     DEGREES)? 5, 135
AIRSPEED -6.086553 M/S
```

(A wind of 12 meters per second coming from west-northwest while the bicycle is moving at 5 meters per second southeast is perceived as a tailwind of a little over 6 meters per second.)

Variables:

VA   airspeed, m/s

VG   ground speed, m/s

VW   wind speed, m/s

ZG   ground azimuth, degrees

ZW   wind azimuth, degrees

How it works:

Lines 20–30 collect inputs (two values per line). Line 40 calculates the airspeed as the sum of the ground speed and the component of the wind speed in the same direction. Note that the difference of the angles is converted to radians. Line 50 displays the result.

Although input and output speeds are in mks units, any consistent unit may be used without a conversion factor. For instance, to enter and display results in miles per hour, merely change "M/S" to "MPH" in lines 20, 30, and 50. For azimuth, however, a unit other than degrees will need a different conversion factor from the one given in the program.

6. Acceleration/Deceleration, ACCEL.BAS

This program simulates a bike that is accelerating (or decelerating) as a result of pedaling, braking, gravity, rolling resistance, aerodynamic drag, and the moments of inertia of the wheels. It displays the resulting time, distance, and speed at the end of the acceleration period. The program can be used for three different types of problem: acceleration for a specified length of time, acceleration over a specified distance, or acceleration up to (or down to) a specified speed.

The user enters the wind and slope conditions and an initial speed. The program requests the final conditions signaling the end of the acceleration period: a maximum duration (time), a maximum distance covered, and a final speed. The final speed may be either higher or lower than the initial speed, depending on whether the user expects the bike to accelerate or decelerate. The user enters these, then enters the power applied through pedaling (if any) and the braking force (if any). Using a short time increment, the program iterates until any one of the final conditions is met. Then it displays the time (duration of acceleration), distance covered, and speed attained when that final condition is met.

The program is set up for our standard rider and normal conditions. The notes in the Velocity to Power program apply.

Constants and input and output values are in mks units. The notes in the Velocity to Power program apply here also. For example, to input and output values in this program in miles per hour, change the "M/S" in lines 130, 150, 190, and 560 to "MPH" and insert lines 135 VW = VW * .44704, line 155 VG = VG * .44704, line 195 VF = VF * .44704, and line 555 VG = VG * 2.2369.

Also see the notes on wind speed and grade in the Velocity to Power program.

If the bicycle is coasting, power is zero. Otherwise power should be a positive number of watts from pedaling. If the bicycle is not being braked, braking force is zero. Otherwise, braking force should be a positive number of newtons, viewed as a force in the direction opposite the bicycle's motion. Normally at least one of these numbers is zero. Note that though the bicycle is being pedaled, it may still be decelerating (into the wind, for instance), and though the bike is being braked, it may still be accelerating (downhill, for instance). The final time and distance constraints help keep the program from running indefinitely in case the bike is doing something unexpected.

```
10   REM ACCELERATION FROM ONE SPEED TO
     ANOTHER (HIGHER OR LOWER)
20   M = 90
30   G = 9.8017
40   FM = M * G * .7
50   CR = .003
60   CD = .88
70   FA = .36
80   RHO = 1.205
90   MF = .0938
100  DF = .668
110  MR = .0938
120  DR = .668
130  INPUT "WIND SPEED TOWARD RIDER,
     M/S"; VW
140  INPUT "% GRADE"; GR
150  INPUT "INITIAL SPEED, M/S"; VG
160  PRINT "FINAL CONDITIONS OR
     CONSTRAINTS"
170  INPUT " MAX DURATION, S"; TM
180  INPUT " MAX DISTANCE, M"; DM
190  INPUT " FINAL SPEED, M/S"; VF
200  IF VF > VG THEN AC = 1 ELSE AC = -1
210  INPUT "POWER, W"; P
220  INPUT "BRAKING FORCE, N"; BF
230  DT = .1
240  T = 0
250  D = 0
260  VA = VG + VW
270  IF VG = 0 THEN AF = 0 ELSE AF = CD *
     FA * RHO * .5 * VA ^ 3 / VG
280  RF = G * M * CR
290  GF = G * M * GR * .01
300  IF VG = 0 THEN PF = FM ELSE PF = P /
     VG
310  IF PF > FM THEN PF = FM
320  T = T + DT
```

```
330  A = (PF - GF - AF - BF - RF) / (M +
     .25 * ((MF / DF ^ 2) + (MR / DR ^
     2)))
340  DV = A * DT
350  DP = D
360  D = D + (VG + VG + DV) * .5 * DT
370  VP = VG
380  VG = VG + DV
390  REM PRINT "T "; T, "D "; D, "V "; VG
400  PR = 2
410  IF T < TM THEN 440
420  PRT = (TM - T + DT) / DT
430  IF PRT < PR THEN PR = PRT
440  IF D < DM THEN 470
450  PRD = (DM - DP) / (D - DP)
460  IF PRD < PR THEN PR = PRD
470  F AC * (VF - VG) > 0 THEN 500
480  PRV = (VF - VP) / (VG - VP)
490  IF PRV < PR THEN PR = PRV
500  IF PR > 1 THEN 260
510  T = (T - DT) + PR * DT
520  D = DP + PR * (D - DP)
530  VG = VP + PR * (VG - VP)
540  PRINT "DURATION ", T; "S"
550  PRINT "DISTANCE ", D; "M"
560  PRINT "FINAL SPEED ", VG; "M/S"
570  END
```

Example run (user responses are underlined).

In this example, the bicycle is initially heading into a wind of 3.2 meters per second and down a 1.6% grade at 6.7 meters per second. If it is being pedaled with a power of 150 watts, but not being braked, what is the time, distance, and speed when it has accelerated 15 seconds, covered 90 meters, or reached a speed of 7.5 meters per second, whichever comes first? (User responses are underlined.)

```
WIND SPEED TOWARD RIDER, M/S? 3.2
% GRADE? -1.6
INITIAL SPEED, M/S? 6.7
FINAL CONDITIONS OR CONSTRAINTS
MAX DURATION, S? 15
MAX DISTANCE, M? 90
FINAL SPEED, M/S? 7.5
POWER, W? 150
BRAKING FORCE, N? 0
DURATION 12.82043 S
DISTANCE 90 M
FINAL SPEED 7.245299 M/S
```

(The bicycle covers 90 meters in 12.82 seconds, reaching a speed of 7.245 meters per second.)

Variables:

A acceleration, m/s^2

AC acceleration flag, 1=accelerating, 2= decelerating

AF aerodynamic drag, N

BF braking force along line of bike motion, N

CD coefficient of aerodynamic drag

CR coefficient of rolling resistance

D distance, m

DF diameter of front wheel, m

DM maximum distance, m

DP previous distance, m

DR diameter of rear wheel, m

DT time increment, s

DV speed increment, m/s

FA frontal area, m^2

FM maximum force (limited by tires etc.), N

G acceleration due to gravity, m/s^2

GF gravitational force (drag), N

GR grade, percent

M mass, kg

MF moment of inertia of front wheel, kg m^2

MR moment of inertia of rear wheel, kg m^2

P power, W

PF pedaling force, N

PR pro-rating factor, minimum of PRT, PRD, PRV, and 1

PRD pro-rating factor due to distance

PRT pro-rating factor due to time

PRV pro-rating factor due to speed

RF rolling drag, N

RHO air density, kg/m^3

T time, s

TM maximum duration, s

VA airspeed, m/s

VF final speed attained, m/s

VG ground speed, m/s

VP previous speed, m/s

VW wind speed toward rider, m/s

How it works:

Lines 20–120 set constants, both physical constants such as acceleration due to gravity and air density, and data describing the bike and rider. Lines 130–220 accept user input. Lines 230–250 set the time increment and initialize time and distance. Line 260 is the beginning of a loop, an iterated section of the program. Lines 260–290 calculate airspeed and the forces due to aerodynamics, rolling resistance, and gravity. Lines 300 and 310 do the same for pedaling forces, except that they limit such forces to some practical but arbitrary maximum (see line 40), 70% of the total weight. (When the bike is motionless, too much applied power would just spin the rear wheel, snap the chain, etc.) Line 320 increments the time. Line 330 calculates acceleration from force and mass, including moment of inertia. Lines 340–380 calculate the change in speed and distance and save the values from the preceding iteration. Line 390 is provided for those who would like to see the values of time, distance, and speed at each iteration step; just remove the "REM" if so. Lines 400–490 test the final constraints (time, distance, and speed). If any one of those constraints is met, the program will interpolate between the last two sets of values, one set from the step just prior to meeting the constraint(s) and one step from the step that meets the constraint(s). To allow interpolation, it computes a pro-rating factor between 0 and 1 for that constraint. If more than one constraint is met, the program picks the minimum pro-rating factor, that is, for whichever constraint would have been met first. Line 500 tests whether the pro-rating factor has been set (meaning that a constraint has been met); if not, it loops back to do the next iteration. Lines 510–530 do the interpolation; the remaining lines display the interpolated values.

7. Air Density, AIRDENS.BAS

This program may be used to calculate air density, if a more accurate value than the constant in V2P.BAS, P2V.BAS, and ACCEL.BAS is needed. The user enters the temperature, the relative humidity, and the actual barometric pressure (not "reduced" to sea level); the program displays air density. See Equations, Barometric Pressure, to compute barometric pressure from elevation.

A third-degree polynomial is used to calculate a value for water vapor pressure in moist air. Because that method gives only an approximation, do not expect more than 3 or 4 digits of accuracy when the relative humidity is above zero. Also because of that approximation, the program is limited to temperatures between 0 and 40 C (32 and 104 F).

Input temperature is in degrees Celsius. To change to Fahrenheit, change the "C" in line 30 to "F" and insert line 35 T = (T — 32) * 5 / 9. Barometric pressure is in millimeters of mercury. To change to inches, change the "MM" in line 80 to "IN" and insert line 85 B = B * 25.4. The output density is in kilograms per cubic meter, which is numerically the same as grams per liter.

```
10   REM COMPUTE AIR DENSITY FROM
     TEMPERATURE, BAROMETRIC PRESSURE,
20   REM AND RELATIVE HUMIDITY
30   INPUT "TEMPERATURE, C"; T
40   IF T >= 0 AND T <= 40 THEN 70
50   PRINT "TEMPERATURE OUTSIDE PROGRAM
     LIMITS"
60   STOP
70   E = (((4.59926E-04 * T +
     3.49094E-03) * T) + .39302) * T +
     4.52
80   INPUT "RELATIVE HUMIDITY, %"; H
90   E = E * H * .01
100  INPUT "BAROMETRIC PRESSURE, MM HG";
     B
110  RHO = 1.2929 * (273.15 / (T +
     273.15))
120  RHO = RHO * (B — .3783 * E) / 760
130  PRINT "AIR DENSITY "; RHO; " KG /
     CU. M"
140  END
```

Example run (user responses are underlined:

```
TEMPERATURE, C? 25
RELATIVE HUMIDITY, %? 70
BAROMETRIC PRESSURE, MM HG? 742
AIR DENSITY 1.146649 KG / CU. M
```

(At 25 C [77 F] and 70% humidity with a barometer reading of 742 mm of mercury [29.21 inches], the density of air is about 1.15 kilograms per cubic meter.)

Variables:

B   barometric pressure, mm Hg

E   water vapor pressure, mm Hg

H   relative humidity, percent

RHO air density, kg/m^3

T   temperature, degrees C

How it works:

Lines 30, 80, and 100 collect user inputs. Lines 40–60 ensure the temperature is within limits for reasonably accurate calculations. Line 70 uses a third–degree polynomial to calculate (approximately) what the water vapor pressure would be in saturated air at the specified temperature. Line 90 multiplies it by the relative humidity, giving the actual (but still approximate) vapor pressure. Line 110 computes the density of dry air at that temperature and standard pressure (760 mm Hg), using a standard value for density and the general gas law, which calls for absolute temperatures (K). Line 120 modifies the density according to barometric pressure, again using the general gas law but also accounting for the pressure of water vapor. Line 130 displays the result.

Glossary, Including Abbreviations

(Note: Where possible, equivalences between units are given either exactly or to 10 significant digits. See the Introduction for help in converting an expression from one unit to another.)

acceleration The rate of change of velocity (speed, direction, or both) with respect to time. In the mks and SI system, acceleration is expressed in meters per second per second, or meters per second squared (m/s^2). Linear acceleration refers to motion in a straight line, and is the change in speed along that line per unit of time. A positive value for acceleration means that speed is increasing; a negative value (also called deceleration) means that speed is decreasing. Lateral acceleration, also called centripetal acceleration, refers to motion along a circle, and equals the square of the linear speed divided by the radius of the circular path. Lateral acceleration is always positive (or zero) and directed toward the center of the circle. See also angular acceleration.

acceleration due to gravity Gravity acting on a freely falling body causes it to accelerate; the amount of this acceleration, called the acceleration due to gravity, acceleration of gravity, or simply g, is about $9.8 \ m/s^2$ or 32 feet per second per second. At any given spot on the earth, the acceleration due to gravity is constant, but the precise value varies slightly from place to place depending on latitude and altitude, as a consequence of the law of universal gravitation: see Equations. The International Committee on Weights and Measures has adopted $9.80665 \ m/s^2$ ($32.17404856 \ ft/s^2$) as the standard value, used for defining weights in terms of mass.

aero Aerodynamic. Said of components and attire that have been designed to lower aerodynamic drag.

aerodynamic
1. Relating to the interaction of air with a moving object.
2. Having a low coefficient of aerodynamic drag; streamlined.

aerodynamic drag A force acting on a moving object (the bicycle and rider) opposite to the direction of motion, resulting from the interaction between the moving object and the molecules of the air. Also called aerodynamic resistance, or more loosely, wind resistance.

aerodynamic resistance Same as aerodynamic drag.

airspeed The speed (of the bicycle and rider) relative to the air. It depends on the speed relative to the ground and the wind speed and relative direction.

alpine A system of gearing in which the chainwheels are 1.5 steps apart in size compared to the single steps between cogs.

angular acceleration The rate of change of angular velocity (speed of rotation). Angular acceleration is measured in a unit of angle (such as radians or degrees) per unit of time squared (such as s^2).

atmosphere A unit of pressure equal to 14.69594878 pounds per square inch or 101,325 newtons per square meter. In barometric terms, 1 atmosphere is 760 mm of mercury or 29.92125984 inches of mercury.

attack To increase speed greatly, in an attempt to break away from a group or to wear out one's opponents.

average speed Distance covered divided by elapsed time. By definition, average speed includes any stops within the time interval. If a cyclist turns off his cycle computer during stops, or if the computer turns itself off because the instantaneous speed drops below some built-in limit, the computer is no longer measuring average speed: see pace.

azimuth Direction, measured in degrees clockwise from due north. A bicycle facing due southwest, for instance, has an azimuth of 225 degrees.

bead
The thickened edge of a clincher tire, often reinforced by a metal or composite wire, and the corresponding projecting or hooked edge of a clincher rim. The beads help prevent the tire from blowing off the rim under high pressure.

bearing
A device used to reduce friction between rotating parts, usually between one that rotates and one that is stationary. For example, a wheel axle is stationary: it is clamped or bolted onto the bicycle frame. The rest of the wheel must of course revolve. Inside the wheel hub is a bearing that allows the rotating part of the hub to revolve freely around the stationary axle. The bearing usually also reduces wear, prolonging useful life, and may help prevent unwanted motions, such as sideways sliding or eccentric wobbles. Bicycles may have "standard" bearings, in which small steel balls (also called bearings, specifically ball bearings) revolve between a cup and a cone, or "sealed" or "cartridge" bearings, in which the bearing mechanism is a self-contained, plug-in unit, relatively impervious to dirt and water. A device labeled "sealed mechanism" usually has a standard bearing with internal baffles to help keep out contaminants. The mechanisms of "roller" or "taper" bearings use small cylindrical or conical elements instead of ball bearings. See also cup and cone.

blade
See fork.

block
To impede the mobility of one or more opponents intentionally, for example to allow a teammate to break away or to discourage an opponent from chasing down a break group containing a teammate.

bottom bracket
The portion of the bicycle frame that contains bearings and the spindle to which the crankset is attached. On a conventional diamond frame bicycle, the bottom bracket is the lowest part of the frame, at the bottom end of the seat tube and down tube and at the forward end of the chainstays.

braze-on
A permanent fitting on a bicycle frame allowing attachment of a water bottle cage, a pump, a rack or fenders, shift levers, a particular type of brake, etc. On a steel frame these fittings may be added during assembly by brazing (soldering with brass or silver), but they may also be attached by some other means, such as welding or glue.

break
To increase speed enough to escape, alone or with a small group, and establish a position well ahead of the peloton. The rider or group breaking away is called the break (or breakaway) rider or group; the act of escaping is called a break, breakaway, escape, or flyer, and is not necessarily successful or permanent.

brevet
See randonneur.

butted
Thicker at one end ("single butted") or both ends ("double butted") than in the middle, to reduce weight while retaining strength where it is most needed. The diameter of a butted spoke varies along its length; through clever manufacturing, butted frame tubes have thinner walls in their middles, yet maintain a constant outside diameter. Compare straight gauge. Fork tubes in which the gauge tapers from one end to the other are also sometimes called butted.

cadence
The rotational speed of the crankset and feet, usually expressed in revolutions per minute (rpm). To measure, count the number of downstrokes of one pedal (say the right pedal) within one minute.

CD
Properly, C_D or C_d. Coefficient of aerodynamic drag or resistance.

cantilever brake
A brake with two separate halves, each pivoted at one end. On traditional cantilevers, a cable pulling from top center pivots the halves toward the rim. On more modern V- or direct-pull brakes, a cable from the side pulls the tops of the halves together.

Celsius
The temperature scale formerly known as "centigrade" because it has 100 degrees between the freezing point of water (0 degrees C or just 0 C) and the boiling point of water (100 degrees C

or 100 C). Expressed as a temperature change, a Celsius degree is 1.8 times as large as a Fahrenheit degree, but the Fahrenheit scale starts at a different point, complicating the conversion (see Equations). Some of the most useful equivalent points are 0 C = 32 F, 20 C = 68 F, 25 C = 77 F and 37 C = 98.6 F. See also kelvin.

center of mass
The point within an object or collection of objects at which the mass can be considered to be concentrated. Also called center of gravity.

centimeter
One hundredth of a meter (0.01 m), abbreviated cm. 1 cm = 0.3937007874 inch.

century
Used alone in a bicycling context, a ride of 100 miles in a day. A metric century, however, is a ride of 100 kilometers (62 miles); a double century is 200 miles, etc. Sometimes used loosely to mean any event that offers the option of at least 100 kilometers or miles.

chain
A loop with a flexible series of links connecting a chainwheel to a cog. The physical spacing of chain links is the same as the spacing of teeth on the gears; for derailleur bicycles, it is one half inch.

chain angle
The sideways deflection of the chain. In a properly aligned derailleur bicycle with a double crankset, chain angle should not be a problem except when the rider selects the small (innermost) chainwheel and small (outermost) cog, or the large chainwheel and large cog. Triple cranksets, wide freewheels, and short chainstay lengths may aggravate chain angle problems slightly.

chainring
Same as chainwheel.

chainstay
One of the relatively narrow tubes, which on a diamond bicycle frame connect the bottom bracket with the rear wheel axle.

chainwheel
A gear that is attached to the crankset and revolves at the same rate as the pedals. It drives the chain. Also called chainring.

chase
To pursue the leading rider or group. A small break group of riders attempting to bridge the gap between the peloton and the leading group is called a chase group.

circuit race
A race on a closed loop course, usually comprising multiple laps.

cleat
A device that secures the cycling shoe to the pedal for optimum power transfer when pedaling, but which allows release when desired. Cleats designed for clipless pedals are released by a twist of the foot or some other motion that is not encountered in normal pedaling.

clincher
One of the two types of bicycle tire and rim. Clincher rims grip the tire by the bead at its edge (in the same way that an automobile rim does); a separate tube enclosed by the tire and rim holds the pressurized air. Called "wired-on" (tyre) in Great Britain.

clipless pedal
A pedal designed to accept a particular kind of cleat that holds the shoe in position without the need for auxiliary toeclip or strap.

cm
Centimeter or centimeters.

coefficient of aerodynamic drag
A dimensionless quantity used to describe the aerodynamic properties of a particular shape, such as a rider crouched upon a bicycle, and to calculate the amount of aerodynamic drag force associated with that shape. Abbreviated CD (or more properly, C_D or C_d).

coefficient of friction
One of two dimensionless quantities, measures of the friction between two surfaces. The coefficient of static friction is the maximum tangential force that can be applied without causing the surfaces to slide with respect to each other, divided by the normal force pressing the surfaces together. The coefficient of kinetic friction is the tangential force needed to slide one surface over the other at a constant speed, divided by the normal force pressing the surfaces together. ("Tangential" here means parallel to the two surfaces; "normal" means perpendicular to the two surfaces.) Note that the coefficient of friction does not apply to just one object, such as a tire, but only to pairs of objects, such as a tire and a particular road surface.

coefficient of rolling resistance A dimensionless quantity used to calculate the amount of drag force associated with the wheels and drivetrain of a vehicle as it moves. Abbreviated C_R. See also rolling resistance.

cog A gear that is attached to the freewheel or directly to the hub. When power is being applied, the driven wheel rotates at the same rate as the cog.

component 1. A part of a bicycle, such as a stem, crankset, or brake, but usually excluding the frame.

2. In the context of vectors, one of two other vectors, which together add up to a given vector and which are in specified directions, usually perpendicular to each other. For example, a 2.8-mph wind blowing from the northeast may be considered as the sum of a 2.0-mph component from the north and a 2.0-mph component from the east.

cone The approximately conical (but more often slightly concave) device that confines the ball bearings against the cup and can usually be adjusted to vary the amount of play or pressure. The bearings run in a circular path between the cone and cup. See also cup.

crank Loosely, crankarm or crankset.

crankarm One of the solid bars that connect the pedals to the bottom bracket spindle. The right one usually includes "spiders," arms that support one or more chainwheels.

crankset An assembly consisting of the two crankarms to which the pedals are attached, plus one or more chainwheels. The crankset spins on the bottom bracket. Power applied to the pedals is transmitted through the crankset to the chain. Called "chain-set" in Great Britain.

criterium A type of bicycle race featuring repeated laps of a relatively short closed loop or circuit, often with many sharp turns.

crossover 1. A shift of the front derailleur, moving the chain from one chainwheel to another.

2. A method of gear selection that emphasizes keeping the chain on one chainwheel or the other, shifting between them (crossing over) only occasionally as conditions change.

crown See fork.

cup The concave surface along which a ball bearing rolls. Hubs, bottom brackets, headsets, pedals, etc. that take standard ball bearings all contain cups. Whatever analogous structure a sealed bearing may have is internal to its cartridge. See also cone.

cyclo-cross A bicycle race on a course with a variety of conditions, usually including both on- and off-road surfaces, including some that require the competitor to dismount and run with the bike. Cyclo-crosses are particularly popular as an off-season training activity in Europe. A cyclo-cross bike is often just a road racing bike fitted with wide, knobby tires.

deceleration See acceleration.

degree 1. A unit of angle, 1/360th of a full circle or .01745329252 radian.

2. A unit of temperature. See Celsius and kelvin.

density The ratio of mass to volume, usually expressed in grams per cubic centimeter (in which case its value is almost identical to specific gravity) or, in mks, kilograms per cubic meter (kg/m^3 SI).

derailleur A device that causes the chain to shift from one gear to another. The front derailleur moves the chain between chainwheels; the rear derailleur moves the chain between cogs and has a spring-loaded mechanism that wraps up excess chain to keep it from hanging loosely when smaller gears are selected. Also called "changer," especially in Great Britain.

diamond frame The standard frame configuration for a bicycle, named for the shape suggested by the top tube, down tube, chainstays, and seatstays. Recumbents, mixtes, "ladies'" and other less-common frame

	designs depart from this standard in various ways.
direct-pull brake	See cantilever brake.
domestique	A utility rider on a racing team who plays a supporting or even sacrificial role to help his team win, but is seldom afforded the chance to win himself.
double	Loosely, a crankset with two chainwheels.
double-pivot brake	See sidepull brake
down tube	One of the main tubes of the diamond bicycle frame, running from the bottom of the head tube down to the bottom bracket.
draft	To ride in the slipstream of another rider or riders, to take advantage of the reduced power needed in such conditions. Called "pacing" in Great Britain. The slipstream itself is also called the "draft."
drag	A force retarding motion, especially aerodynamic drag.
drivetrain	The collective term for the components of the bicycle that transmit power from the rider to the driven wheel, including the pedals, crankset, chain, freewheel, and hub.
drop	To leave (a rider) behind despite his efforts to keep up.
dropped handlebars	Handlebars with drops (see).
drops	The ends of the curved handlebar usually found on road bicycles, usually 12 or more centimeters below the level top part clamped by the stem. In the standard racing crouched position, the rider's hands rest on the forward portion of the drops, thumb side up.
dropout	The slotted end of a fork blade, or the similar fitting at the junction of the seatstay and chainstay, which accepts the end of the wheel axle.
elasticity	The ability of a material that has deformed under stress to return to its original shape after the stress is removed.
elastic limit	See yield point.

energy	The ability of a body to do work. See potential energy and kinetic energy. Energy spent is the same as work done. The mks unit of energy is the joule. Other units of energy are the foot-pound and the kilowatt-hour. See also work.
escape	See break.
fairing	A shield-like device, like a curved windshield, mounted on the bicycle and used to reduce the aerodynamic drag of the rider (or the rider and bicycle).
field	Same as peloton.
flyer	See break.
foot	A unit of distance, abbreviated ft. 1 ft equals 0.3048 m.
foot-pound	A unit of energy, 1.355817948 J.
force	In general terms, a push or pull in a specific direction. A force causes an object to accelerate (or decelerate). The mks unit of force is the newton; the English unit is the pound.
fork	The joined pair of tubes that support the bicycle frame on the front wheel axle. The tubes (called fork blades) are usually raked (curved forward) and are connected at their top by the crown, to which is attached a steerer tube that rotates within the head tube, providing steering. On a "unicrown" fork, the blades and crown are all one bent piece. Some forks, especially for mountain bikes, use internal springs and shock absorbers instead of the elasticity of the blades.
freehub	A freewheel mechanism built into the rear hub.
freewheel	A mechanism with an internal ratchet that enables the bicycle rider to transmit power to the wheel when pedaling and to coast when not pedaling. It is fitted with one or more gears (cogs); on a derailleur bicycle, the multiple cogs are parallel so that any one may be selected by the rear derailleur. A freewheel may be a separate unit that threads onto the rear hub, or it may be integral with the hub, in which case it is usually called a freehub, or (rarely) it

	may operate at the crankset end of the chain.
frontal area	The area of the apparent largest cross section of an object (such as a bicycle and rider) as seen from the front, along the line of the object's motion.
ft	Foot or feet.
ft-lb	Foot-pound or foot-pounds.
g	1. Acceleration due to gravity (see). 2. Gram or grams.
gear	1. A toothed wheel used to transmit power and motion, sometimes called "sprocket," although that term is more correctly applied to one of the teeth. On bicycles, there are normally two types of gears: cogs and chainwheels (also called chainrings). The teeth on these gears mesh with the spaces between the links of a chain running between them. Some bicycles also have a hub with internal gears. 2. Short for "gear combination" or "gear ratio" (see).
gear combination	The connection of two particular gears, one a chainwheel, the other a cog, via the chain. The combination is selected using the shift levers and derailleurs, and it is associated with a particular gear ratio.
gear-inches	The unit for expressing a gear ratio value. Pedaling in a gear ratio of 100 gear-inches is equivalent to pedaling directly a wheel whose diameter is 100 inches.
gear ratio	The effect of a particular gear combination, expressed by the size of the chainwheel divided by the size of the cog and (to make gear ratios comparable between different bikes) multiplied by the diameter of the driven wheel. The gear ratios of internally geared hubs can be calculated in a similar way. If the wheel diameter is in inches, the value of the gear ratio will be in "gear-inches." A high gear ratio has a larger numerical value of gear-inches than a low gear ratio.
grade	A measure of the inclination of a slope. Grade is the vertical increment divided by the horizontal distance, and is

	usually given as a percentage. For example, a slope that rises 3 feet in 100 is a 3% (up-) grade. Also called gradient.
gram	One thousandth of a kilogram (0.001 kg).
granny, or granny gear	A very low gear ratio, or the small chainwheel or large cog capable of providing such a ratio, used for climbing steep hills.
half-step	1. Approximately half the perceived difference in gear ratios between successive cogs on a freewheel; the square root of one step (see). 2. A system of gearing in which the chainwheels are one half step apart in size compared to the single steps between cogs.
headset	The bearing assembly within the head tube that allows the fork to rotate freely around the steering axis.
head tube	The tube of the bicycle frame that (aside from the fork blades) is farthest forward, housing the headset. In a diamond frame, the top tube is attached to its top, the down tube to its bottom.
head tube angle	The angle between the head tube axis (the steering axis) and the ground, as viewed from the side; usually between 60 and 80 degrees.
heat	A preliminary or qualifying race to reduce the field to a suitable number of strong contenders. For example, the organizers may assign each racer in the total field to one of three heats, usually taking care to distribute the top seeds evenly; the highest-placed finishers in each heat earn a spot in the final. See also repechage.
horsepower	A unit of power, equal to 745.6998716 watts. Abbreviated hp.
hp	Horsepower.
inch	A unit of distance, equal to 2.54 centimeters or 0.0254 m.
J	Joule or joules.
jockey wheel	One of the pulleys, usually toothed, in the lower cage of the rear derailleur.
joule	The mks unit of energy, 1 newton-meter or 1 kg-m^2/s^2 SI. A joule is the work done when a force of one newton moves an object one meter in the same

keirin

direction as the force. Abbreviated J. One joule equals 0.7375621493 foot-pounds; there are 3,600,000 (3.6 x 10^6) joules in a kilowatt-hour. See also energy.

keirin A form of track racing combining motor pacing and sprinting. A relatively small number of riders (usually 9 or fewer) are assigned random starting positions. At the start, they sprint to catch the pace vehicle (a motorcycle or occasionally a tandem bicycle) and attempt to place themselves in a favorable position in the draft and for the finish. They may change positions (voluntarily or through coercion) but are not allowed to pass the pace vehicle, which gradually increases speed, then pulls off, leaving the field to sprint to the finish. In Japan, keirin is a professional parimutuel sport.

kelvin The SI unit of temperature. Expressed as a change in temperature, 1 kelvin = 1 degree Celsius, but whereas the zero point on the Celsius scale is at the freezing point of water, the Kelvin scale begins at absolute zero, the lowest possible temperature: 0 kelvin (0 K) = –273.15 C.

kg Kilogram or kilograms.

kilo- A prefix meaning 1,000. For example, there are 1,000 grams in a kilogram.

kilogram The mks and SI unit of mass, abbreviated kg. A mass of 1 kg weighs about 2.2 pounds on the earth's surface, but the pound is a unit of weight (not mass) and thus the weight depends on the local value of the acceleration due to gravity. Using the "standard" value of the latter, a 1 kg mass would weigh 2.204622622 lb (avoirdupois).

kilometer 1,000 meters, abbreviated km. 1 km = 1,000 m mks or SI; 1 km= 0.6213711922 statute mile.

kinetic energy The ability of a body to do work by virtue of its motion. See also energy.

km Kilometer or kilometers.

lateral acceleration See acceleration.

lb Pound or pounds.

ladies' or lady's (frame) A frame design with no top tube but instead a tube above and parallel to the down tube. Originally designed to be suitable for a lady wearing a long skirt.

lead out To begin a high-speed effort while a teammate drafts immediately behind, exhausting oneself short of the finish line but setting the teammate up for a sprint and possible win.

linear acceleration See acceleration.

m Meter or meters.

m^2 Meters squared. See square meters.

madison A track points race between several two-person teams in which only one member of each team is actively racing at a time. The inactive member stops or rides easily near the top edge of the track and rests. About once a lap the team members exchange functions: the inactive member drops down into position and the active member grabs his hand and slings him into the race, transferring his momentum to his teammate. The sustained high speeds, precision maneuvers, near collisions in close quarters, and team tactics make this an exciting, if confusing, event. Named for Madison Square Garden in New York City, where track racing was once popular.

main triangle The roughly triangular arrangement of the four main tubes of a diamond frame, the top tube, head tube, down tube, and seat tube.

mark To shadow or stay close to a rival in an attempt to ensure that if he makes a break, he will also tow the shadowing rider along in his draft. A team that is not necessarily strong itself may mark the strongest riders on opposing teams to try to place at least one rider in a successful break group.

mass A basic property of a physical object, a measure of its resistance to acceleration. The mks and SI unit of mass is the kilogram (kg). Mass is not the same thing as weight, but because the acceleration due to gravity is nearly constant on the earth's surface, an object's weight anywhere on the earth is very nearly proportional to its mass. At any particular place on the earth, the ratio of the weights of two objects will be exactly the same as the ratio of their masses.

match sprint A race between only two riders, usually held on a track, and usually only 1,000 meters or less in length. Because tactics may play as important a part as outright speed, often the pace will be slow until the final 200 meters or so.

meter The mks and SI unit of length or distance, abbreviated m. One meter equals 39.37007874 inches or 3.280839895 feet or 0.0006213711922 ($6.21\ldots \times 10^{-4}$) statute mile.

meter-newton The mks unit of torque, abbreviated m-N, equal to 1 kg-m^2/s^2 SI. One meter-newton equals 0.7375621493 pound-feet.

meter per second The mks and SI unit of speed, abbreviated m/s. One meter per second equals 2.236936292 statute miles per hour or 3.6 kilometers per hour.

meter per second squared The mks and SI unit of acceleration, abbreviated m/s^2. One meter per second squared means one meter per second per second, and equals 3.280839895 feet per second squared or 2.236936292 statute miles per hour per second.

metric The international decimal system of weights and measures. In this book, most of the metric units are those of the "mks" (meter-kilogram-second) system, rather than the "cgs" (centimeter-gram-second) system. See also SI.

mile A unit of distance, sometimes called "statute mile" to distinguish it from the nautical mile. One statute mile equals 1,609.344 m. Abbreviated mi.

mile per hour A unit of speed (one statute mile per hour) equal to 0.44704 m/s. Abbreviated mph.

milli- A prefix meaning one thousandth. For example, there are 1000 millimeters in one meter.

min Minute or minutes.

miss-and-out A track bicycle race in which the last rider across the line on each lap is eliminated, until only a few (say, 3) are left for a final sprint. Also called "devil take the hindmost."

mixte A bicycle frame with no top tube but instead a pair of stays, one on each side, running from the top of the head tube to the lower part of the seatstay.

mks Meter-kilogram-second. The metric system has many different units of measurement; for example, distance may be measured in millimeters, centimeters, meters, kilometers, etc. The mks system chooses the meter, kilogram, and second as the standard units of distance, mass, and time, respectively, and bases its other units, such as the newton, on these. Another common metric system is the cgs: centimeter-gram-second. See also SI, a system that is based on the mks.

mm Millimeter or millimeters, one thousandth of a meter (0.001 m).

modulus of elasticity A measure of a material's resistance to deformation, it is the ratio of stress to strain. This book uses only Young's modulus, for elongation or bending, but there are other related measures for compression and shear.

moment of inertia A measure of a physical object's resistance to angular acceleration, as determined by its mass and the distribution of its mass about the axis of rotation. See Equations for the precise formula. Also, if M is the total mass of an object and k the radius of gyration, the moment of inertia is Mk^2.

mountain bike A bicycle characterized by wide tires, low gears, and (usually) straight rather than dropped handlebars, such as may be suitable for mountain trails or other off-road conditions.

mph Miles per hour. 1 mph = 0.44704 m/s.

m/s Meters per second. 1 m/s = 2.236936292 mph.

N Newton or newtons.

newton The mks unit of force, abbreviated N. It is the force required to accelerate a mass of 1 kilogram 1 meter per second per second in the same direction as the force, equivalent to 1 kg-m/s^2 SI. One newton equals 0.2248089431 lb.

nipple See spoke.

normal	Perpendicular; at a right angle. Normal is used especially to describe a line that is perpendicular to a plane surface: a line normal to a plane meets the plane at a single point and makes a right angle with every line in the plane that passes through that point.
pace	The rate at which movement proceeds, also called "rolling average" or "average riding speed." This book recommends use of this word to mean the covered distance divided by the total time the bicycle is actually moving. Adopting this recommendation would not only provide a neat, compact term, but avoid confusion with average speed, which as defined in science may include periods of no motion. (See average speed.) Some cycle computers with an automatic on/off feature compute pace but mislabel it "average speed." Whatever it is called, this number has mostly entertainment value: a cyclist can stop and rest often to keep the pace number high, while under the same conditions true average speed inexorably declines. To calculate the difference between pace and average speed, one can also estimate the fraction of time the bicycle has been stopped and multiply it by the pace.
pack	Same as peloton.
pannier	A bag designed to be mounted on a rack.
peloton	The main group of riders in a bicycle race.
π (pi)	A constant, about 3.14159265359, which represents the ratio of the circumference of a circle to its diameter. It is symbolized by the 16th letter of the Greek lower-case alphabet.
points race	A track race, several laps long, in which the object is to accumulate the most points, or to lap the field. Points are awarded to the first riders across the line on designated laps throughout the race, in addition to the last lap. Final placings are determined first by laps completed and then by points, so that riders who have gained one or more laps place ahead of riders with fewer laps but possibly more points.
potential energy	The ability of a body to do work by virtue of its position or state. For example, a bicycle at the top of a hill has greater potential energy than one at the bottom. See also energy.
pound	A unit of force, abbreviated lb. One pound = 4.448221615 newtons or kg-m/s^2 SI. A pound is most often used as a unit of weight (a particular kind of force), and is the weight of about 0.4536 kilograms most places on the earth's surface. The pound is also used in the pressure unit pounds per square inch, abbreviated psi; 1 psi equals 6,894.757293 newtons per square meter or kg/(m-s^2) SI. It is also used in the torque unit pound-feet; 1 pound-foot equals 1.355817948 meter-newtons or kg-m^2/s^2 SI.
power	1. The rate at which work is done or energy is expended; work or energy per unit of time. The mks unit of power is the watt. Another unit of power is the horsepower. 2. An exponent, denoted by a superscript, indicating a mathematical function of a number. Four raised to the third power (4^3, 4 cubed) is three fours multiplied together: 4 x 4 x 4, or 64; four raised to the ½ power ($4^{0.5}$, the square root of 4) is that number which when multiplied by itself gives four, namely 2.
pressure	Force per unit of area. In mks, pressure is expressed in newtons per square meter, unfortunately an awkwardly sized unit for bicycles. Pounds per square inch is the more commonly used unit. See also atmosphere.
prime	A prize awarded to the first rider to cross some intermediate point in a race, such as the end of a particular lap or the crest of a climb. From French, and therefore pronounced "preem," its spelling is sometimes Americanized to "preme." Primes are used to reward outstanding riders who may not be in contention at the finish, to keep speeds (and spectator interest) up when they might otherwise begin to lag, and to showcase event sponsors.
psi	Pounds per square inch.

pull	The period of time during which a particular cyclist rides at the front of a group, letting the others in the group draft him. In a group working together, each rider takes his share of pulls.
pursuit	A track racing event in which two cyclists (or two teams of cyclists) start at opposite sides of the track and attempt to overtake each other. Because with near-equal competitors overtaking rarely occurs before the specified distance is completed, a pursuit is like two time trials conducted simultaneously. Some forms of individual pursuit feature more than two cyclists spaced equally or unequally according to their estimated speed.
quick-release	A device used to facilitate loosening or removal. It consists of a cam and finger-operated lever. When the lever is closed, the cam tightens, for normal operation; when the lever is open, the cam loosens. Types often found on bicycles include the wheel quick-release, at the end of a spindle inside a hollow hub axle, for removing a wheel without a wrench; the brake or brake lever quick-release, to splay the brake arms for pad clearance when a wheel is being removed or replaced; and the seatpost binder bolt quick-release, for easy saddle height adjustment or removal. Toe straps and tire pump heads often have a similar mechanism. Sometimes abbreviated QR.
rack	A frame securely attached to the bicycle frame or fork and designed to carry panniers or other equipment for touring or commuting. Called "carrier" in Great Britain.
radian	The most natural unit of angle in mathematics. Because there are 2π radians in a full circle (360 degrees), 1 radian = 57.2957795131 degrees.
radius of curvature	A measure of the sharpness of a curve. Because most curves follow a circular arc for much of their length, the sharpness can be quantified by measuring the radius of that circle.
radius of gyration	A measure of the average distance of the mass of a rotating object from the axis about which it is rotating. See moment of inertia.
rake	The amount of bend in the fork, measured perpendicularly from the steering column axis to the front wheel axis.
randonneur	A non-competitive long-distance cyclist, particularly one who rides events called brevets. Brevets are group rides of usually 200 to 1,200 kilometers, often with a time limit. Brevets in which riders choose their own pace are also called randonneurs; those in which a group moves at a basically fixed pace are also called audaxes.
rear triangle	The portion of a bicycle frame aft of the seat tube. The triangular arrangement of the seat tube with the thinner chainstays and seatstays forms a sort of suspension for the rear wheel.
recumbent (bicycle)	A bicycle designed to be operated by a rider in a reclining position, as opposed to the standard bicycle in which the rider is upright or bent forward.
repechage	A second chance for riders who failed to qualify in a previous heat. For example, the total field for a keirin or scratch race may be divided in thirds for three qualifying heats, the top two finishers from each heat guaranteed a start in the final. To make up the final field of eight, the organizers may allow some or all the non-qualifiers to compete again in a repechage, the top two from that heat also making the final. From French, and pronounced REP-uh-shahzh, a repechage is far more sporting (and far more interesting to spectators) than the "consolation round" typical in American sports.
rigidity	Stiffness: resistance to bending, twisting, and stretching.
rim	The outer edge of a wheel, which supports the tire. On most bicycle wheels, the rim is a separate component connected to the hub by individually adjustable spokes under tension. See also clincher and tubular.
road bike	A bicycle designed for use on mostly paved roads. Although the definition should also include touring bikes, the term is nowadays commonly used to mean road *racing* bike.

road race	A race held on roads, usually a relatively long distance point-to-point or on a relatively long circuit, as opposed to a criterium.
rolling average	See pace.
rolling resistance	A force acting opposite the (bicycle's) direction of travel, caused by the absorption of energy by the contact between tires and road, friction in the drivetrain and wheels, flection and vibration, etc., as the bicycle moves at constant speed. Some sources restrict the term to the resistive force from tire-to-road contact, which is the dominant force among those listed above; others may use the term more loosely to include gravity or moment of inertia.
rpm	Revolutions per minute. Loosely, cadence or engine rotational speed. Either foot of a rider pedaling at a cadence of 80 rpm completes 80 full circles within one minute.
s	Second or seconds.
scalar	A quantity completely specified as a magnitude. Speed, mass, temperature, time, energy, etc. are scalar quantities. See also vector.
scratch race	A race in which all riders start together (from scratch) and the first rider to cross the finish line wins. Compare points race.
seatpost	The column, which on most bikes attaches the saddle or seat to the frame. Saddle height adjustment is accomplished by inserting more or less of the seatpost into the seat tube, then clamping it in place, usually by tightening the seatpost binder bolt. Called "seat pin" in Great Britain.
seatstay	One of the relatively narrow tubes, which on a diamond bicycle frame connect the top of the seat tube with the rear wheel axle.
seat tube	One of the main tubes of the diamond bicycle frame, running nearly vertically from the seat down to the bottom bracket.
seat tube angle	The angle between the seat tube axis and the ground, as viewed from the side; usually but not necessarily close to the head tube angle.
sew-up	A tubular tire (see). Called "tub" in Great Britain.
shift pattern	A diagram, real or imaginary, that shows an ordered progression of chainwheel-cog combinations, particularly those combinations that produce all the available gear ratios from highest to lowest or vice-versa.
SI	*Système International d'Unités*, the International System of Units. Often used interchangeably with "mks," SI employs the same elemental units (meter, kilogram, second, kelvin, and others that do not concern us here, such as ampere and candela), but tends to be more strict about retaining them rather than combining them into new units. For example, mks uses the watt where a strict SI advocate may prefer $kg\text{-}m^2/s^3$.
sidepull brake	A brake with two curved arms operated in scissors action toward the rim by a cable at one side. On traditional sidepulls, both arms have a single central pivot. On more modern double-pivot brakes, one of the pivots is offset on the arm with the central pivot.
slipstream	The "draft" or air current behind a rider or riders.
specific gravity	The ratio of the mass of a solid to an equal volume of water at 4 degrees Celsius; practically the same as density in grams per cubic centimeter.
speed	1. Magnitude of velocity; rate of distance traveled per unit of time, such as miles per hour or (mks and SI) meters per second, m/s. Because the term speed does not necessarily imply a particular direction of motion, velocity is a more meaningful term than speed whenever direction is important.
	2. Loosely, an available gear, gear combination, or gear ratio, as a 9-speed freewheel (one with 9 cogs) or an 18-speed bicycle (one with 18 different gear combinations, such as available from 2 chainwheels and 9

spin   freewheel cogs, which may give 18 or fewer distinct gear ratios).

spin   To pedal at a rapid cadence: 80, 90, 100 or more rpm. A cyclist who has reached his maximum cadence is said to have "spun out."

spoke   One of the rods connecting the rim and the hub of a wheel. Most spokes have a bend and an enlarged head at the hub end and are threaded like a bolt at the opposite (rim) end. The spoke nipple, projecting toward the hub from inside the rim, acts as a nut, allowing the spoke to be tensioned.

sprint   An all-out burst of speed, usually to the finish line. A race finish contested by several riders in the peloton is called a field sprint. Sometimes short races for only a few riders are called sprints; see also match sprint. In a track or circuit race, designated intermediate laps at which points or prizes will be awarded are occasionally called sprints.

square meter   The mks and SI unit of area, equivalent to that of a square one meter on a side; abbreviated m². One square meter equals 10.76391042 square feet or 1,550.003100 square inches.

stage race   A bicycle competition consisting of multiple events (called stages) held on two or more consecutive days. Stage races may include road races, criteriums, and time trials (or occasionally their off-road equivalents), and usually include competition between teams as well as individuals. They are usually scored based on overall time, that is, the sum of a rider's times for the individual stages, possibly deducting bonuses for stage wins and intermediate sprints.

stay   One of the narrower tubes of a bicycle frame. See chainstay and seatstay. Some frame designs have additional stays for extra bracing, or replace one of the standard frame tubes with stays.

step   The approximate ratio between successive cog sizes on a freewheel, or an equivalent perceived difference (actually ratio) between gear ratios. A step is an idealized or average value, considered constant even though the actual ratios vary somewhat from one pair of cogs to the next.

straight gauge   Having uniform thickness, as a spoke or the wall of a tube. Compare butted.

strain   A deformation resulting from a stress, the ratio of the change in some dimension (for example, length or volume) to the total value of that dimension. It has no unit.

stress   A force per unit area that deforms a material or object, that is, changes its shape or volume. Stress is measured in newtons per square meter or pounds per square inch.

suspension   The mechanism that supports a vehicle on its wheel axles, usually including springs of some sort. On a standard bicycle, the front suspension is the fork, and the rear suspension is the rear triangle; but some bicycles replace or supplement these components with coil springs, rubber doughnuts, vibration-damping mechanisms, or other devices. The suspension helps both to isolate the rider from road shock and to keep the wheels firmly in contact with the ground.

tandem (bicycle)   A bicycle designed to be operated by two (or more) riders, one behind the other.

tangential   Along a tangent. A tangent is a straight line touching a circle (or a sphere, etc.) at one point and perpendicular to the radius at that point. The ground, for example, can be considered tangential to a bicycle wheel at the bottom point of the wheel — at least in an idealized drawing. We use the term tangential force when we discuss torque because only the component of force along a tangent to the pedaling circle matters. For example, suppose the rider is standing and applying force straight downward on the right pedal. When the right crankarm is at the 3 o'clock position (90 degrees past straight up), force applied straight down to the pedal is tangential to the pedaling circle; 100% of that force is applicable to torque. However, at the 4 o'clock position (120 degrees past straight up), only part of that force, namely the sine of 120 degrees times the force, is tangential to the pedaling circle. The tangential force in that case is 86.6% of the total force.

Tangential can also mean parallel to a surface at some point, that is, perpendicular to a line normal to the surface at that point.

tensile strength The maximum longitudinal (elongating) stress a material can withstand without tearing apart, e.g. cracking.

time trial A race against the clock, in which competitors are usually started at intervals of 30 seconds or more and drafting is not permitted; minimum time on the course wins. A time trial usually has a standing start (requiring a helper or stand to hold the bike upright) and may be held on road or track or off-road. A consistently uphill time trial is usually called a hill climb. Time trials may be "solo" or "individual," for individual competitors, or "team" for teams of a specified number of riders who ride as a group and are allowed to draft each other and trade places at the front. In a team time trial, it is often not the first but, say, the third rider of the team whose finishing time counts.

tire The wheel component that contacts the ground. Made of rubber or a similar flexible synthetic material, the tire is held in place by the rim and provides adhesion and insulation from shock. See also clincher and tubular.

toeclip A curved piece of metal or plastic that attaches to the front of the pedal, for proper foot positioning and increased pedaling efficiency.

toe strap A strip of fabric or leather, often with a buckle, which threads through the pedal and (usually) toeclip, to secure the foot to the pedal for increased pedaling efficiency.

top tube One of the main tubes of a diamond bicycle frame, running nearly horizontally back from the head tube to the top of the seat tube. In other kinds of frames, the top tube may be replaced by one or more tubes that connect the head tube to a lower spot on the seat tube or the seatstays.

torque Also called moment of force, a measure of how effective a force is at producing rotation (circular motion about an axis). It is the product of the tangential force (for example, the force applied at the pedals perpendicular to the crankarms) and the distance between the axis and the point at which the force is applied (for example, between the bottom bracket and the pedal spindle). The mks unit of torque is the meter-newton.

touring Bicycling in which the sights and experiences of the trip are more important than the speed. As used in this book, touring usually implies long-distance, multi-day trips with baggage such as panniers, but the term is often used to mean any sort of riding other than competition, training, and commuting.

touring bike A bicycle characterized by medium to wide tires (or at least the ability to accept them), long wheelbase, moderate frame angles, usually dropped handlebars, and usually the ability to attach racks, suitable for long rides on paved or reasonably smooth unpaved roads. As with racing, actual touring with such a bike is strictly optional.

track See velodrome.

track bike A bicycle characterized by narrow tires, short wheelbase, dropped handlebars, a single fixed gear (no freewheel) and no brakes, designed for racing on a velodrome. Slowing is accomplished by applying backward pressure to the pedals.

trackstand A maneuver occasionally performed by the lead rider in a match sprint in an attempt to force his competitor to take the lead. It requires balancing on the stopped bicycle without putting a foot down. The banking of the track and the direct fixed gearing of the track bicycle make the feat easier to accomplish than, say, on a derailleur bicycle at a stoplight.

trials A non-racing form of off-road competition rewarding superior bike handling skills, such as rock climbing, turns in

	very tight quarters, negotiating slippery conditions, etc. Competitors are penalized for touching a foot to the ground or planting a foot on the ground to retain balance.
triple	Loosely, a crankset with three chainwheels.
tubular	One of the two types of bicycle tire and rim. A tubular rim provides only a shallow concave channel to support the tire, which is held in place by glue; the tubular tire (also called a sew-up) is sealed and does not need a separate tube. In Great Britain, tubular rims are referred to as "sprint" rims, tubular tires as "tubs."
ultra-marathon	Very long distance, usually involving several consecutive days of cycling 200 or more miles with little sleep.
V-brake	See cantilever brake.
vector	A quantity specified as a magnitude and a direction. Velocity, acceleration, force, displacement, etc. are vector quantities. See also scalar and component.
velocity	Speed in a particular direction. When the direction is fairly obvious, such as the direction the bicycle is moving, this book uses the term speed. The mks and SI unit of velocity is the meter per second, m/s.
velodrome	A bicycle racing facility, outdoor or indoor, usually constructed as a banked oval. Also called a track. Assuming the facility is in good repair, its surface of concrete or polished boards is very smooth, for minimum rolling resistance (and, during falls, minimum abrasion).

W	Watt or watts.
watt	The mks unit of power, abbreviated W. One watt equals 1 joule per second (1 kg-m^2/s^3 SI) or 0.00134102209 (1.341022090 x 10^{-3}) horsepower.
weight	The force gravity exerts on an object, equal to the product of the object's mass and the acceleration due to gravity, directed approximately toward the center of the earth. This book refers to weight only in the context of gravity. See "mass," which is the more general concept.
wheelbase	The distance from the center of the front wheel to the center of the rear wheel.
work	Force acting over a distance. Work done is equivalent to energy spent. The mks unit of work is the joule (kg-m^2/s^2 SI). See also energy.
yield point	The amount of stress a material will sustain before it deforms permanently. Also called the elastic limit, the value of the yield point is usually slightly below the ultimate tensile strength. Some materials, such as steel and titanium, can rebound completely from any number of lower-magnitude stresses; others, such as aluminum, develop minute cracks and (if the stresses continue) eventually fail.
Young's modulus	The modulus of elasticity in length, defined as longitudinal (elongating) stress divided by longitudinal strain, but also applicable to bending stress and strain. Expressed in units of pounds per square inch or newtons per square meter.

Bibliography

Richard Ballantine and Richard Grant. *Richard's Ultimate Bicycle Book*. New York: Dorling Kindersley Inc., 1992. Glossy coverage, recent developments.

Allan V. Abbott and David Gordon Wilson (Eds.). *Human-Powered Vehicles*. Champaign, IL: Human Kinetics, 1995.

B. A. Adeyefa. *Determination of the Loads, Deflections and Stresses in Bicycle Frames* (Dissertation). Manchester, England: University of Manchester Institute of Science and Technology, 1978.

R. J. Barlow. *Statistics, a Guide to the Use of Statistical Methods in the Physical Sciences*. Chichester, England: John Wiley and Sons, 1989. Assessing confidence in experimental results.

Arthur Beiser, *Physics*. Reading, MA: Addison-Wesley, 1991. General text.

Frank Berto, Ron Shepherd, Raymond Henry. *The Dancing Chain: History and development of the derailleur bicycle*. San Francisco: Van der Plas Publications, 2000.

George S. Brady and Henry R. Clauser, editors. *Materials Handbook*. New York: McGraw-Hill Inc, 1991. Properties of materials of all kinds.

Jobst Brandt. *The Bicycle Wheel*. Menlo Park, CA: Avocet Inc, 1981, 1983. Wheel technical analysis, wheel building.

F. Bueche. *Technical Physics*. New York: Harper and Row, 1977. General text.

Frederick J. Bueche. *Schaum's Outline of Theory and Problems of College Physics*. New York: McGraw-Hill Inc., 1989. Loaded with practical examples.

James W. Daily and Donald Harleman. *Fluid Dynamics*. Reading, MA: Addison-Wesley, 1966. Aerodynamic drag and much more.

John Forester. *Effective Cycling* [6th Ed]. Cambridge, MA: MIT-Press, 1992.

J. E. Gordon. *The New Science of Strong Materials*. Princeton, NJ: Princeton University Press, 1968. Properties of materials; beam stressing.

James Greene et al. *Bicycle Accident Reconstruction and Litigation* (4th Ed.) Tucson, AZ: Lawyers and Judges Publishing, 1995.

Albert C. Gross, Chester R. Kyle and Douglas J. Malewicki. "The Aerodynamics of Human-powered Land Vehicles." *Scientific American*, December 1983. Much data on different types of bicycles and other human-powered vehicles.

Douglas Hayduk. *Bicycle Metallurgy for Cyclists*. Grand Junction, CO, 1987 (an updated version of this text is included in Greene et al listed above.)

Raymond Henry. *Du vélocipède au dérailleur moderne*. St. Etienne, France: Association des amis du musée d'art et d'industrie, 1998.

Charles D. Hodgman, editor-in-chief. *Handbook of Chemistry and Physics*. 44th edition Cleveland, OH: Chemical Rubber Publishing Company, 1962. Tables galore: mathematics, physical properties of elements and alloys, gravity, atmosphere, etc. For this classic reference book, the older editions, such as this one, are often more valuable to the non-professional.

Michael J. Kolin and Denise M. de la Rosa. *The Custom Bicycle*. Emmaus, PA: Rodale Press, 1979. Informative if slightly dated coverage of custom bicycles and builders; more detail on setup and fit than most books.

John Krausz and Vera van der Reis Krausz. *The Bicycling Book*. New York: The Dial Press, 1982. Amazing variety of coverage, enjoyable reading.

Russell Langley. *Practical Statistics Simply Explained*. New York: Dover Publications Inc., 1970. Assessing confidence in experimental results.

David R. Lide, editor-in-chief. *CRC Handbook of Chemistry and Physics*. 72nd edition. Boca Raton, FL: CRC Press, 1991. See Hodgman above.

Peter Matthews, editor. *The Guinness Book of Records 1993*. New York: Facts on File, 1992. Cycling speed records.

L. A. Milne-Thomson. *Theoretical Aerodynamics*. New York: Dover Publications, Inc., 1958. Formidable mathematical treatment.

Tony Oliver. *Touring Bikes: A practical guide*. Ramsbury, England: The Crowood Press, 1990.

David B. Perry. *Bike Cult: The ultimate guide to human-powered vehicles*. New York: Four Walls Eight Windows, 1995.

Arnold L. Reimann. *Physics*. New York: Barnes and Noble, 1971. General text.

Marc Ross and John DeCicco. "Measuring the Energy Drain on Your Car." *Scientific American*, December 1994. For cyclists, an interesting analogy.

Archibald Sharp. *Bicycles and Tricycles: An elementary treatise on their design and construction*. First published London, New York: Longmans, Green, 1896. Reprint edition Cambridge, MA: MIT-Press, 1977.

George Shortley and Dudley Willrams. *Principles of College Physics*. Englewood Cliffs, NJ: Prentice-Hall, Inc., 1959. General text.

Hans-Christian Smolik and Stefan Etzel. *Das grosse Fahrradlexikon*. Bielefeld, Germany: BVA-Verlag, 1997.

John L. Synge and Byron A. Griffith. *Principles of Mechanics*. New York: McGraw Hill, 1959. Detail on plane statics of rigid frames.

Paul A. Tyler. *College Physics*. New York: Worth Publishers, Inc., 1987. General text.

Rob van der Plas. *Bicycle Technology*. San Francisco: Bicycle Books, 1993.

Manfred Vötter et al. "Betriebslasten an Fahrrädern" (Operating Loads Placed on Bicycles, German with English Summary). *Fahrzeugtechnik*, No. 27. Bergisch Gladbach, Germany: Bundesanstalt für Straßenwesen, 1999.

Robert C. Weast, editor. *CRC Handbook of Chemistry and Physics*, 65th edition. Boca Raton, FL: CRC Press, Inc, 1984. See Hodgman above.

Frank Rowland Whitt and David Gordon Wilson. *Bicycling Science*. Ergonomics and Mechanics. Cambridge, MA: MIT Press, 1976. Comprehensive though somewhat dated technical treatment. Abundant references, more detail on some of the topics in this book, plus comparisons with other forms of transportation.

The catalogs of the major bicycle mail-order companies are also a valuable source of information regarding the availability and weights of components.

Index

H

hair, 142
half step, definition, 40
half-step plus granny system, 44
half-step system, 41
hand strength, rider, 91
handlebar bags, 122
handlebar height, *see* stem adjustment
handlebar, riding position, 90
handlebars, aerodynamic, *see* aero bars
handlebars, pulling on, 54
handling, standards, 112
hardness, tread, 131
head tube angle, 116
headset, 125
heart rate monitor, 170
heat during braking, 97
heat during inflation, 133
heat treating, 153
Hegg, Steve, 77
height, saddle, 50, 90, 130
helium, 134
Helmert's equation, 171
helmets, 142
Hetchins, 129
high altitude records, 23
high-wheeled bicycle, 31
hill climb, 84
hills, 33, 66, 70, 80
hub shell, 159
hub, occlusion of front, 51
hubs, 126
human performance, testing, 169
human-powered vehicles, 146
humidity, 23
hydroplaning, 132

I

industry, bicycling, 11
inertia, *see* moment of inertia
inflation pressure, *see* tire pressure
inflation, heat during, 133
insight, technical, 13
International System units, 20
intervals, 76

J

jockey wheels, 125
journalists, 11

K

keirin, 84
Klein, 128

L

ladies frames, 129
laminar flow, 148
layers inside tire, 132
lean angle, 103, 108, 174
leaning the bike less than the rider, 109
leaning, obstacles, 107
leg flexibility, 53
leg length, 53
leg strain, 58
Lehigh Valley Velodrome, 60, 77
length, crankarm, *see* crankarm length
leverage, crankarm length, 52
lift, aerodynamic, 22
lift, wheel, 86, 88
lifting the inside pedal, 108
lightweight components, 152
limitations, 13
limits to sustained power, 59, 61
loads and handling, 122
lockup, wheel, 91, 93, 94
Longo, Jeanne, 23
lubrication, chain, 127

M

madison, 84
magnesium, 155
making up time, 75
manganese-molybdenum, 152
maps, topographic, 167
mass and acceleration, 156
mass and braking, 156
mass and coasting, 156
mass and cornering, 104
mass and weight, 22, 156
mass savings from other gases, 134

mass, effect of geometry on, 155
mass, minimizing, 156
mass, rotating, 157, 158
mass, sprung and unsprung, 110, 113, 137
mass, wheel, 114, 159, 160, 161
masses, force of gravity between, 174
match sprint, 84, 146
materials, properties, 152
mathematical expressions, 15
mathematical tables, use of, 15
metric system, 20
mileposts, 166
mind, role of, 9, 145, 165
miss-and-out, 84
mks system, 20
modified alpine system, 42
moment of force, *see also* torque
moment of force, 86, 88
moment of inertia and torque, 176
moment of inertia vs. aerodynamics, 161
moment of inertia, 157, 158, 159, 161
momentum and tandems, 156
Moser, Francesco, 23
Moulton, Alex, 114, 160
mountain bike race, 84
mountain bike wheel, 114, 131
mountain bike, 49, 107, 130
multiplication sign, 15

N

natural selection, 11
New Zealand cycling team, 77
nitrogen, 134
normal force, 88, 91, 175
notation, scientific, 19
numbers, 14, 15, 19, 46
nylon, 155

O

obstacles to leaning, 107
one-and-a-half-step system, 40
one-hour record, 23
opponents, 80, 81, 82
ordinary high-wheeler bicycle, 28
oscillation, 118, 120, 123
out-and-back course, 101
oval frame tubes, 145
overlap, toeclip, 53
overlapping wheels, 150
oxygen consumption, 170

P

pace, controlling, 148
pacing, *see* drafting
pack, 81
PAN, 153
panniers, 122, 145
parentheses, 15
pattern, shift, 45
paved surfaces and rolling resistance, 136
pedal position, 163
pedal speed, 54
pedal system, 55
pedal width, 107, 108
pedal, inside, 108
pedal, rolling resistance, 126
pedaling circle, 56
pedaling circles, 53
pedaling force, 54, 175
pedaling in a curve, 108, 109
pedaling position, 49
penny-farthing bicycle, 28
performance evaluation, 169
performance, 10, 81, 164
period of vibration, 173
physical attributes, using to advantage, 82
physics terms and units, 20
pitch, 153
pointing the knee, 109
points race, 84
polyacrylonitrate, 153
position, 49, 73, 90, 139, 140
position, pedal, 163
potential energy, 175
power and cadence, 58
power and force, 24, 163

Other Cycling Resources books from Van der Plas Publications (http://www.vanderplas.net)

Lance Armstrong's Comeback from Cancer

A Scrapbook of the Tour de France Winner's Dramatic Career
Samuel Abt
Photos by James Startt
ISBN 1-892495-25-2
Trade paperback, 6 x 9 in.
176 pages text with 12-page color photo insert and 30 black & white photos
U.S. list price $16.95
The dramatic "comeback" biography of Lance Armstrong, the American racer who won the 1999 Tour de France, just 2½ years after being diagnosed with cancer.

The Dancing Chain

History and Development of the Derailleur Bicycle
Frank J. Berto, Ron Shepherd, Raymond Henry
ISBN 1-892495-21-X
Hardcover, 8½ x 11 in.
352 pages with 1,000 black & white illustrations
U.S. list price $49.95
Unlike other books about the history of the bicycle, this one focuses on how the modern lightweight derailleur bicycle and its gearing system evolved.

The Unknown Tour de France

The Many Faces of the World's Biggest Bicycle Race
Les Woodland
ISBN 1-892495-26-0
Trade paperback, 6 x 9 in.
192 pages with 50 black & white photos
U.S. list price $16.95
After nearly 100 years, the Tour de France is still the sport's premier event. Les Woodland recounts many of the fascinating episodes from the Tour's past and present in a knowledgeable and humorous style.

100 Years of Bicycle Component and Accessory Design
The Data Book

ISBN 1-892495-01-5
Hardcover, 7 x 10 in.
212 pages with 1,200 black & white illustrations
U.S. list price $39.95
This classic book containing a vast collection of superb illustrations is an inspiration for the design of bicycle components and a delight for any bicycle aficionado. Includes English translations of original Japanese texts.

In Pursuit of the Yellow Jersey

Bicycle Racing in the Year of the Troubled Tour
Samuel Abt and James Startt
ISBN 1-892495-15-5
Trade paperback, 6 x 9 in.
192 pages text with 16-page color photo insert and 30 black & white photos in text
U.S. list price $16.95
Bicycle racing has lost its innocence, and in the 1998 season, doping scandals and sponsorship battles were as prominent as the racing itself. It made for an interesting season, superbly described.

The Birth of Dirt

Origins of Mountain Biking
Frank J. Berto
ISBN 1-892495-10-4
Trade paperback, 5½ x 8½ in.
128 pages with 50 black & white illustrations
U.S. list price $12.95
Although the mountain bike has been around for only 20 years, it already has a rich history. Based on the author's quest to settle once and for all who (if anybody) "invented" the mountain bike, this book traces the beginnings of the machine and the sport.

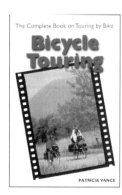

Bicycle Touring

The Complete Book on Touring by Bike
Patricia Vance
ISBN 1-892495-27-9
Trade paperback, 6 x 9 in.
224 pages with 60 diagrams and black & white photos
U.S. list price $16.95
Bicycle touring is one of the greatest ways to see the world. World traveler Patricia Vance gives all the advice needed to make any long or short bicycle tour a success.

Buying a Bike

How to Get the Best Bike for Your Money
Rob van der Plas
ISBN 1-892495-17-1
Trade paperback, 5½ x 8½ in.
96 pages with 50 black & white illustrations
U.S. list price $16.95
Clearly illustrated and concisely written, veteran bicycle writer Rob van der Plas explains what to watch out for when buying a bike and other equipment.